# THE ESSENTIAL KAFIR

Plate 1.

ESSENTIALLY KAFIR: OLD MOLIWASH.
A Tembu "Headman."

# THE
# ESSENTIAL KAFIR

### BY
### DUDLEY KIDD

WITH SIXTY THREE FULL-PAGE ILLUSTRATIONS
FROM PHOTOGRAPHS BY THE AUTHOR

 BOOKS FOR LIBRARIES PRESS
FREEPORT, NEW YORK

LIBRARY
WAYNE STATE COLLEGE
WAYNE, NEBRASKA

First Published 1904
Reprinted 1971

INTERNATIONAL STANDARD BOOK NUMBER:
0-8369-6656-2

LIBRARY OF CONGRESS CATALOG CARD NUMBER:
75-179527

PRINTED IN THE UNITED STATES OF AMERICA
BY
NEW WORLD BOOK MANUFACTURING CO., INC.
HALLANDALE, FLORIDA 33009

# PREFACE

A GROUP of tribes may be viewed from many standpoints, according as we are interested in anthropology, history, social problems, economic questions, travel, sport, or missionary work. The Kafir is not exclusively viewed from any of these standpoints in the following pages, which are intended to serve as a warm-blooded character-sketch of the South African natives. Everything that is of broad human interest takes precedence of departmental aspects of the subject.

The word *Kafir* is used in its broadest sense, so as to include all the dark-skinned tribes of South Africa, though the word has been used by others in the most varied connotations. The word does but mean *an infidel*, and has been confined frequently to a few tribes living south of Natal. But the title is often used in South Africa as a synonym for the word *native*, and it is in this sense that it is used here. It is thus equivalent to the word *Bantu*.

But why use the phrase *Essential* Kafir? some one may ask. Ever since the discovery of gold at the Rand the native has been regarded as essential to the economic success of South Africa; yet it is not alone in this sense that the phrase is used. The title refers primarily to that essential spirit which

# The Essential Kafir

underlies all the variations of the outer life of the many tribes included under the name of Kafir. It is with the essential spirit or personality of the Kafir that these pages deal.

Browning has said, with great truth but with his usual over-emphasis, that little else besides the development of a soul is worth study. It is the development of the soul of the Kafir people that forms the central interest of these pages, customs and beliefs being described so as to bring out clearly the nature of Kafir personality.

The aim has been to preserve, as far as was possible in print, the sympathetic juices, the hopes, the fears, the joys, and the sorrows, of these people. Occasional remarks calculated to indicate the points at which the Kafir is connected with the great broad ranks of humanity are given from time to time. To enable a reader to see the world through Kafir eyes, and to feel it through Kafir finger-tips, it is essential to conserve all the living juices of a strange personality, not fearing to show up the vices and foibles of the native, for it is just these human failings and foibles which touch us with a sense of pathos and endear to us many a friend.

In a word, it is an artistic presentation that is offered, in order that when the reader puts down the book he may feel not so much that he knows a great deal *about* the Kafirs—this he may better do by reading other books—but that he *knows the Kafir*. To know a person is a very different thing from knowing a great deal about him.

The method adopted in writing was as follows : A skeleton

# Preface

note-book was prepared in which was entered a mass of details selected from personal experiences of the various South African tribes. Having, during the last dozen years, visited Pondoland, Basutoland, Tembuland, Bomvanaland, Natal, the Transvaal, Zululand, Swazieland, Gazaland, Bechuanaland, Mashonaland, Matabeleland, and the Sena-speaking tribes above the Zambesi as far north as Blantyre (some of these districts being visited four or five times), I found myself in possession of a great mass of information. The result of a thousand talks with natives, traders, magistrates, old residents in the country, and missionaries, was added to the note-book, and, having read rather extensively on the subject, I collated nearly every fact which bore upon native character in the fifty books referred to under the heading of Bibliography. This united mass of information was then classified, and passed under systematic consideration; of which processes this book is the outcome. A great deal of matter was rejected during the sifting; yet even Blue Books have been found useful, though there is rarely much red blood in them. At least one humorous passage was discovered in a Blue Book a dozen years ago, and, as well as I can remember, it ran as follows: The Government instructed all magistrates to gather the natives and ask them a series of questions, in order to gain light on native ideas. One question was somewhat like this, "What do you conceive 'Government' to be?" An old chief stood up and told a magistrate that they were not so ignorant as he seemed to imagine: they knew very well that Government was an old man with a white beard, that he

# The Essential Kafir

was occasionally seen walking in the streets of Cape Town, and that *very* occasionally he went across the sea to visit the Great White Queen. Thus it is evident that there are purple patches even in a Blue Book, the crimson being supplied by the generous and rich blood of the Kafirs, for it is ever the case that "the dulness of the fool is the whetstone of our wits."

It may be well to point out that no single tribe has been singled out and isolated in the description of the Essential Kafir. Details have been taken from the various tribes in as far as their combination was thought to throw into relief the genius or spirit of the Kafir. The portrait presented is a composite one. Therefore, if a person who is living among a special tribe finds that the details of some custom are not in accordance with those familiar in that tribe, he must remember that there is great variation to be found among the many tribes which go to make up the generic Kafir. In no single tribe can all the customs mentioned be found in full swing. Some of the customs long ago became obsolete, and others have undergone great modification through the influence of Europeans.

With regard to system, at one moment the method adopted is frankly impressionist, the broad effect of light or colour being all that seemed of interest, while at another time the study is minute in its attention to detail.

In taking photographs of the Kafirs my aim has always been to throw the background out of focus on purpose, so that the personality of the Kafir may stand out from his

# Preface

surroundings, and unnecessary or conflicting detail has been frequently sacrificed. The same holds with regard to the verbal descriptions offered. After travelling for years among the Kafirs, I have a very strong impression left on my mind as to their personality: what I wish to do is to infect others with this feeling.

With regard to the spelling of names, every author seems to choose his own method. One writer talks of hassagayes, another of assagais, a third of hassagais, and a fourth of assegais. Similarly we meet with Chaka, Tshaka, Chsaka; Kaffir, Kafir, Caffre, Cafir, Kaffer, Caffir; Dingan, Dingaan, Dingarn, &c. I have sought to strike an average, always avoiding native names when possible, as the book is not intended for those already familiar with the natives, and I have no wish to burden the reader with a glossary of native names and words. Certain words became current coin since the Boer war, and these are sometimes introduced, together with a few untranslatable expressions.

The reason that so few references are made to authorities in the text is as follows: It is quite impossible to decide, in most cases, whose name should be mentioned. Writers borrow so much from one another that, though I have usually sought to verify all quotations in the original works, so as to secure the greatest possible degree of accuracy, it is impossible to be sure that the bed-rock has been reached. When a person observes a fact with his own eyes, and then finds it described by a man who has borrowed from some old writer, who yet again borrowed from another, it is impossible to say whose

# The Essential Kafir

name should be mentioned. For this reason I have given a short Bibliography.

It may well be said, "*Semper novi quid ex Africa.*" But, if some one wishes to quote the well-known aphorism about new and true things, all I can plead is that I was intent to supply fresh and living information rather than new. The photographs, at least, are my own, and, though two or three have appeared in a small local monthly magazine in South Africa, the great bulk were specially taken for this work, of which they are intended to form an integral part.

Thanks are due to my friend Mr. Rendel Harris for kindly reading through the proofs during my absence in South Africa.

JOHANNESBURG, *January* 1904

# CONTENTS

## CHAPTER I
INTRODUCING THE KAFIR . . . . . . . . . 1

## CHAPTER II
NATIVE BELIEFS . . . . . . . . . . 63

## CHAPTER III
MAGIC . . . . . . . . . . . 131

## CHAPTER IV
THE WITCHDOCTOR . . . . . . . . . . 153

## CHAPTER V
CUSTOMS—BIRTH TO DEATH . . . . . . . . 195

## CHAPTER VI
GENERAL CUSTOMS . . . . . . . . . . 255

## CHAPTER VII
MENTAL CHARACTERISTICS . . . . . . . . 275

## CHAPTER VIII
WAR AND THE CHASE . . . . . . . . . 299

## CHAPTER IX
ARTS OF PEACE AND DOMESTIC MATTERS . . . . . 321

# The Essential Kafir

## CHAPTER X
LEGAL MATTERS . . . . . . . . . . 349

## CHAPTER XI
FOLKLORE . . . . . . . . . . . 363

## CHAPTER XII
THE KAFIR—WHAT IS TO BECOME OF HIM? . . . . . 391

## APPENDIX
HEITSI-EIBIB, A HERO OF THE HOTTENTOTS . . . . . 409

BIBLIOGRAPHY . . . . . . . . . . 417
INDEX . . . . . . . . . . . 429

# LIST OF ILLUSTRATIONS.

| Plate | | | |
|---|---|---|---|
| " | 1. Essentially Kafir—Old Moliwash | *Frontispiece* | |
| " | 2. A Zulu kraal, Lake St. Lucia | *Facing page* | 16 |
| " | 3. In a Natal kraal | " | 17 |
| " | 4. A Gazaland hut | " | 32 |
| " | 5. In a Zulu kraal | " | 33 |
| " | 6. A Pondo girl with baby | " | 36 |
| " | 7. A Pondo dandy | " | 37 |
| " | 8. A Pondo boy | " | 44 |
| " | 9. A Bomvana family | " | 45 |
| " | 10. Kafir spirituality | " | 48 |
| " | 11. The hair-dresser | " | 49 |
| " | 12. Trimming the hair | " | 64 |
| " | 13. Back from the hairdresser | " | 65 |
| " | 14. A Pondo dandy | " | 80 |
| " | 15. Interior of a native hut | " | 81 |
| " | 16. "Feeding the baby" and "The napkin" | " | 96 |
| " | 17. A Swazie making fire by friction | " | 97 |
| " | 18. A Pondo mother | " | 112 |
| " | 19. A Pondo woman going to fetch water | " | 113 |
| " | 20. How a Zulu hut is built | " | 128 |
| " | 21. Interior of a Zulu hut | " | 129 |
| " | 22. A Gazaland witchdoctor | " | 144 |
| " | 23. A Zulu witchdoctor, ready for dancing | " | 145 |
| " | 24. A witchdoctor | " | 160 |
| " | 25. A witchdoctor | " | 161 |
| " | 26. A Pondo woman | " | 168 |
| " | 27. Disconsolate | " | 169 |
| " | 28. A Pondo girl considering a bargain | " | 176 |
| " | 29. The bargain completed | " | 177 |
| " | 30. Self help | " | 192 |
| " | 31. Self help | " | 193 |
| " | 32. A Tembu boy | " | 208 |
| " | 33. Pondo sweethearts | " | 209 |

## LIST OF ILLUSTRATIONS (Continued).

| | | | |
|---|---|---|---|
| Plate | 34. Dressed for a wedding | Facing page | 224 |
| ,, | 35. A married Zulu woman | ,, | 225 |
| ,, | 36. A Swazie headman and his two wives | ,, | 240 |
| ,, | 37. Bushman drawings | ,, | 241 |
| ,, | 38. A Swazie beauty | ,, | 256 |
| ,, | 39. Extracting a thorn | ,, | 257 |
| ,, | 40. A native evangelist | ,, | 260 |
| ,, | 41. A Zulu warrior | ,, | 261 |
| ,, | 42. A Swazie warrior | ,, | 268 |
| ,, | 43. Zulu children setting bird-traps | ,, | 269 |
| ,, | 44. A Gazaland game-trap | ,, | 292 |
| ,, | 45. Stripping the mealie field | ,, | 293 |
| ,, | 46. In the harvest field | ,, | 300 |
| ,, | 47. A basketful of grain | ,, | 301 |
| ,, | 48. A Zulu woman threshing Kafir corn | ,, | 304 |
| ,, | 49. A Pondo woman winnowing the corn | ,, | 305 |
| ,, | 50. A Pondo woman grinding mealies | ,, | 320 |
| ,, | 51. A native blacksmith on the Zambesi | ,, | 321 |
| ,, | 52. A Pondo playing an ugwali or gorah | ,, | 336 |
| ,, | 53. A Zulu woman playing the igubu | ,, | 337 |
| ,, | 54. The spitting game | ,, | 352 |
| ,, | 55. { Zambesi boys playing at horses <br> { Zambesi boys standing on their heads for fun | ,, | 353 |
| ,, | 56. Pondo men smoking Indian hemp | ,, | 372 |
| ,, | 57. A Zulu woman carrying water | ,, | 373 |
| ,, | 58. Pondo women thatching a hut | ,, | 380 |
| ,, | 59. A Gazaland carrier | ,, | 381 |
| ,, | 60. Blantyre Church | ,, | 384 |
| ,, | 61. Sawing mahogany near Port Herald | ,, | 385 |
| ,, | 62. Going to school in Tembuland | ,, | 400 |
| ,, | 63. The lesson | ,, | 401 |

*Sketch map at end of volume.*

# INTRODUCING THE KAFIR

What is the course of the life
Of mortal men on the earth?—
Most men eddy about
Here and there—eat and drink,
Chatter and love and hate,
Gather and squander, are raised
Aloft, are hurl'd in the dust,
Striving blindly, achieving
Nothing; and then they die—
Perish,—and no one asks
Who or what they have been,
More than he asks what waves
In the moonlit solitudes mild
Of the midmost Ocean have swell'd,
Foam'd for a moment, and gone.

MATTHEW ARNOLD.

# THE ESSENTIAL KAFIR

## CHAPTER I

### INTRODUCING THE KAFIR

FAR away, lost in the pearly haze of the horizon, lies the kraal we are about to visit. The chief lives under the shadow of that grey-blue kopje which rises out of the boundless plain, and we have many a dusty mile to travel ere we reach his kraal. If that hill were in Europe we should judge it to be about ten miles distant; but out here, in this thin, clear air, distances are very deceptive. The character of the natives is still more deceptive, and it has suffered much unfair criticism from hasty travellers, who too often have been more occupied in imparting their own ideas to the natives than in getting to know what they think. Consequently, the judgments of these "swallow travellers" are frequently based on inadequate information. Moffat describes how one of them asked his guide the name of the place he had started from. The Kafir did not understand the question, and asked, "What did you say?" The hasty gentleman took out his note-book and entered this question as the name of the place from which he had started.

Great difficulty arises from the fact that the ideas of the Kafirs seem at first sight so very topsy-turvy, their customs so very silly. Yet when we come to understand the silliest of

# The Essential Kafir

their customs we are surprised to find how it fits in with human customs the whole world over, and forms some of the primordial stuff out of which modern European usages have been evolved. To dismiss such customs as silly is to advertise our ignorance. There is scarcely a custom which will not be seen, on mature examination, to rest on some basal fact or deep-seated need of human nature, which has found expression in similar customs in all other parts of the world. Still, the fact remains that, from our European standpoint, many of these customs seem exceedingly silly. When the Matabele first saw a locomotive engine at Bulawayo, that ancient fortress of heathenism, they declared that it was a large animal which fed on fire ; that it hated work—else why did it scream before it moved ?—and that it suffered badly from malaria. Did not the white doctor pour medicine into it whenever it groaned ?

When the pigmy Bushmen first saw ox-waggons they noticed that some were large and some small ; they came to the conclusion that the small waggons were daughters of the large. This seems grotesque and absurd until one remembers that when they had previously noticed the spoor of the waggons in the sand they at once decided that these could only have been caused by animals, for they had never seen any spoor marks except those left by animals. And if the waggons were animals, why should not the small ones be children of the large ?

More laughable still is the incident which happened in another tribe. When the first waggon appeared in their midst, the people of the kraals all turned out to see the new wonder —a hut which moved on wheels. Mile after mile the people clapped hands, and cheered the little wheels, which seemed to form the centre of attraction. On being asked what they saw in the small wheels to make them so excited, they replied that they thought it was so plucky of them to be able to keep up with the large ones. These people, then, clearly have good

# Introducing the Kafir

sporting instincts: their sympathy goes out to the weaker side.

Quite in keeping with those ideas is the story told by Captain Cook, how that in Tahiti the natives bought some large nails from him with the idea that these would by-and-by bear small ones. I doubted this story till I recollected a case in which a South African woman once obtained some huge safety-pins from me, and came back next day with a very long face, because some one told her they would not bear small safety pins.

World-wide is the idea that emetics or purgatives can dispel false notions. A Kafir woman was very indignant that her son had renounced heathenism and embraced Christianity. She promptly administered a strong emetic and purgative to dispel the hated religion.

Anything new sets natives wondering. Great was their excitement when they first saw a man wash himself with soap. They declared that the European was washing in boiling water. Yet they cannot distinguish as to relative values. A railway engine is not more wonderful to them than a sixpenny jack-in-the-box; indeed, a native once told me that he thought the latter far more wonderful than the former.

The desire to give some account of causation is at the root of all religions, and we have only to remember how recently Europe was confused on this point to be very charitable towards savages. A Kafir cannot distinguish between *post hoc* and *propter hoc*. Europeans are still apt to be very confused over this subject, and medical science has the greatest difficulty sometimes in distinguishing between cause and coincidence. The natives come to conclusions with but little thought, and so the mistakes they make are infinite. Here is an example: A certain missionary always wore a thick dark suit on wet days; the natives came to the conclusion that this dark suit was the

# The Essential Kafir

cause of the wet weather, and so in a time of drought sent a deputation to the missionary begging him to put on the dark suit, as they were very anxious to have some rain.

And the moment the Kafirs come to live in our houses as servants these odd ideas become still more marked. It is hard for us to imagine how very novel and strange all our things must seem to them at first. When a raw boy—and a Kafir sixty years old is still a " boy "—goes to a town to act as cook or general servant, he finds himself in a new world where everything is mysterious and strange. People thoughtlessly blame him for not instantly divining the function of some weird implement like a kettle. As if he could evolve from his inner consciousness the use of such an article! One of these raw boys was told by a friend of mine to take a kettle and fill it with water. As waterworks were few and far between in those good old days, the water was kept in a bucket, and a cup was used for ladling out the water. The boy was told to take a cup and to fill the kettle. He glanced at the kettle with an air of great sagacity, and yet did not know how to take hold of it. The fact that his master was looking on made him nervous and shy: so he grasped the kettle by the spout and vanished into the kitchen to begin operations. As these were very prolonged, his master went to inquire what the boy could be up to, and was amused to find him carefully pouring the water out of the cup down the spout of the kettle. How could the boy know that, if he used force, the lid, which of course had become jammed, could be removed? The same boy was told to light a fire in the kitchen. He went and sat down before the stove and scratched his woolly head, wondering where he ought to put the wood. He had never seen a stove before, and set to work to light the fire in the oven, as it seemed to be the place intended for the purpose.

Such a mistake is not at all more stupid than the way in

# Introducing the Kafir

which an average person handles a kodak for the first time. He generally forgets to wind up the spool, or to set the shutter; possibly he leaves the shutter open all the time and snaps away for a whole day. I have seen even intelligent people, who were handling a camera for the first time, point the lens at themselves instead of the object to be photographed, expose twelve pictures on the same piece of film, hold their thumb over the lens during exposure, and generally do a dozen bizarre bits of absurdity.

The Kafirs differ from us in their ideas *toto cœlo*. No wonder that since the war the most astounding statements concerning the Kafirs are in circulation in England. In nearly every family there is some member who has "been to South Africa, you know," and who is said to know the natives. But to understand the Kafirs a person must do more than see them amid abnormal surroundings and unnatural conditions: he must do more than travel by rail from Cape Town to Kimberley, Bulawayo, Bloemfontein, Pretoria, Johannesburg, Ladysmith, and Durban: he must do more than see native drivers of mule-teams during war-time. He might as well think that he knew lions and tigers because he had walked round the Zoological Gardens at feeding-time, and heard lion stories of a tall nature at his club; or he might as well think that he understood how the poor live because he had watched the waiters at some hotel, seen flower-girls at Regent Circus or match-sellers in Piccadilly. He needs something more trustworthy than smoking-room gossip, or club yarns, or views from train or hotel windows. "Height is not reached in a hurry," say the natives; and Kafir character is not understood at the first glance.

So let us get on horseback, strap our month's luggage on our saddle, and shake ourselves loose from civilisation and white faces; for we must live among the Kafirs, sleep in their huts, and eat out of their pots, if we would really know how

# The Essential Kafir

they live and what they think about. And let us start by watching our native guide.

Until you are accustomed to this land of great distances you will be for ever asking him how far it is to the journey's end. And hour after hour the good fellow will lift himself in his stirrups, and make a curve with his hand, saying, "Yes, baas: it is just over the rise." He always begins with *Yes*, even when the next word is *no;* he always raises himself in the saddle when he points to the goal; he always declares the end of the journey is just over the rise. This he does out of natural politeness, for he is not troubled with our Western conception of truth. Politeness is far more important in his eyes than truthfulness; he consequently tells you the thing he thinks you would like to hear. An old author describes how he had been asking the natives about strange animals, and among other things he had made inquiries about a unicorn. The natives, wishing to agree with the white man, assured him there was a unicorn some way off. At considerable difficulty this traveller went out of his way for a day, and saw this wonderful unicorn. It turned out to be an old he-goat which had lost one of its horns. The natives did not mean to deceive. They meant to please.

If they can both please you and tell the truth they will do so. They have no objection to truth *per se*. But if a choice has to be made they prefer to be polite first and truthful afterwards; facts have to be adjusted as most convenient. A native will never differ from you if he can help it. He has no objection to truth viewed in the abstract or *in vacuo*, nor has he any preference for deception; but why should he worry himself over such an unimportant thing as truth? His use of language is analogous to his use of a horse: the one he uses to kill time with, and the other to kill distance; and just as he lets his horse jog onward any way it pleases so long as it covers the ground, so he lets his tongue wag that he may pass the time

# Introducing the Kafir

pleasantly. There is this difference, however : he talks for pleasure, but rides for business. (He is everlastingly amused with white men who go out walking just for walking's sake; he is hopelessly at a loss to know why he should do anything so foolish.) His horses are the most woe-begone creatures imaginable, Basuto ponies excepted. Where they find them is a mystery; but, having got them, they put on the horse's back a thing that was a saddle half a century ago—what it is now no one knows—they then fasten it with old bits of string, worn-out bootlaces, or decayed straps; and, being mounted, they place the stirrup between the great toe and the next, hit the horse on the rump with a stick or piece of strap, and the animal starts off with the queerest action. It may be cantering with its hind legs while it trots with the front ; yet the Kafir sits on it in stately dignity, with a perfectly grave face. He frequently rides bareback, with his blanket thrown over his shoulder, and never seems to get stiff or sore, though he covers incredible distances without stopping.

After riding for about two hours we suggest an "off-saddle," and so dismount close to a stream, and knee-halter our horses, allowing them to roll or graze at pleasure. The Kafir thinks this a most unnecessary work of supererogation. Why should a horse be given any rest ? Is it not an animal whose only use is to carry men ? If the rider wants a rest, well and good; but if he is consulting his horse's feelings his action is most uncalled for and gratuitous. That any one should be merciful to an animal, and consult its feelings, never enters a Kafir's head, never rises above the threshold of his mind.

After a short rest, we "saddle up" and continue our journey. When we come to a river we notice that the raw Kafir spits on a stone and throws it into the water, a custom believed to be what a biologist would call a *vestige*, indicating

## The Essential Kafir

an obsolete usage of offering some propitiatory sacrifice to the river-spirit. The natives in olden days were in the habit of either sacrificing some animal or offering some grain to appease ancestral spirits living in the river. The Bushmen used to offer up some game they had killed, or in the absence of that would offer up an arrow. It is very doubtful whether the natives have any fully formed conception of what we call a river-spirit; it seems more probable, on the whole, that they imagined some ancestral spirit to be living in the river, or that some fabulous animal had its home in the water. All the Kafir does now is to throw a stone into the water as some dim recognition of the old custom. It has been suggested that the inveterate way in which even civilised people feel constrained to throw stones into water has some dim connection with this old custom, which makes itself felt through heredity. It is not at all clear that the anthropologists are not putting the cart before the horse in such cases, for why should it not be a natural thing to pick up a stone and throw it into the water without any previous reference to appeasing spirits? Might it not be that people felt the need of developing or accounting for this habit, and so coupled it with the idea of a river-spirit to whom they were offering a stone? In that case the belief would be grafted on to the custom rather than the custom on to the belief.

When the native has advanced into the stream he usually pauses, fills his mouth with water, and, looking round to take his bearings, deliberately spits the water in the direction of his greatest enemy, or in the direction of the kraal where, he fears, they are using magic against him. Action at a distance is a primitive conception with these people, in spite of Sir Isaac Newton. Natives place great faith in spitting in the direction of an enemy: they frequently chew medicines and spit them out in the direction of their enemy: they get their ill-will " off

## Introducing the Kafir

the chest" by this action. They combine self-protection with the expression of contempt for their enemy by this explosive outlet for their venom, and it is but natural to suppose that this custom, which is found in the aborigines of nearly all lands, is at the bottom of the universal habit of spitting at a person as a sign of contempt and malice. Having thus done his duty, the fellow mounts his nag and trots along with a serene mind which is the direct result of the conviction that he has once more balanced accounts with the world.

At last we come in sight of our goal, and see, perched on the side of a kill, a kraal, whose mushroom-like huts are placed in a circle or in the shape of a horse-shoe, so arranged that the drainage naturally flows down to the cattle kraal which is placed on the chord of the curve. Natives always work in circles if possible : the huts are circular; the fireplace is circular, and it is placed in the centre of the hut; the huts are arranged in circles; the cattle kraal is usually circular. The very children can draw perfect circles without the use of any compasses, and in their games they frequently sketch out kraals in the dust with marvellous neatness, the circles being perfect.

This tendency to do things in circles surprises Europeans at first. It will not do to jump to the conclusion that these people have read Mr. Ruskin and so know that a circle is a symbol of rest. A little reflection will supply us with a simpler explanation. It is far easier to build in circles than to build in any other way, and it is far more economical of material. Any one who has tried to mould the corner of a cornice or of a wainscot knows that the chief difficulty comes in with the angles. Any one who has tried to thatch a roof knows how difficult it is to make the corners watertight. The great advantage in living in a circular hut consists in the obvious fact that a slovenly woman cannot leave things to accumulate in the corners. A Kafir hut is bad enough as it is—the roof is a

# The Essential Kafir

general receptacle for every odd article which can be either shoved into the thatch or hung from the rafters; the floor is littered with calabashes, mats, and other rubbish. Give but a woman a corner and see how rubbish will accumulate in it. This can be observed by looking into a Basuto hut, which is frequently made square.

Viewed from a distance a kraal looks something like a fairy ring of mushrooms; but if you want to cherish this pleasing fancy, if you wish to retain this picturesque fallacy, you had better pass on and spend your night in the veldt. To-day you may imagine the country peopled with fairies; to-morrow the feat will be quite impossible, for reasons which will ere long appear.

Before we ride up to the kraal, it may be well to pause and explain the meaning and structure of a kraal. The word kraal does not connote a single hut; it is a collection of huts. It is sometimes called a village; but, for no manifest reason, people always speak of a kraal in one district and a village in another. The terms are interchangeable. As to the origin, the word is said to be a Hottentot corruption of a Portuguese word, and in old works is often spelt *coraal* or *crael*. Some writers say it is derived from the Spanish word *corral*; others say it is derived from the Dutch *kuraal*; or the Portuguese *curral*; or the English *corral*, which comes from the Spanish *corro*—a circle. Authorities can be quoted for each of these derivations, and we may safely leave the origin of the word undetermined. It is spelt in a dozen ways, according to the whim of the writer.

The true Zulu type of kraal is built in a circle, with the cattle kraal in the centre. This cattle kraal is usually a large enclosure, made of sturdy sticks or brushwood—occasionally of stone—with a single opening which can be closed by two or three stout poles. Round this cattle kraal the huts are arranged in a circle, and yet again round the entire kraal there is some-

# Introducing the Kafir

times a palisade which serves to keep out wild animals. Outside the stockade may frequently be seen a few store-huts for grain, in shape like beehives or shocks of corn. In Zululand grain is also kept in huge baskets which are literally built into the huts, though these baskets are becoming scarce.

The shape of a Pondo kraal is a little different. In Zululand the huts look like Brobdingnagian beehives, the thatch extending right down to the ground. In Pondoland the huts look like large mushrooms, the walls being built of wattle and mud, over which is fixed a curved roof of thatch. In Bomvanaland the two types of hut can be seen in the same kraal. The Pondo kraal is usually built in the shape of a horseshoe, the cattle kraal being placed in the mouth of the shoe. The hut facing the cattle kraal belongs to the chief or " great " wife. Often the chief marries her long after he has had several wives, for her son succeeds to the chieftainship, and if he were born at the same time as several rival brothers he would stand a poor chance of surviving all the intrigue and fierce light which beats around a native throne. If he is born in the midst of many rival brothers, their rivalry will be in his favour, and combination against him will be rendered difficult. On the right-hand side of the great wife is the hut of the right-hand wife. She is usually the first wife; but her son cannot succeed to the chieftainship till all the other wives have failed to supply a son. The medicines and the family charms are kept by this "house," and the chief lives in it during many ceremonies. Though it has not the rank of the house which the left-hand wife creates, yet it sometimes gains great power by means of the family charms ; and in case the old chief dies while the young son is a minor, this right-hand house assumes the regency. In certain tribes the son of the right-hand wife has a portion of the tribe allotted to him, and so he forms a new clan. The left-hand wife is called the wife of the ancestors,

## The Essential Kafir

for upon her rests the responsibility of providing an heir in case the great wife or her "Rafters" have no son. It is but six generations ago that this function was instituted. Before this, only one son of a chief was allowed to live. The left-hand wife is sometimes called the Beam, while the lesser wives are called the Rafters; and are all attached to one of these three main houses, which they are supposed to support. In a polygamous family it is necessary that each wife should have a hut to herself to prevent endless squabbles. It should be noted that in ordinary families not related to the chief the first wife married is usually the great wife. Hence a hut-tax practically becomes a wife-tax. The details of these domestic matters vary in different tribes; but the above may be taken as an average of the Xosa Kafirs. It should be added that some of these customs are rapidly dying out, and innovations are being instituted. Further details on these matters will be found in the tenth chapter. But to return to the kraals.

The Swazies build their huts in beehive fashion, but usually place reed fences around them, a practice which the Basutos also adopt. This fence gives a little protection from the weather as well as a rudimentary kind of privacy, and the women frequently cook inside the reed fence instead of inside the huts. In Gazaland the huts are built with short thick stakes of wood, which are more or less—generally less—plastered with mud. The shape of the kraal is not so well defined, however. As one approaches the Zambesi the huts become square, and show signs of rudimentary verandahs. Above the Zambesi it is quite common to find special huts made for the pigeons. These huts are raised above the ground on poles which are some ten feet high, thus giving the birds protection from wild animals and dogs. (An example of one of these pigeon huts can be seen in the photograph of the

# Introducing the Kafir

Native Blacksmith, plate 51. The blacksmith is sitting under this hut.) On the Zambesi and Shire rivers the huts are often placed in long strings on the river bank, while the villages in the plains seem to be constructed on no fixed principle, the huts being dumped down in great confusion. (Examples of these various shapes of hut can be seen at a glance in plates 2, 3, 4, 5 and 51.)

As we ride up to the kraal and dismount we are met by a motley crowd, many of the inmates having watched our progress for fully half an hour. We are far away from civilisation, and it is years since a white man was seen in this kraal. So we have to undergo the ordeal of curiosity and close scrutiny. The children have never seen white men, nor have the girls; but the men have travelled and so are familiar with our appearance.

We are surrounded by a ring of eager faces, and wonder is the order of the day. The bolder children stand in front of the men, and show immense delight in what, to them, is almost a circus-show, the timid children half hiding behind their mothers' blankets, or clinging to their elder sisters, who are giggling in the background. These girls are very excited, and convulsively clutch one another and laugh when any special feature in this novel scene strikes their fancy or sense of humour. The small children, who were bold enough while we were at a safe distance in the saddle, set up a howl on our dismounting, and fly incontinently to the nearest cover, dropping anything they chanced to be holding in their arms —sometimes it is only a baby that is dropped through the inhibition of fear; but that does not matter much, as "it" cannot break. These children have nerved themselves up for the last half-hour to face the white foe that could be seen advancing; but the very action of our dismounting from our ponies had caused the native hue of resolution to be sicklied

## The Essential Kafir

o'er by the pale cast of thought. The children have fled away pell-mell into the bush, just like so many little wild animals. It is the funniest sight to see the babies who are only old enough to crawl. They look on calmly at first; but no impression seems to pierce its way or to struggle through their dull and torpid intelligence. Then slowly they evidently perceive that something is wrong—you can almost see the message travelling up the nerves to the brain—and instinctively make a bee-line to their mother's blanket, in which universal harbour of refuge they hide their woolly heads and lusty yells. No wonder they are frightened at the apparition of white men, for their mothers have often used the bogey of the white man to still their chatter and noise, English nursery fears and methods ruling in Kafir kraals with white substituted for black. The young men greet us with a grin and are quite at their ease, showing considerable interest in our buttons, gaiters, whip, watch-chain, and other trifles. We are in a country where criticism is untrammelled by considerations of European etiquette. Here comment is free of all artificial standards of shame. As soon as the young women and big girls see that it is all right they draw nearer, impelled by that feminine prime mover, curiosity. Presently the children who have run off into the bush, and have been keenly surveying the scene behind the safe cover of some shrub, are convinced that matters are not so grave as they at first imagined, and so they slink out of their hiding-places to join the rear of the spectators, and in a few minutes are examining us, open-mouthed. One little chap goes to the bushes and assures a more timid sister that the white men do not really eat black babies, as their mothers said they would, and comes back very proud in his superior boldness. These children are the most delightful little animals, and are nearly always laughing, so that they display a splendid set of ivory-white teeth; they always have grotesquely fat stomachs, and

Plate 2.

A ZULU KRAAL, LAKE ST. LUCIA.
The interior of the hut on the right, surrounded by a fence, is seen on plate 21.

Plate 3.

IN A NATAL KRAAL.
The Huts are built on the Pondo pattern.

## Introducing the Kafir

are as plump and jolly as sandboys. We may as well look round and take stock of our new friends. Let us take the people in order.

*And first the children.* The tiny boys and girls walk about in stark mother-nakedness and are not ashamed. They are generally guiltless even of a rag, being but slightly differentiated from the animals. Sometimes the little girls have a single thread of beadwork strung round their loins; but this is calculated rather to accentuate than to hide their nakedness. Their black skin and utter absence of self-consciousness is, however, an adequate covering. The most noticeable thing about the little children is the fact that they are all plump, their little beer-barrel "corporations" giving them a delightfully comical appearance. They look quaintly top-heavy, being in a state of unstable equilibrium. They are always grinning, except when they are crying; yet they make such woe-begone faces when they cry that one can hardly help laughing. Thus some one is always laughing, you or they. As a rule their anxious mothers tie charms round their necks, their faith in such things being absolute; no English patent soothing-syrup ever inspired such absolute faith as these charms. The children play together like little animals, and their habits might well convert the most rabid anti-Darwinian.

As the children grow older they annex or "commandeer" some rudiments of dress; the girls affecting a very scanty embryonic petticoat which is made out of cloth of uncertain age and manufacture torn from their mother's old blanket, the original hue being past finding out, as it has been coloured with red ochre and well soaked in grease. Strapped on to the back of each girl is a baby, which she has to nurse for its mother, the nurse frequently being but little larger than the baby. In Pondoland the children have their hair cut in the most fantastic patterns, reminding one of nothing so much as

## The Essential Kafir

poodle dogs, the shaving of the hair being done by means of a piece of broken glass or old hoop iron sharpened up for the purpose—no soap is considered necessary.

*The elder girls* are well clad from the waist downwards, though they vary much as to the covering of the upper part of the body. It is said that in Chaka's days the young unmarried girls were not allowed to dress at all; but if this is not an exaggeration, the custom must have changed considerably. One rarely sees such obtrusive nakedness as one might expect after looking at the photographs thrust into view in the shop windows of Cape Town, Johannesburg, and Durban. At dances and other functions the people put aside their clothing and dress in beadwork. I have travelled for many years among the raw Kafirs, and yet have been far less conscious of their nakedness in real life than when looking into shop windows of colonial towns, where photographs of Kafir nakedness—for that is what photography of the nude too often comes to—are exposed to view. Protesting, one day, with a dealer in these objectionable photographs, I showed him those appearing in this book, and he admitted that mine were far more true to nature than his—he even tried to purchase mine—but said that he had to supply the other kind, as the demand for them was great.

*The women* invariably have a fine carriage, the curve of their backs being very graceful and stately; it is the natural result of their carrying heavy weights upon their heads. They are all physically well-conditioned, their value as an asset turning largely upon their good physique and ability to work well. They consider fatness to be an essential condition of beauty, and to call a woman "a lump of fat" is a high compliment. The women are all large footed and sturdy-limbed, frequently being more muscular than their husbands.

The petticoats the women wear are usually made from oxhide, which is soaked in water until the hair can be easily

## Introducing the Kafir

removed; after this the skin is rubbed and frayed until it is very soft and limp. It is then well rubbed with charcoal to make it black, and after this it is scratched with thorns until a pleasant nap is obtained.

The women are, in body, buxom, round-limbed, deep-bosomed, broad-hipped; in face they are dark-eyed, thick-lipped, large-mouthed; in carriage they are erect and graceful; in manner unconstrained.

The mothers and fathers are always lenient to the female children, for fear lest any rough treatment should diminish their market value—they are often sold in marriage to the highest bidder. The men, however, frequently scold the boys and hit them freely—they have no market value, and rough usage does but the better fit them for the battle of life, which among Kafirs is fairly serious and severe.

Some old writers declare that the women usually have ten children ; Theal places the average number at five, and his estimate is derived from an amateur census compiled by some missionaries. Yet I think that, as the death-rate is very great among children, it would be safer to say that only three or four children per wife survive the risks of infancy. Most Kafir women live in strict seclusion from their husbands while they are suckling their children, a process which frequently lasts for three years. This custom helps to keep the desire for polygamy alive.

As to ornament, the fashion changes as often as in Paris. During one season the people are all wearing safety-pins as ear-rings; the next season no one will look at them, for pins are " out " and buttons are " in." In one tribe blue-spotted cotton handkerchiefs are all the rage; but fifty miles away no one will look at such things—they want cotton shirts. The only universal ornament, perhaps, consists in bead-work. Some tribes, such as the Fingoes and Zulus, take to bead-work more

## The Essential Kafir

than others; the one thing they are all consistent in is a strangely good taste for colour combination. They never indulge in the combination of gaudy colours, never affect an inharmonious colour-scheme, thus strikingly bearing out Ruskin's statement that bad taste in colour does not arise in people who are left to themselves and nature. Bracelets, armlets, necklaces, anklets, and similar "lets". around the upper part of the calf, the thigh, and the waist, are always more or less in fashion, finger-rings being strangely rare. These bangles are made of iron, copper, brass, or grass; occasionally of ivory in the case of chiefs. The Bomvanas seem to love shell ornaments; but the Tembus living beside them seem to despise them. Some women have so many solid brass bangles round their arms that they keep the arm flexed to prevent the weight dragging on their wrists.

Anything is capable of being turned into an ornament by the ingenuity of a Kafir. Thus old cocoa-tins are very useful (see plate 7); the empty brass cartridge-cases of the old Martini-Henri rifles make excellent snuff-boxes, and are worn in the pierced ear. The natives have a curious belief that a person cannot hear well unless the ear is bored. Buckles of old straps, old keys, spoons, combs, feathers, chains, grass rope, string, and such-like articles, are all pressed into service. I once saw a man with a wine-glass fixed into his hair, with a collar round each leg, and no other dress except the skin apron round his waist: the effect was decidedly bizarre.

Boots are rare except near centres of civilisation. When they are worn it is simply for show and effect. Natives living near a mission station will frequently keep a Sunday-go-to-meeting pair of boots. These they carry on their arm till they are near the church; they will then sit down and solemnly put them on, walking into church with conscious and manifest pride, making all the clatter they can, so as to attract attention;

# Introducing the Kafir

but as soon as they are seated you hear the boots being taken off, and all is decorous till the closing periods of the sermon, when you hear a shaking among the dry boots, for the natives must walk out of church with boots on if they wish to be thought correct. Once out of church the congregation will sit down by the road-side and take their boots off, carrying them home under their arm. The boots are then hung up in the roof of the hut, for they will not be wanted again till the owners go to church once more. A native has no real need for boots, for the soles of his feet are covered with a pad of horny skin, the thickness of which amazes any one who extracts a thorn from a native's foot.

With regard to sense of delicacy, the women vary much. Some will instinctively cover their bosoms when a white man is seen approaching; others would no more think of doing so than of standing on their heads. One occasionally sees a woman with a baby strapped on her back who without a blush throws one of her very pendulous breasts over her shoulder and suckles her child; or she will sit on the ground before a stranger and cast off all the covering from the upper part of her body and allow her child to suck its fill from her ample bosom. It is surprising how the sense of shame varies in different races of mankind. We always imagine ourselves to be the pink of perfection and true standard in such matters, being ignorant of the ideas of others. Many a Hottentot woman would expose her bosom quite freely without a thought; but if a small cap came off the back of her head she would suffer torments of shame. An English woman would reverse all this, much to the scandal of her Hottentot sister. Some Eastern races will expose portions of the body which we instinctively cover, and yet they cover up their face in public, and would feel degraded and humbled if they exposed their face in the streets as a European woman would. Each is scandalised by the other's

# The Essential Kafir

lack of delicacy. What woman would walk in the street with the low-necked dress in which she will appear at dinner without any sense of indecorum? A Jew and a Christian differ in their ideas of decency in respect to the wearing of a hat in a place of public worship, and all those who are familiar with the customs of the different South African tribes will recall many strange usages in this connection, which are quite unintelligible to Europeans at first, and cannot be described in print.

*The old women* are scraggy, withered, and shrunken, their skin hanging on their bones. After a certain age they take but little interest in their personal appearance, and allow their hair to go unkempt and dishevelled. They are allowed to break many restrictions which are placed on younger women, being sometimes called men. They lose the grace of past days, and their bodies become bent and deformed. They are always horribly dirty. The natives are respectful to men in old age; but old women are excluded from such attention, so that their lot is sad indeed. A Kafir once said to me, " They are cast-off things ; their use is over." Women have practically no rights, and their function is to work in the fields and bear children and generally administer to the pleasure of the men. If they cannot cook, or till the fields, or bear children, what can they do? They are frequently left to starve or die of exposure and neglect, for they have to depend on the charity of the young and strong, and that is a precarious source of supply to count upon in heathen kraals. The one weapon they have is their curse, which is a thing greatly dreaded by the people. But to be set off against this is the fact that they are frequently accused of being witches, and nothing is easier than to get a witch doctor to " smell out " any old hag who makes herself objectionable. He must have a hard heart who does not feel a lump in his throat when he hears how these poor old creatures are slowly burnt to death because they will not give

## Introducing the Kafir

up the medicines which they are supposed to have used to cause sickness among the cattle or people in the kraal. No wonder that old women sometimes make away with themselves. Kafirs believe that any one who eats a certain tongue-shaped lobe of the liver of an animal (the *Lobus Spigelii*) is sure to forget the past. Only old women eat this, so that they may forget their sorrows—a fact that throws a lurid light on the sad lot of old women, and on the pleasurable nature of life in the case of the men, who have no wish to forget the past.

I shall never forget the picture presented by an old hag in Swazieland who managed to get a little girl to lead her out of her dark hut to beg from me. With great difficulty and after much shouting, she understood that a white man was at the kraal and that it was a good chance to beg for food. The old woman was literally bent double with age, the upper part of her body being parallel with the ground, so that she was like an inverted letter L, her body being supported by her hands, which clutched her thighs as if they were the angle-bits of a bracket. Her nose was eaten away with disease, and she was blind and deaf. I had never seen such a shrivelled, dried-up specimen of woe-begone humanity: her scraggy and pendent breasts were like empty bags of dirty skin and were hanging from a wrinkled, shrunken body. It was long since she had a tooth in her head, and handsful of skin could have been taken up at any part of her body, as if she had been a starved pug dog. She piteously begged for a little salt.

As will be seen later, this lack of respect for old women is a part of the natives' religious system, and is connected with their conception of a future life in which women play a subordinate part, their spirits not being able to cause much trouble and therefore not being of much account. Yet by virtue of their expressive and forcible language they manage to shift for themselves through life, and to keep their heads above water in a striking way; their husbands often have to give in before the blast of their abusive and never-slackening fire of words, in which they do not hesitate to make the most abominable charges against their husbands, without any regard for truth. So fierce is the fire of their raillery and the endless clatter of their unwearied tongues that the men get into despair and know not how to evade the all-penetrating sound of the woman's voice. The woman begins abusing her husband in public—I have often heard it—charging him on the vilest and most obscene accusations, screaming out in frenzy so that all may hear her shameful words. The man at first sits silent under the lash of her scourging tongue, and bears, in strange meekness, the hot abuse. In philosophic calmness he mutters some Kafir proverb, which says, "The mouth is a tail to drive away flies with," or " Water is never tired of running." All this does but irritate the woman, who redoubles her abuse. His philosophy begins to grow thin as he quotes another proverb : " The fly irritates the sore." The woman, baffled and angered by his calmness, turns her back on him in high disdain. She turns from her worm of a husband to the other women, stalking off in hauteur. She goes to her hut, which is a Kafir woman's castle, talking all the time with great volubility. The torrent of her talk pours at white heat from her swelling bosom. She retires, discharging her artillery as she goes, and continues to scream out her vile talk when she is in her hut. For hours she will keep up this stream of vituperation, her voice sounding like some spluttering or murmuring of a distant thunderstorm. The husband's philosophy and patience at length become exhausted, and he walks off to visit his friends.

The moment the wife hears the sound of her husband's returning footsteps she renews the torrent of her abuse. He comes near to the hut and hears the ominous rumble of

## Introducing the Kafir

her fury. She withers him with her ceaseless fire, till sometimes—very rarely—the man goes away in despair and either kills himself or returns to kill the woman, being unable to stand the everlasting clatter of her tongue.

Passing from the women to *the boys*, we find them clad in a small rag, a worn-out piece of wild-cat skin, or a part of an old blanket. Far up north the boys wear a loin-cloth, which is quite the best garment they could adopt, even though it will not remain clean and white for half an hour after it is washed, which is very rarely. The advantage of a blanket, however, is that it can be easily carried on the arm when the weather is hot, and then thrown round the body when entering a kraal. It can also be disposed of about the body in a picturesque way, the folds adding to the graceful effect. It is a sad lapse from an artistic point of view when a native discards his blanket, which is generally coloured red with ochre, for a pair of worn-out second-hand trousers or coat. The traders are guilty of committing much artistic sin when they sell old clothes to the natives. As soon as a decent-looking Kafir gets into European clothing he looks slovenly and awkward. Similarly, when a woman encases herself—we cannot say dresses herself—in old European skirts she looks slatternly and uncouth. It is a thousand pities that the missionaries did not invent some rational dress for the natives long ago.

The small boys are quite naked, and with their large heads look very top-heavy and ridiculous until they grow up a little. However, they are dear little podgy things, with great protuberant stomachs, which swell visibly after food. They never feel the irony of waistcoats in the way in which the little schoolboy did (in *Punch*) who said he could eat more dinner if he might go and " take his beastly waistcoat off" and put his football jersey on instead. A Kafir boy always eats till there is either no more food or no more room for food. As the boys

# The Essential Kafir

grow up they become shy and pass through an awkward stage, just as our boys in England do. Their skin is generally of an earthy grey colour, for it is covered with thorn-scratches ; and they present an ashy appearance, for they lie about in the dust a good deal. After a little while they enter the dandy stage and become very careful of their personal appearance, hold themselves erect, are fastidious as to ornament, display inordinate vanity, cultivate the three hairs which are growing on their chin, take great trouble with their hair, and generally try to take themselves seriously. All Kafirs have great respect for hair on the face, and they imagine a man with a beard to be a great personage, because they have so much difficulty in cultivating a beard themselves.

*The young men* are dressed much like the boys, only more so. Their mode of dress varies a good deal in different tribes ; but usually it consists in a strip of hide, or a few tails of wild cats, which are hung round the loins. An apron of skin is fastened on behind. Men nowadays frequently wear nothing more than a blanket, or a large kerchief or a strip of "limbo." If they have been to Johannesburg—"Goldi" or "Josaberg" is what they usually call it—they will probably have brought back with them a great variety of things, including spats, watches, chains, old neckties, shirts, bunches of useless keys, "swear words," the love of spirits, conceit, disease, and sometimes militant Atheism, all of which things they take to as if to the manner born. Not that it is only at Johannesburg they get these questionable things : they pick up dirt by instinct, and in all conscience were full enough up with conceit, lust, and desire for drink, before they left their kraals. They knew how to emphasise their talk with expletives without European tuition.

But naturally at Johannesburg they are free from what little restraint exists in the tribe, and the virulent germs of their nature find a suitable nidus for a quick "culture." Not

## Introducing the Kafir

that Johannesburg is the unmitigated and blatantly wicked place that many good people at home seem to imagine. Both goodness and badness are apt to assume a vigorous and outspoken tone on the Rand, for there is less conventionality there than at home, and, thank heaven, there is less hypocrisy. Considering that Johannesburg is a young mining city, there is an amount of public order that is surprising. It is quite common for a newcomer to say, at the end of his first day, that the place is not half so wicked as he had been led to expect. The besetting sins of the town do not parade in public in a blatant way : one sees but few drunkards in the streets, though vice is said to have been brought to the perfection of a fine art in more private circles.

But to return to the young men at the kraal. They have brought back old soldiers' coats, marvellous waistcoats, watches which will not go except when well shaken—these they buy from Jewish pedlars—pocket looking-glasses, and in fact everything from a pin to a toothbrush. When a big boy first sees a waistcoat he is much puzzled to know how to get into it ; he tries to put his head through one of the arm-holes, but, finding that impossible, even with the help of his little brother who applies *vis a tergo*, he decides to use the article as a pair of trousers, thrusting his legs through the holes and buttoning the waistcoat up behind. Finally he hitches the whole concern up by a piece of grass string which acts as a pair of braces. He immediately remembers that he has a pressing matter of business at the next kraal and starts off, followed by half a dozen admiring boys. The love of display is very strong in a savage.

Young men like an old pair of trousers, which seems somehow to appeal to their imagination; the more patches it has the better, especially if the patch work is made from cloth of a different pattern from the trousers. They prefer loud check-

# The Essential Kafir

patterns, for these are discordant and attractive. It is surprising to see what good use a boy can make of half a pyjama, or an old stocking, and the cover of an umbrella; or give him a boot and an old shirt and he will tour the surrounding country, causing pangs of jealousy and envy in the hearts of his dandy friends. If any one thinks that this is an exaggeration let him turn to plate 9,, where he will see a boy clad in an old umbrella from which the stick has been removed.

In Swazieland the young men roam about the country in small parties, clad in aprons of skin or bunches of wild-cat tails, carrying assegais and shields. The effect is very good, for these Swazies are splendid fellows, with fine physique and manly bearing. They even surpass the Zulus in appearance. Like all natives, they have but little personal courage in isolation; but let them be infected by the influence of numbers and they are capable of unbounded prowess, especially if they feel sure that victory has been secured by magic, through a great "doctor."

The men are big-limbed, large-boned, well-covered specimens of humanity; they are usually full-blooded fellows with supple limbs, though they are a trifle flabby. However, their pectoral and deltoid muscles are well developed, especially on the Zambesi, where they do a great deal of paddling in canoes. Their skin is always well filled out with underlying connective tissue and fat, so that there are no creases. They remind one of prize animals in a show, and tempt one to dig them in their well-padded ribs with one's fingers. Their lips are usually thick, sensual, and protruding; their noses are flat, broad, and spread out. They are usually courteous and merry, with a well-developed sense of humour. They know how to conceal all emotions except surprise, which they betray by placing a hand over the mouth as they utter some exclamation. They are rarely caught off their guard, and the result is

## Introducing the Kafir

that their carriage is distinctly dignified. In short, the average Kafir is every inch a man.

The Portuguese make the natives grovel in the dust before them, and thus degrade both their own manhood and that of the natives. It is most striking to pass out of Portuguese into British territory and see what a different bearing the natives show. An English official tells the cringing Portuguese native to stand up like a man and not demean himself.

*In old age* the men turn a little grey, become thin and scraggy, and present very bleary eyes with a well-marked *arcus senilis*. In very old age their hair turns white; they grow deaf and infirm, though they retain much of their dignity unimpaired. Noticing that grey hair is connected with old age, they sometimes mistake effect for cause, and consequently pull out all white hairs that they may ward off old age, of which they have a great dread. Especially was this the case with chiefs in olden days, for a chief used to be deposed for no other reason than approaching age, which would render him less fit in war. The great Chaka and Dingan refused to marry, saying that they were too young. They would carefully remove all grey hairs, and became quite excited when they heard that the white men had ointments which would prevent the hair from turning grey and the skin from becoming creased. Chaka was inordinately keen to obtain such a priceless boon, for he feared that his soldiers would kill him when he began to show signs of old age.

Yet the natives show extraordinary respect to old men, and usually a man is quite safe in handing over his possessions and affairs to his son when old age is creeping on him. If the son neglected his father in his old age he would be hounded out of the tribe as an utterly worthless fellow. It is difficult to guess the age of a Kafir, for he looks much younger than a European of the same years would. They never know their age, which

# The Essential Kafir

can only be reckoned by finding out what events in their tribal history they witnessed.

The old men are less particular about their dress, renouncing the vanities of youth. The skin of a wild cat or a blanket is all they need. Still for what, they lose in dress they add in dignity. Their faces betray a long life-history of slyness and cunning; yet they look dignified, if not imperious. A hundred contending passions leave their traces indelibly fixed in the countenance, and one can often see the effect of deceit, fear, suspicion, amusement, authority, sensuality, and many other emotions recorded in their faces. A good specimen of a man verging on old age is represented in the frontispiece. In the case of Old Moliwash we see "a smile striving with a wrinkled face," on which are left traces of a whole lifetime of cunning, dignity, sensuality, cruelty, and good-natured humour. No geological record could be more of a tell-tale than this face. Contrast with this the face of the boy in plate 10, which illustrates the nearest approach to Kafir spirituality I have yet seen. This boy, however, is far from being overweighted with an ethereal nature. On one occasion, at a Mission Station, he was being instructed on the subject of prayer. His teacher wished to interest him and draw out his latent spirituality. Consequently, he asked him to name the one thing above all others which he loved best. With praiseworthy promptitude he answered, "Grub," to give a schoolboy equivalent to his answer. Later he was asked to name the one thing above all others he would like to pray for, and he briskly said, "A pig." Who would care to prophesy what his face will be like when he is as old as Moliwash?

No description of first impressions would be true to life that excluded the all-important question of red clay. A native's dress is never complete without this cosmetic. Red ochre and oil are rubbed into the skin, and frequently into the blanket.

## Introducing the Kafir

When this latter is done by a tribe the people are called Red Kafirs, or merely "Reds." The effect of the anointing with oil and clay is to form a splendid protection against the sun and the rain ; and I think that, objectionable as the practice is from many points of view, it undoubtedly improves the colour of the native, whose skin is more of an ashy or slate-grey than a rich brown. The effect of the red clay is to make the skin the colour of chocolate. I have often tried to match the colour by placing patches of paint against the skin, and have always found that a piece of ordinary chocolate exactly matched the skin.

The women frequently rub red clay and oil into the hair, which is dressed into the most fantastic shapes according to the whim of the tribe. In Pondoland the children's heads are shaved in poodle fashion, patches of hair being left in odd shapes here and there. The girls are very fond of plaiting their hair into long string-like strands. One would imagine it to be a mass of dirty string fitted as a wig. A Pondo woman asks a friend to trim her dirty locks. The method adopted is as follows : The hairdresser places a strap on the forehead and then cuts the hair level by means of a knife, cutting down on to the strap, which protects the skin. (See plate 12.) The kindly office of hairdresser is performed by one girl, who expects her subject to operate on her by-and-by. "The cow licks the one that licks her," say these people; and this custom of returning a kindly office is universal among the natives. They always share food with one another, and no one needs to wait for an invitation to join in a meal.

If you are travelling with twenty boys who are carrying your loads, and happen to give one boy a single sardine, he will share it with all the rest, and every one will get a taste of it. They say, "Throats are all alike in swallowing," which means that if you do not give me now, I will give you tit for tat

# The Essential Kafir

when you want my food. They have numberless proverbs on this point, such as "The wooden dishes go backwards and forwards"—that is to say, the man who offers you meat on a wooden dish will have his kindness returned one day. They also have many phrases which act as delicate hints that they want some food. Thus they say, "Thanks for a pinch of snuff," which implies that they would like to remind their friend that they expect hospitality, and that the mouth needs attending to as well as the nose. If they want a little more beer they will say, "The dance is sweet by repetition." If it is more food they require they will change the metaphor and say, in feigned excuse, "If a dog eats bones it will get to like them." At first one is apt to regard this trait in their character with admiration, for it seems to be splendidly unselfish and generous. I hope it is so, but I will not do more than say with the Scotsman, "I ha'e ma doots"; it may be mere self-preservation which has led to this custom.

But to return to the hairdresser. When the whole day has been spent in dressing the hair the operation cannot be repeated for a month—it is so tedious and laborious. Comfort must give way to appearance, and the hair must not be allowed to rest on the ground at night, lest the labour of the day be thrown away. Consequently, the pillows consist of blocks of wood, on which the nape of the neck has to rest, the head being thus raised off the ground. There is no need to give a picture of one of these pillows, which are well known, and can be seen in the picture of the interior of a hut (plate 15). The pillows in the British Museum which were taken from Egyptian tombs are very similar to those still used in South Africa, though not so elaborately carved.

In olden days the tribes used a blue sparkling mineral powder, made, it is said, from mica-schist, with which to dress the hair. This is now much less common.

Plate 4.

A GAZALAND HUT.

Plate 5.

IN A ZULU KRAAL.

# Introducing the Kafir

In Zululand the women dress their hair in a peculiar fashion. As soon as they are married, or betrothed, they begin to train their hair into a cone-shaped mass, red clay and oil helping the process. The women take great pride in this top-knot, and the woman whose portrait appears in plate 35 flatly refused to be photographed at first, for she dreaded the effect of the witchcraft which lurked in the camera ; but when I told her that I wanted friends across the sea to know what beautiful hair the Zulu women had, she readily succumbed to the soft flattery and allowed the photograph to be taken as she was standing in the fields. The hair of the men is managed in a simpler fashion, except in the case of the Pondos. In Zululand and Swazieland, and other tribes descended from a common stock, the men wear rings on their heads, which distinction is much coveted, for the ring may not be worn till the chief gives them permission. (See plate 17.) Only married men are allowed to wear this ring, and when once they are allowed to adopt it they feel important, for they are regarded as warriors of the nation and are consulted more or less in tribal concerns. The ring is made in various ways. Sometimes the natives take the mid-rib of a date-palm, and twine it into the hair ; over this they spread the dried juice of a small insect, mixed sometimes with powdered charcoal; the whole is then polished. Sometimes the ring is made from the tendon of a cow, though this seems to be an obsolete custom as far as I have been able to discover. Some old writers state that beeswax was used for making the ring. A piece of rush was twisted with a sinew of an ox, and this was sewn into the roots of the hair, beeswax being rubbed into this ring. One of the greatest insults that can be offered to a man is to pull his ring off : that is taken as an affront to his manhood and to the chief who allowed him to wear it. Frequently the rest of the hair is shaved off, usually with a piece of broken glass or a

## The Essential Kafir

piece of hoop iron sharpened up. The shaving is done, as in the case of the children, without any soap; but the skin of the Kafir is so thick that he does not object to the scraping process.

In Pondoland the big boys and young men take inordinate care over their hair: they frequently pull out a few peppercorn masses and wrap grass round a small bunch of hair so as to make it stand out. These masses are cut to the same length and remind one of the stump-end of matches stuck into a pumpkin. Some strands of hair are allowed to grow extra long at the back of the head. Frequently two or three metal combs, bought at a trading store, are kept fixed in the hair, and these young dandies show great vanity in their mode of hairdressing. Fortunately, this quaint desire to become a dandy does not last long: the young fellows present a very laughable appearance while the fit of vanity is on them. (See plates 7, 8, 13, and 14.)

But no description of the outward appearance of the Kafirs would be complete if we failed to refer to the omnipresent odour which streams from these people. It would be impossible to do better than quote an old writer (1577) who says quaintly, " Because they allways annoint themselves with grease and fat, they yeeld a ranke smell." Other old writers keep on insisting throughout their pages that the Kafirs " delight in dirt and filth," that they take supreme pleasure in them, that they are never happy unless dirty. But this is an exaggeration. The men wash a good deal, though the women might well wash more.

All this time the chief has pretended not to see us; he has left us to chat with the people, for it would not be good form to take notice of us too soon. The details of etiquette vary somewhat in different tribes, and also according to the greatness of the chief. Visitors to Lobengula were sometimes kept waiting at a distance for several days, until their capacity of

## Introducing the Kafir

giving presents was considered exhausted and the chief's dignity duly respected. When visiting the old Swazie Queen, many years ago, I was kept waiting outside the kraal—a huge place consisting of about three or four hundred huts—for an hour or longer; then I was admitted inside, but had to wait for half an hour near the cattle kraal, chatting with some old men; by-and-by the Queen, a coarse, greasy old woman, "fat and scant of breath," came waddling like a duck through a reed fence which surrounded her royal hut, and sat on the ground for fully five minutes, pretending not to see me. But on visiting a small chief there is much less delay, and only small presents are required to be given. If the chief is one of medium dignity and greatness a blanket is quite enough to "open his eyes," as the native phrase goes. My work has led me to visit a good many chiefs during the last dozen years or so, including such people as the great Kreli (Sareli) of the Gcalekas, Nqiliso of the Pondos, the old Swazie Queen, the young King Bunu and his mother, as well as several Zulu, Tembu, Basuto, Bomvana, Gaza, and Sena chiefs.

The finest specimen of humanity was undoubtedly Kreli. The local magistrate, Mr. Morris, had kindly offered to take me down to see Kreli at his kraal, and Dr. Soga accompanied us. Altogether we made up a party of about a dozen mounted men, which party included some native policemen who helped to maintain the dignity of "Government" and of the representative of the Great White Queen. What names to conjure with among the natives! Kreli had gathered four or five hundred of his warriors to greet us; and this old chief, who kept the British at bay in the bush for so long, met us at the head of his small force. He was clad in his well-known leopard-skin kaross, and had a huge ivory bangle above his elbow. He stood before us with a proud bearing. Napoleon clad in a leopard skin could not have carried himself with

## The Essential Kafir

greater dignity. As soon as we halted, the old chief lifted his hand up to the sky and said, "Chiefs," and instantly four hundred deep-throated voices thundered out, "Chiefs!" The roar reminded me of old Homer's "loud-sounding sea." Kreli apologised for having so few followers to greet us with, but said Government had taken away his warriors and left him "like a baboon on the top of a hill."

When a chief sends for his men and they come riding up to his kraal, or the Great Place, as they call it, they dismount a little distance away, and, bunching up their blankets in their left hands, point to the sky with their right, calling out the name of the chief. In Tembulandi I saw the leaders of the tribe coming to consult with Tyelenzima, their chief. As they dismounted they all pointed to the sky, calling out his name in rapid succession—"Tyelenzima!" "Tyelenzima!" "Tyelenzima!" The effect was very fine and quite added to the dignity of this young chief. The method of salutation varies greatly in different parts of the world. The Esquimaux are said, perhaps wrongly, to pull one another's noses when they meet; a Malay sits in the presence of his superiors; a Chinaman is said to put on his hat; some Indian tribes are said to show respect by what schoolboys call "cocking snooks," only they place the thumb on the forehead; the natives had to crawl on their knees to Chaka, probably to prevent them from taking him at a disadvantage. In several tribes in South Africa natives now shake hands—or two fingers—adopting the European custom. Other tribes have an attractive custom: when they meet their friends they all sit down and clap their hands. They then ask the news, and when they hear anything pleasant they start clapping again. When there is a natural period in the conversation they start clapping. This custom is practised in Bechuanaland, Gazaland, and above the Zambesi. Kissing is usually said to be a modern importation from Europeans; but

A PONDO GIRL WITH BABY.

A PONDO DANDY.

# Introducing the Kafir

there is evidence that it was an old custom among the natives. A century ago men always kissed their wives and sisters when returning from war or a long expedition. They may have adopted this system from Europeans. Writers in the eighteenth century talk of it as an old custom in South Africa, and the folklore of the people contains references to kissing. In addition to this, the natives sometimes call a thorn-bush, which Europeans name " Wait-a-bit," by the expressive name " Come and I'll kiss you."

But the commonest greeting among ordinary Kafirs is to say " I see you " ; to which the answer comes back, " Yes.' When a native passes a European away from civilisation he will frequently not wait for the white man to say " I see you," but will start off with a loud " Yes."

But, instead of describing any exceptional visit to a chief, let us select an average visit, choosing a chief of medium greatness, such as the late Nqiliso of Western Pondoland.

This chief had been expecting us to stay the night at his kraal, which we reached on horseback at about an hour before sunset. The old chief was sitting near the cattle kraal engaged in trying a case which had been brought to him. He was consequently surrounded by his old councillors. Nqiliso was an immensely fat man and could hardly walk. He was clad only in a dirty old flannel shirt, and was sitting on a sheep-skin kaross, and by his side was a fine ebony stick, beautifully carved, which had been given him by a former visitor. There sat the old chief at the entrance of the cattle kraal, much as old-time patriarchs might have sat at the gate of the city, dispensing justice. The chief was just finishing the case, and after pronouncing judgment turned to us, chatting a little to his councillors. It would have been rude for us to speak first: so we sat in silence, and pretended not to see him. At length he looked up at us and said, " I see you," and the ice was broken.

# The Essential Kafir

We grunted an approval of the sentiment and said the proper things. Of all ways of expressing sentiment, grunting, as it is done by the Kafirs, takes pre-eminence. Their simple grunt can express a whole world of sentiment. After hearing natives express so much by grunting one does not despair of the very pigs learning to speak. They have many very expressive exclamations, such as " Yo ! " when they wish to show contempt, " Hau ! " when they show surprise, " Wow ! " and many other similar utterances.

The conversation with the chief developed naturally. He wanted to know first why we had left our home across the sea, and why we came to his country ? Did we not want to eat up his land ? Was our country such a bad one that we had to come to his ? If not, why ever did we leave a better country for a worse ? How long did we mean to stay in his country ? What did we want to come and see him for ? Had we ever seen the Great White Queen ? What was she like ? Was she greater than South African Chiefs ? Were there more Boers or English in the world ? Why did not the English turn the Boers out of the country ? How big was London ? Was it as big as his kraal ?

When the questions began to be a little too personal we told our native servant to fetch the blanket we had brought with us in order to open the chief's eyes ; possibly, if we opened his eyes we might shut his mouth. When we gave him the blanket he looked at it and gave a grunt which was one of moderate and guarded approval, but yet distinctly one of approval. He felt the qualities of the blanket with his fingers, placed it to his skin to feel how warm it would be ; he then showed it to his councillors and asked them bluntly what they supposed it had cost. When he was satisfied that it was better than any kept by local traders he gave another grunt of approval which plainly said, " Thanks ; I think that on the

## Introducing the Kafir

whole it is not bad; I have seen better, but it will do all the same." Then he said in words, "Now my eyes are open and I can see you." In fun, I began to chaff him and said, "Well, if you can see us now, will you tell us what you can see?" Did you ever expect to get the better of a native in talk? Vain delusion! Swift as light came the answer, "I shall know what I see when the night is cold and I wrap the blanket around my body." A native never commits himself if he can possibly help it. After a little more desultory conversation the chief thought it was time to end the indaba—" to hem up the fringes of the talk with the thread made from the sinew of an ox," as their expressive phrase runs, for the sun was nearing the horizon and was flooding the whole country with golden-orange light. With great difficulty I persuaded him to let me take his photograph: he had much antipathy to the process. I photographed him just as he stood.

Crouching on his heels close to the chief was an attendant, who had nothing to do but to watch every movement of his master. This fellow was a splendid piece of human flesh and as lissom as a tiger. He seemed to divine the least wish of the chief, but was never the least fussy; in fact, he was a perfect servant. He moved about with an indescribable softness as if he were a cat, and a mere glance and sign from the chief told him to go and fetch the dinner. All the chief did was to pat gently that portion of his enormous body which ought to have been covered by the fifth waistcoat button, and the attendant ran off like a flash of light. He took a huge chunk of boiled beef from the wives of the chief, who were doing the cooking, and placed it with his hands on a greasy wooden plate or dish. He then placed a small grass mat before the chief, and with a wooden probe prodded the meat to find the most tender part. This he cut off with a penknife and handed to the chief on the mat, kneeling on his knees all the time. Without any ceremony the chief began to tear the meat with his teeth, using a jack-knife to cut his mouthful off from the chunk, which he held up to his lips with his left hand. By this time the attendant had cut off another chunk of meat, which he gave with his hands to the chief, who passed it on, with his fingers, to his chief councillor, who received the meat in both hands to show his belief in the chief's boundless liberality, and said "Chief!" as he took the food. When all the important men had been similarly helped by the chief, the attendant simply threw masses of meat to the lesser ones, calling out their names as he threw the lumps. In a few moments there was a remarkable silence, as all jaws were hard at work, to say nothing of fingers, which, however, they managed to keep uncommonly clean. Nothing was offered to us—to our joy, for the sight was very unappetising.

All this time the dogs were lying on the ground, seemingly asleep; they knew by long experience that there was no hope for them. But suddenly these dogs all jumped up and began to show great delight, some almost dancing, and others literally grinning. Wondering what caused this sudden change, we looked round and saw two small boys leading a sheep up to the kraal. The dogs knew instantly what this was for. It was the chief's return present to us, and the dogs knew they would get some of our dinner. It was "only a chicken," the chief said to us in a very deprecatory tone, snapping his fingers to add to the dramatic effect, "just to open your eyes."

By this time the chief had finished his food, and a hungry Pondo, who had so far received nothing, was given the empty wooden dish to lick, which he did with great gusto. Not a particle of meat was left, and the very fingers were licked clean. So we signed to our boy to lead away the sheep and kill it, for it is customary to give most of the meat to the people of the kraal. A chief may be as vain as a peacock; but he always

## Introducing the Kafir

speaks disparagingly of his present. Nqiliso apologised for not giving us an ox, by saying the rinderpest had killed them all off; yet he knew that we knew that he knew this was untrue. To give oxen grieves the natives to the heart, for all their delight is placed in three things—oxen, grain for beer, and women, which constitute the Kafir trinity of delight.

While our sheep was being killed we thought we would test the marvellous memory of these old men: so we asked for a list of ancestors. The Kafirs have no written language of their own, and they have therefore to trust to their memory, which is consequently marvellous. In a few moments I had written down in my note-book the following list. I dare say that it will convey some idea of the sound of Kafir names: Nqiliso, Damasi, Faku, Ngqungqushe, Nyawuza, Tahle, Ndayimi, Citwayo, Bala, Kangata, Cabe, Ncindise, Msiza, Tobe, Hlamandane, Hlamba Ncububende, Ziqelekazi, Dlemini, Mkondane, Sihula, Santsabe, Umpondo, Sibisidi. As far as I can find out, this takes us back to about the beginning of the sixteenth century, for it goes back twenty-three generations. The striking thing about this list was the unanimity shown by the majority of old men: only now and then was there any discussion as to the right order, and probably none of these old men had thought of the order for more than fifty or sixty years.

The subject then turned to religion, and the old chief explained his ideas on cosmogony and kindred subjects. When we asked him whether he intended to become a Christian he laughed and said, " When I can become one by swallowing some medicine I will do so." This is a common answer for a native to give: he has such unbounded faith in the power of medicine and witchcraft that there are no limits to what is possible in this direction. The witch-doctors are often consulted by relations who wish to get some medicine which will

## The Essential Kafir

counteract the influence of the missionary, who is supposed often to act on people by magic. The only objection to medical missions is the way the people at first think the missionary is using powerful magic; yet this soon wears off as the natives mark the kindliness of these admirable men.

Looking round, we were surprised to find that the sheep was already killed; and the dogs were licking up a little blood which had been accidentally spilt on the earth. The Kafirs eat the blood of their animals—except when they are offered in sacrifice. Not a sound had betrayed the suffering of the sheep, and this is why the natives usually choose a goat or an ox for a sacrifice to the spirits of their ancestors. Goats and oxen make a noise when they are being killed, and thus attract the notice of the ancestral spirits. A sheep is dumb before her slayers.

The chief suggested that it was time for us to see the hut set apart for us, and he led us into a large hut some twenty-five feet in diameter, which had been cleared out for us and our party. Some of his wives had swept the hut out, making a broom from a few twigs of the nearest bush. The floor of a hut is usually made with the earth of ant-heaps, which forms a very hard and firm cement; this is smeared with cowdung at frequent intervals. To a new-comer the practice seems very dirty; but a short stay in the country will convince him that it is an excellent plan, for it helps to keep vermin away. The Dutch also adopt this method of keeping the floor polished and clean; but whether they learnt it from the natives, or *vice versâ*, I cannot tell.

As the chief retired for the night, that he might leave us free to cook our food, an old rogue of a councillor came up to me and pulled my sleeve; with an expressive grunt he made it clear that he was going to be very confidential; then he began

# Introducing the Kafir

to beg for the skin of the sheep, in order that he might make a kaross for one of his children. No sooner had he gone away satisfied, than another old fellow came up and said that he hoped that I would give half the sheep to him, to divide among the people of the kraal. This request was considered quite an ordinary one. I believe a Kafir could give lessons in begging even to a Neapolitan mendicant. The very Prime Minister of Swazieland came up to me once and begged for a box of matches!

A dozen willing hands set to work to skin and clean the sheep, and in a few minutes several fires were blazing, for a great treat was about to start. It was most surprising how people from the neighbouring kraals had got wind of our arrival, and discovered that they had very important business at the Great Place. They tried to give the impression that they had come quite accidentally. Of course, they needed no invitation to remain. A great many people live close to a chief, for they feel safe in his presence. They say the chief has a long shadow, or a large kaross; which means that the area of his protection is large.

And now the feast began in real earnest: there was no waiting for a preliminary grace. Charles Lamb has traced, in a charming and well-known essay, the custom of saying grace before meat to those savage times when the whole family gathered round the captured game, and danced for joy in prospect of a good meal. And if Jean Ingelow is right in saying that " Joy is the grace we say to God," then the Kafirs say grace with a vengeance. Meat is a great treat to them, and if they know that there is a chance of getting meat to-morrow, they will do what many a child does who is going to a Sunday-school treat : they will half starve themselves in advance and tighten their belts. I once accused a Kafir of being greedy : I shall never do so again, for he turned on me such eyes of reproach as he said, " Me greedy,

# The Essential Kafir

Baas? It takes *two* Kafirs to eat a sheep in a day, but only *one* Hottentot: Hottentot greedy, not Kafir." An old writer declared he saw five Kafirs eat an ox in a day and a half. To eat well is but to do one's duty, and it is a thing to be rather proud than ashamed about. Bunu, the late king of Swazieland, once said to his warriors, " Which of my men can eat the most ? " A great strapping fellow, whom I knew, said that he could. Thereupon the king gave him a quarter of an ox. No one else volunteered to beat him at this work. The fellow sat up all night eating, and as the sun rose in the morning all the meat was gone, and he was breaking the bone to get the marrow out! Then the king declared he was the best man in his kingdom. Chaka told visitors who brought him presents of medicine for his soldiers that they did not need them : " Beef is the best medicine," said he, " for my soldiers " : and he added that when they could not eat that it was time they should be killed off, for they could do no fighting.

A Hottentot or a Bushman can eat meat that is quite putrid, with no ill effect. The ordinary Kafirs cannot do this, though they can enjoy meat that is, from our point of view, hopelessly bad. They always eat the animals that die of sickness, and when a friend of mine expostulated with a Pondo for eating the oxen which had died of rinderpest, the man grinned and said, " When a white man has an ox that dies he buries it in the ground ; but when a Kafir has an ox that dies he buries it also—he does so by eating it."

A sheep is only a small feast : you should see an ox being devoured ! The animal is hacked into chunks which are boiled in irregular-shaped masses : the viscera are roasted on the embers and eaten uncleaned ; some pieces of meat are roasted on wooden skewers, and portions are swallowed almost raw. The "lights" and other parts of the viscera are frequently given to the herd-boys, who eat them raw. They smear the faces of the

Plate 8.

A PONDO BOY.

Plate 9.

A BOMVANA FAMILY.

# Introducing the Kafir

small boys with blood, so as to make people believe they have shared the meat with the children; consequently, to say "You smear me with blood" is a forcible way of saying "You accuse me falsely." The dogs prowl round and devour all they can seize, frequently stealing pieces from the very embers when the cook's attention is suddenly called away. They wait till they see a small child with both its hands and all its teeth busy struggling with a hopelessly large portion, and then they make a sudden raid on the child and run off with the meat, leaving the forlorn child howling, amid the chaffing and laughter of its elders, who think that the dogs have a right to what human beings cannot defend. Thus the children are trained in a stern struggle for existence. The mothers are responsible for the boldness of the dogs, for they use them as napkins. This may seem an exaggeration to those who have never seen these people at home; but it is quite common to see a baby being fed with clotted milk out of the hand of its mother; the child's face gets smeared all over with milk, and, as these people have no handkerchiefs, the mother calls up one of the dogs and gets it to lick clean the baby's face. I have photographed this scene because I found that people did not believe the statement. (Plate 16.) The photograph is an end of strife.

When the meat is all gone the men gnaw the bones, and finally break them to get the marrow out; and what remains of well-sucked bones is thrown to the dogs. Darkness mercifully descended on the scene, so that we saw only the swaying of black bodies and gleaming of white teeth, lit up by the glare of the smoky fires. Within three hours there was nothing left of the sheep except the skin, which was pegged out on the ground to dry.

I have gone into unnecessary length, it may be thought, to prove that the natives are coarse, for it is necessary that at the start we should agree that, whatever else the natives are, they

# The Essential Kafir

certainly are animals. They are hardly the "dear creatures" who figure in enthusiastic missionary meetings.

To return to our kraal. When living in a state of nature man gets into the habit of going to bed at a shockingly early hour, especially if he has been in the saddle since five in the morning. All this time we had been sitting in the cool night air, and now we began to discuss the everlasting question as to the earliest hour a person can decently go to bed. One generally comes round to the conclusion that this is half-past seven—one *may* go to bed earlier, but it is hardly decent. To-night we are turned into Kafirs, and so can retire as soon as we like, for we shall have quite half a dozen natives sleeping in our hut. But, as we should be sleeping in unusual conditions of refinement at the chief's kraal, let me rather describe an average night spent in a hut which we have stumbled on in the dark: thus we shall really sleep with the family and see how the natives live amid ordinary conditions.

On dismounting in the dark at a kraal we come to the small door of the hut, which is about two feet high, and, kneeling down, signify our presence by a grunt. Being told to come in, we find it easier said than done. Crawling "on all-fours," we push our head into the hut and then draw it back, feeling as if we had been struck in the face: this is caused by the dense smoke—thick enough to be cut with a knife—and Kafir odour. It is far worse than a good London pea-soup fog of the most virulent type. Filling our lungs with the fresh night air, we crawl quickly into the hut, and a strange sight slowly becomes unveiled before us as we grow accustomed to the darkness and the smoke.

Everything is of a red-brown colour, the very people looking as if they had just been fashioned out of the earth or dirt of their kraals, which seems to cling to them. The first thing we clearly distinguish is the fire, which is placed near the centre of

# Introducing the Kafir

the floor ; the smoke rises into the hut and escapes as best it may, causing the roof to have the appearance of the deepest jet-black polished ebony. As the thatch may be several feet thick, the smoke finds great difficulty in escaping, and wanders round the hut. It is true that in some tribes the main cooking is done outside the hut, behind the reed wind-screen ; yet one cannot help smiling at some of the recent war-books when dealing with native matters. One writer makes the serious statement that " Fires are apparently made outside," and goes on to say that these huts are " sometimes thatched with grass." This is modesty where one expected something very different. Or did the writer mean to say that the huts are usually thatched with slate ? Kafir huts are invariably thatched with grass, and even if the cooking is occasionally done outside, a fire is almost invariably found inside the hut.

On the left of the fire we dimly discern the outline of a dozen women and as many children ; half a dozen babies are squalling lustily, for they are being told to go to sleep, and resent the intrusion of nasty white men. They are being put to bed— that is to say, in plain language, they are being rocked to sleep after being tucked into the blanket on their mother's back. The children are visible chiefly on account of their white teeth, which reflect the glare of the fire, and by their glistening eyes. Some of the children are busy roasting mealies in the ashes of the fire, while dogs and hens are prowling round seeking for food. As a dog puts its head into some calabash, two or three sticks are hurled at it from different directions, the only effect of which is to send the hens flying through the fire and frightening the babies. On the right side of the hut we see six or seven men who are squatting on their haunches. The mother and the daughter are allowed to cross to the right side of the hut; but the daughter-in-law may not, a custom which will be explained later. We notice that none of the people

# The Essential Kafir

sit with their back to the fire : the Basutos say that a person is in danger of becoming a monkey if he allows his back to become heated by the fire.

We were just beginning to explain our plight and to ask for a night's lodging, when a dog began to curl itself up in a large basket ; it had evidently never studied the science of statics, for it upset the balance of the basket, which rolled over it, causing a tremendous noise and general shouting of strong language. We now notice that there is an old man close to us sitting on a mat : he holds out two fingers to us, which we shake. He grunts approval of nothing, and then offers us a seat : we must use this word, though the article was a Kafir pillow made out of a branch of a tree. Our eyes are now becoming accustomed to the smoke, and we notice that the roof is filled with articles of all sorts : calabashes hang down from it ; pegs are fixed in it to hold old blankets, dirty pots, medicines, spoons, an old pair of soiled trousers, and other articles. Away in the background we notice a calf tied up to one of the roof-poles, while feathers of birds are nailed on to the wall in one place. Against the wall are heaps of mats, assegais, sticks, and dried ox-skins.

On the left side of the hut is a woman suckling a baby quite unabashed. Another baby is sitting on her mother's lap, sucking her necklace and two or three fingers. It is strange that fir children suck their fingers and not their thumbs. (See te 27). While we are talking to the old man two or three blackbeetles run under our boots, and a big boy close by gives a yawn and without ceremony rolls himself up in his blanket and goes off to sleep, almost with a bang. He is snoring now to his heart's content. But inadvertently a small child has disturbed the roosting hens, which fly all round the hut. An old cock lights on the sleeping beauty, who awakes with great anger and indignation. Every boy and girl in the hut suddenly

Plate 10.

KAFIR SPIRITUALITY.
A Tembu Boy.

Plate 11.

THE HAIRDRESSER.
Red clay and oil is being rubbed into the hair.

## Introducing the Kafir

seizes the nearest article it can find and hurls it at the peccant hens, who finally retire once more to their rest, after giving forth a loud expostulation over their unkindly and indecorous treatment. The disturbance being quelled and the enemy driven off, the mothers tell the children to make the beds; this only means to clear out some of the rubbish and place mats and wooden pillows on the floor. These pillows seem to be made on the principle involved in the hoary old story of the Irishman who slept one night on a single feather. In the morning he is reported to have said, " Bedad, if one feather is so hard, what must a lot be like ? " and ever after used a stone for a pillow. The Kafirs, therefore, make their pillows of the hardest material they can find.

As the mats were being spread, other animals came to light; there were two or three cats, several goats, and a sickly sheep. Without any ceremony, the people lay down and were soon snoring, while we looked round, scratched our heads, and began to take our coats off. These we rolled up and decided to use for pillows. But first we went outside to see that our horses were right. We unstrapped our blankets from the saddle, and once more turned in for the night, to find all the natives caught in the meshes of sleep, for " all day they sweat in the eye of Phœbus, and all night long sleep in Elysium." Taking a small piece of candle out of our pocket, we lit it at the dying embers, and looked round for a moment: then we made a rampart of " Keating " round the area we meant to annex, sprinkled the powder over the blanket, and prepared to lie down.

Soon all was perfectly silent—except the rhythmic breathing of the people and the heavy breathing of the animals. We wished one another a good night and blew out the candle. All went well for two minutes: we felt drowsy, and waited quietly for sleep to come down from the blissful skies. An

## The Essential Kafir

occasional cluck of a hen was most disturbing, and undid the good of the last two minutes' attempt to sleep. Then another hen thought her sister was taking up an undue share f the perch and objected in a querulous tone. Again all was still. Then I felt myself rapidly falling into a delicious doze, until the thought dawned on me that something was crawling on my blanket. With a great mental effort I tried to ignore it : the effort only roused me ; I felt hot, uncomfortable, and tossed over from side to side ; at last I became quite delirious and determined to strike a match, but feared to wake my friend. Soon I noticed by his breathing that he was as wide awake as I, and so I struck a light, just in time to see half a dozen blackbeetles crawl away from my blanket, like guilty things surprised. We both sat up and shook the blankets and had a good laugh. Then, seizing the "Keating" tin, we emptied its contents all over the place till we sneezed so loudly that we awoke dogs, hens, goats, cats, and old men. The whole thing was so laughable that I asked my friend a South African riddle: "How does Keating kill——?" He indignantly denied that it did kill, and I said, "Why, it makes them sneeze so that they break their backbones." He tried to laugh, and mumbled out, "I wish it did."

It will be safer to say no more about the agonies of the night. All who wish to know more of such experiences are referred to the amusing description in Kinglake's delightful "Eothen," where he has a most eloquent passage, which I will not spoil by quotation, merely giving the first sentence. He had settled for the night in some old Eastern church in Palestine and was badly treated by the vermin. He says, "The congregation of fleas which attended my church alone must have been something enormous. It was a carnal self-seeking congregation, wholly inattentive to the service that was going on, and devoted to the one object of having my

# Introducing the Kafir

blood." He then describes the congregation which attended at his church.

At about an hour before the first streak of light in the east, an old cock awoke us all with his strident greeting, and for a moment there was a clatter on the hen-roost and among the animals ; however, all soon found out that it was a false alarm. I then sank into the most delicious sleep, as though I had been some sick child after a delirious night, when suddenly this dreamless sleep, or sleep which was "bordered with dim dreams," was rudely disturbed by two great flapping wings brushing past my face, as a fat old hen came to rest on the floor near the fire. It then raised itself up and began to flap its wings violently, causing a miniature hurricane among the ashes of the fire. Lighting a candle, I began to think of getting up, and was just fumbling in a pocket for my watch, when another fat hen came hurtling through the air and flew about the hut, the wind blowing out the candle which had just been kindled. I lay back disgusted, and in semi-drowsy stupor began to mutter to myself, " Wings of the wind," " Wind of the wings," " No—Wings of the——" when some one threw down the small wattle fence which served as a door to the hut and a stream of rosy light burst in. In a few moments we were all in the open air, trying to forget the agonies of the night.

Soon the babies started the music for the day, the hens were turned out of the hut, and the men emerged one by one on their hands and knees : a boy blew up the embers of the fire, which never seems to die out, and in a few moments a thin wreath of smoke was curling up into the fresh morning air. When the fire has actually gone out it has to be kindled by friction if there are no matches handy, though usually nowadays matches are found in every kraal. The mode of making the fire by friction is very interesting.

A native takes two special sticks, made of a light wood.

# The Essential Kafir

One of these he points : this is called the male-stick. He then makes a conical hole in the centre of the other stick, which is called the female. Placing the female-stick on the ground, he holds it firmly by his feet—a native finds no difficulty in this, as he can easily pick things off the ground with his toes if his hands are full. He then places the pointed stick into the conical hole, and slowly twirls the male-stick between his hands. He does this while using a good deal of pressure, and the wood becomes powdered, lying round the revolving point in a little heap of dust. When he thinks he has made sufficient of the wood dust, he twirls the stick very fast and in a moment the powder bursts into flame, which he uses to set fire to some dried grass. (See plate 17.)

Having cooled one's head in the fresh morning air, all one needs is a wash and a brush-up. If there happens to be no river near, one must rest content with a lick and a promise, in which a native will gladly render his aid. The method is very simple. Fetching a small pannikin of water which holds about half a pint, he will let it slowly dribble in a thin stream over your wrists and hands, while you rub yourself; then, when your hands are clean, he will let the water drip slowly over your head and neck as you stand half-stripped in the open air, for *al fresco* is the order of the day. It is surprising how well a man can wash in half a pint of water on this method; and, as the water has to be fetched from a long distance, it is a very convenient method to adopt. The natives help one another at this operation; but if no friendly help is near the fellow will fill his mouth with water and let it dribble slowly over his hands. Many a mother have I seen give her baby a morning bath in this fashion—seen and photographed too ! (See plate 18.)

Having washed, you begin to admire the view spread before you, for the blood-red sun is rising above the horizon. The natives are singularly deficient in æsthetic taste, and they have

# Introducing the Kafir

not even a rudimentary sense of beauty; yet the degraded Bushmen, whom the Kafirs heartily despise and regard as animals, have left their drawings on the rocks and caves where they once lived. These drawings will be described in a later chapter. The only beauty the Kafirs recognise is the fatness of their women and the colour of their oxen. That any one should admire the beauty of scenery never enters a Kafir's head. I once asked an old Bomvana chief, who had selected the site for his kraal amidst the most beautiful scenery, whether he admired the view. The old man did not want to be rude, but knew not how to conceal his merriment; he went off into a hearty chuckle or series of explosive eruptions, and said he only chose the site that he might be able to feast his eyes on his cattle feeding and corn ripening in the valley beneath, and be safe in case of a surprise attack from some foe.

And so, when we delight in the gorgeous sunrise, the natives do not know what we can see in it: can we eat it? If not, what is there to admire in it? Yet I must try and describe a sunrise I once saw on the Drakensberg Mountains. It was in the middle of an eight-hundred-mile ride, and we had stopped at a trader's shanty over night. Long before dawn we were up and getting ready for an early start, as we had to cross Ongeluck's Neck and make for Morosi's mountain. We fed our sturdy little Basuto ponies and packed up our saddlebags, and were soon on the edge of Basutoland, that Switzerland of South Africa. The Kafir track over the mountains led to a precipitous pass which was known as Ongeluck's Neck, over which Kock had led his people many long years ago. How he managed to bring his waggons down these precipitous rocks is a mystery, even though one knows that he tied the wheels and fastened his ploughs behind his waggons to act as breaks. To get up some parts of the road we had even to dismount from our Basuto ponies, which would almost ride up one side of a house and canter down the other, and we had to clamber up on hands and knees, leaving our ponies to follow as they pleased. We reached a pinnacle, and sat down to rest in order to regain our breath before mounting our ponies.

Below us lay the sleeping country spread out in the sunrise. The grey dawn was brooding over the land, and here and there faint streaks of crimson were fretting the sky. This was clearly to be no " morn in russet mantle clad," but a " rosy-fingered morn " that would have delighted the old Greeks. Away a thousand feet below us lay the country extending towards the sea as far as eye could pierce, and the morning mists were thick in all the valleys, looking exactly like some ocean of silver foam. Here and there a hill-top pierced the foam and rose like some volcanic island out of the ocean. The sun rose apace, and very soon a ruddy light suffused the mist, causing it to look like the pink foam of some wine-red sea. The sun thrust up his rosy fingers into the air as if he were trying to climb above the horizon. Hill after hill rose out of the ocean of mist, as the power of the morning sun dispelled the products of the darkness. Small clouds of the deepest crimson flecked the pale orange-coloured sky; but as the burning sun shone on them they slowly dissolved away in light. Little by little the valleys emerged from the chilling mists, and we scampered up to gain a vantage-ground from which to get our last glimpse of the glorious scene ; but all had vanished and faded into the light of common day. The native guide looked on impassively : to him there was no beauty in the sight : he would prefer to look at a good fat ox being skinned. So let us leave the sunrise and return to the kraal where we spent the night.

Our companions, sitting out in the sun, are indulging in snuff. The taking of snuff is a great ceremony among the natives: they can do nothing without this. In olden days it was

# Introducing the Kafir

considered " bad form " to offer snuff to a person. The greatest man in the company considered it to be his right to supply it, and thus show his wealth and importance. The people would ask him to give them snuff, and etiquette would lead him to refuse, in order that he might be asked again. He would then give a tardy consent. If he showed any anxiety or hurry in acceding to the request he would be thought to be offering them some snuff with bewitching medicine in it, and any illness which followed his offer of snuff would be put down to his evil designs, and might cost him his life. So he would most reluctantly give in after being pressed for snuff. When people take snuff they must not stand up : to do so would be very rude. This habit is the survival of a practice current in olden days. When a man wished to kill another he would ask him for snuff, and as his friend was fumbling in his bag for his snuff-box he would suddenly kill him. It was a famous way of taking a man at a disadvantage. Thus it became bad form to stand up when taking snuff, for when men were all squatting down no evil could be intended. The great person pours out some snuff into the middle of his left palm, and offers it to the people in turn.

Nowadays every one has snuff; and the people, both men and women, keep it in curiously-made boxes, which are devised out of many articles, such as old Martini-Henry cartridge-cases, small gourds, bottles, tin boxes, pieces of horn, and so forth. Great ingenuity is shown in the manufacture of snuff-boxes, which are often wonderfully worked up and ornamented with brass and copper wire. The snuff is made from crude tobacco, grown at every kraal; this is powdered up and mixed with the ash of the aloe, and the whole is carefully ground on a stone and slightly damped. If the snuff does not bring tears to the eyes the people press their fingers over the lachrymal duct, drawing a finger down from the eye to the corner of the mouth, to stimulate the tears. When they sneeze they say "Chiefs," or "May the chiefs bless me," much as people in the lower classes in England say "Lor' bless you." To sneeze is thought to be a very good sign. In ancient days, when a Zulu chief sneezed all the people near would say, "May the chief live long," or "May he grow greater." If a sick person begins to sneeze the people say it is a sure sign that he is about to get well, for the spirits are pleased. The taking of snuff has given rise to a very good proverbial saying. If a person makes a stupid mistake a man will say, "I sent him for snuff and he brought me ashes"—a saying which expresses great contempt for any error.

As soon as the people are refreshed by snuff they begin to think about the day's work. Women set off with huge pots on their heads to fetch water (see Plate 19); some go to the field to bring food; others go to bring firewood. It is marvellous to see how the women can carry great weights. Turning to a man on your left, you ask him if he can lift yonder huge earthenware pot. He laughs at the question, and says that of course *he* cannot, but that his wife could do so quite easily. This he says with no trace of shame. It is the most natural thing in the world, he thinks, that a woman should lift a larger pot than a man. Is it not her work? Was she not made for this?

The natives are not very particular about the water they drink: they do not need Pasteur filters, for they prefer the water to be fairly thick and strong. But, fortunately, they know nothing about microbes and bacteria: consequently, they take no harm from contaminated water, for "there's nothing either good or bad, but thinking makes it so."

The natives fetch the water early in the day in tropical districts, because the pools shrink away during the day and fill up at night.

# Introducing the Kafir

As soon as the women are back from the river they set to work at all kinds of odd jobs : some mend the thatch ; others grind the grain, or make Kafir beer. This beer is made, as a rule, from Kafir corn, which is soaked and allowed to sprout ; it is then dried and powdered up and soaked in water ; sometimes special roots which contain a ferment are added to help the process. The stuff, which is a sort of thin dirty gruel, acts as both food and drink. It seems to be very healthy in moderate quantities, though its effects are bad when drunk to excess. In handing the beer to a stranger a native will always taste a little first to show there is no danger of poison.

And what are the men doing all this time ? They lie about and smoke and chat—what else should they do ? If the weather be cold, they wrap themselves up in their blankets and lie in the sun, looking like a brood of hairy caterpillars ; if the weather be hot, they throw off their blanket and lie about almost *in puris naturalibus*. Possibly they kill time by making bangles out of brass wire, or carve sticks, or make dishes out of logs of wood. They think nothing of cutting a milk-pail out of a solid mass of wood. · If by chance a stray visitor has turned up at the kraal there will be a great discussion of the news. The first question a Kafir asks when he meets a person is, " What's the news ? " That fellow sprawling on the ground over there is telling how one of his cows has a calf ; and this all-absorbing topic of conversation may last several hours, for the exact colour, size, shape, value, and other characteristics of the calf will be fully discussed. If a man tells a very tall story the people say, " You milk the cow with calf," or else, " You are big in the mouth." They have endless proverbs which they address to boasters, while to a liar they say, " You are with a tongue." If no stranger has come along with exciting news, the men will fill up all the interstices of their talk, after exhausting the subjects of cattle and crops, with obscene conversation.

# The Essential Kafir

The hours of eating vary greatly. It is impossible to make a hard-and-fast statement, as some writers do, unless we confine ourselves to a single district or tribe. Natives often eat any food left from over-night as soon as they awake; yet some boys I have walked with never touched food till noon; others carried their loads all day and never tasted food till night. Others would take three meals a day. If you have to supply the food they will probably eat at all hours; if the natives have to supply their own food they eat less frequently; yet they can eat enormous quantities at a sitting. "Pots are made while the clay is in good condition," is a saying of theirs, which means, Make hay while the sun shines. They eat when they get the chance, for they add, "It is never safe to depend on the well ahead." Food also provides the subject-matter for proverbs. Thus they say, "The buck has got out of the pot," where we should talk about "many a slip 'twixt the cup and the lip." They also say, "I returned with only a feather," when they just miss doing a thing—the bird having escaped. To say that a person is "like a dog well stuffed with food" implies that he is well pleased with himself. To a greedy man they say, "Are you a hawk, that you do not hide your eyes when you see food?" To a man pursuing evil ways they say, "You will never eat out of your children's dishes." Children eat when they like, and frequently men will roast some mealies at any odd hour. Sometimes they will take two meals, sometimes three, in the day. There is as much variation as to the hours of milking the cows. On this point I have read the most absolute statements which even a brief journey would prove incorrect.

Sometimes the cows are milked at sunrise. (This I have frequently seen, though some writers deny the assertion.) Sometimes they are milked at nine o'clock; in other districts or tribes, at noon. As a rule, the cows are tied up to milking-

# Introducing the Kafir

posts by their horns, while their back legs are tied together. Then a young man throws off his blanket, and in stark nakedness sets to work to milk the cow into a tin or pail, which is often held by a small boy. When the milking is over the milk is taken into the hut, and is immediately placed in the milk sac or calabash. This is never cleaned out, but contains a strong ferment which makes the milk clot immediately. Sweet milk is but food for babies, and only a few tribes would drink it. But clotted sour milk is food for men. The calabash has a small plug at the bottom by which the natives let off the whey, the curds being the only part they care for. Milk formed the staple article of their diet in olden days; but, since rinderpest has carried off most of their cattle, they have a good excuse for drinking beer. They treat eggs and chicken with the same scorn as sweet milk. Hence one can often buy a dozen eggs—mostly bad, unless one knows the natives—for a box of matches.

The hens and eggs should always be bought from the women or children, who, by the way, are not allowed on any account to touch the milk sac. To do so would be a gross breach of order, for in that case the cows would die, and the hapless woman would be sure to be accused of seeking to bewitch the people by contaminating the milk. In fact, any breach of custom is put down to the desire of exercising witchcraft, and in olden days would frequently lead to death.

The men take care of the cattle, and in most districts are particular not to let them leave the cattle-kraal till the dew is off the ground, for this is supposed to be a safeguard against disease. I have for days together timed the hour at which the oxen were led out of a certain kraal; and, though the natives only tell time by the sun, I found that every day for a fortnight the oxen were let out within five minutes of nine. The hour varies according to the season. One has to be very chary in

# The Essential Kafir

jumping to conclusions from a few isolated observations. It will not do to follow the German method adopted by a young man who was visiting an English family I know. He happened to notice one day that the husband went to London first-class; the mother followed later in the day second-class, and one of the sons went up third-class. He was writing a book, and eagerly put down the conclusion that in England men go first-class, women second, and young men third. This type of generalisation will not apply to the Kafirs.

Natives in olden days never kept all their cattle at one kraal —for fear of being "smelt out," or fear of sickness. The men sit down when the news is all told and feast their eyes on the cattle, which the little boys have to herd during the day. Then the men have to devise a way of killing the time. Among the methods adopted must be mentioned that of asking riddles, though it is not resorted to so much as it used to be in the good old days. One man will say, "Tell me the name of the longest snake in the world," and back will come the answer: "*A road.*" This is too well known to be repeated often. "Who is it that always stands and never sits?" "*A tree.*" Then a man says: "I puzzle you with a goat-ram which grazes with white goats; they move about much, yet they eat in one place." The answer is, "*The tongue and the teeth.*"

Some excellent riddles are given in Callaway's books; and as these were long ago out of print, and are scarce, I will give one from his collection, slightly altered. "Guess ye a man who makes himself a chief. He refuses to do any work, and simply sits still in the kraal, and looks down on the ground. He makes all the people work for him, but will do no work himself. He takes his people by the hand and leads them to where there is food, and they have to carry it back to their homes, while he will not lend a hand. At first the people disputed his authority, and said, 'You cannot be a king if you

# Introducing the Kafir

sit still and do nothing : as for us, we cannot see in what your kingship consists : we cannot see the power of your majesty.' But he merely replied, 'Since you say I am not a chief, I will just sit still and do nothing : I will merely look on the ground. Then you will all fall into pits and over precipices, and your land will be desolate ; and you will be eaten by the wild beasts and die, because you will not be able to find food.' Then the people owned that he was a chief, for they said, ' If we die of famine, then the majesty we are claiming for ourselves will come to an end, for we are kings by living.' So the country was peaceful. And now the king simply sits still ; he never washes, and if he is ill the whole nation mourns, and the people are afraid to go out of their huts ; they long for the king to get well again, and when he is well every one rejoices greatly." The answer to this lengthy riddle is, of course, " *The eye.*"

As an example of Basuto riddles I give three taken from Casalis : " There is a thing which falls from the top of a mountain to the bottom without breaking itself : do you know what it is ? " Answer : " A waterfall."

" Can you tell me who that quiet and unmovable little boy is who dresses warmly during the day and is left bare during the night ? " Answer : " A clothes-peg."

" Do you know a mountain-peak leaning over a ravine ? " Answer : " The nose placed over the mouth."

I have frequently drawn the natives out and learnt new riddles from them by telling them an English allegory which is just after their heart. Every one knows the children's story of the tongue which is likened to a little red dwarf living in a cave. This dwarf sends out invisible warriors, who do ever so much mischief in the country ; these warriors or words hurt and sting people, but kind words gladden the country. This story can be easily made to taste of the true Kafir flavour, and the natives sit listening open-mouthed to the description of the

# The Essential Kafir

*minutiæ* which one invents on the spur of the moment to mystify them. It never fails to interest them.

This aimless life, then, is the natural course of most Kafirs. They go through the years chatting, eating, idling, hating, loving, taking their fill of sensual pleasure; and so they leave no trace behind them, unless some man arises like Chaka, who dyes his hands in blood, and impresses the imagination of the people. They are splendid triflers with time, know how to kill it without *ennui*, do as little uncongenial work as possible, never being troubled by the desire to live up to any great ideal. They are highly evolved animals, and to our first view are gifted with minds that are almost blank. They are often jolly, good-natured, ease-loving, selfish; their nature is well rooted in red earth; and if we do not like to look on them as bone of our bone, they certainly are earth of our earth, and claim kinship with us through the lowest strands of our animal nature. "Let us eat and drink, for to-morrow we die"—that is their philosophy.

# NATIVE BELIEFS

Plate 12.

TRIMMING THE HAIR.

Plate 13.

BACK FROM THE HAIRDRESSER.

## CHAPTER II

### NATIVE BELIEFS

WE are now on speaking terms with the natives, but only know them on the outside. Many of our first impressions need considerable modification, for we have but taken swallow flights on the topmost froth of Kafir habits and thought. To understand a people we need to know, not only what they do, but also why they do it. It is unfair to judge a people from their actions divorced from the underlying motives. We must now try to get inside a Kafir's skin, that we may look at the world through his eyes, and feel it through his nerve-endings. We must try, in imagination and sympathy, to bridge that estranging sea which makes each individual an island floating in an impassable ocean.

We must first try to find out what a Kafir believes about the world and about human life.

It is notoriously difficult to view the world from any other person's standpoint, for the grace of detachment is a very rare possession; and it is specially difficult to enter into a Kafir's view of things—for many reasons. To start with, he greatly dislikes to find Europeans investigating his customs, and usually hides all he can from them, and takes a sporting pleasure in baffling and misleading such inquisitive white men; for the Kafir has a truly Johannesburg delight in the gentle game of bluff.

You must not be surprised, then, if the native will not really

## The Essential Kafir

give you the facts of the case. If he can put you off the scent by telling you a falsehood he will gladly do so, a lie being wrong in his opinion only when it is found out; nor is it so much wrong in that case as silly. He thinks that to tell a lie successfully is a smart thing, but to be found out implies one is dull and clumsy.

One soon gets tired of the everlasting answer that meets your questioning at every turn, "It is our custom." No doubt in very many cases it is all a Kafir could tell you, even if he wished to be very communicative. You might as well stop a well-dressed man in Pall Mall and ask him why he wears a silk hat with a coat of a certain cut and not with others. If he stopped to answer you at all he would probably tell you that he did so because it was the custom. If an enormous amount of our life is a mass of custom, much more is it so in the case of the Africans. From the moment that a Kafir baby is rocked, muling and puking, in his mother's blanket—a "naked forked radish"—to the moment he is carried to his last long home, and is placed in a sitting posture in the rude grave scooped out of mother earth at the edge of the cattle kraal, his life is rigidly confined by the power of custom, as if by some fated Destiny; all that is left for him is to spin more or less merrily down the ringing grooves of custom. Wordsworth might well have been speaking of a Kafir baby, just about to open its eyes on this weird strange world, when he said:

> Full soon thy soul shall have her earthly freight,
> And custom lie upon thee with a weight,
> Heavy as frost, and deep almost as life.

Custom will thus be seen to cover a large extent of the life of a Kafir, who can give you no information about the origin or reason of many of his practices.

## Native Beliefs

If the native is disinclined to talk about his customs, still less is he willing to tell you what he thinks about witchcraft; and so our difficulties are very greatly increased. It may be well to give an example in illustration. If you will join that party of women who are all sitting outside yonder kraal, you will find that they will chat to you quite freely about the cattle, the hens, the mealie crop, or the next beer-drink. That old toothless woman on your right will talk with a volubility that will surprise you if you have never spoken to one of these old crones before; she will answer your questions and return your banter and chaff. But lead the conversation round to the subject of the native belief in witchcraft: immediately the flow of conversation is stopped. Without betraying the least emotion, the old woman will look you in the face and calmly say, "I am very old and deaf: so I cannot hear what you are saying." You repeat your question still more loudly, imagining in your ignorance that she is telling you the truth. All the women present will join in a chorus of grunts, and will add that it is quite true what the old woman says: the poor thing has been growing deaf of late. The dame will then look you in the face very solemnly, and, after grunting to give her approval to the last remark, will add, "It is quite true what these women have told you: I have been growing very deaf of late, and can't hear what is said." She will then change the subject without showing the least sign of embarrassment or uneasiness. It only needs to be said that this is not a hypothetical case: it actually happened. It is quite useless seeking to squeeze information from such unwilling witnesses: you might as well put Sam Weller into the witness-box to find out Mr. Pickwick's weaknesses.

The next time you try to get information you may find the Kafir most obliging while you are talking generalities, and you begin to think, possibly, that you are about to gain some

# The Essential Kafir

sound and valuable information. But as soon as the native finds that you are getting him into a corner he will ask you whether your last question was addressed to him or to somebody else. As there is no one else close by, you are apt to wonder what game the man is up to. He is merely trying to gain time so that he may think how to avoid your questions. You therefore tell him that, of course, you are speaking to him. He will then try to get you off the track by asking you whether you want to know what the Zulus or the Pondos think on the subject. You point out that the conversation all along has been concerning what the Pondos think, and that you have not once mentioned the Zulus. He will assent instantly, and tell you that you are quite right : you did not mention the Zulus. He will now pretend that the subject is fully exhausted and will sit in silence. As he shows no inclination to speak, you again ask your question, and the native looks very wise and pretends to be thinking out the subject, but will probably ask you whether you want to know what the Pondos as a whole think, or what he, as a Pondo, thinks on the subject. You feel inclined to dig the old humbug in the ribs, knowing that he is making fun of you, and would be laughing up his sleeve if he had one. But you tell him as quietly as you can that, of course, you want to know what he himself thinks ; and then he will seem quite satisfied, and say that he has really quite forgotten the original question during this long indaba. You repeat the original question, which was, " What happens to a Pondo after death ? Does he die like the cattle ? " " Yes," he answers gravely : " the cattle do indeed die: many died recently from the rinderpest." You tell him that you are quite aware of that fact, but want to know what happens to a Pondo when he dies. He sees he is in a corner, looks very wise as if hunting for an answer, and presently glances up at you and says with dry wit, " Well, as I never was

## Native Beliefs

dead, I do not see how I can know." And, though he keeps up a perfectly solemn face, you know he is laughing at you inwardly. So you repeat your question once more, explaining that you know he has not been dead, but may nevertheless have some theory on the subject. At this he looks very wise and says, "I do not know." This is the ultimate answer to all questions about native beliefs, just as "It is our custom" is the final answer to all inquiries concerning customs. These two answers are evidently twins. The native then looks as if he wanted to speak, and you wait for his remark. He merely says that, as you have been talking about the cattle, he now remembers that he must go off to look after some straying oxen; and, gathering his blanket round him, he hitches it over one shoulder, takes a pinch of snuff with great deliberation, and walks away.

You are left to think over your methods, and realise by this time that frontal attacks are quite useless when you want to know what a native really believes. He must be taken unawares in the flank if you would succeed, and to know how to do this you must understand the country over which you have to manœuvre. It is here that books like Callaway's "Religion of the Amazulu" and Bleek's "Folk-lore" stories are so useful: from them you can gain some outline of what a native thinks.

To him that hath, to him shall be given. If you know a single native belief, you can use it as a basis from which to extend your knowledge. For example, take one of the Zulu or Hottentot beliefs mentioned in these books, and begin to explain it to the natives of some different tribe. It will often be found to be a good plan to pretend to turn stupid, and purposely to give a distorted account, trading on the tribal prejudices which are so rife. The unsuspecting Kafir will possibly try to put you right. Tell a Zulu what a Pondo believes, and probably before you have finished talking the

# The Essential Kafir

Zulu will interrupt you and tell you that the Zulus believe differently—the Pondos are so foolish. If he has not suspected that this movement is a feint on your part to draw him out, he will give you more trustworthy information in five minutes than you could get out of him by weeks spent in making direct inquiries. But every piece of information will need to be checked and counter-checked by information gained from other Zulus. If you fail to do this your information will be valueless.

When information is obtained from some Kafir who has renounced heathenism you will need to be doubly careful lest he mislead you inadvertently, for he will be in danger of importing the new conceptions gleaned from missionaries into his old beliefs. Natives are singularly deficient in critical or analytical faculties, and, as their original ideas are very misty and ill-defined, they can import European conceptions into their old beliefs unawares. The natives have no writing of any sort, and so all beliefs have to be handed down from mouth to mouth. Even now it is easy to trace European traditions, received from people who have been wrecked on the coast, intermingling with pure native beliefs. In Bomvanaland I was once standing on a hill, and noticed three natives down in the valley. A native said to me, "Do you see those two white men down in the valley walking with a native?" When I declared that the three were all natives, my informant loudly objected, declaring two were whites. It turned out that these so-called white men were the great-great-grandchildren of some white people who had been wrecked on the shore, and had intermarried with the natives. It is easy to see how such marriages would tend to corrupt the purity of native tradition, and thus we find current among the Zulus traditions which remind us of many old Bible stories.

When one considers these difficulties in gaining trustworthy information, it is manifestly absurd to suppose that by taking a

## Native Beliefs

hurried trip over the railways of South Africa, in which places such as Cape Town, Kimberley, Bulawayo, Johannesburg, and Durban are visited, one can get anything but a distorted idea of what the natives are really like. This cannot be done by a bustling traveller from the hotel or club windows of some South African town, where the natives are seen merely on the surface, for, like Englishmen crossing the Channel, they leave their religion behind at their kraals, or else mask it from observation. Even a year or two spent at a place like Johannesburg is still more apt to mislead people, for they grow familiar with native faces, while the true character is hidden. On the top of these difficulties we find others crowding. For example, the natives have not yet arrived in the course of evolution at that stage in which they can safely make any critical examination of the content of their own consciousness. Their self-realisation has hitherto been sought solely along the line of their animal nature. They cannot tell you what they believe, for the very good reason that they hardly know this themselves. As psychologists would say, their "threshold" is very high, and they are but dimly conscious of large tracts of their own individuality which lie below the level of full consciousness. The unconscious mind presents large proportions in their case: the subliminal self is enormously greater than that portion of it which rises to full self-consciousness. In a word, though they believe a very great deal, they do not quite know what they actually believe, for they never sit down and reflect on their beliefs. And the moment you try to find out what the Kafir believes, your very questions, unless carefully thought out beforehand, are sure to suggest to them ideas which they can easily fit in with their other ideas. Like the Greeks, they have plenty of room for unknown gods. Your very question will cause the development and crystallisation of their ideas, and they will present this crystallisation, which your question has

# The Essential Kafir

effected, as their own. If you supply them with a new idea they can readily fit it in the loose and elastic region of their belief. After some European Paracelsus has fed up his Kafir Michal with new ideas, he can turn to her and say, " Dost thou believe this?" and the answer is sure to come back as of old, " I ever did believe it."

Suppose you ask some old Kafir, who is bunched up in his blanket, a few questions, and see how he will answer you.

" Do you believe there is a God?" you ask.

" Yes, Nkos," he answers.

" Do you believe there are twenty Gods?"

" Yes, Nkos."

" Do you believe there is only one God?"

" Yes, Nkos."

" Come! you can't believe both of these things: you don't believe in any God at all—do you?"

" No, Nkos."

" Which do you mean? Do you or do you not believe there is one God?"

" Nkos, I don't know; yes; no; perhaps; you know better; we Kafirs know nothing."

It is no exaggeration to say that much information which is gravely recorded in books is deduced from such conversations, and is therefore quite valueless. The man will tell you just what he thinks you wish to hear, and then he will give a grunt of satisfaction, as much as to say, " There: that is nicely settled now."

Your question instantly causes some flocculent precipitate of conviction—that word is far too strong—which is readily soluble in the information derived from your next question. A Kafir's thought reminds one of some of those flasks of supersaturated solutions of Glauber's salts with which Professor Tyndall loved to interest his audience at his lectures.

# Native Beliefs

The flaskfull of solution was carefully cooled and isolated from all vibration and foreign matter. The least shake, or introduction of a crystal of the salt, or a few grains of dust, would set the whole mass crystallising in a moment. The native mind is supersaturated with beliefs—with "extra beliefs"—and so your very question causes some of the vague ideas which are floating in his mind to crystallise out into clearly defined thoughts. The Kafir may feel that the thing you suggest is not exactly what he always believed; but it is all of a piece with it. It was implicitly there before, and your question makes it explicit. You bring many of his vague feelings above the "threshold," and they become definite and clear-cut; and so he recognises them as his own thought. Out of his mental fog arises a belief which your questions have suggested.

It is extremely difficult to make arm-chair critics feel the full force of this fact. It is comical to see how those who write books on anthropology, without a first-hand knowledge of the Kafirs, contradict one another, though they all borrow from the same common stock of books. One will tell you that the Kafirs are Atheists; the next passionately denies this, while a third classes them as given up to Totemism, and a fourth to Shamanism. All the anthropologists I have studied seem to me to miss the peculiar flavour of the Kafir mind, and choose from the weltering mass of contradictory statements of travellers what suits their own preconceived theory. They have their pet authors, and set off one writer against another. This type of anthropology is but a pseudo-science, based on individual whim, the evidence not being sufficiently clear for us to say that "these are the facts on which the science is based." It reminds one of a sort of astrology where personal whim rules the science. The "will to believe" rules the creed of the writer. It is not yet time to build up a constructive science:

# The Essential Kafir

what is needed is a careful sifting of evidence, that we may arrive at the bed-rock of fact. It will be time to begin to think of building when we get the ground clear. At present it is littered with a hopeless jumble of discordant opinion. (I do not refer to that branch of anthropology which is truly scientific—the branch which consists in measurements of physical features and physiological tests of the various functions and senses. I refer to that which deals with civilisation, beliefs, and customs.)

With regard to the Kafirs, we must try and grasp the fact that they are capable of entertaining contradictory ideas at the same moment. Until some one points out the contradiction, a Kafir sees no difficulty in believing that his grandfather "went out like a candle" at death, while at the same time he will tell you that his grandfather visited the kraal yesterday in the form of a snake. Later he will tell you that all yesterday his dead grandfather was living below the ground in a splendid world of enjoyment. This grandfather's spirit can be both material and immaterial, and it can exist and not exist at the same moment. When you point out how contradictory these statements are, the Kafir will re-examine the question, and his answer will turn on the mood he happens to be in. Opposing statements of fact vignette off in his mind into one another, apparently without passing through any region of conscious untruth or mental incompatibility. A little reflection should show us that the average Englishman's ideas concerning such a subject as religion, which he may cherish with a keen dogmatism, are often quite as incompatible. They are often kept in separate watertight compartments of his mind, and he shrinks from testing them along the lines of rigorous logic. When this European expects the Kafir to have his ideas clearly cut, his demand is unreasonable.

## Native Beliefs

Then, again, the Kafir's notions are changing by slow natural growth, assisted by the accretions of European thought, and the various tribes differ among themselves as much as Roman Catholics and Protestants. A single trip to the mines at Johannesburg affects a Kafir's belief, frequently turning him into an Atheist. I have sometimes met these objectionable Johannesburg gentlemen at their kraals, and their Atheism was more blatant than one would have expected.

Max Müller seems to see these difficulties, for he says in one place, writing in 1865: "As it happens, we know from other sources enough to explain the appearance in South Africa of stories about Reynard, by referring them to European influence." Yet, strangely, he wrote two years later—speaking of different tribes, it is true:—" If we admit for the present, in the absence of any evidence to the contrary, that the Zulus were free from the influence of German missionaries or Dutch settlers in the formation of their popular stories, it is certainly surprising to see so many points of similarity between the heroes of their kraals and of our nurseries." All the time this writer must surely have known that there were numerous wrecks along the coast, and that thus many white people became incorporated into native tribes—to say nothing of Portuguese influences. (For details of these wrecks, see Theal's "History of South Africa.") Kafir folklore is full of ideas borrowed manifestly from European sources, as any one can see who reads Callaway's works.

I think, then, it may safely be said that it is impossible to draw up a code of native belief that will hold even for a single tribe : all that can be done is to try and catch the spirit of their creed, which, fortunately, is the same all over the country. The spirit of their belief—the essential conception underlying their view of life—this can be found, and this is what is really of vast importance. Let us, then, try to catch the typical Kafir

# The Essential Kafir

attitude in the face of the world-problems which beset and often oppress him.

One of the keys to the subject will be found, I think, in the attitude of natives towards death and the life beyond the grave. Let us, then, start with this. Later we can examine their ideas concerning cosmogony and magic.

If you talk to natives about death they will say that you are a bad friend to speak of anything so unwelcome and dark. They have the greatest dread of death, and an unspeakable horror of a dead body. No Greek ever loved to see the light of the sun more than a Kafir. No Browning or Walt Whitman ever rejoiced more fully in the " sheer joy of living " than the Kafirs. Death is such an omnipresent fact that it casts its shadow over most events of life. It tinges and colours all the imaginations of the Kafirs. Yet they strongly dislike thinking about it, or about what follows death. As Lubbock shrewdly says, to ask a Kafir what happens to him after death is to ask him a question he has never seriously thought about in the past, and does not consider worth thinking about in the present. They are true Positivists in their attitude towards metaphysics. Thus, they are easily satisfied with the following fable about the origin of death:

Long, long ago, Umkulunkulu (of whom more later) wanted to send a messenger to earth to tell men that they were to live for ever. Looking round for a messenger, he saw a chameleon and promptly sent it off to earth with the message of life. As the chameleon is the sleepiest of animals, it dawdled on the way, and, passing a tree, climbed up in it to bask in the sun. The lazy creature filled its belly with flies and then fell asleep, and so loitered on its journey. Umkulunkulu seemingly changed his mind and wished to send a message of death to the world. Looking round again, he saw a lizard. He told it to hurry off and tell men that they were to die. It ran off

## Native Beliefs

instantly, and never stopped till it came to men, who believed its message. By and by the chameleon awoke, and came along to the top of a hill from which it could see men ; it then said that Umkulunkulu had sent it to say that men were to live and not die. But the lizard slapped it in the face and said, "Get you gone : the message is that men are to die" : so the people said that they would not believe it, for the lizard had long ago arrived with the message that men were to die. Consequently they began to beat the chameleon and throw stones at it, telling it not to tell lies. The chameleon is therefore hated by the natives to this day, and they often kill it, saying, " But for you we should never die." This is the Kafir version

> Of Man's first disobedience, and the fruit
> Of that forbidden tree whose mortal taste
> Brought death into the world, and all our woe.

The variations of this story are infinite, and sometimes cause the fiercest arguments among the natives. Some will declare that it is literally true ; others say that it is only an old woman's story. Natives differ on this point as much as religious people do over Adam and Eve ; yet among the Kafirs, as in Europe, the subject is generally considered to lie outside the sphere of practical politics. It is only when people argue against cherished beliefs that the *odium theologicum* gains strength ; as a rule people leave the subject undiscussed.

It would seem that this story is really of Hottentot origin. They have many stories about the subject in which it is a hare that was sent to the world by the moon with the message, " As I die and dying am born again, so shall you die and dying live again." The hare got confused over the message and put a "not" in. It thus reversed the message, saying, "As I die and dying am born again, so you shall die and dying *not* be born again." When it returned to the moon and explained how

# The Essential Kafir

it had delivered the message the moon was angry with it for being so stupid : so the moon took up a stick and hit the hare on its nose, thus splitting its lip. Ever since the hare has had this split lip. According to one version of this story, the moon sent an insect with the message ; but the hare volunteered to save the insect the trouble. (See Bleek's " Hottentot Fables," p. 69.)

The Bushmen have yet another story. According to them, Urezhwa created men, and then took to himself a wife. The wife fell sick, and so Urezhwa shut her in a cave and went away on a long journey to fetch medicines. He told the people who watched her on no account to bury his wife if she died in his absence. However, she died soon after he left, and the people were so disgusted with the dead body that they buried it. When the creator came back he found what they had done, and in anger said that if they had only obeyed him he would have raised her up to life, and would have given them power to become alive again after death. Now they must suffer for their disobedience. He then went above into the heavens, where he is often seen to pass with a bright light, and his voice is heard during thunder. This story is probably based and built up on the wonder caused by meteors.

There is a preliminary story—which also has countless variations—that in olden days was attached to the Umkulunkulu myth. It is said that long before the chameleon was sent with its message the people used to live in bliss : there was no sickness, no need to eat, no propagation of the species: in fact, it was a golden age. But one day, much to every one's consternation, a baby appeared. The mother was ill and in pain : so the people gave her pumpkins to eat, thinking they would poison her. (In another account it was a rival wife who gave her corn, thinking to kill her by it.) Yet the woman got well and fat on the pumpkins, and so the people began to eat

## Native Beliefs

them. It was after this that Umkulunkulu sent his message of life to the world.

It would be possible to trace out a dozen variations of these myths; yet the spirit underlying them all is the same. When we come to the question as to what happens after death, we find great uncertainty and diversity of opinion. And the progress of civilisation has infected the people with ideas that were not indigenous. Garbled reports of what missionaries teach have reached every kraal in the country, and this fact alone would account for many modes of belief which are now current. Yet it is not so difficult to trace the underlying backbone behind the soft flesh of personal opinion. It is in ancestor worship that we find the spirit of the belief. But the worship of ancestors would seem to be very different from that which is found in countries like China.

The Kafirs live in a very circumscribed environment, and the memory of an old man's personality would pervade all associations of the kraal in which he lived. It was only yesterday that they buried the old man, and to-day at every turn they half expect to find this old familiar face fronting them; the power of association would bring him to their thoughts a thousand times a day, and the spot close to the cattle kraal where they buried him would seem to be the focus of these memories. The natives draw omens from every trifling incident of life, and would connect the memory of the old man with all their fortunes. He would seem to them to be alive in some dim way, and the sense of his presence would specially haunt the tree under which he was buried, or the stones or bush placed over his grave. All their joys, fears, hopes, and sorrows would be connected with this dead man's personality, and, since the Kafirs have great respect and veneration for old age, they would consider that he sent the fine weather or the good crops —at least, he would be connected somehow with these things.

# The Essential Kafir

Calamity also would be naturally traced to his displeasure, for during his life could he not stop much of the pleasure if he were cross and angry or displeased? The old man is by their laws more or less responsible for all that happens in the kraal. Their respect for old age is perhaps the closest feeling they have to worship, and from the respect for their headman to veneration or dread of displeasing his spirit would be but a step.

Then the troublesome European comes along and wants everything defined in black and white. In what sense does the man survive death? The natives do not naturally trouble their heads about this problem; they feel dimly he is present, even as we feel the dead often to be near us, so that it would hardly surprise us to find our dead friend meeting us as we turn the corner of the street into the old familiar lane where we used to walk with him. But if the European insists on knowing where the man lives, the natives naturally say that he lives below the ground near the cattle kraal, at the distance from the surface that he was buried. The body and the spirit seem to them to be closely connected, if not identical.

Then the troublesome European wants to know what the dead man does. Is he happy? Does he have plenty to eat and drink? Has he oxen, and dogs, and sheep, and wives to minister to his needs? "Well," thinks the Kafir, "if you press me to answer, I suppose he can shift for himself in death as he did in life." On this he develops a long story about a fine world below the ground where there is no sickness, no death, no dearth, no drought, but plenty of food, beer, wives, and all other good things. This is strictly in keeping with the way the Greenlanders conceive a heaven of sunshine and no night, with plenty of fish, reindeer, and good water; or with the Jew, who loves to think that in heaven there will be "no more sea." People who live in hot countries make

A PONDO DANDY.
This is a typical case of hairdressing for a young man of the "awkward age."

Plate 15.

INTERIOR OF A NATIVE HUT.

In the middle of the picture is seen a native pillow; in front of this is a Kafir pot, and in front of that the fireplace. Blankets, calabashes, and other articles can be seen in the background.

## Native Beliefs

heaven cool and hell hot ; those who live in cold climates make heaven warm and hell a place of frost and icicles. If you wish to know whether men who have been a trouble to the chief, who have stolen, killed people, broken native customs, or ill-treated others, live in happiness hereafter, the Kafirs argue from analogy that the old men turned such rascals out of the kraal and left them to wander where they could : so it must be much the same below. Has death made the old men silly ? If not, then of course these worthless fellows have to wander about in the air.

After this the natives hear that missionaries talk of heaven being above. They then add to their stock ideas, and say that heaven is just above the tree tops ; that the world is built in double stories, and that men could climb up into the heavens like Jack-and-the-Bean-stalk. When Dos Santos, writing in 1684, tells us that the natives of Sofala believed in twenty-seven paradises and thirteen hells, we note that he is speaking of natives who had been in touch with Portuguese Roman Catholic missionaries. And so the belief grows according to the fuel supplied to the flame. In Chaka's days the Zulus said that the spirits of the dead men lived beneath the ground and had plenty of nice girls. It is well-nigh impossible to be quite sure what the natives believed before white men visited them ; the early writers asked them far too many leading questions for their evidence to be of much value, and, unfortunately, we cannot travel backward in some " time-machine " and investigate the subject in a more scientific way. The chance has passed and can never come back again. All we can say is that the earliest conceptions were very vague and ill-defined : that the people imagined the dead man to move about a short distance from his grave, which, however, he could leave at times (the Bushmen believed that if any one watched till the dead man left his grave he could intercept the spirit and

# The Essential Kafir

prevent it from getting back into the grave),—and that he was supposed to have cattle and wives and dogs to keep him company (they made sure of this by killing off his wives and favourite animals in olden days, not as a sacrifice, but to enable him to have companions to administer to his pleasure). They would also bury his assagai and shield, together with his snuff-box and other possessions, possibly to make it useless for people to kill men in order to get their possessions, and partly to let the dead man have his possessions with him in case of need.

I doubt very much the theory of a writer—apparently he has not been to South Africa—who elaborates a wonderful hypothesis that the natives imagine that a man's possession must pass through death to become immortal and capable of being used. This is too finespun a theory for a Kafir's brain. The articles would be broken, not to enable them to pass through death and be born anew, but for a much more prosaic reason, namely, to prevent people from being tempted to steal them and use them for magical purposes. So strong is this dislike to possess dead men's property, that I have several times found native Christians very much scandalised when white men keep any articles as mementoes of dead friends. They say that if they did so they would certainly be accused of witchcraft.

Use has been made of the phrase *spirits of ancestors* because it was inevitable. But how does a Kafir conceive of a spirit? They have many ways of viewing the subject; but all are delightfully vague and ill-defined. The nearest English word would possibly be *personality*, though that would be but an approximation. This word has a very vague connotation to those who have not studied psychology, and its vagueness makes it suitable in this connection. The Kafir idea of spirit is not at all the same as our religious conception of a soul or

## Native Beliefs

spirit. Some natives say a man's soul lives in the roof of his hut; you can hardly keep a "theological soul" there. It would be nearer the mark to connect it with the body, though that would be incorrect. So vague is the word that it is confused with a man's shadow, which is supposed to dwindle as he grows old. A man's shadow is supposed to vanish or grow very slight at death; most naturally so, for the dead body lies prone. This shadow, then, is connected with the man's personality and forms a basis for the ancestral spirit. You may call it a ghost if you like, but must be careful to strain off most of our European ideas connected with this word. The natives think that this shadow, or spirit, can leave the body during sleep, and that it actually visits the places dreamt of; and if a man dreams that another person visited him—it may be a dead man who visits his dreams—he thinks that the man's shadow or spirit (or some emanation of his personality) has actually come to him during sleep and told him things. If it can do this, why should it not survive death? The natives occasionally fix ox-horns in their roofs and say that the spirit of the chief lives in these horns and protects the hut; these horns also protect the hut from lightning, though not in virtue of their spiritual connections. (They are also used simply as ornaments.)

So strongly do they feel the connection between a man's shadow and his personality that the women hang up the sleeping-mat of their husband when he is away at battles; if the shadow grows less they say the husband is killed, but if it retains its usual proportions they say the man is uninjured. A man's personality haunts his possessions, and even in Europe we feel that there is some dim and lingering presence at a grave. A wife weeps at the tomb of her husband, feeling that his presence is there. The Kafirs feel this sentiment ten times more strongly. They show great dislike when they find

# The Essential Kafir

Europeans ploughing the ground where some ancestor was buried. Some natives very much dislike any one to stand on their shadow, for they think they can be influenced for evil through it. Owen describes how a boy who had been working for the Portuguese was asked about a future life. He pointed to his body and said, "Me stop here," and then pointing to his shadow said, "Dat man go dere," pointing to the sky. The distinction is not much greater than that made by a lunatic I saw when I was walking the wards of an asylum as a student. The doctor told him that if he did not keep more quiet he would put him in a strait-waistcoat. The poor fellow drew himself up with hauteur, and said in withering scorn, "Put *me* in a waistcoat? You may put *this*" (pointing to his body); "but you cannot touch *me*." Madame Guyon in the Bastille could not be more "detached." In burial the body does not seem to be destroyed; and so a Bushman, who was troubled with a quarrelsome wife, not only killed her, but smashed up her head into a jelly to prevent her troubling him after her death. He felt that there was some connection between the body and the woman's unpleasant personality, and wished to make an end of it. The very same device is frequently resorted to in the folk-lore of this people.

This conception of a spirit soon gets corrupted, and we find the natives associating the spirits of their ancestors with some special animal, most commonly with a snake, though in some tribes with crocodiles, lions, elephants, and so forth. These animals then serve as a modified totem, and it is most unlucky to kill them even by mistake,—a sacrifice being required to put matters right. They would apologise to the slain animal, and say to the elephant, for example, "The elephant is a great lord, and the trunk is his hand; he must excuse us for killing him, but we could not help it." The natives who regard a certain animal as sacred never eat that animal; they dance to it, if

## Native Beliefs

they do not worship it. Yet the tribe a few miles away might eat it quite freely.

Travelling with native carriers one frequently sees this. A boy catches a small lizard or iguana; some of the boys join in eating it, while the others call them all the insulting names they can think of for doing so.

By far the commonest belief is that the ancestors visit the living in the shape of, or through the medium of, snakes. Thus, a chief is supposed to go into a boa constrictor, as in the case of Chaka; other chiefs go into Mambas; while the lesser fry go into small snakes, and the women into sleepy old fat lizards, which are most contemptible creatures. I once asked a native who pointed out a snake that had just visited the kraal where we were sitting, " What would happen to your ancestor in that snake if I were to kill it inadvertently ? " The man said that it would not matter at all, for the ancestors do not live in the actual individual snakes, but in the genus. (Of course, he did not use the word *genus;* but this is what he meant.)

Serpent worship is common all over the world, being found, according to Lubbock, in Egypt, India, Phœnicia, Babylonia, Greece, Italy, Persia, Cashmere, Cambodia, Thibet, certain parts of China, Ceylon, Abyssinia, Guinea, Peru, and other countries. Lubbock gives six reasons which have been advanced, by others, for this worship; these reasons are as follow :

(1) Because of its beauty.

(2) Because of the brilliance of its eyes.

(3) It is a type of growth and health.

(4) Fear of the snake leads naturally to flattery and worship.

(5) Totemic in origin.

(6) The quickness of the effect of its poison makes it seem

## The Essential Kafir

to kill without means, and it is a natural thing to think such a creature to be divine.

Lubbock admits that the fourth, fifth and sixth of these reasons may hold good, but seems very doubtful of the others.

Where the authorities differ one should speak with caution; but may it not be that in South Africa (I do not speak of other countries) the people notice that the snake comes, they know not how, out of the wattles of the cattle kraal? They would associate this with the grave of the ancestor who was buried there, and would suppose the snake had come out of the grave. This would fit in with the strange fact, which no one so far as I have read has tried to account for, that a Kafir who venerates a special kind of snake will freely kill it if he finds it in the veldt away from the kraal. He often says this cannot be his ancestor, who never wanders far from his grave. A snake is known to be an ancestral spirit only when its entrance and exit to the kraal cannot be observed. The Kafirs will sometimes tell you that it is the shade of the dead man who enters the snake that makes it love to haunt the kraal for the sake of company. They also say that if the snake attacks a man he is quite right in killing it, for no ancestor would be so utterly silly as to kill his offspring who habitually offers him beer and praise. All that a snake which was an ancestor would do would be to crawl over the body of a person without doing him any harm. It is a strange spectacle, when sitting with some Kafirs at a kraal, to see a snake suddenly glide out of the cattle kraal. A stranger picks up a stick to kill it; but the people say, "Hold! Do you not know that this is our ancestor? Would you kill our ancestor?" He answers, "Eh, sirs, I did not know it was your ancestor. I thought it was merely a snake. I am glad you have told me it was your ancestor; or I should certainly have killed it."

## Native Beliefs

When the snake makes its appearance there is great joy in the kraal; the people say, " Our ancestor has come to visit us." They then fetch an ox to kill in its honour. They watch the snake to see what its habits are like, and if it moves quickly they will say that it is So-and-So, who used to walk very fast. If it has a scar on one side, they will say it is some other ancestor, who had a wound on the same part. The identification of the ancestor is fairly easy; for it is only the chief ancestors who would return, and their characteristics are well known.

If you press for further information they will tell you that the reptile is the man's backbone which has become changed into a snake. Others maintain that it is the man's entrails which have formed the animal. A very simple explanation of Kafir veneration of snakes is thus presented. There is no need to look for highly-wrought theories. What a pity that there was no Kafir William Blake to give us some designs of the snake coming out of the dead body of a chief!

While the women are supposed to go into lazy old lizards or harmless black snakes, or into irritable lizards on account of their natural quarrelsome nature, children are said to go into gentle and harmless snakes, which are often used by the diviners, as these spirits of children are supposed to be very beneficent and kindly. A woman who has borne no children has no spirit, being quite a negligible quantity.

Thus, there are many ways in which the dead are supposed to live. They may be living under the earth in much the same way in which they once lived above ground; they may have plenty of cattle, and wives, and "no rinderpest," as a man gleefully said to me once; they may live in snakes, or in the sky; or, yet again, they may haunt woods and rivers and have furniture in their spirit world. The earth is peopled more by spirits than by living men, and if a Kafir has to travel by night the rustling of the wind in the leaves makes him think of shades, or spirits, or ghosts.

Yet there is no need for the spirits to have a continuous mode of existence. Being is not necessarily continuous according to Kafir ideas. As Frazer has pointed out in "The Golden Bough," savages have no idea of eternal duration. The North American Indians were asked whether the world was made by the good or the bad spirit. They said it could not be by either of them, for the original ones must have died long ago—they could not possibly live so long. And the Kafirs seem to think that ancestral spirits slowly vanish, much like the Snark. As soon as people forget the great things they did, and their praise-giving names, they practically cease to exist. Their life after death is vaguely dependent on the memory of the living. When people forget an ancestor he practically ceases to exist. The man can exist and not exist at the same time. You can no more take hold of a Kafir by logic than by the coat-tails he has not got.

The one thing that can be said of these spirits is that they are intensely human. The Kafir, like all of us, has no religion or science that is not strongly anthropomorphic. Only his anthropomorphism is more frankly crude than ours, which in the case of natural science is often hidden and implicit. Instead of worshipping Mathew Arnold's "magnified non-natural man," the Kafir worships a magnified *very natural man*. The ancestral spirits love the very things they loved before they passed through the flesh; they cherish the same desires and have the same antipathies. The living cannot add to the number of the wives of ancestral spirits; but they can kill cattle in their honour and keep their praise and memory alive on earth. Above all things, they can give them beef and beer. And if the living do not give them sufficient of these things the spirits are supposed to give the people a bad time: they

## Native Beliefs

send drought, and sickness, and famine, until people kill cattle in their honour.

When men are alive they love to be praised and flattered, fed and attended to; after death they want the very same things, for death does not change personality. Thus, after any calamity, or after the appearance of a snake in the kraal, or a vivid dream of some dead relation, the men will select and sacrifice an ox to coax the spirit into a good temper. Some writers call this a sin-offering; but we must be careful not to import too much meaning into this phrase. The chief sin they would confess over the slain ox would be the failure to praise the dead man enough.

In time of drought, or sickness, or great trouble, there would be great searchings of heart as to which ancestor had been neglected, for the trouble would be supposed to be caused by the neglected ancestor. Most of the people would get the subject on their nerves (at least, as far as a Kafir could get anything on the leather strings which do duty for nerves), and some one would be sure to have a vivid dream in which an ancestor would complain that the people had not praised him half enough of late. So an ox would be killed, either by the head-man of the kraal or by a diviner. Then the man would say over the ox as it was being killed, " Cry out, ox of So-and-So; listen to us, So-and-So; this is your ox; we praise you by all your laud-giving names, and tell of all your deeds; do not be angry with us any more; do you not see that this is your ox? Do not accuse us of neglecting you; when, forsooth, have we ceased to praise you and offer you meat and beer? Take note, then, that here is another ox we are offering to you."

When the ox is dead some of the meat is mixed with herbs and medicines and placed in a hut with a bowlful of blood. This meat is placed in the part of the hut where the man loved to sit while he was alive, and some one is told off to guard the

# The Essential Kafir

sacrifice. The meat is left for a night, or longer, and the spirits are supposed to come and enjoy the smell, or drink the serum which oozes from the meat, and to inhale the smell of the beer. The priest or diviner will then sprinkle the people and the huts with medicine made from the contents of the stomach of the ox. He places a little on a sherd ; when this is dry he burns it and calls on the spirits to smell the incense. After the meat has been left for a certain time it is taken out and cooked, and eaten by the men near the cattle kraal in public. To eat the meat in secret would be the basis of a charge of witchcraft. The diviner, of course, manages to get a good portion of the meat for himself.

If now you ask the natives why they do all this they will say, " The white men pray by saying words ; we also pray, but we do it by the act of eating the meat." And if the children say to their parents, " How is it that you say the spirits eat the meat ? We notice that there is always as much left after the spirits have eaten it as there was before, yet you say the spirits eat the meat." The old men then tell them to hold their tongues ; they laugh and say, " O, the spirits drink the blood, or drink the odour ; this is all they care for." Or else they will say, " The spirits licked the meat." To pray by eating is "going one better" than doing so by a water-wheel.

Yet this custom is very common. Certain tribes in India give the breath of the sacrifice to the spirits or idols, and keep the meat for themselves ; in Guinea they simply smear the idol with the blood and eat the meat themselves ; in other tribes they merely paint the idol with symbolic red ; in Fiji the gods have the soul of the beast and the men have the flesh. And did not the Jews believe that Jehovah delighted in the smell of the burnt offering ?

If the trouble does not vanish after this ceremony the people get angry and say to the spirits, " When have we ceased to

## Native Beliefs

kill cattle for you, and when have we ever refused to praise you by your praise-names? Why, then, do you treat us so shabbily? If you do not behave better we shall utterly forget your names, and then what will you do when there is no one to praise you? You will have to go and live on grasshoppers. If you do not mend your ways we shall forget you. What use is it that we kill oxen for you and praise you? You do not give us rain or crops, or cause our cattle to bear well; you show no gratitude in return for all we do for you. We shall utterly disown you. We shall tell the people that, as for us, we have no ancestral spirits, and this will be to your shame. We are disgusted with you." Shelley's Prometheus could not speak more disdainfully to Zeus.

Lubbock gives some interesting quotations to show how savage tribes treat their idols or gods. An old Arab woman, who could not persuade Allah to cure her toothache, prayed, "O Allah, may thy teeth ache like mine!" The negro in Guinea beats his fetish if his wishes are frustrated, and hides it in his waist-cloth when he is about to do something of which he is ashamed, for he does not want his fetish to see him then. In some parts of China the lower people get very angry with their idol if it does not give them what they want. They then say, "How now, dog of a spirit? We give you lodging in a magnificent temple, we gild you handsomely, feed you well, and offer incense to you; yet after all this you refuse to give us what we ask!" They then pluck it down and drag it through the mud and dunghills as punishment. If after this they get what they want, they wash the idol clean, take it back to its temple, and make excuses for what they have done, pointing out that it was all its own fault for being so tardy in answering their prayers.

If the Kafirs had idols they would probably do exactly the same thing to them. Having no idols to abuse, they turn their

## The Essential Kafir

attention in other directions and do the next thing—that is to say, they abuse their ancestral spirits in order to shame them. This expression of their disappointment is more pathetic than comical, for the native feels in some dim way that the power behind phenomena is personal. After much searching of heart he has failed to propitiate this weird power, and day after day he feels disappointment eating into his bosom. He has sacrificed his best oxen to the spirits; he has consulted great diviners; he has done all he knows: yet he is only brought face to face with the grim tragedy of life and the impassive countenance of the Sphinx. There is none that hears or regards. The skies remain like brass, and the sick are unhealed. His disappointment and disgust are too keen and cruel for words. He must battle on all alone against fate, while his more fortunate neighbours have Amatongo or ancestral spirits to help them. The man's heart grows bitter under the weight of this whole Iliad of woes. Life looks weary, stale, flat, and unprofitable. Bah! let us eat and drink, for to-morrow we die. He has stood on the ocean of mystery, stretching out his hand into the dark void, and no answering hand has come to meet his own. He has looked for help from the unseen world; he has looked into the dark cheerless grave: but all in vain. "As for us, we have no Amatongo, and we may as well perish." *In his failure he shows that he is more than animal.*

The most important part of the whole matter seems to be the praising of the ancestral spirits. It is as important as the sacrifice. During life these old ancestors loved praise above all things: what could be more calculated to please them now that they are dead? To be ignored is the cruellest of fates; to be cursed is better than to be ignored. So all chiefs keep a Court Praiser, whose business it is to go in front of the chief and sing his praises. The insignificant Hottentots love to call themselves the Men of Men, and the pigmy Bushmen delight

## Native Beliefs

in being told that they are so big that they could be seen from the top of a mountain on the far-off horizon.

Here is a good example of the absurd excess to which this praising may be carried : Bunu, the Swazie king, was extraordinarily cruel and proud. One day he went out hunting with a hundred warriors, and after a whole day's effort managed to kill one miserable little hare. Yet the Court Praiser ran in front of the King, calling out, " Bunu, the King of the Swazies, the chief of chiefs, has killed a hare. Let all the people listen : it was as big as an ox, as fierce as a lion, and as swift as a buck. The brave King Bunu killed the hare all alone. He killed it with his assegai. Listen, ye people : Bunu the King has killed a hare. Without any help the King has killed the hare. It was as terrible as a tiger, as large as an elephant ; its eyes were flames of fire : and yet Bunu the great King has killed the hare." This long rigmarole was then repeated *ad nauseam*, while the King followed behind with great gravity.

Arbousset gives the following translation of the praise given to an ancestral spirit : " He glides into the fold like a fish into water ; he roars like a hyena, and, like it, tears the prey ; the bravest are speared to death by his assegai; the strongest are crushed to death by his club. With a vigorous hand he lays hold on the thigh of the swiftest of foot ; he hurls them to the ground ; he rains stones on the heads of his enemies, and burning torches on to their huts." Here also are the Ode to Dingan, given by the same author, and a song in honour of Chaka, given by Grout.

### ODE TO DINGAN

Bird of the morning ! Give in secret thy commands
To thy soldiers ; to the veteran and to the more youthful.
They will go before the dawn of day,

# The Essential Kafir

To ravage every place whithersoever thou may'st command them
To carry desolation.
Of night we know nothing.
Formerly we used to say of him,—He is a man of no importance.
We did not know thee!
But now we know thee:
For thou hast cast a death-spell on the Chaka.
Ravisher, thou art held in repute amongst the Basutos,
At Khobas, and amongst the Balunques.
Thou hast plundered the cattle of the Amakozas,
Of the Suquentos, of Cutene, and of Maculoge.
Thou art the purple dawn of the morning.
Thou art beautiful as an isle in the Mosiniati.
Thou art the salvation of the towns of Kankela, of Mabese.
Thou puttest to death the Basuto—to death the old men.
Thou hast despoiled the troops of Makheta.
The smiths themselves are torn in pieces by thee,
Without their hearing a breath of thy approach.
Thou puttest nations to silence,
As thou wouldst silence thy cooks.
In the race, by thy agility, thou causest to pant
The lungs of the Basutos.
Dost thou not say to them: "Ha, ha!
When they speak they tell lies"?
Thou thunderest like the musket.
At the fearful noise that thou makest
The inhabitants of the towns take to flight.
Thy granaries are larger than those of Kokobane.
Thou art sagacious as the elephant.
Thou slaughterest the nations as thou slaughterest a lamb.

(Quoted from ARBOUSSET.)

## SONG IN HONOUR OF CHAKA

Thou striker of poison into every conspirator,
As well those abroad as those who are at home;
Thou art green as the gall of the goat;
Butterfly of Punga, tinted with circling spots,
As if made by the twilight from the shadows of mountains,

# Native Beliefs

In the dusk of the evening, when the wizards are abroad;
Lynx-eyed descendant of Punga and Makeba,
With looking at whom I am ever entranced.
What beautiful parts! a calf of the cow! *
The kicking of this cow confuses my brain,
Kicking the milker and upsetting the holder.

(Quoted from GROUT.)

The moment a man's praise-giving titles are forgotten it becomes impossible to worship him in any full sense, for wherewith shall the people praise him? He then drifts out of the sphere of practical politics, even though he may retain some vitality in the folk-lore of the people. One or two exceptions could be found to this rule; for if ever the aphorism is true that the exception proves (or tests) the rule, it is true in the case of the Kafirs. In certain tribes they still, for example, offer a sort of worship to the Queen of Heaven, though they do not know her praise-giving names.

If this account of Kafir conceptions of the life after death seem unsatisfactory from its vagueness, all that can be said is that in this respect it is true to fact. The natives do not seek to construct a philosophy which shall be self-consistent. They have the vaguest ideas on the subject, and it is quite easy to make them contradict themselves when they talk with you. Like their own children, they see through the absurdity of offering meat to the spirits; but, for all that, they love to make-believe about it. They neither believe nor disbelieve the things they profess; they simply do not think about them; and if you ask them why they continue to offer meat to spirits who manifestly do not eat it, they will laugh and say, "We do it because it is our custom." That answer, with a Kafir, is the end of all argument.

* A "calf of a cow" is about equivalent to our "chip of the old block."

# The Essential Kafir

## UMKULUNKULU AND CREATION

We now come to the subject of Umkulunkulu, and shall find at least as much haziness of thought among the Kafirs, and as much dispute among the anthropologists in Europe, as we do with regard to the Amatongo or spirits.

A study of origins is always interesting; yet with regard to Umkulunkulu the Kafirs talk as if it were a matter of no practical interest. If they forgot all about him it would not affect their lives one iota. The natives are not capable of sustained thought in speculative matters. When you seek to sift critically the evidence given you by a Kafir concerning Umkulunkulu, the one thing which comes out clearly is " the natural fog of the good man's mind." One native will give you information which will lead you to consider Umkulunkulu as the Creator or First Cause ; the next native's evidence will put the matter in quite another light. They are not even agreed as to whether he had a wife or not, whether he is still alive or not, whether he was an ordinary man or a superior kind of being, whether he had a father or not.

Zulu scholars tell us that if you ask a Zulu the name of his father, grandfather, great-grandfather, and so on, after some five generations he comes to the word Umkulunkulu. Here he stops, and all older ancestors go by the same name. The word means *The Great One*. Some missionaries, who are keen to use this word to translate our word *God*, are inclined to press the word to mean "great" in the sense of infinite. But it seems originally to bear the meaning of "great" which it has in the word *great*-grandfather. A man can hardly remember the praise-giving names of his ancestors for more than five generations back : it becomes too great a tax on the memory. Yet tribal chiefs of importance can be remembered

Plate 16.

"FEEDING THE BABY" AND "THE NAPKIN."
The dog is the napkin.

Plate 17.

A SWAZIE MAKING FIRE BY FRICTION.

## Native Beliefs

for many more generations. So a man has an Umkulunkulu of his family, and also an Umkulunkulu of his tribe. From this it is but natural to conclude that there was an Umkulunkulu who was the common ancestor of all black men. But no one would know his names, for there would be no one interested in remembering them. In case of sickness or trouble the people would praise and pray to the ancestors who were recently dead. They would be supposed to take greater interest in the people than those chiefs who died ages ago. Thus, the old Umkulunkulus get forgotten, and remain simply as postulates for thought. Let us keep clear in our mind that the word " Great One " does not imply infinity, but that it connotes the conception of age, much as Sam Weller's phrase, "The Ancient," was used for the word *father*. To have a single word to express your great-great-great-great-great-great-great-*ad-infinitum*-grandfather is a manifest economy of thought and time. Thus, Umkulunkulu comes to have much the same value to a Kafir that the name Adam had to millions of people in pre-Darwinian days. It furnished a point from which thought could start.

But this is not all. It would be very simple if the subject could be dropped here. The natives worship their ancestors because they consider that during life the head of the family is responsible for all that happens in the family. He is ultimately responsible for them all : they consider that he gives them all things, which they hold in tacit dependence on him. His father gave him all things, and again that ancestor's father gave him all he had, and so on *ad infinitum*. As whatever is done in the kraal the father is the doer of it, so whatever is done in the tribe the chief is the doer of it ; he is responsible for his tribe : so most naturally the oldest grandfather, or originator of the tribe, is considered the one who gave the tribe all its possessions. He continues, of course, to carry on his function of preserver and supplier of needs after his death. Therefore, the oldest Umkulunkulu was the one who must be supposed to have originated all things, if indeed they need have any origin. Umkulunkulu thus begins to take on a little of the function of a creator. If people give way to evil habits they will often say, "That is no business of mine: did I make myself? Umkulunkulu made men, with their nature, and the responsibility for what I am doing rests with him: he told us to enjoy ourselves, to multiply, and to gratify our desires: if there is any blame, it is his." I have even heard Christian natives excuse themselves when detected in evil by saying, "It is no fault of mine that I have these strong desires: the blame is his who put this heart in me." Umkulunkulu is often used as an excuse for living a sensual life.

Some writers maintain that Umkulunkulu is worshipped in certain districts. Thus, a tribe in Zululand is said to have worshipped Umkulunkulu in olden days, slaying an ox and saying, "Hear us, Umkulunkulu: may the sick recover. Hear us, Baba: may we never stumble." I have little doubt but that these people were praying to the founder or Umkulunkulu of their tribe. The people have forgotten Umkulunkulu's praise-giving names, and so can hardly worship him in any sense which is adequately Kafir. It is true that sometimes children are told to go out into the veldt and call to Umkulunkulu to send them rain and good crops; the people will also sometimes say during thunder that Umkulunkulu is talking. Yet this praying to Umkulunkulu is rare, because, as Callaway points out, the Kafirs say that people prefer to pray to the Amatongo or spirits of people whom they have seen with their eyes rather than to Umkulunkulu, whom they have never seen—that the Amatongo, or ancestral spirits, have taken away any worship that may have been offered to Umkulunkulu. People now

## Native Beliefs

ask for food and health from the spirits (Amadhlozi or Amatongo). No one would call himself the son or descendant of Umkulunkulu, all natives regarding themselves as sons of men of much more recent times; it followed that Umkulunkulu has now no sons, or people who considered themselves of his tribe, to worship him. The people even go so far, sometimes, as to say that they made their own ancestors into spirits, in order that they might have some one less vague than Umkulunkulu to pray to.

Yet they admit that there may have been an Umkulunkulu above in the heavens who made the sun and the stars, the moon and the earth. This may be the same One who made men and women; but they are not at all clear about it. Why trouble about such unpractical things? *Cui bono?* It is true that they feel it difficult to account for the world as it is: it could hardly have made itself, and so a vague, misty Umkulunkulu will serve well as a ποῦ στῶ from which to begin mental operation. "Because there is or is not a name for a thing, we cannot argue that the thing has, or has not, an actual existence." (Jowett, " Introduction to Plato.") The belief in Umkulunkulu is convenient for excusing themselves from any guilt in being lustful and evil, for what have they to do with the will of Umkulunkulu? If he thought it good to give them strong animal desires it was his look-out, not theirs. Theal sums up the question thus: "No man of this race, upon being told of the existence of a single supreme God, ever denies the assertion, and among many tribes there is even a name for such a being, as, for instance, the word Umkulunkulu, the Great Great One, used by the Hlubis and others. From this it has been assumed by some investigators that the Bantu are really monotheists, and that the spirits of their ancestors are regarded as mediators or intercessors. But such a conclusion is incorrect. The Great Great One was once a man, they all assert, and before our

# The Essential Kafir

conception of a deity became known to them he was the most powerful of the ancient chiefs, to whom tradition assigned supernatural knowledge and skill." ("The Beginnings of South African History," page 43.)

This statement is open to a good deal of criticism in certain directions; yet it clearly points out how the conception of God is not explicit in a Kafir's mind, even though it may possibly be implicit.

A few things need to be added. They will only increase the fog; yet they must be told. Natives will sometimes say that Umkulunkulu was created by Umvelinqangi, and that he was "broken off from a bed of reeds" together with a woman who was his wife; that these two people, Umkulunkulu and his wife, who together constitute one Umkulunkulu, gave birth to the present race of people. Others, again, say that Umvelinqangi "broke off" Umkulunkulu from Uthlanga, which word really means *a reed*, or *origin*, or *source of being*. Yet, again, others will tell you that Utixo, who is probably a Hottentot importation, made Umkulunkulu, and that this last-named person managed skilfully to hide Utixo, and so he has managed to *commandeer* all the praise which should have gone to Utixo.

This Utixo is sometimes said to be a word coined by European missionaries; yet there is strong evidence that it was an old Hottentot word in use long before white men visited the country.

Hahn, a great authority, says that the Zulus probably borrowed the myth of Uthlanga from the Hottentots, and misunderstood them into the bargain. The Khoi-khoi, or Hottentots, used a word which meant *offshoot* and not *reed*. Thus we see what a hopeless muddle the whole subject is in. One man says (see Prout) that Umkulunkulu burst out of a reed and made men; others say that "our progenitors were two, Umvelinqangi and Umkulunkulu, who sprang out from the reeds "—that one was a man and the other a woman. Brownlee tells us that Uthlanga simply means *supreme*, and that Utixo means *beautiful*. The Swazies say that Umkulumcande made all things, but that he died long ago, though he gave the first king power to make rain. Another will tell you that it was Usondo who made Umkulunkulu, though others say he is the same as Umkulunkulu. Again, they tell us that Uthlanga begat Usondo, who begat Umkulunkulu. Umvelinqangi, whose name is said to mean " One who made his apppearance," is also said to be the same as Umkulunkulu; or else it is asserted that he made Uthlanga, who was a woman, and that he and this woman begat the human race; or, yet again, that he was Uthlanga, " the origin." *Quot homines, tot sententiæ.* It is impossible to reduce this chaos to order, unless one refuses to accept all evidence that contradicts one's preconceived notions.

And swift upon the heels of these ancient people come other names which must be mentioned.

### QAMATA

The Xosa Kafirs have a dim belief in a person called Qamata, who was once either a powerful chief or some semi-supernatural being. So in times of trouble they will occasionally pray, " O Qamata, help me." They never seem to offer any sacrifices to him, for they do not know his praise-names; yet sometimes when they sneeze they will say, " Qamata, help me." It has been suggested that they have borrowed this personage from the Hottentots, and that he is identical with Utixo. Some Kafirs say that Qamata had only one leg,—an idea clearly borrowed from the Hottentots, for Heitsi Eibib, their great hero, was said to have a sore knee. (See Appendix).

# The Essential Kafir

MORIMO

Morimo may be regarded as the god of the Bechuana. They say he made men and brought them out of a cave, and that his footprints are still visible, but they have no sign of toes.

MOLUNGU, ETC.

As we go farther north we find the natives saying, during a thunderstorm, "Molungu thunders." This person seems to be similar to the Mashona Magondi, who, the Mashonas say, was driven away by the Matabele. Bishop Knight Bruce was asked not to fire guns near a certain kraal, lest he should frighten their god away. The natives in the north of Matabeleland declare that there is a god, whom they call Ngwali, who was wont to be worshipped by the Bushmen. Even Lobengula used to pay tribute to this god. The godship is said to be hereditary, and so we must suppose it to be akin to that of Mbona, the worship of whom is carried on among the Sena-speaking people north of the Zambesi, near Port Herald, for no one is allowed to see Ngwali any more than he is to see Mbona's prophetess. Mbona was a great Rain-maker who died long ago, and an old woman acts as his prophetess. She tours the country occasionally with two old men, who are the only persons that are allowed to see her. As the people hear she is coming they hide in their houses, and she collects the offerings left outside the huts. Some of these she offers to Mbona, and the rest she keeps as her own. The people are most careful to keep in their huts as she is passing, lest they should be stricken with mortal disease if they accidentally saw her. A friend of mine stood out in the street with a native evangelist as she passed, and the people all thought they would

## Native Beliefs

be sure to die soon after this piece of sacrilege. An ancient Rain-maker with a great reputation is apt to be worshipped as if he were a hero, and later as if he were a god; yet it is very doubtful whether the natives mean the same thing by the word that we do.

To show how difficult it is to obtain sound and consistent information on native beliefs, I will close this passage by quoting the words of Captain Allan Gardiner, who visited the great Chaka early in the nineteenth century, and thus had an unrivalled opportunity of gathering information. He says: " The following brief account is all that I have been able to collect on this subject : It is agreed amongst the Zoolos that their forefathers believed in the existence of an over-ruling spirit, whom they call Villenangi (literally the First Appearer), and who soon after created another heavenly being of great power, called Koolukoolwani, who once visited this earth in order to publish the news (as they express it) and also to separate the sexes and colours among mankind. During the period he was below, two messages were sent to him from Villenangi, the first conveyed by a chameleon announcing that men were not to die, and the second by a lizard with a contrary decision. The lizard, having outrun the slow-paced chameleon, arrived first and delivered his message before the latter made its appearance.

" To this want of promptness they attribute our present condition as mortal beings, heaping all the odium of death upon the sluggish chameleon. There are still many legends respecting Villenangi, but none of which my informant could remember, excepting that he enjoined that lamentation should be made over the dead. It is said that many years ago, though not within the memory of the oldest person living, sacrifices of cattle were offered to Villenangi. The generality of the people are ignorant even of this tradition; but since their intercourse with the Europeans the vague idea of a Supreme Being has again become general. At present the reigning king absorbs all their praises, and he is, in fact, their only idol."

This evidence, like the remarks of Theal quoted above, is open to criticism in some directions; but it is very valuable as showing the way in which the great bulk of the natives are ignorant of their own traditions, and alter and develop them after contact with white people. Leaving the subject of Umkulunkulu in a somewhat hazy state, though not more hazy than it is in Kafir thought, let us pass on to examine the various conceptions of creation. It is impossible to be more royal than the king, or more kafir than the Kafirs.

## CREATION

One of the shrewdest guesses as to creation was made by the Bushmen: they said the world was made by a spirit—whether evil or good they did not know—with his left hand. It must have seemed to them "as if some lesser god had made this world." This explanation would seem to them to account for all the tragedies, inequalities, sorrows, and troubles of life. It is a crazy world we are born into. German philosophy was thus long ago anticipated by the Bushmen.

The Hottentots thought that Tixo made the world, and the Kafirs have adopted this idea very largely. One myth runs thus: Teco, or Tixo, made three kinds of men, namely, Hottentots, Kafirs, and white men. A day was fixed for these men to appear before Tixo. As they were gathering together, a honey-bird, which leads people to the place where honey is to be found, came flying about in great excitement. With the Hottentots it is almost a religion to leave any important work unfinished and immediately to follow the honey-bird. So the Hottentots at once ran after it. Tixo was very cross with this

# Native Beliefs

action of the Hottentots, and declared that they should be a vagrant race, living on honey, beer, and wild roots. After this, vast herds of cattle appeared, and the Kafirs were so excited that they began to squabble, one claiming this beast and another claiming that. One wanted this red cow, another wanted that black bull; and so they went on wrangling. Tixo was very cross, and said that they should be a restless people whose chief possessions should consist in cattle. The white men waited patiently, and Tixo was so pleased that he gave them cattle, horses, sheep, and many kinds of useful things; and that is why the white man is so superior to the Kafir. He gained all his useful knowledge by waiting.

There are a dozen variations of this story, which is differently told by the Damaras, Zulus, Pondos, Basutos, and other tribes; but all agree that the white man gained by sitting on his heels and waiting. Some of these stories run thus: When Umkulunkulu made black men, he was not much pleased with his work: so he sent them out into the world and only gave them cattle and assegais and mealies and Kafir corn. The black man was in a hurry and ran away. After this Umkulunkulu made another black man, who sat down quietly and waited, and after some time he began to cast his skin. And since snakes are supposed by the natives to become more perfect by casting their skins, they suppose that the man who cast his skin and became white naturally became more perfect than the one who ran away with his black skin unchanged. (This is not unlike the idea of some Australian natives who said that white men were black men risen from the dead.) The man who cast his skin then "scraped up" all the cunning and knowledge he could, and thus became so clever that of course he could do anything. He got hold of ploughs and guns, and other wonderful things, and he also learned how to make gunpowder.

## The Essential Kafir

This myth shows how strongly the natives feel the superiority of white men, for one does not sit down and invent a story to explain a thing one does not feel. In the light of this legend alone it would seem unwise for missionaries to talk so much about the equality of colour. That is a most thorny subject in South Africa; but a very little clear thinking and speaking would dispel much of the storm raised over it. Obviously it is an absurdity, which needs no exposure, to say that the Kafir is in all respects equal to a white man. Would you like him to marry your sister? If you think him *quite* equal to a white man you should feel no shrinking from this. Do you, for a moment, believe that he is as clever and rational and cleanly in his habits as a white man? Do you think that he has as much balance and grit? Has he the same capacity and sense of the beautiful? Is he as artistic and musical and scientific as a white man? No one in his senses would say that he is. So missionaries cannot mean this when they say all are on an equality. But if the question is, To what class of animal must he be assigned?—Is he a vertebrate, a mammal, a member of the genus homo?—then we all admit he is a human being. He is not a monkey or a dog; he is a man. And though he may be a very depraved man, though he may be very ignorant and dirty and objectionable in his insanitary habits and his morals, yet "a man's a man for a' that." This is also self-evident.

The native is capable of improvement; he can develop, for he has the basal attributes of manhood, though he is at present low down in the scale of civilisation. He has the human qualities of conscience, will, intellect, and affection; he feels many of the emotions which we know; he is a social animal. This is what, I take it, the missionary means. And surely we must have lost our senses if we deny this.

The whole question is, What shall we tell the Kafir? Shall we accentuate this self-evident fact, or shall we lay the emphasis

# Native Beliefs

on his present inferiority? If he is conscious of his inferiority, and if he invents myths to account for it, we can do him little harm by admitting this fact, and by telling him it is high time he began to awake and improve, and leave his dirty habits behind. The lowest members of our great criminal classes in England are men as well as the peers of the realm. But we do not go and tell them that they are as good as dukes, for they are not. It seems to me that missionaries have often, most unwisely, ignored this Kafir myth about inequality; they might have made great use of it to urge the people to be discontented with their low state. As a Zulu would say, I shall not thresh that straw again," or, in other words, I shall not argue that point again."

The variations of the story of creation are very numerous. One legend says that Umkulunkulu split a stone in two, and that man sprang out fully equipped, even as some Pallas Athene from the head of Zeus. The Bechuanas say that Morimo, as well as men and animals, came out of a hole in the earth. The Damaras say they all came out of a tree, and that the men lit a fire which frightened away all the Bushmen and animals: that is why the Bushmen live in holes in the earth, like animals. But the dogs and cattle were not frightened by the fire, and so they became friends with man. Campbell tells how the natives said that the first man's name was Matoome, and that he had a brother of the same name, and a sister named Matoomyan. She was told to go and look after the cattle. However, her brother frightened her away and took charge of them: and ever since then the women are not allowed to have anything to do with the cattle. This made the girl so angry that she instantly ran back into the hole in the earth out of which she had come; she took all the medicines with her, and hence it is that death entered into the world. With regard to this productive tree, the Damaras say naïvely that it is not now worth while

# The Essential Kafir

sitting under it in order to obtain cattle, for its rate of production has been very slow of late. The Basutos also have their story about men who came out of a hole in the ground, and even say they know the spot where the prints of his feet are to be seen. These marks were probably caused by some bird in olden ages which left petrified marks of its feet in the rock. I have seen one such indication of a huge bird close to Morijah, and myths would naturally gather round such a sight. The Swazies told mé that they knew of some marks of one-legged angels on the rocks in the mountains near the king's kraal, but that they disliked showing them to strangers.

In olden days the natives used to say that monkeys were human beings who were dumb, because they knew that if they once began to speak they would be made to work—a most anthropomorphic view of monkeys!

## NATURE

It is surprising how little the Kafirs have thought about nature; and it seems clear that most of their ideas were borrowed from the Bushmen, or Hottentots, whose imagination was extremely fertile. Chaka told a visitor that he thought the sky was caused by the smoke of the fires which mounted upwards. I once asked an old man if he thought this was correct, and he said, "Yes: the sky is formed by the smoke of our fires"; and he then went on to volunteer the following information unasked, a very rare thing for a Kafir: The rain comes down through the sky because its surface is covered with little holes, which let the light through at night, thus forming the stars. The sun, he said, was supposed to turn round after it set; it then shone on another part of the world, if, indeed, we could believe the old women; but, as for himself, he doubted this very much. Other natives believed, he said,

# Native Beliefs

that the sun goes down into the sea, and travels through the water till it comes to the east; it is then warmed up afresh in a cave and comes out once more. Kafirs think they also came out of this cave in the east, or else from the north. He declared that some natives said the sky was not smoke, but was a great arch of rock, and that it was full of people, but that the sun, moon, and stars were between us and it. He, however, expressed his doubts on these latter points. When I told him that the Bushmen thought that the moon was a piece of bullock's hide which some one threw into the sky, and that the stars were lumps of food, he grew scornful and said that that was only what the Hottentots thought. They all knew that the moon was the servant of the sun; it died every month and came to life again, or else a new moon was made. The days devour the moon, and when it gets very small it hides itself in the sun. "But," added he, "we are only black men, and know very little about these things."

Other natives say that there is a great fire in the sea, and that sun and moon come out of it; the sparks from the fire form the stars. I even once found the idea which many small European children have invented, namely, that the stars are made from the old moons, which are cut up for this purpose.

An eclipse of the moon is taken to be the sign that a great chief has died. The Hottentots declared to Moffat that the sun was cut to pieces after it set, and was fried in a pot, and put together again in the morning. The sun had to move in the sky to make way for the moon. The Mashonas say that every morning the stars fall on the earth as soon as they hear the cock crow, and I fancy they got this idea from the Bushmen. Some tribes spit on the ground when they see a shooting star, crying out, "Go away all alone," lest it should make their cattle ill. The Namaquas think that a falling star is a sign that the cattle will get ill. When they see a shooting star they cry out to it, and tell the number of cattle they have, begging it to go away. Some tribes declare that the moon is a hole in the sky; but it is reserved to the Bushmen and Hottentots to develop theories which would not form a bad basis for Greek myths. Those who wish to study their ideas should certainly read Hahn's works, which are extremely valuable and interesting. The Hottentots welcome the new moon, and hold dances in its honour. This moon worship has been asserted and contradicted and reasserted by travellers; but it was certainly a religious function. Even in Chaka's days the Zulus used to beat drums when they saw the new moon, and no one worked in the garden next day, for they believed they would never reap the benefit of that work. Yet most of the natives pay but little attention to the heavens, though they know the sowing time by the position of the Pleiades in the sky. This method of telling the seasons they probably got from the Hottentots, who have strange myths on the point.

We come now to the subject of wind. It is the Bushmen who suggested that the wind was a person. With keen suggestiveness they said that it was a person who sometimes changed himself into a bird; that it lived in a hole in a mountain and went out day by day to catch food; then it returned into the mountain at night to rest. On one occasion a Bushman saw the wind. He was about to throw a stone at it, mistaking it for a bird, when the seeming bird suddenly burst and blew hard in his face; and, raising a terrible dust, went up in a whirlwind into its home in the mountain. This story is most valuable, for it shows how easily the myth could arise. In South Africa small whirlwinds are very common, and it would often happen that Bushmen would be aiming at a bird when the wind would suddenly come with a gust and hide the bird in dust; the Bushman would then think that the bird had changed back

## Native Beliefs

into the wind, which vanished in a whirlwind up the sides of the mountain.

A whirlpool, in a similar manner, is supposed to be caused by a bird with huge wings. Diviners often declare that they have been carried down below the surface of the water by whirlpools, where they learned many wonderful secrets about medicine and magic. A Kafir cannot always distinguish between his dreams and his waking life, and his visit to the bottom of the river must be regarded, not as a lie, but as a dream-experience. He thinks that his dream-experiences are quite real, and believes he went to the place he dreamt of; and this fact will account for some of the untruthfulness of Kafirs.

The natives are much afraid of looking into deep pools. They think that a fabulous monster lives in some of them, and that this monster has the power of laying hold of a man's shadow, by which it can drag him into the water. Crocodiles also are supposed to be able to do the same. If a man falls into a pool when his friends are looking on, they will frequently leave him to drown, while they run to the cattle kraal and drive a cow of a special colour to the pool. They then either throw the cow into the water or kill it on the bank, in the hope that the fabulous monster will send the man back in exchange. They think, also, that some men's spirits live in the water after their death, and consequently sacrifice to these spirits, who are supposed to be able to take hold of a man by his reflection. A native cannot always distinguish between a photograph of a man and the man himself; the image seems to them a part of the man. They have often asked me why I want to get their image on to a piece of paper, and said they did not like it, for I could easily bewitch them through this emanation from themselves. Why did I want to have their image? they asked. They feared that after their death I could still have a hold on them through this shadow, reflection, or likeness.

# The Essential Kafir

Passing on, we find that the world itself is sometimes regarded as a huge animal which is alive. The trees are sometimes supposed to be able to hear what is said under their shadows. They can drink beer which is poured over their roots or leaves. The birds can talk at times—at least, to those few people who have ears to hear. The Bushmen said they thought that the cattle could fight and use bows and arrows and so forth if only they had the implements. In their folk-lore tales the stones open as in "The Arabian Nights," huts build themselves and as suddenly vanish; and if you ask them if they actually believe this to be fact they cannot give you any consistent answers. One man thinks it actually happens; but the next man is given up to philosophic doubt.

One of the most picturesque pieces of their natural philosophy is found in their ideas about the rainbow. The beauty and rareness of the sight appeals to a savage mind, and many are the stories invented to account for it. They say the rainbow is a sign that the weather is about to clear. The bow is declared to be some of the wattles of the hut of the Queen of Heaven, or a queen in heaven. The wattles of a hut are bent in a similar curve during building operations, and a half-finished hut shows this structure to perfection; but the shape can be seen even in a finished hut (see plates 20 and 21) Some missionaries think that this Queen of Heaven is a development of the story of Jeptha's daughter, which they imagine to have been known to the original Kafirs who came down from the north. The idea of Jewish influence is founded on a wholly inadequate basis, and it will be discussed in another chapter.

When the natives worship this Queen of Heaven, the girls take off their petticoats and put on the loin-skins of the young men; they then rush into the cattle-kraal—a thing absolutely forbidden at other times—seize the oxen, and drive them out

Plate 18.

A PONDO MOTHER.

She is washing her baby with a mouthful of water which she squirts on to it.

Plate 19.

A PONDO WOMAN GOING TO FETCH WATER.

# Native Beliefs

into the veldt. They herd them all day and night. Next morning the girls drive the oxen up to the kraal, and the cattle are milked by the men. The girls go to their own huts and prepare food and make beer. Also they select some seed for sowing and go off into the veldt to a specially selected spot of land, where they plant the seed after they have hoed up the ground. They pour some beer into a pot, which is placed in a hole in the ground. When the grain is grown it is considered sacred, and is left for the Queen of Heaven, who is supposed to come down in a mist to consume the food and the beer.

But there are many other suggestions concerning the rainbow. Sometimes it is said to be a sheep that comes out of a pool. I could never find any explanation of this idea. When I have asked natives for fuller information they have said, laughingly, "This is all we know: it is a sheep." If a rainbow is seen to rest on a pool, the people are afraid of bathing in it, though witchdoctors love to bathe in such water; they say it enables them to divine with great success. The Mashonas say that if any one manages to run to the spot where the rainbow rests on the earth he will find a large brass ornament. (A similar belief prevails amongst English children.) No one ever seems to find this ornament, and so the story is on a level with our advice to children about catching birds by placing salt on their tails.

Other natives say the rainbow is a disease, or causes a disease, and that if it rests on a person he is sure to die. Yet again it is said to be a snake in the sky.

### RAIN-MAKING

The rainfall is an all-important subject in South Africa. If it is plentiful the crops will be abundant; but if there be a drought the natives are sure to be pinched by famine. The methods adopted by the Kafirs to make rain find their counter-

# The Essential Kafir

part in nearly every country under heaven; these methods are so varied in detail that we shall have to confine our attention to Kafir customs.

In very old days the chief was the great Rain-maker of the tribe. Some chiefs allowed no one else to compete with them, lest a successful Rain-maker should be chosen as chief. There was also another reason: the Rain-maker was sure to become a rich man if he gained a great reputation, and it would manifestly never do for the chief to allow any one to be too rich. The Rain-maker exerts tremendous control over the people, and so it would be most important to keep this function connected with royalty. Tradition always places the power of making rain as the fundamental glory of ancient chiefs and heroes, and it seems probable that it may have been the origin of chieftainship. The man who made the rain would naturally become the chief. In the same way, Chaka used to declare that he was the only diviner in the country, for if he allowed rivals his life would be insecure.

It may be well to pass in review some of the methods adopted to secure rain. The Swazies seek to make rain by throwing water high up into the air, and expect that as the water falls in drops it will stimulate the clouds, which will fall in rain in sympathy with the artificial shower. The Pondos kill certain birds with bright red feathers on their breasts; they hunt for these in times of drought; and when they have caught and killed the birds they throw them into the river, this is a practice which is probably a remnant of some old custom of offering a sacrifice to an ancestral spirit living in the water. The Bechuanas refrain from telling folk-lore tales before sunset, lest the clouds should fall on their heads. When the people near Delagoa Bay want rain, the women dress in petticoats of leaves and put on a head-dress of grass. They then dance to a rough chant or tune, and go to the water-holes,

## Native Beliefs

in order to clear away the mud that has accumulated in them. They go to the hut of a woman who has recently had twins, and drench her with water. During this ceremony the men are not allowed to see the women. Afterwards the women go and pour water on the graves of some ancestor.

In Zululand the native girls form a procession and carry large pots of water to a certain tree which happens to be on a mission station; they dance around the tree and pour the water on its roots. My friends who were living at this station were surprised at the ceremony, and asked the girls what they were doing this for. They said that an old ancestor of theirs had been buried under the tree, and that, as he was a great Rain-maker during his lifetime, they always came and poured water on his grave in time of drought, in order that he might send them rain. In the Basuto mountains I saw the natives offering beer to the spirits by pouring it into the earth at the edge of the mealie field. This is supposed to ensure a good crop and plenty of rain. The Matabele and Zulus frequently light fires to windward of their fields, and place medicines in the flames, that the smoke may doctor and improve the crop.

But the most powerful charms are "worked" only through the official Rain-doctors, who devote themselves to this special branch of magic. They smear themselves with mud and sacrifice oxen as an essential part of the process; almost everything turns on the colour of these beasts. Umbandine, the old king of the Swazies, had enormous herds of cattle of a peculiar colour, and as a result tribes far away to the north or south would send deputations to him, paying him large sums in order that he might make rain for them by sacrificing his cattle. He could threaten to "bind up the skies" if they did not pay him what he demanded, and thus exercised enormous power. When the ox is killed the blood is caught in calabashes, and is on no account allowed to fall to the ground. The dish of blood

## The Essential Kafir

is then placed in a hut, together with the meat of the dead ox, which is left untouched for the night; on the morrow the meat is eaten, and on the third day the bones of the ox are burnt. The priest is said to confess over the beast the sins of the people; but this confession of sin is little more than an admission that they have not honoured the ancestral spirits sufficiently.

Of course, it sometimes happens that rain actually follows these sacrifices. The Rain-makers are very shrewd men, and, as a rule, do not offer to make rain unless they think the wind is in a favourable quarter. A few years ago the Swazies urged Bunu, their king, to make rain for them. He was very chary about doing this; but they bothered him so much that finally he said, " Sacrifice a beast on the mountains, and rain will come." It so happened that rain actually fell after this sacrifice, and the people came to the missionary and said, " You see now that our king is powerful to make rain." These doctors work on the imagination of the people to an extraordinary extent, and declare that serpents sit on their medicines, thus rendering them very powerful.

If the doctor thinks that the sky shows no signs of rain he will probably manage to keep putting off the people by a dozen dodges. He will say, "Very well : I will make rain for you, and you will then see that I am a real Rain-maker." He tells them to go and hunt the country for some special animal, which must be of a certain colour, and must also be free from blemish. He knows that the men will spend days hunting for this impossible thing ; or he may tell them to catch some animal, such as a baboon or a leopard, alive, and bring it to him. If, after this delay, he fails to bring rain, he will invent a hundred excuses, and say the people have not paid him half enough ; or that the cattle sacrificed were not quite the right colour ; or he will declare that some one is using magical practices to

## Native Beliefs

prevent the rain from coming, and this excuse is final and universally accepted. After this statement there has to be a great smelling out of the culprit, and if the wind still keeps in the wrong quarter he tells the men to drag stones up the mountains and roll them down in certain directions, that the wind may be turned back. By such means he gains time, and the process may go on so long that rain is almost sure to come. If, however, he utterly fails, he has a never-ending excuse that no one would dare to gainsay : he declares that the Amatongo, or spirits of the ancestors, refuse to send the people rain. Who can deny this ? Occasionally the people turn on the Rain-maker and in disgust throw him into the river ; and indeed it is commonly said that nearly all diviners die a violent death.

In addition to these regular Rain-doctors there are many women who are supposed to be fairly skilled in making rain. They sometimes cut out the gall-bladder of a black sheep or goat and drink some of the gall, using the rest to wash their bodies with, having mixed the gall with medicines. The black colour of the animal causes the clouds to turn black. The goat is roasted on a fire, which must not be kindled from any ordinary source, but has to be made by friction with special pieces of wood. The dark smoke of the fire helps to turn the heavens black by sympathy. The woman then goes out to harangue and scold the heavens. The effect of this ceremony is to make the heavens black, and the shouting adds to the efficacy of the charm.

In Zululand the women sometimes bury their children up to the neck in the ground, and then retire to some distance and keep up a dismal howl for a long time : the heavens are supposed to melt with tenderness at the sight. The women then dig the children out and feel sure that rain will follow. They say that they call to " the lord above " and ask him to send them rain. If it comes they declare that "Usondo rains."

Among the Sena-speaking people above the Zambesi the natives worship a great Rain-maker named Mbona, who is supposed to have died ages ago. There is an old prophetess (referred to on page 102) who is said to make rain for the whole country. Her village is so sacred that the people take off their hats and sandals when entering it, and if they happen to be carrying any weapons they lay them down on the ground at a distance from her hut.

Not only do these Rain-doctors profess to produce rain : they profess to stop it when it is too plentiful. In this case they burn the skin of a rabbit, or even kill a bird and throw it into the river, to make the heavens sorry for sending so much rain. They cry out, "The rabbit is burning ; the rabbit is burning," and this makes the heavens relent. The Hottentots try to stop the wind by hanging up skins on poles ; the wind is supposed to expend its energies in blowing about the skins.

Moffat tells a good story of one of these doctors, who had been "working" hard for rain for a long time without any success. At last rain came, and the people went off to thank the doctor. They found him asleep in his hut. This was a disappointment to them, for they thought he was working very hard to make the rain. So they asked him why he was sleeping. The acute fellow saw that his wife was churning butter in a calabash, and he said, "Don't you see that my wife is churning the rain for you as fast as ever she can ?" The people went away quite satisfied.

# Native Beliefs

## THUNDER AND LIGHTNING

Thunder deeply impresses the native mind. Storms in South Africa are usually very fierce: the weather rarely loiters over its work as in England. If it rains, it rains with a vengeance, and clears up. If it thunders there can be no mistake about it. And the hail! It sometimes comes down in pieces as large as pigeons' eggs, and pierces corrugated iron. It has several times been my misfortune to be caught in it when riding through the country. One's ears and hands begin to bleed with the small ice pellets which bombard the country; the horses refuse to move and turn their backs to the storm. One has often to take off the saddle from the horse's back and place it over one's head to prevent being injured. No wonder the natives seek to charm away such a troublesome thing, which ruins the crops in many cases. Natives sometimes say that thunder is caused by thieves, who eat thunderbolts (or attract them). When the thunder begins they say, "We do not eat the wealth of others." They spit on the ground, and assure one another, "We do not eat the wealth of others." The sin of the thief is supposed to attract the thunder.

The people have a vague idea that lightning and thunder are caused by some old ancestor; but they are somewhat hazy on the point. In olden days they used to say, "Usondo rains," or "Usondo thunders." Similarly the natives on the Zambesi still say, "Molungu rains," or "Molungu thunders." When a man has been struck by lightning the people say that no one must mourn: the ancestral spirits want this man in the other world, and this is the way they sent for him. They feel that if they were to murmur it would show "a will most incorrect to heaven."

Yet some tribes seem to think that the lightning is caused

# The Essential Kafir

by hostile spirits. Thus the Bushmen will throw stones or shoot poisoned arrows at the lightning, hoping to drive it away. The Bechuana are said to curse it, while others offer sacrifices to it. The conception that thunder is caused by some one scolding in the heavens is very natural. All who have read that delightful book, "Elizabeth and her German Garden," will remember how the children used to say during thunderstorms, "There's lieber Gott scolding those angels again"; and they added naïvely that they wished he would get the scolding done in the daytime. In Devonshire the farmers will greet you on a stormy day by saying that the weather is "very cross." The natives are not much behind this stage, though sometimes their ideas on the matter are confused and fantastic. The natives in Zululand believe that if one examines the spot where lightning struck the ground the shaft of an assagai will be found. The lightning is thus thought to be some dazzling spear hurled through the air. Others maintain that a special brown bird will be found at this spot, which is supposed to be surrounded by a mist or haze—probably their interpretation of the dazzling of the eyes by the bright light. This idea is modified in Pondoland, where the natives assure you that lightning is caused by a brown bird which spits fire down on the earth. The Bomvanas modify this, again, by saying that the bird sets its own fat on fire, and throws it down on earth. I was on the point of shooting one of these birds, and the natives cried out in horror, begging me not to "shoot the lightning."

On this bird hypothesis it is easy to account for thunder. It is caused by the flapping of the wings of the bird. When the thunder is loud and crackling the people say it is caused by the female bird; when the thunder is far off and rumbling they say it is caused by the male. In Natal one frequently hears it said that lightning is caused by a white bird of enormous size which comes down and flaps its wings. An

## Native Beliefs

old native became quite indignant with a missionary who contradicted this assertion. The old man wanted to know how such a person could ever presume to teach the natives if he did not know that thunder was caused by a bird. In Mashonaland the people say that the thunder is caused by a fat baby which descends from the heavens at the spot where the lightning struck the earth. When the baby crawls on the ground it causes the thunder. If you ask why no one has ever seen such a baby, which, *ex hypothesi*, should be a fairly large monster, the people look at you in scorn and say that of course the baby is instantly taken up into the skies again.

There are many ways of warding off the lightning, and these customs find their counterpart in other countries, as, for example, in North America, where the Red Indians offer up some tobacco to appease the thunder. The Kafirs sometimes place assegais through the roof when the storm begins, thinking that these will ward off the lightning. Other tribes place a hoe standing against the outside of the hut to perform the same function. On the Zambesi the natives place pieces of ostrich egg-shell on their huts. They told me they did this as a protection against lightning. The Zulus and the Pondos frequently place the horns of oxen over their huts. There are many reasons given for this practice. Natives have often assured me they simply do this for ornament; others say that it wards off the lightning.

But there are regular men whose function it is to doctor the heavens. These are sometimes called " Heaven-herds " or " Hail-doctors," and their work is to take care of the clouds and drive them about just as small boys do the herds of oxen. They keep the capricious heaven from breaking beyond bounds and destroying the crops by hail and lightning. These Heaven-herds collect the assegai shafts left in the ground where lightning strikes it; they collect the lightning birds and use their feathers as medicines for the skies; they even eat the birds themselves, that they may be strong to fight the storm and drive it off, vanquished; they make charms which the people wear round their necks when the sky is very dark—these are certain safeguards against being struck by lightning.

As soon as a storm is seen brewing in the distance the women scream out against it, and some Heaven-herd has to begin operations. As one of their proverbs puts it, "It is better to turn back the enemy on the hill than to drive him out of the village." Prevention is better than cure. It is said—and one can quite believe it—to be much harder to turn away a storm which is breaking over one's head than to drive it away when it is on the horizon. So when the storm is seen to be brewing on the horizon the doctor runs to his hut and takes his hail-shield and goes out into the open air. (If he is away on a journey, his blanket or sleeping-mat is hung out to represent him.) Quickly he lights fires all around the gardens, and puts slow-smouldering medicines in them. The country is soon filled with numberless bluish columns of smoke which curl up into the sultry air. The doctor then fights the storm by crying out at it, just as if he were shouting at the oxen; he tells it to go away and not injure the crops. The people all gather at the kraal; and no one speaks, lest the heavens should not be able to hear all that the doctor says. He has fasted for some time, or, in other words, he has abstained from food *and work*. If he fails to drive away the storm the people say he has been eating and working too much.

The doctor sends off all the people to fetch their charms as soon as he sees the storm gaining on him. Also he fetches a calabash of medicines, into which he dips the tail of a cow, which has been fastened on a stick; with this he sprinkles the huts and the people. It is a weird picture—the doctor "working" against the storm at night-time. The thunder is

## Native Beliefs

spluttering and rumbling in the distance, and the cattle are all huddled together in the cattle kraal, knowing that a storm is coming. The sky is as heavy and dark as lead, and one can see the naked body of the doctor lit up by the fitful flashes of lightning as he goes round sprinkling medicine on the fires. The storm comes nearer, and every one in the kraal holds his breath; all are anxiously watching this man, in whom they have unbounded faith. He sends off some young men to blow horns on the hilltops: this is supposed to frighten the storm away. One can see these dark figures clambering up the hills, blowing the horns as loudly as they can, as if everything turned on the noise they made. The thunder peals louder and louder, and drowns the sound of the horns, while the people begin to gain courage as they hear the doctor shouting at the heavy storm-clouds overhead, which begin to fall in heavy drops. Suddenly there is a vivid flash of lightning in the distance, which shows up the silhouette of the doctor athwart the sky; his naked and skinny arms are raised in threatening gesture against the clouds, which he is defying with all his energy. Columns of smoke can be seen drifting in the gusts of wind which eddy about and are but the prelude to a fresh outburst of storm. There is suddenly a fearful crash of thunder just overhead, and every one feels as if the whole heavens were about to fall and crush the earth; the rain comes in torrents, and the children scream out in terror, while the doctor yells at the vivid lightning. Every now and then the noise of the horns pierces in fitful blasts through the pattering rain.

The doctor gets into a frenzy and screams out at the storm with fury, while the bleating of the goats in the kraal is all the response he hears. The hail begins to patter on the ground, and flash after flash of lightning defies the wise man's magic, and soon the heavens seem to be pouring out streams of water

## The Essential Kafir

mixed with livid fire. Clap after clap of thunder rends the air, and the din is continuous. The horn-blowers are beaten back, drenched, to their huts; they are terrified by the deluge of water and fire. The doctor alone stands out in the open air, with his hail-shield held over his head. The lightning seems to stream on his dripping but devoted brow, and the flashes remind one of the quivering tongue of an angry snake as it darts at some irritating object.

The doctor sees that the whole sky is a mass of fire, and runs back drenched and baffled into the hut, terrified in his defeat and quaking in every limb on account of the enormous expenditure of nervous energy; he cries out that he is overcome and can no longer keep back the heavens. For ten minutes the storm rages as peal after peal of thunder rolls along the hills, showing a thousand krantzes brilliantly lit up, while the children all join in a chorus of wailing. Suddenly there is a final volley of liquid fire and a clap of thunder, as if some wicked witch, after finishing all her mischief, were calling her children around her to tell them that the work is done. There can be no mistaking the sound of this clap: it is the *finale* of the concert; and slowly the dense black masses of cloud roll back like some heavy curtain, and in an incredibly short time the eternal heavens are seen to be calm and spangled with myriads of stars; all is as quiet as a nun at prayer; not a cloud is to be seen in the tranquil sky; and the onlooker finds it hard to believe that such fury and indignation could ever have ruffled the firmament.

If a cow is killed by lightning it must not be eaten (and I believe that this is the only occasion on which dead animals are not eaten). Where a kraal or a person is struck by lightning the people are considered unclean and are placed in the strictest quarantine. They are not allowed to drink milk; they may not sell cattle to their neighbours or hold any communication

# Native Beliefs

with them. It may be weeks before they are allowed to act as ordinary mortals and receive *pratique*. So great is the sense of pollution that frequently the hut, or even the whole kraal, is deserted and burnt with all that it contains.

### THE CLEANSING

A special doctor or priest is called in, and begins the cleansing process. The first thing he does is to place charms on the necks of all the people, that they may profit by the ceremony to follow. The men who are to bury the slain animal are specially doctored to make them strong to dig the grave. Their nerves are shaken and need the sedative of assurance. If a man has been killed by lightning the doctor chooses an ox, which is slain and offered to the ancestral spirits. Some of the flesh of the ox is charred over the fire, after being mixed with medicines; this mass is then powdered and mixed with milk, and the people have to drink some of the mixture. The doctor then makes incisions in various parts of the bodies of the people, as if he were about to vaccinate them; into these incisions he rubs medicines made from the charred remains of the ox. After this the people have to shave their heads. Then they are considered clean.

When the natives go to a trader or missionary to borrow a spade or wheelbarrow to help them in digging the grave, they will come back by-and-by, and pay, perhaps, half a crown, to " cleanse the spade," as they say. It is a rare thing for a native to insist on paying; but in this one instance they are urgent that the money should be accepted.

The process is sometimes modified thus, as in the case of Swazieland: The doctor, on arriving at the kraal, sends off the girls to fetch huge earthenware pots full of water. Some twenty girls may be seen wending their way to the river

# The Essential Kafir

to do this. In the meantime an enormous pot is placed in the kraal, and the doctor puts in it sundry roots which have emetic properties. The girls all pour their water into this immense vessel, and the doctor churns the whole mass up with a long stick. The people of the kraal form a circle, and one after another they have to drink their fill of the nauseous mixture. Up they come in order : first the old men, with their wrinkled faces ; then the young men ; the girls and the children following. As soon as the liquid is finished the doctor digs a huge hole in the ground, into which he makes the people vomit. When all is done the hole is filled up with earth, and the doctor tells them that they have now vomited up all the beasts which had taken possession of them, and that they will be troubled no more. The process is a splendid cure for hysterical people, who feel much better after the odious operation.

### DEMONS, SPRITES, HAUNTING SPIRITS, AND FABULOUS MONSTERS

The world is supposed to be filled with numberless monsters and spirits, which give the people no rest. Not a glen or stream but some haunting spirit is associated with it. In Zululand the people believe in a monster called an Isidawane, which is said to be as large as a cow. It has a great hole in its back, and at night comes to the kraal and calls out a person's name. The man goes out to see who is calling him, and then the Isidawane takes hold of him, places him in the hole in its back, and runs off to feed on the man's brains. The people declare that this monster frequently carries people off thus, and, if any one expresses doubt, they add that people have been actually caught by the animal and rescued by their friends.

## Native Beliefs

Then, there is a wicked little dwarf called Tickoloshe or Hili, who appeals strongly to the Kafir imagination. This dwarf is of a very amorous nature, and lives in the reeds. At night he is said to come and milk the cows and make the women fall in love with him. He sometimes beats the children till they are black and blue. A Christian native evangelist once declared to me that he believed in this little imp. He told me a long story of how he abandoned his belief in Tickoloshe when he became a Christian, but that many years after that he was sleeping in his hut with his wife and children. The children awoke him by their screams, and declared that Tickoloshe had come into the hut and beaten them till they were black and blue. And when the evangelist examined his children he found them covered all over with bruises. How could he doubt the existence of Tickoloshe after that? he asked. I thought the explanation very simple. Most Kafir children are usually covered with bruises and scratches; in their sleep they had dreamt about Tickoloshe and had possibly fallen out of bed, or fought with one another in their fright. But the evangelist thought this explanation would never do.

The Zulus have a great story about a fabulous animal called Isitshakanamana, which lives in deep pools. A man was once fishing in a pool, and this fabulous monster caught hold of his hook. The man wondered what heavy fish could have taken his bait, and he pulled the monster up on to the land. The monster cried out that it was afraid of the sun, and begged to be put back into the pool. Suddenly, as the man was hardening his heart and preparing to kill the creature, his eye rested on the eye of the monster. The sight instantly held him spellbound: the eye and mouth and nose of the beast were all in one spot! The man left his things and ran to the kraal, crying out that the eye of the monster was devouring him. He induced the people to pile a heap of blankets over his head, but found the eye glaring at him all the same. He then begged to be placed in the mealie-pit, which is excavated in the ground of the cattle kraal. They put him in it and covered him with blankets, sealing up the small opening of the pit with a large stone. Still the man shouted out that the eye was devouring him, and when, by-and-by, the people opened the pit they found that the man was dead. Some natives declare that this really happened; others laugh and say it is only a fairy-tale.

David Leslie gives a striking account of a haunted wood which runs as follows: The Esimkovu are supposed to be people who have been dead and have been raised from the dead by witches. The witches clip off the tips of their tongues, so that these risen people may only be able to wail out, " Maieh, maieh," which is a sound like the soughing of the wind. When people hear this sound in the woods they run away to their huts and chew a little medicine. (There are other people who have been dead and raised to life again; these are sent back by the Amadhlozi, or spirits, and they come only in the form of snakes.)

Now, a certain man died and was buried; but the next day he was seen walking in his kraal as usual, as if nothing had happened. He told the people that he had indeed been buried, but that the Amadhlozi in the under-world had sent him back to earth. He said he had been in a fine country where the cattle were all very fat. In that world he met a cousin who had died many years previously, and this cousin sent him back to the world from which he had come, telling him that if he once ate food in the spirit-world he could never return to earth. After this he remembered nothing until he found himself lying on the ground.

For days this man lived in the kraal with the people who had buried him, and they noticed that he was constantly sighing for the good land which he had seen when in the lower world.

Plate 20.

HOW A ZULU HUT IS BUILT.

The man pushes a wooden needle through the wickerwork, and a boy on the other side returns it. Native grass is used for string.

Plate 21.

INTERIOR OF A ZULU HUT.

This is the hut shown on Plate 2. It belonged to a chief, and was therefore very clean.

# Native Beliefs

So the people said that he must be one of the *Esimkovu, and should be put to death. However, his brother suggested that he should be allowed to take him to a wood which was haunted by these Esimkovu; if he fraternised with them, and they with him, then it would be proof that he was a real Esumkovu, but if he recoiled from them it would be a proof that he was no Esumkovu. To this plan the people agreed.

These brothers entered the wood and heard the wind rising with a moaning, soughing sound among the trees. The suspected man was quite at ease; but his brother was much frightened. The brother cut a wattle and heard a sound come near and all round him; there were semi-human ejaculations, which seemed even to come from the interior of their own bodies. The brother cut another wattle, and there was a sound as of surprise heard on all sides; the noise grew louder and louder, and a heavy pressure seemed to take hold of the one who had cut the wood. Then something seemed to hold the axe he was wielding. At length the suspected man became excited and frightened, for he felt things to be very uncanny. The brother gave another desperate cut at the tree with his axe, and there was instantly the sound of a rushing wind, which seemed like that of a swollen river, and there were exclamations of " Wow, wow, who comes here ? So they dare us ! " Some unseen power twitched the axes out of their hands and took away their assagais; and suddenly showers of sticks and stones were hurled at them, till the two brothers fled in terror. As soon as the people heard that the Esimkovu had treated the suspected person thus, they declared that he could not possibly be one of them, and so his life was spared.

### CONCLUSION

Such is the crazy world in which the Kafirs live. To experiment, and so to eliminate impossible theories, never enters

*Esumkovu, singular; Esimkovu, plural.

# The Essential Kafir

their heads. On all sides whim of spirits, capriciousness of monsters, and uncertainty of natural processes, seem to reign. In this soil witchcraft can luxuriate, for no one is in a position to point out the absurdity of the superstitions. We are now prepared to study the subject of magic. In sifting evidence supplied by natives we need to be constantly reminding ourselves what hopelessly bad observers of phenomena they are.

# MAGIC

Never fear but there's provision
  Of the devil's to quench knowledge
Lest we walk the earth with rapture.
                    ROBERT BROWNING ("Christina").

# CHAPTER III

### MAGIC

(1) *Explanation of Sickness.*—The natives have no classified system of medicine, because they have no classified system of anything. Certain theories float through the minds of the natives concerning sickness; yet those ideas are never reduced to order. For all that, their ideas on the subject may be roughly classified under three headings by European observers.

To start with, there is sickness which is supposed to be caused by the action of ancestral spirits or by fabulous monsters. Secondly, there is sickness which is caused by the magical practices of some evil person who is using witchcraft in secret. Thirdly, there is sickness which comes from neither of these causes, and remains unexplained. It is said to be "only sickness, and nothing more."

This third form of sickness is, I think, the commonest. Yet most writers wholly ignore it, or deny its existence.

It may happen that an attack of indigestion is one day attributed to the action of witch or wizard; another day the trouble is put down to the account of ancestral spirits; on a third occasion the people may be at a loss to account for it, and so may dismiss the problem by saying that it is merely sickness.

It is quite common to hear natives say that they are at a loss to account for some special case of illness. At first they thought it was caused by an angry ancestral spirit; but a great doctor has assured them that it is not the result of such a spirit. They then suppose it to be due to the magical practices of some enemy; but the doctor negatives that theory. The people are, therefore, driven to the conclusion that the trouble has no ascertainable cause.

In some cases they do not even trouble to consult a diviner: they speedily recognise the sickness as due to natural causes. In such a case it needs no explanation. If they think that some friend of theirs knows of a remedy, they will try it on their own initiative, or may even go off to a white man to ask for some of his medicine. They would never dream of doing this if they thought they were being influenced by magic or by ancestral spirits.

The Kafirs quite recognise that there are types of disease which are inherited, and have not been caused by magic or by ancestral spirits. They admit that some accidents are due to nothing but the patient's carelessness or stupidity. If a native gets his leg run over by a waggon, the people will often say that it is all his own fault through being clumsy. In other cases, with delightful inconsistency, they may say that some one has been "working" magic to cause the accident. In short, it is impossible to make out a theory of sickness which will satisfy our European conception of consistency. The Kafirs would delight in Emerson's saying (if they only knew it) that a "foolish consistency is the hobgoblin of little minds."

It would be pleasant to be able to bring forth some clear-cut theory that all sickness is due to magical practices, and it would be easy to get some isolated Kafir to tell you that this was a full account of native ideas; yet, for all that, the theory would not be true. There is a class of doctors that claim no special relation to the ancestral spirits, and no knowledge of magic; these people simply deal in a few well-known drugs, which they dispense without any ceremony. The diviner may

# Magic

send a patient to one of these people, saying that, as his illness is not caused by magic or by ancestral spirits, all that is needed is a course of medical treatment by a herb-doctor. This man no more professes to cure disease in a marvellous way than an old housewife in England who administers a few simples pretends to be able to ride on broomsticks. The stock of medicines used by the native herb-doctors consists of such things as aloes, nux vomica, castor-oil plant, fern root, rhubarb, and the bark of various trees, many of which have purgative or emetic properties.

Again, when a man has a toothache the people may trace the cause to the magic of an enemy or the anger of ancestral spirits; but it is far more usual for them to say that it is only toothache. In this case some person who is skilled in extracting teeth sets to work. He fastens a sinew of sheep or ox to the tooth and winds the rest of the sinew round a stick. He twists this up until the tooth is firmly grasped, and then begins to lever and prise the apparatus until something gives way; it may be the sinew, or it may be the jaw, or possibly it may, occasionally, be the tooth. Or else he may dig round the roots of the tooth with an old rusty nail and set up an abscess, so that after long torture the offending member is sloughed out. Another successful plan is to take a bar of iron and place one of its ends against the root of the tooth. All that is needed is to hit the other end of the iron bar with a small piece of rock, when the tooth is sent half-way down the patient's throat. If there should happen to be a white man near who has a pair of forceps, he is frequently consulted, and the operation is performed so easily that the delighted patient feels in his mouth with one of his fingers, and points out one or two other teeth which he would like to have extracted. If the white man expostulates with him and says these other teeth are quite sound, the native will admit the soft impeachment,

## The Essential Kafir

but will say with a naïve grin that they may possibly go bad when there is no white man near to extract them: so they may as well be pulled there and then.

When a native suffers from a dislocated joint he is usually treated without consulting any diviner. The people make a deep hole in the ground, into which the man inserts his arm or leg, as the case may be. They fill in the earth round the limb, and press it well down with their feet. Two men take hold of the patient and forcibly pull him away from the affected joint until it yields to the treatment. The dislocation is thus effectively reduced.

The reason why travellers have so often failed to recognise the fact that the natives consider that much illness is "simply sickness" and nothing more is not far to seek. The imagination is much impressed by stories of magic or ancestral interference, and when a man is writing up his journal he enters all the facts which seem bizarre, and forgets to take note of the more commonplace explanation, if, indeed, he has noticed it. But native conceptions are sufficiently strange without our exaggerating them.

The Kafirs are very rough and ready with their methods of using medicine. They think that a drug can act well at a distance. A man went to a European doctor whom I know and obtained some ergot for a certain woman who was in trouble. This drug acted so very powerfully that he placed the rest of the medicine about a hundred yards from the kraal, hiding it under a stone, so that the drug might not act powerfully on all the other women of the kraal. A native will also sometimes take medicine by proxy. Thus, a man once came to me and complained of a long list of symptoms, and said he badly wanted some medicine. For a *placebo* I gave him some jalap and a dose of salts. As he was licking up the last few grains of Epsom salts with his tongue—how they love to have ill-

# Magic

flavoured medicine, and to eat it slowly!—he thanked me for the dose, and said that he hoped the medicine he had just taken would do his wife good, for the pains were hers and not his.

Headaches are sometimes cured by administering a good shaking and pounding to the sick person, or else by making a set of scratches over the temple; a cupping horn is applied until there is a great swelling. This is a splendid cure for headache. A native loves to have a really good substantial dose of medicine. When Chaka was given some medicines, he called up one man and gave him a spoonful of calomel, and then threw a box of pills to another, telling the man to swallow the whole boxful. When a white man expostulated with him, he said that no one could have too much of a good thing—that if a small dose of medicine cured a man slowly a large dose should certainly cure him quickly. He then mixed a number of medicines in a calabash and gave spoonfuls all round to the people, saying that he did not know much about these medicines of the white man, but that if one medicine in the mixture did not touch the spot, probably another would. I have seen the Dutch do precisely the same thing. When I was in a store one day, a Dutchman came in and bought a bottle of every kind of patent medicine in the shop. He told me, with a knowing wink, that he always mixed these medicines in a basin, and then gave a spoonful to any member of his family who should happen to get ill: if one drug did no good, probably one of the other ingredients would.

Sickness which is due to the interference of ancestral spirits is much more picturesque. It is treated with a very marked ceremonial, and appeals strongly to our sense of the bizarre. A priest or doctor selects an ox, which is killed in the cattle kraal. The spine of the animal is cut out from the head to the tail. This is placed by itself in a hut, while the blood and fat are placed in the hut of the sick person. The people of the kraal eat the meat; but after two days the blood is buried in the cattle kraal, and the spine is burnt, together with the fat. The theory is that the spirits send sickness to show their displeasure with the people of the kraal. This is one of their ways of calling attention to the fact that the people have neglected to offer sufficient sacrifices of late; or it may be a way of informing the people that some of the ancient customs have been neglected, or broken. It is a common saying that if the ancient customs are not kept up the people will find their teeth falling out. In that case not even an American dentist could help them. A diviner would be called in to find out the culprit, and some one would be accused of sorcery, for the hypothesis is that no one could wish to break old tribal customs unless he wished to gain power over others through magic. Thus custom is most tenacious of life: it has managed to get the diviners on its side.

This conception of the cause of sickness is of very ancient date, and has existed ever since the first glimmerings of historical record. In Chaka's days the Zulus said that most sickness was caused by Vagino, or evil spirits, who made people ill out of revenge, or because some enemies had bought over these Vagino by offerings and sacrifices. These spirits were supposed to come and dwell in the bodies of the sick, and cause all their pains and aches. Relics of this theory are still extant in Swazieland, where the people consider certain forms of epilepsy to be caused by enraged ancestral spirits, who stab people from within, thus causing the convulsions. It also happens that the Kafirs sometimes think sickness to be due to the spirits of ancestors or fabulous monsters living in the rivers. In such cases cure is sought by throwing oxen into the river to appease the spirits. A description of some of these diseases and modes of cure will be given by-and-by.

# Magic

But the chief cause of sickness is probably to be traced to the influence of the magical practices of some envious person. Magic touches every part of a Kafir's life, and to fail to understand his ideas on this one point is to fail to understand the Kafir at any point. It is said that in European political life the only subject on which all parties are agreed is the Multiplication Table. The one subject that all Kafirs are agreed upon is the reality of magic. No Kafir in his senses dreams of doubting the tremendous power of magic. If there is one thing in the whole world about which all natives are agreed it is that the power of magic is the one reality of life. A Kafir might possibly doubt whether the grass were green; he might doubt whether sunshine were warm; he might doubt whether night followed day : but he could never doubt that magic is a reality. It is the one subject on which there can be no controversy.

There lies a man in the sunshine, curled up in his blanket; he has been ill for some time, and the women are all screaming out at you excitedly, saying that this very morning they saw three hundred and one blackbeetles crawl out of his brain; that these beetles were placed there by the magical practices of a man fifty miles away. They no more dream of doubting the magic than they do the blackbeetles, and they no more doubt the blackbeetles than they do the sickness; and they no more doubt the sickness than they do their own existence. You might argue with them till doomsday; but you would never shake their conviction that the sickness was directly caused by magic, and that this is a full, exhaustive, sufficient statement of the cause of the trouble.

It is quite recently that Europe has been emancipated from the belief in magic, and it is truly difficult to understand a Kafir's thought on the subject. Still, let us try.

Frazer has pointed out in his admirable work, "The Golden Bough," that there are two basal conceptions underlying ideas on magic. One is that like produces like ; effect resembles cause. From this, savages infer that they can produce a desired effect by imitating it, and from this conception arises imitative or *mimetic magic*. The second thought is that things which have once been in contact, but have ceased to be so, continue to act on each other as if the contact persisted. From this, savages conceive that they can influence people at a distance by any article belonging to these people. This leads to *sympathetic magic*. (Yet Frazer would use the phrase " sympathetic magic " for both forms. See " Golden Bough," vol. i. pp. 9 and 10.)

This statement is, perhaps, the best general analysis of the essential conception underlying native thought that could be given ; but it is a little too abstract for people who are not immersed in the study of anthropology or well-read in folk-lore. Let us, then, try to break up these beams of elementary thought into their component colours, remembering that it is impossible to reduce native belief into any theory which would seem to the European scientific mind to be consistent and complete. From the standpoint of South African natives, the subject may be stated thus :

(1) Qualities of men and animals are resident in their various parts or organs.

(2) The qualities of things are transferable. Thus, courage resides in the liver or the heart, and a man can, therefore, increase his stock of courage by eating the heart and the liver, or drinking the gall, of his slain enemy. An animal has a protruding under lip : if a girl eats that under lip she will become ugly, for her lip will tend to take the shape of the one she has eaten. A rat has the knack of evading things thrown at it : to twine the hair of a rat in one's own hair imparts this quality to a man, who can then easily evade the assegais thrown at him in war.

# Magic

(We have already seen how throwing water into the air in imitation of rain causes the clouds to fall, and how the sacrifice of black goats turns the clouds dark by sympathy. The number of such sympathetic charms is endless.)

(3) Anything which a person has possessed or touched can be used by an enemy to influence that person by. Therefore, men hide the parings of their nails, destroy the hair they have cut, stamp their spittle and other secretions into the ground, lest an enemy should get possession of these things and influence them for evil through their means.

(4) In failure to obtain possession of anything which has been in contact with a man, an image or some symbol can be made to represent him; it is possible to influence a person through this image or symbol.

(5) Sickness is capable of being transferred to an article or animal; the disease will then pass into any one who touches this article or the animal.

(6) A person can be temporarily changed into another person by the power of magic, and by the same power he may be rechanged into his original form.

(7) Medicines and charms can act at a distance, the effect generally being lessened in proportion to the distance; one medicine or form of magic can counteract the influence of another, a strife arising in some invisible sphere of action.

There may be other root-conceptions which should be added to the above; but these seven rays of thought will fairly well account for the full white light of a native's conceptions. The whole subject of magic is so shadowy and hazy that it is impossible to make any dogmatic statement of value. Still, a possible hypothesis may be built up as follows, though it must be distinctly understood that the scheme put forward is purely tentative.

Nothing is more natural than for people to suppose that

# The Essential Kafir

they absorb the qualities of the things they eat. Eating beef makes a man strong and forceful; food imparts to men the strength they need. Where shall the line be drawn? In the absence of any experimental research, or clear inductive reasoning, people would naturally suppose that all qualities of the animal they ate could be assimilated. A glance at savage races shows how universal this idea is. In Guinea men and women abstain from certain animals before the birth of a child, lest it should be born with the likeness or qualities of the animal. In New Zealand some tribes make children swallow stones, to make them hard-hearted and fit for the grim struggle of life. The Caribs abstain from eating tortoises or swine, lest their eyes should become small. In Borneo the people avoid eating deer, lest they should become faint-hearted. The Malays eat tiger-flesh, to gain sagacity and courage. The Namaquas in South Africa abstain from eating hares, lest they become faint-hearted: they devour lions, to get courage, and drink the blood of leopards, to be fierce. Many tribes in South Africa believe that if people eat the incinerated bones of animals they will live as long as the animals. The Basutos used to cut out the heart of a brave enemy and eat it so as to gain his courage. Many Australian tribes do exactly the same thing, and so do the Amazons. At the rite of circumcision, the boys of many Kafir tribes eat similar " medicines," to give them courage and boldness. The Bechuanas avoid eating kidneys, lest they should lose their power of having children. The only men who would eat the kidneys are very old men, and so the phrase *kidney-eater* signifies an old man. Men drink the gall of a conquered chief, to gain his courage. A Pondo chief in very olden days, on accession to the throne, would kill one of his brothers and wash in his blood, to strengthen himself, and then would keep his medicines in the skull of the dead brother—a practice which raised the power of the

## Magic

medicines to the *n*th, as mathematicians would say. The practice ceased with Faku, who was unable to catch his brother.

Among most South African tribes, when an army is going out to war, the warriors are smeared with medicines made from the dried flesh of leopard, elephant, and snake, and have to eat meat dipped into such medicines, so that they may obtain the qualities of the animals used. If a warrior of conspicuous bravery is killed in war, his body is made into medicine and administered to the young men, to make them brave—a practice which may well have been the basis of cannibalism. Various parts of the body are selected for the medicine. Thus, the ears are the seat of intelligence; the skin of the forehead, where perspiration is seen, is the seat of perseverance; other organs have their special qualities.

There is also supposed to be some sympathy existing between a warrior and the foe he has slain. For this reason a native punctures the abdomen of a dead foe, lest his own body should swell in sympathy with that of his slain enemy.

So ingrained are these conceptions that when white men expostulated with the Swazies concerning the untold cruelties of their King Bunu (to be described later) they admitted that it was indeed very shameful, yet said in apology, "But what else could you expect? It is not his fault, for when he was a child the old man fed him on the hearts of lions and tigers, that he might become fierce and cruel." This conception is not unknown in England, and I can well remember small boys at school asserting that those who devoured the eyes of fishes were enabled to see well under water.

From these fundamental conceptions natives soon advance to fresh ideas. If a person absorbs the qualities of what he eats, then any evil worked on his food should affect him. Therefore, one of the most powerful ways of influencing a person is to get possession of some of his food, on which magic

# The Essential Kafir

is "worked." And if qualities of things are absorbed by eating, why not by rubbing them on the body? The chiefs, therefore, give their warriors special medicines, called Intelezi, with which to wash their bodies. They go to the river and stand in the water; they then bruise the medicines and let the juice run down the body, in order to counteract the magical practices of the enemy, and also to increase their strength.

From this it is but a step to the conception that a thing worn on the body or placed on the neck should influence the person who wears the charm. If some quality resides in a rat's whiskers, then any one twining the rat's hair in his own should absorb the properties of the rat. There is nothing on earth that is devoid of properties, and consequently the resources at the disposal of those who wish to work magic are endless.

Passing on, we find that a man's shadow or photograph can be "worked on" by magic, for it is supposed to be an emanation from the personality. And the connection between a man and his picture is thought to hold even after the man's death, and that is why so many natives are terrified at the sight of a camera. They usually run away when they see the lens (or eye), declaring that the white man is about to bewitch them. It is this dread of witchcraft that makes it so difficult to obtain photographs of natives in their kraal, while it is quite easy to dress up some civilised native in a studio in a European town. From this idea it is but a step to the conception that a thing can be set up as a symbol or representation of a man and magical practices worked on this symbol to affect the person represented. The best collection of such magical arts that I know of is to be found in the first chapter of Frazer's "Golden Bough," to which I am indebted for many of the following details, which are chosen out of a great wealth of lore. Thus, in Australia people imagine that a man can be killed by an enemy who makes an image of him.

**A GAZALAND WITCHDOCTOR.**

The man is clad in a cotton shirt; his medicines are placed in the buck-horns forming his necklace; the gall-bladder of a goat is fastened into the cap.

Plate 23.

A ZULU WITCHDOCTOR READY FOR DANCING.

This is the woman represented on Plate 25. Round her ankles are the cocoon-like seed-pods which are referred to on page 171.

# Magic

Needles are stuck into the image, through vital parts, and it is supposed that the person at a distance will be affected similarly. Then, again, people in Fiji take a cocoanut which is supposed to represent some enemy; this nut is buried under the hearth, and a fire is lighted over it. The eye of the nut is placed uppermost, and as the fire slowly bakes the nut, the person represented is supposed to be similarly affected. In North America a picture or a small image representing a man is made, and medicines are applied to it, or else its heart is pierced, the idea being that the person represented is sure to be similarly injured by sympathy. In India, magicians do the same thing—only, they mutilate the image, expecting similar mutilations to result in the person represented. The men of some Australian tribes adopt the following plan when they wish to grow beards. They take a pointed bone and prick the skin of their chin with it, and then stroke the marks with a magical rod, which represents the whiskers of a rat. The virtue of the rat's long whiskers passes out into the man's skin. Natives no more doubt these things than an English housemaid doubts that a fire will promptly burn up brightly if she places a poker in front of it. In Central America some tribes plant canes to represent their friends who are on a journey, and if these canes thrive they suppose their friends at a distance are well. The Maoris, and, strange to say, the Zulus, before going out to war place sticks in the ground to represent the rival armies. If the wind blows one stick down it means that the side represented is about to lose the fight. The Zulus take two oxen, which are made to represent the rival armies. These oxen are then skinned alive, and the ox that dies first indicates which side will lose in the fight.

From representation of armies or individuals by animals or sticks it is but a step to the idea of the transference of sickness or evil. Consequently, we find that in Southern Europe girls

# The Essential Kafir

sell nosegays which have been taken from the sick-bed of some friend, in the hope that the illness will be transferred to the person who smells the flowers—a truly charitable process.

From this custom in Christian Europe it is but a short way to the custom which I found universal above the Zambesi among the Sena-speaking people. When any one is ill the doctor makes a small image of straw in the shape of a pig; by a ceremonial process the sickness of the person is transferred to the small image, which is then placed on the ground where two paths meet. This place is said to be selected for the reason that the image would not be easily observed in that position, and would stand a good chance of being kicked by some traveller. Any one who accidentally kicks the image is said to be sure to absorb the disease from the sick person. When I took one of these straw pigs up and packed it in a Gladstone bag to take away to Europe, the natives were furiously excited and assured me I should certainly die in a short time. When I was taken ill with malaria a week later they all said that it was manifestly caused by my touching this straw image.

The Bechuana cure their chief's headache by driving up a bull, which is thrown on to the ground; the chief sits on the head of the animal and water is thrown over him. The headache is supposed to be transferred to the ox, which is killed by having its head held under water.

When the Matabele are troubled with caterpillars in their crops they put a few ears of corn in a calabash and fill it with caterpillars. They set this vessel on the path which leads to their neighbour's kraal, in the hope that all the other insects will migrate thither. Did not the Jews imagine they could transfer sin to a scapegoat?

Advancing from our present position, we come to the idea that a man may use animals as his agents for bewitching others. And among the natives the baboon is quite as powerful, from

# Magic

an imaginative point of view, as the witch's broomstick of Europe. Kafirs love to think that wizards, witches, and sorcerers ride about on the backs of baboons, or employ them to go and administer medicine to cattle or to sleeping people. Tiger-cats are in the service of wizards, and if these animals are seen to be prowling about a kraal the people say it is a sure sign that wizards are not far off.

Once we have come as far as this we need not try and trace out any development of thought : if these things are possible, what is impossible, or even unlikely ? A doctor will undertake to whistle to elephants, declaring that they will come to him and allow him to cut off their legs. He offers gaily to kill the rhinoceros by planting a bulb in the sand, saying that as soon as the animal comes within the influence of the bulb it will be unable to move away and will therefore be easily killed. Another doctor lightly offers to turn all the lions out of the country by magic, and sets to work in full faith that he can perform the marvel. Wizards are said to dig up dead bodies, cut out their tongues, and bring them to life again. They then burn a hole in the head and make the bodies into the shape of cats, owls, or wolves. When this is accomplished the sorcerer sets the animal to work in his garden, and as soon as his good fortune attracts attention the wizard flies for his life ; the dumb animal cannot inform against him. So strong is this fear of being accused of getting rich by magic that many people purposely refrain from undue cultivation of their land, lest others should accuse them of using magical practices to increase the fertility of the soil. A witch can also cause weeds to grow in the garden of a person whom she hates. There is little hope for the elevation of these tribes until the fear of the accusation of witchcraft is removed.

The highest conception of virtue which most natives can form consists in obedience to the chief ; the lowest depths of vice into which a man can fall is to use sorcery. Here we have the limits of light and shade in our native portrait. I have sought in vain through scores of books to find any method of distinguishing between magic and witchcraft. When is it highly praiseworthy to use magic, and when is it the most wicked of sins? The main occasions on which it is legitimate to use magic, are as follows: If the chief wishes to counteract the magic used against his nation by some rival tribe, he is bound to use his fullest knowledge of magical practices to hinder the enemy and strengthen his own people; secondly, if a diviner is assured that a certain person is being injured by the magical practices of some enemy he is bound to counteract the witchcraft, if he can, by more powerful methods or medicines; thirdly, duly recognised people are allowed to improve the crops or the weather, or to drive off locusts and birds and other pests by magical practices. It is thus seen to be legitimate to use magic for the benefit of the tribe or for common interests; it is wicked to use it for private or personal ends. In this case it is anti-social. Only chiefs or duly initiated diviners have any right to use magical practices; any of the common people supposed to have made use of magic run a tremendous risk of being put to death, for they are not doctors but sorcerers—a distinction of immense importance. The sorcerer is the most abandoned scoundrel in the country, and even his relations will say that he is worthy of death. He has not been authorised to use such practices; he has disregarded the common interest of the tribe to further his own private ends; he is an enemy to the tribe and a source of tribal weakness. No one in the whole country will stand up for him, unless it be some rival diviner who is paid to say that the diviner who accused the man of using magical practices was mistaken. If he can convince the people that the first diviner was wrong it will go badly indeed with that fellow, and he will

# Magic

probably be put to death. It thus happens that diviners rarely die natural deaths, unless they are of no great importance.

There are, in the main, two reasons which lead people to the illicit use of magic. The first and by far the commonest in South Africa is the desire to injure an enemy. The second reason is probably connected with the relics of cannibalism, which is now practically extinct in South Africa. On the Zambesi the people still believe that it is possible for a person to change himself into a crocodile or a lion by magic, and to lie in wait for and devour some fat woman, and then to change himself back into an ordinary human being once more, thus practising cannibalism without being suspected. On this hypothesis, the lion would watch for a person in the bush and devour him, or the crocodile would wait for the woman in the mud of the river bank, and seize her when she came down to wash or to fetch water. So absolute is this belief in sorcery for such ends that natives freely bathe in pools of the Zambesi which are infested with crocodiles. If you expostulate with a woman whose sister, but a few days ago, was taken away by crocodiles from the pool she is about to bathe in, she will tell you that her sister did not get the right medicine to sprinkle in the pool, and so the magic of others was too strong for her. Then she will tell you that she had been to a very clever man who has given her medicine which never fails to counteract all magic. She will sprinkle the medicine into the pool and bathe without any fear, and will most probably get caught by the crocodiles. Deaths are occurring daily on the Zambesi as a consequence of this belief, the strength of which will be seen when dealing with the subject of ordeals in the next chapter.

The crocodile appeals to the imagination of the natives very forcibly, and they believe that certain parts of its body are effective when used as charms. If a person were willing to make money out of the superstitions of natives he would do

# The Essential Kafir

well to sell portions of crocodile to them—a practice which sometimes obtains among a certain type of traders. The profit is said to be enormous.

If it be asked why the chiefs do not protect people from being put to death on the charge of magic, it only needs to be pointed out that they fully believe these people to be scoundrels, and they also know how immensely they gain from this belief. Is any man getting a little too powerful or too rich? What is easier than to get up some trumpery charge of witchcraft, and prime the doctor as to the person to be found guilty? The man is then either killed or turned out of the tribe, and all his possessions are divided between the chief and the doctor. The offending person is "smelt out" and "eaten up."

In Europe people were in the habit of using the most extraordinary concoctions to bewitch people. Thus we read of snake's fat, pigeon's blood, lion's blood, fat of an unbaptized baby, ointment of scorpions, stag's antlers, snake-skin, wolf's flesh, snails, owl's feathers, and a hundred other things. Who does not instinctively think of one of the witch scenes in *Macbeth?*—

>Fillet of a fenny snake,
>In the cauldron boil and bake;
>Eye of newt and toe of frog,
>Wool of bat and tongue of dog,
>Adder's fork and blind-worm's sting,
>Lizard's leg and owlet's wing,
>For a charm of powerful trouble,
>Like a hell-broth boil and bubble.
>
>. . .
>
>Scale of dragon, tooth of wolf,
>Witches' mummy, maw and gulf
>Of the ravin'd salt-sea shark,
>Root of hemlock digg'd i' the dark,
>Liver of blaspheming Jew,
>Gall of goat, and slips of yew
>Sliver'd in the moon's eclipse,

# Magic

> Nose of Turk and Tartar's lips,
> Finger of birth-strangled babe
> Ditch-deliver'd by a drab,
> Make the gruel thick and slab,
> —&c.

The list would exactly suit South African witches, who even steal European babies, when possible, to make into medicine. A most distressing case of this once came under my notice. A trader went down to bathe in the river, and was followed by his small son, who was about three years old. The father sent the boy home to his mother by a native servant, who disappeared with the child. All search proved fruitless: no native would give information of a black man to the Europeans. There was no doubt at all but that the native stole the child to make portions of its body into bewitching medicines.

Though the endless subject of magic has only been touched on briefly, we must pass to consider the modes used in detecting witches and wizards.

# THE WITCHDOCTOR

## CHAPTER IV

### THE WITCHDOCTOR

THE main function of a witchdoctor is the detection of people who are using magical practices or sorcery ; but in addition to that he is open to consultation about a thousand other things. Particularly is he importuned to supply what we should call love philtres and antidotes to the magic of others. This must be a remunerative part of his business. Witchdoctors are men or women who specialise in the direction of " smelling out " sorcerers ; but there are many other doctors who specialise in other branches of the science. Thus, there are special doctors for rain, crops, hail, lightning, locusts, birds, war, and herbs, and I know not what else. The main work of the true witchdoctor is to " smell out " the person using magic, and to get into contact with the ancestral spirits, who are supposed to make their wishes known through him. This man is sometimes called a priest, and indeed he frequently takes that function upon himself; yet in olden days the chief would maintain that he was the only person who could make rain, smell out witches, and interpret the wishes of the ancestral spirits. Slowly the various functions became divided, and now witchdoctors are universal in South Africa. Let us begin a study of the subject by examining the mode of his initiation.

It is quite common to hear Europeans talk of the witchdoctor as a person who *uses* magic for evil purposes ; they seem to think that he is a sorcerer or wizard, and this fallacy is actually recorded in print by "swallow visitors" to the native tribes. To call one of these doctors a sorcerer would be the very grossest insult you could possibly offer him. You might as well call policemen a set of men whose main duty it is to steal property and fatten on society. The witchdoctor is the protector of society, and his work is to detect the worthless people who are injuring others by magical arts or sorcery. He is specially authorised to use magical practices in constitutional and legitimate ways for the good of society. The sorcerer acts on his own initiative for private and forbidden ends.

No man can take upon himself the honour of detecting witchcraft: he has first to undergo a regular course of training, which is so severe that it kills many natives. The ranks of the diviners or doctors are recruited mainly from the more intelligent and clever members of the tribe. To be a successful doctor a man must have keen powers of observation, a good supply of mother-wit, and an endless stock of barefacedness. As a rule he has a neurotic tendency, and is predisposed to see visions and dream vivid dreams. In a word, he must be susceptible of psychic influences.

The first symptom which attracts notice is usually the succession of very vivid dreams in which ancestral spirits visit the imagination of the dreamer. If these dreams persist the young man (or woman) imagines that the Amatongo, or ancestral spirits, are anxious to use him as an intermediary with the people. The chief is ere long informed of the fact; and he usually decides that some well-known diviner of great sagacity shall take the person in hand, and test him, so as to see whether it really be the case that the spirits of the ancestors wish to communicate information through the young person.

Voices now seem ever to sound in the ears of the novice, and he begins to lose his appetite—a thing about as rare in Kafirs as in dogs; he becomes capricious about his food, avoid-

# The Witchdoctor

ing certain articles which he liked before. In olden times he would first begin to learn about the properties of certain herbs; but this seems rare nowadays. He wanders off into the veldt alone and hides in kloofs, dives into deep pools of which others are afraid, declares he sees ancestral spirits below the water, who give him valuable information. He only comes back to his kraal at night, for he spends the whole day roaming on the hills talking to the birds. He falls into trances, and declares that he has just seen the Amadhlozi.

The diviner who has taken him in hand gives him medicines, which only aggravate all these symptoms, and if the diviner thinks the case genuine he initiates him into certain customs and rudiments of knowledge which are known to the diviners only. The young person now wears on his head an isala, which is a head-dress made out of a bunch of feathers. If the case progresses well, the man becomes very thin, and all the symptoms are aggravated, and he begins to waste away. The natives have but little faith in a fat diviner. As the sickness grows more alarming the man tries to kill himself, and throws himself into the water, or tries to jump off krantzes; so that his friends watch him all day and keep him from killing himself. Later, the people are horrified to find him coming back from the veldt at night with a number of poisonous snakes coiled round his neck and waist. He charms snakes, which never seem to bite him, and behaves in a very weird manner. Other doctors are called in, and sometimes a good deal of dirty linen is washed in public, one diviner calling the other a worthless and ignorant fellow, who has been using dangerous medicines. He changes the treatment, and gives special charms to the young person to wear round his neck.

Under this regimen the fits grow less frequent, the man's violence diminishes, his appetite returns, and his dreams become less vivid. He begins to declare that he is a new creature, and

# The Essential Kafir

that the spirits speak to him in their proper whistling tone. He begins to find lost articles, and shows signs of possessing a sort of second sight. At length the diviners say that they think it is time for him to be initiated fully into the mysteries of the profession and to recognise him publicly. They tell him to kill off all his cattle and feast his friends, for he must cast off all that appertains to the old life. He has to undergo the ordeal of finding lost articles, which are hid in huts, under bushes, in the rivers, and on the mountains. The onlookers unconsciously help him in this task, as will soon be apparent. When he has found all the things that were hidden he will claim that he is a diviner. There is a feast at the kraal; and his friends send him presents of various sorts, to enable him to start in life.

Yet this is not all the capital with which he is set going. By far the most important part of his capital consists in his shrewdness and mother-wit, without which equipment he could do but little in his profession. A short course of tuition shows him how very easy it is to deceive the people when he puts on a bold face and makes a high claim. Such a comparatively simple thing as finding a hidden article carries great conviction to the minds of the spectators, and the young doctor soon finds that he can account for his failures by saying that the spirits will not tell him what he wants to know; these spirits are, *ex hypothesi*, so very capricious that no one can gainsay this statement. If a patient dies it is very easy to say that this special kind of disease is not in his line, and that a different kind of doctor should have been sent for. It reminds one rather of Mr. Dooley's account of our English and American specialists, one of whom he humorously describes as declining to treat a case by saying that he does not treat below the chin.

As soon as the young doctor is attached as an assistant to a great diviner, his eyes are opened to the immense amount of trickery used, and so great is this that even natives will some-

# The Witchdoctor

times throw up the life of a diviner in disgust. I have met one such, and he told me that he began to get quite accustomed to the fraud. He went round Mashonaland for some time with a great doctor, who frequently used to run away from a kraal when he thought his patient was about to die. But this old rogue never forgot to get his payment first, which usually consisted of a hen or a goat. As the rule is supposed to be, No cure no pay, this was contrary to correct custom. On one occasion, after administering medicine to a sick man through his nose,—a plan supposed to be very efficacious—the old doctor saw that the man was about to die. Looking about carefully for a moment when all the people in the kraal were occupied, he cautiously caught up the hen which had been agreed on previously as his fee, and ran off into the bush, leaving his assistant to face the music. This was too much for the assistant, who chased his principal and finally caught him up at a great distance from the kraal. On expostulating with the doctor, he was surprised to hear him defend his action. The old man said that it would be best to cook the hen speedily and eat it, so that even if they were caught the fee could not be taken away. The young man said, " Father, why did you run away like that when you saw the patient was dying ? You ought to go back and return the payment." " No," said the old man : " that would never do : it would be a disaster to be there when he died." The young apprentice in disgust left the doctor and earned his living by other and more honest methods, and now it is very entertaining to hear him argue with the natives about diviners. They are puzzled and embarrassed when he begins to expose the trickery used ; but, of course, the people do not abandon the custom, which is deeply ingrained.

With regard to the methods in divining, at least nine of them must be mentioned :

(1) Divining by asking questions.

(2) Divining by bones.
(3) Divining by crystal-gazing.
(4) Divining by lifting a basket.
(5) Divining by sticks.
(6) Divining by familiar spirits.
(7) Divining by the mantis.
(8) Divining by subjective methods.
(9) Divining by poison, boiling water, and other ordeals.

In olden days, if a person died without having been attended by a doctor the people of the kraal were fined, although before any one could consult a diviner he had to get permission from the chief; but nowadays this is rarely done. A person wishing to consult the doctor goes to this man's kraal and sits down outside the place with a number of his friends; in a few moments the man comes out and greets the people. If they simply ask for tobacco he knows that the call is not professional, but simply an ordinary visit. The people consulting the doctor usually sit in a semicircle, and then the diviner calls out some of his own people, who complete the circle. The diviner retires to his hut in order to put on his full dress, and the preliminary dance begins.

The dress of the witchdoctor is usually very striking. He is clad in skins of wild animals, with a profusion of tails and feathers. Often he wears a fur cap, in which is placed the gall-bladder of the goat which was killed for him at his last successful case. He wears this for ornament, and also as proof that he is a great and successful diviner. It is true that other people sometimes wear these gall-bladders when they are considered great personages and have had oxen killed in their honour; but usually the gall-bladder is a sign of a diviner. The man frequently has a string of buck-horns tied round his neck; in these horns he keeps his medicines. He has about his body ornaments made from snakes, or else a necklace made of the teeth

Plate 24.

A WITCHDOCTOR

Is here seen "dancing" to a tune which the people are chanting.

Plate 25.

A WITCHDOCTOR.
The onlookers were chanting a dirge and clapping their hands to assist her.

# The Witchdoctor

of baboons, or of tigers, or of lions. (See plate 22.) The style of dress varies greatly as to detail; yet the type of dress is well marked and could hardly fail to attract attention. These diviners generally avoid white people: they feel that "Government" is opposed to them, and they fear lest Europeans should inform against them. So it happens that many Europeans who have lived for years in the country have never seen these men in their full dress, much less seen the dances held when they are divining. I have been most fortunate in seeing quite a number of these, some of which I have even photographed, though the natives dislike that process.

When in presence of a case the diviner will sometimes begin by asking questions, so that he may find out the nature of the trouble about which he is being consulted; or, yet again, he may insist on having a good dance first, that he may get into a frenzy, in which state the spirits are supposed to speak to him. As a dance will be gone through next day, when the sorcerer is to be "smelt out," we may as well describe it later. It is not always held at the preliminary stage.

The diviner gets the people to sit down, and then gives them pieces of leather, on which they have to beat with sticks as he asks them questions. He tells by the way they beat the sticks—frequently they beat the ground, not using the piece of hide to strike on—whether he is "hot" or "cold." As he makes a random guess at the nature of the trouble about which he is being consulted, he ends up with the question, "Agree ye with me?" or else leaves this to be understood. The people then all sing out, "We agree," or "We hear," the answer varying in different tribes. By the way the people beat the leather or the ground with their sticks, and by the way they answer his question, he tells whether he is getting near the mark or not. The natives are excited when he is nearing the truth, and beat vigorously or answer excitedly; if he is going farther away

# The Essential Kafir

from the matter they beat softly and speak calmly. This is necessary to success. It is the means by which a diviner discovers what is the trouble concerning which he is consulted ; for we must remember thàt when natives go to a doctor they do not tell him what is wrong ; it is his business to find this out. If he were to ask the cause of the visit they would answer that it was his business to discover the trouble : how could they have any faith in his medicines if he could not discover, unaided, what was wrong ? If he was not clever enough to find this out, how could he be clever enough to cure the sick person ?

So the doctor begins questioning :

" Good day ! Ye have come to me because ye are in trouble ? "

The people say, " We agree." They beat the ground strongly and speak out loudly, because it is obviously true.

" Your chief is a great man and has great possessions ? "

" We agree," say the people firmly.

" It seems to me that something is lost ? "

" We agree "—very indifferently.

" It seems to be something soft ? No ! It is metal ? "

" We agree," say the people coldly.

The man sees he is on the wrong tack, and continues :

" It is something soft that is lost ? Something that people carry ? "

" We agree," say the people calmly.

" No ! It is a thing kept in the hut ? No ! Something in the field ? "

" We agree," say the people, who manifestly do *not* agree.

" Perhaps it is the cattle that are not all well ? "

" We agree," say the people without special emphasis.

" It is the cattle that have been straying ? "

" We agree,"—most mechanically.

The doctor knows he is on the wrong tack, and proceeds :

# The Witchdoctor

"No! I knew it was nothing of the sort. I only asked these questions in pretence. You will soon have abundant proofs that I am indeed a great diviner. The cattle are all well."

"We agree," say the people with marked emphasis for the first time.

So the trouble has nothing to do with the cattle. The diviner then selects the next most probable subject, and says, "Some one at home is ill?"

"We agree," say the people excitedly.

"I knew one of the children had a pain in the stomach," says the doctor, adopting a very safe line. Yet the people do not agree very warmly: so the diviner tries again and says, "No! It is a woman in trouble?" Violent beating of the sticks, or vigorous agreement, instantly follows, and this would show even a fool that he was on the right tack. So the diviner narrows the circle down until he has fixed the suspicion on one of his audience who has been showing symptoms of having pain in her side, for she has been rubbing it. The diviner says: "Now I will tell you what the spirits told me last night, and by this you will see that I am a truly great diviner." He then jumps up and pounces on the woman who is ill. The people are lost in amazement, and place their hands over their mouths in astonishment, and own that he is a great diviner indeed.

The rogue then explains that he will call at the woman's hut in the morning and smell out the thing which is causing her pain; he promises to consult the spirits during the night and to make the woman quite well next day. The woman begins to feel better, and the people retire after the important subject of the fee has been settled.

A most amusing exposure of the method used by the diviners in finding out what is the matter is given by Callaway in "The Religious System of the Amazulu." A sceptical fellow called

# The Essential Kafir

John went to consult a diviner about his sister's illness. The account is given by a native as follows:

"John, for example, went to inquire of a diviner when his sister was ill, wishing to know what was the cause of her illness. But when he smote the ground he smote mechanically, assenting to everything the diviner said; for he said to himself, 'For my part, I know nothing. It is the diviner that shall point me out the real facts of the case.'

"The diviner reproved him, saying, 'Surely, my friend, did you ever inquire of a diviner in this way before?'

"John replied in the affirmative, saying, 'Oh, it is I indeed who inquire, for I am now the responsible head of the village; there is no other man in it; there is no one but me.'

"The diviner said, 'I see. You do not know how to inquire of a diviner.' At length he devised a plan with one of his own people, saying, 'This man has not the least notion of divination. Just go and ask him, that he may tell you why he has come, that you may smite the ground for me in a proper manner.'

"So indeed the man said to John, 'The diviner says you do not know how to divine. Tell me the cause of your coming. You will see that we smite the ground for him vehemently when he speaks to the point; but if he does not speak to the point we do not smite much.'

"John said in answer, 'For my part, I do not understand what you say. I have merely come to the diviner for no other purpose than to hear of him the nature of a disease. I did not come to talk to you about it. For my part, I shall hear from the diviner what the disease is.'

"So he refused to tell him; and the man went back to the diviner. He said, 'Let him come to me again, that we may hear.'

"So John again smote the ground mechanically, and thus

# The Witchdoctor

expressed his assent to everything the diviner said. Until he became quite foolish, and said, 'O my friend, I see you indeed do not know how to inquire of a diviner.' He said this because there was no point where John assented very much, nor where he assented very slightly, that he might see by his assenting slightly that he had not hit the mark. So he left off divining, and said, 'No, my friend: I never met with a man who inquired like you.' He could do nothing.

"John said, 'O then, my friend, as you do not see the nature of the disease, now give me back my shilling, that I may betake myself to another diviner.' So the diviner gave him back his shilling."

As one looks on, the whole thing seems childishly absurd—it is so transparent. And yet the people have absolute faith in their diviners. Once I met a trader who told me that he wanted to prove to his native boys that this mode of divining was all nonsense. When they refused to be persuaded he said: "Well, let us hide something in this hut, and then you can all go and fetch your wonderful diviner, and let us see if he can find it." They all agreed, and hid some article in a calabash in a particular corner of the house. Then the trader sent off the boys to fetch the doctor. They ran off in high glee, certain of victory, for their diviner was a cunning man. But in the meantime the trader took the hidden article—a candle—and put it in a different place.

When the diviner came he squatted on the floor, and began to divine by the method of asking questions, and soon discovered what sort of article was lost or hidden. Pursuing his questions, he had some difficulty in locating the lost article, and the excitement of the natives grew very great when the doctor detected the direction by watching the involuntary movements of their eyes. At last he declared the lost article to be hidden in the original corner agreed on. As there were not many vessels large enough to hold a candle, the doctor said that the candle was hidden in the calabash. The boys were beginning to glory in their success when the trader said calmly to the doctor, "Go then, and fetch it, and prove you are right." With consciousness of his success the doctor walked jauntily to the corner, looked in the calabash in which the article had been hidden. But his face fell as he found it empty. So upset was the diviner by his failure that he refused to search any more. The trader then explained what he had done, and tried to persuade the boys as to the method by which the doctor divined the whereabouts of the article, but of course in vain; it was mere waste of breath, for superstition dies very hard.

To return to the sick person. The diviner went over in the morning and decided to cup the woman in the side, and to put a large cow-dung poultice on the seat of the pain. He said the spirits had told him during the night that the woman had been bewitched through a lizard, and that he would prove this by extracting it from her side. The sick woman had to swallow a nauseous mixture of medicines made from small pieces of skin and bones of various wild animals, powdered teeth of baboons, dried entrails of cows, fur of cats, or of rabbits, or of tigers, and so forth. When she had swallowed these abominations a charm was tied round her neck, and the operation of extracting the lizard which was said to be causing the disease was begun. The children were sent out to fetch some cow-dung, which was made into a poultice and put to the side of the patient, after a cupping horn had been applied.

Let me describe an actual case that I recently saw in Tembuland. The diviner was an old hag without a tooth in her head; as she opened the proceedings she stripped herself half-naked, only keeping her skin petticoat on. She began to chant a dirge, and worked and kneaded up the cow-dung poultice with both her hands, smearing her own body and face

# The Witchdoctor

with the material. She kept on at this process for some time, making terrible grimaces, and turning her back to the audience. She made the people so excited that their attention was distracted from her operations, and I noticed that she skilfully took a lizard out of a secret pocket she was wearing beneath her petticoat and shoved it into the poultice.

These people are frequently very skilful in sleight-of-hand tricks, and the silly onlookers are very easy to deceive. As soon as she knew that her lizard was inside the poultice she became very theatrical in her actions, and began to shriek out a weird chant. She then put her face down to the side of the woman and sucked very vigorously for some time, and, seizing the poultice, threw it on to the floor with a gesture worthy of any actor, as if to say, " There, the matter is over : the disease is in that poultice." She told the people to examine the poultice, and, of course, the lizard was found struggling in the mass.

When the people saw this they became excited, rushing out of the hut as fast as possible, lest they should be infected with the disease, and they began to sing the praises of the old hag as if she were a hero. The diviner was paid her fee ; and then she walked off, giving the people no time to see if the patient were cured or not. Poor thing ! She was so excited that she could hardly tell whether she was ill or well ; and the people all seemed to think that if she was not cured it was very unthankful of her, for she certainly ought to be cured after the lizard had been extracted from her side. She would not dare to say she was still in pain. I then explained the hoax to the natives, who simply laughed, and quite agreed with me that the whole thing was imposture ; yet the next time any of them might happen to be ill they would undoubtedly send for this old hag again. If confronted again with absurdity they would settle all dispute by saying, " It is our custom."

# The Essential Kafir

Similar practices are known in all parts of the world. Thorns, beetles, worms, frogs, and other things are supposed to be the cause of disease in Paraguay, Brazil, Australia, and other countries. It has even been surmised that our modern saying to children, " Let me kiss the part and make it well," is a relic of this old custom of sucking out the disease.

Missionaries have frequently exposed the trickery of these diviners, and have demonstrated to the people the mode in which the supposed cause of disease has been sucked out from the seat of pain. The doctors sometimes swallow the articles they wish to "extract" from the patient; possibly it may be some small insect or a few grains of Indian corn. A small quantity of tobacco is also swallowed, in order to induce vomiting, which is controlled by a string tied tightly around the stomach. By this means the doctors manage to bring up the supposed cause of the disease at the right moment.

Yet it is but love's labour lost to point out the fraud to the people, or to explain the sleight-of-hand trick whereby lizard, or snake, or frog was inserted into the poultice. The natives do not want to be undeceived. They cling with a marvellous limpet-like tenacity to their old customs, and are as impatient with those who would fain put them right as is any religious crank who has the absurdity of his extravagances demonstrated to him.

The diviner has now removed the immediate cause of the disease; but he has to determine whether some enemy put this lizard inside the patient by magical practices or whether it came there by the will of some ancestral spirit. He may even say that the lizard entered the woman of its own free will, and that no other cause can be traced. In this case the matter is at an end.

But if the diviner decides that the true cause of the sickness lies in the action of ancestral spirits he will order a sacrifice,

A PONDO WOMAN.
She is seen in the act of "dancing."

Plate 27.

DISCONSOLATE.
Note that this Pondo baby is sucking its finger, not its thumb.

# The Witchdoctor

determining the colour of the beast to be offered while he is in a state of frenzy when the dance is being held. (It sometimes happens that the people of the kraal decide to offer a beast before they consult the diviner ; yet the head of the house only does this on very rare occasions. The headman of a kraal or village may occasionally act as priest, though the doctor more frequently exercises the function. The national witchdoctor is the national priest, and ought to conduct all tribal ceremonies, such as doctoring the soldiers before war.)

When an ox is sacrificed to the spirits, the doctor, or, in his absence, the headman of the village, decides which beast shall be killed. The blood of this beast has to be carefully caught in a calabash, and none of it is allowed to fall on the ground. Then the fat and the bones are burnt, and as the smoke ascends into the air the doctor addresses the spirits, saying : " Ye who are above, see this ox which we are offering to you. Look on us graciously and take away the sickness. We repent and offer this sacrifice : see, it is yours. Relent and be kind to us and remove the sickness." The doctor cuts the animal down the spine, and one half has to be eaten by the people in public, while the other half is the portion of the diviner and his relations. None of the meat is allowed to be eaten in private, or a charge of sorcery against the culprit will be sure to follow.

If, however, the diviner says that some one has been using magical practices and has thus caused the sickness, a dance has to be held, that the spirits may reveal the name of the culprit, or enable the doctor to smell the sorcerer. This dance is a great affair. Every member of the kraal has to be present, lest suspicion should be fixed on the absentee. It generally happens that the doctor is told in advance the person whom it is proposed that he should find guilty. When every one is present the dance begins. To make the matter concrete, I will describe a dance which I saw close to the Zambesi. It will indicate

# The Essential Kafir

the customs which existed in Zululand a hundred years ago, though some of the details of the ceremony have been forgotten in the south in recent years. I was unable to take a photograph of the scene, but give two pictures which I took of other dances in Swazieland and Zululand. (See plates 24 and 25.)

We were crossing a large plain which extends between the Zambesi and Shire Rivers, and were making for the hills which overlook Port Herald. Hour after hour, as we lay sleepily reclining in our machilas, we could hear a number of drums being beaten, the rumble of which came floating over the plain. The day was sultry and fiercely hot; yet our native boys carried the machilas with good humour and fun. A machila is a hammock suspended from a large bamboo pole, in which the traveller lies, while two or four boys—in our case four—carry the pole on their shoulders. A machila team generally consists of a dozen boys, four of whom carry the traveller, while the other eight follow at a jog-trot. When one set of boys is tired they call out to the others, and four fresh boys run in and take the places of the tired boys. The tired boys " rest " by running along behind, waiting till their next turn to carry comes.

As we drew closer to the hills we could hear the noise of the drums growing louder and louder, but could not see the village from which the noise came, as the bush was dense. Suddenly we burst through the bush into a large kraal and found a witchdoctor's dance in full swing.

The scene beggared all description. Ranged in a row were five drums. These were placed in due order, the largest being at one end, and the size diminishing in order down to a small drum at the other end. The largest was on the left, and a tall man was busy beating this big drum with all his might. He was a picture of lusty manhood. The next drum was smaller, and a smaller man was beating it; then came a still smaller

# The Witchdoctor

drum, which was being beaten by an overgrown boy. The smallest drum was being beaten by a tiny urchin.

Our presence made no difference to the dance. Every one pursued the even, or uneven, tenour of his way quite unconcernedly. The drums were kept going with savage glee and fury. On the left of the drummers twenty or thirty women and children were grouped ; some were squatting on the ground, and behind these others were standing up. All were keeping time to the chant by clapping their hands. The smallest children were pressed into this service, and seemed to enter into the spirit of the affair.

In front of this motley crowd a witchdoctor was dancing ; she was an ugly old withered hag, clad in a monkey-skin skirt, from which a dozen long tails were flying at a tangent. Round her waist was a belt of beadwork, and a couple of jangling bells were fastened to her skirt. Round her ankles were some dozen circular cocoon-like hollow balls filled with seeds, which rattled as she moved. (These can be seen in the picture of the witch-doctoress on plate 23.) On her head was perched a battered old straw hat of sailor type, and her face was rendered doubly hideous by the semi-drunken leer which disfigured it. In her hand she held a native battle-axe, which she brandished in the faces of the women and children. It might well have been one of the witches in *Macbeth* come to life and drugged with drink. She was the very picture of drunken devilry.

The dance was kept up at a furious pace, as she stamped about the open space in front of the drummers with a vigour that was surprising. She suddenly stopped dancing, placed her head on one side,* as if listening for some voice beneath the ground, and then jumped about furiously and rushed at the

---

\* This can be seen in the photograph of the Zululand witchdoctoress dancing (plate 39). In this photograph the woman is at the extreme right of the picture, looking down at the ground.

drummers, or the women, as they increased their noise. Suddenly she pretended to be in a frenzy and *en rapport* with the ancestral spirits. She began to behave in an amazing fashion. Her body was seized with irregular jerking spasms; her head kept quite steady as she stamped at a tremendous rate with her feet; then the lower part of her body vibrated rapidly, as if the muscles were seized with a tremulous motion. After this she stood still while the upper part of her body was racked with the most tempestuous jerks, the outcome of nerve storms in her brain cells.

When one of the five drummers became slack in his work she darted over towards him and brandished her axe at him, and he hastily started beating his drum with fury, as if he were intoxicated, laughing immoderately all the time. Meanwhile the witchdoctor and the people were yelling different tunes of their own, and clapping their hands in rhythmic sequence. When the women grew slack in their chanting or clapping, the old crone rushed at them with her axe and set them off singing at a brisk rate. Suddenly the witchdoctor ceased dancing and looked down at the earth, bent her ear to the ground, and made weird noises, which seemed to come from her stomach, listened again to the earth, made loud expostulations, and set off dancing again. In a moment every muscle in her whole body began to vibrate, jerk, twinge. She jumped up in the air, stamped upon the ground, ran furiously at the men, glided over to the women sideways, moving her feet so swiftly that her legs seemed rather to vibrate than to stamp, while she kept the upper part of her body perfectly steady and free from jerks. Then she moved back to the men in the same way, the vibration of her legs being so rapid that one could scarcely see more motion than in the case of a bee's wing in flight. Finally, she gave a piercing yell, pulled a bangle off from her ankle with a furious jerk, and gave it to the third drummer boy, who seemed

## The Witchdoctor

inordinately delighted and started doing his best to break his drum by furious beating. If the performance could but be enacted on the stage while Wagner's "Ride of the Valkyries" was being played by an orchestra, the effect would be extraordinary.

Thus ended the first part of the concert or *séance*, and, as our time was limited, we got into our machilas and continued our journey, the sound of the drums being wafted to us over the plains for an hour or longer.

So much for a dance on the Zambesi. Those I have seen in Swazieland, Pondoland, and Zululand were much the same in general outline; drums are but rarely used in these more southern tribes nowadays, though they were in universal use some fifty years ago. They are still used in Gazaland, and are often kept going half the night, much to a man's discomfort when he is trying to sleep after a long day's walk. The picture of a doctor's dance in Swazieland, given on plate 38, differed but little from this one on the Zambesi, except that the doctor reminded one of a Scotsman in kilts dancing the Highland Fling to a tune that was far above the average of native compositions.

The close of a witchdoctor's dance ends in one of two ways. If he pretends that he has been told the name of the sorcerer by the spirits during his frenzy, he may go up to the chief and whisper the culprit's name in his ear. In that case his work is over, and the chief then tells his executioners to catch the man indicated on his way home from the dance; or if the chief is inclined to be merciful he gives the man a hint to fly out of the country, and in that case the chief and the doctor, and a few important people, divide the man's property among them. The man is said to be "eaten up." The same division of property would be made if the man were put to death.

# The Essential Kafir

But the dance may end in a more dramatic way than this. When the diviner has made the people thoroughly excited he will sometimes go round the circle of dancers, smelling each one in turn, and will then suddenly pounce on the guilty person, or jump over his head as he squats on the ground. In a moment every one flies away from this guilty person in horror, and he is left stupefied in his isolation. The man is "smelt out." The diviner asks him to confess that he used sorcery, and conjures him to reveal the medicines he employed for the purpose. The man may passionately declare his innocence; but no one will believe him until he can prove that he is guiltless—among Kafirs an accused man is considered guilty until he proves his innocence. Sometimes the man will confess his imaginary sin and will involve another person in his crime, and then this second person also is isolated. Or the man may say that he is innocent, and may challenge the diviner to find the medicines he has used to bewitch with.

The diviner is supposed to be bound to find not only the culprit but also the magic medicine used. He will then grub about in the cattle kraal and pick up some pieces of horn, or some hairs from a cow's tail, and declare that these were the bewitching medicines which were used. Generally the diviner hides some such thing about his own person, and so easily finds the stuff which (he says) was used by the guilty man. In one case the diviner produced some hair from a cow's tail, which he had cut off and buried overnight. The guilty man challenged the diviner to produce the bewitching material. The doctor promptly went to the cattle kraal, where he had hidden the hair under the ground on the previous evening. Amid great *éclat* he dug up this portion of hair, with some skin attached to it; but the condemned man had fortunately seen the doctor cut this off a cow the day before, and so he told the chief what he had seen. When the cow referred to was examined, a piece

# The Witchdoctor

of skin was found missing from its tail, and the suspected magical medicine exactly fitted the missing part. The condemned man was declared guiltless.

As a rule, people deny the charge when the diviner accuses them; and then begins the torture which is supposed to make men confess where they have hidden the bewitching medicine. In some cases this is dispensed with, and the man is only fined or turned out of the tribe. In other cases he appeals to a greater doctor, who is paid to give a verdict freeing him from crime. If the appeal is successful the man's character is cleared, and when the punishment is only a fine the man is supposed to be once more a respectable member of society after he has paid up the fine. It often happens that if the sick man gets well the person found guilty is acquitted.

The ignorant people believe the most absurd stories told them by the diviners. A favourite form of accusation is that some person is causing illness through the instrumentality of a baboon which lives in the man's hut. The baboon is supposed to go at night with bottles of medicine, which he pours down people's throats while they are asleep. The explanation quite satisfies the people, who never dream of verifying the story; they never go to see if the baboon is really living in the roof of the culprit's hut, but merely proceed to kill the condemned man. The nation is unanimously against a man who is found guilty of witchcraft. It would be too risky for the nearest friend to stand up for the man: this would only entangle him in the crime. Wherever the *Pax Britannica* obtains such "eating up" or "smelling out" is forbidden. Undoubtedly the customs are still practised in secret; but the evil is enormously abated. The Government is so strict in punishing these doctors that the risk they run is very great, and few would care to take part in the killing of any man. Diviners are so afraid of being found out that they will passionately

# The Essential Kafir

declare to white men that they are not diviners, lest information should be given to the authorities. I have seen these diviners hiding in the bush when they noticed white men coming in the distance.

In olden days the sickness of a chief would sometimes lead to whole villages being killed off because some person who lived in one of them was supposed to have used magic to injure the chief; and when a warrior broke the orders of the war-doctor he, *ipso facto*, declared himself a sorcerer, and his whole village would be wiped out without more ado. When a woman is found guilty and is fined for sorcery, her father, not her husband, has to pay the debt. No father should have a witch for a daughter.

It may be well to try and give some idea as to the amount of suffering which was endured by the people in olden days. The cloud of woe that has rested on Africa for ages in this connection is overwhelming. When I first visited Pondoland it was not annexed to Cape Colony. It was calculated that fully one person was put to death in that district every day, on an average, on charges of witchcraft. I shall never forget my first day's ride through the country. A native guide showed me my way, and pointed out kraal after kraal where people had recently been tortured to death for witchcraft. He specially pointed out one kraal where seven people had been recently killed because the cattle were ill. This harmless-looking kraal was sleeping in the hot sunshine, and the mushroom-like huts which composed it looked innocent enough. The cattle, however, had been ill, and so the diviner was sent for. After searching into the cause of the trouble, he came to the conclusion that the sickness was caused by an old woman who was bewitching the cattle. She was accused of the crime, and denied it. Then she was placed between hot stones and urged to confess her crime and give up her magical medicines.

Plate 28.

A PONDO GIRL CONSIDERING A BARGAIN.

Plate 29.

THE BARGAIN COMPLETED.

# The Witchdoctor

As she finally confessed under the pain of her torture, she was killed by a blow on the head. But the cattle did not get well after this. So the doctor was called in again, and he decided that a certain young girl was bewitching the cattle. In terror she tried to fly out of the country, but was caught and slowly tortured to death. The cattle continued to be ill, and the next victim fixed on was a young man. He was buried in the ground up to his neck, and his brains were knocked out by clubs. Then the doctor declared that a man was keeping a big baboon in his hut, and, by doing so, was causing the disease among the cattle. No one searched for the baboon; but the man was taken to a high krantz and hurled over to the rocks below. The next person accused was a young girl. She was smeared with grease, and tied over an ant-heap, till the torment of the stinging made her "confess." She was then killed out of hand. And so the story went on.

Wondering why the natives submit to this practice, you find, strange to say, that they usually defend it as necessary to the well-being of society: no one expects that he will be put to death any more than a soldier imagines that he will be killed in battle. Also, it is their custom: if they broke it the ancestral spirits would be angry and send them no rain or crops, their women would cease to bear children, and the white man would eat up their country. They will tell you that "the seed waits for its ground"; which is their way of saying that murder will out—that so long as people work magic they must be killed for doing it.

It is difficult for us to conceive the hardiness of a native's nerves. Theal tells in his history how the wife of the Pondo chief Sigcawu was declared to be guilty of using witchcraft. She was stripped naked; her wrists and ankles were fastened to pegs; and she was covered with ants, which were irritated by having cold water thrown over them. She endured this torture and refused to confess her guilt : so the people said that her medicines were stronger than the ants. She was then tied to a pole and slowly roasted over a fire, when she ultimately confessed her guilt. As she did not produce the bewitching medicines, she was roasted three times within two days; yet she recovered ! A European has to remember this marvellous power of resisting pain before he can form a true conception of the suffering of these people ; but, when all true discount has been taken off, what a weight of horror remains !

If the trouble had not been one of human sickness, but simply of lost cattle, the diviner would have depended on his marvellous supply of intelligence concerning strayed cattle. The natives have far more words for describing the colour of cattle than we have, and they never forget an animal when they have once seen it ; thus it becomes fairly easy for them to trace lost cattle. The doctors may be unable to find them; in which case they fall back on the unanswerable statement that the spirits will not tell where the straying cattle are. A Kafir always has a plausible excuse handy for every emergency : you can never " score off him " in an argument. He is also a past-master at speaking a multitude of words without conveying any definite information.

On the whole, however, it cannot be denied that the doctors are very good hands at finding lost cattle. Not infrequently both English and Dutch farmers will inquire of them about straying animals, and if they only pay the diviner well they are fairly sure to regain them. The doctors are so well informed that they need no clairvoyance.

We now pass on to the next mode: *divining by bones*.

Doctors carry about with them small bones, selected from different kinds of animals, which look much like those used by boys when playing at school, though sometimes the natives use cowry shells to divine by. Having discovered by the method

# The Witchdoctor

of asking questions what the trouble is, the diviner proceeds to find out the direction in which the cattle are straying, or the direction of the person who is using sorcery. In Pondoland I have seen the diviner place the bones in a small sort of calabash, which is well shaken. The diviner then chews some medicines and puffs on the bones. After this he throws them to the ground and notes carefully how the bones lie, and he probably throws them a second or third time, till he is satisfied with the indications offered. He pretends to tell by the way the bones lie the direction in which the cattle are straying or the abode of the sorcerer who is bewitching them. If he wishes to find out, not the direction of some straying cattle, but the seat of pain in the patient, he places one bone on the patient's body and then proceeds as just mentioned, and from the way the bones fall divines the seat of disease. But in Mashonaland a different method is used. The diviner chews medicine, and then passes the bones in front of his mouth, that he may breathe on them; or else blows some smoke on them, to charm them. Next he places most of the bones in the hand of the suspected witch or wizard, keeping one or two in his own hand. At a given signal they both throw the bones down to the ground, and the doctor very carefully examines the way in which the bones lie. He notes whether any bones lie on the top of others, and so forth. From these data he forms his decision as to whether the suspected person is guilty or not. As only the diviner is possessed of the information by which one can know what the bones say, he has a splendid chance of carrying out his own wishes, and of trading on the credulity of his dupes.

If he failed to tell by the bones what was wrong, the diviner would say that he was overcome by the bones, and would try another plan. He might adopt the third method—*divining by crystal-gazing*. I have never seen this mode used,

## The Essential Kafir

but have obtained a full account, first hand, from a native doctor's assistant, who has often seen it practised. The suspected people are all arranged in the sunshine in a row. The diviner stands facing them, and takes a special kind of large crystal in his hand, through which he inspects the row of people. He causes the sunlight to be reflected from one of the facets of the crystal on to the people in front of him. Some of the people do not notice the reflection of sunlight on their body, and so remain quite still. If, however, any poor unlucky wretch happens to notice the patch of sunlight on his body, he tries to wash it off or brush it away, for it seems most uncanny to him. The moment he tries to brush it away the diviner pounces on him and declares him to be the guilty person. On my asking the native who told me this whether he did not mean that the diviner saw an image of the guilty person in the crystal, he said that it was not thus the sorcerer was discovered. The diviner saw no image, but merely noticed the patch of light on the body of the suspected person. Thinking that this was but a mode of crystal-gazing referred to in Mr. Andrew Lang's "Making of Religion," I several times cross-examined the native, who had been the assistant of the diviner; but he was quite consistent in his statements, and said the diviner was guided by the reflected patch of light on the culprit's body.

With regard to *divining by lifting a basket*, it seems a little hard to accept all that is asserted. It was the ex-witchdoctor referred to above who supplied me with the information, and he said he had frequently seen it applied successfully. The diviner takes a native basket and places in it various kinds of medicines and charms, together with bones of many wild animals. Each person in the kraal has to come up in turn and try to lift the basket. If he, or she, succeeds in lifting the basket, guilt is instantly disproved; the guilty person comes to the basket, and, though a child had just previously lifted it with

# The Witchdoctor

ease, the culprit finds it quite impossible to move it. It seems as if some electro-magnet were holding the basket down, for the diviner does not tamper with the basket when once the ordeal has been begun. The informant could give no explanation of the affair, his principal not having initiated him into the secret; but he declared he had frequently seen the procedure with the results mentioned. It may be that the man who thinks himself guilty is paralysed by fear; for the dread of an ordeal like this is very great, and it need hardly be said that electro-magnets are unknown to the natives. An intense fear might inhibit the normal action of the nerves and so make the man seem guilty.

*Divining by sticks* is very rare. Never having seen it used, I can only quote a few lines from Callaway's "Religious Systems of the Amazulu." The native called John, recently referred to as having been sceptical about the mode of divining by hitting the ground, went off with his shilling to a man who professed to be able to divine by sticks, without previously asking the patient any questions. "So John came to the sticks. Their owner took them and laid them on the ground; he chewed some medicine, and puffed it over them, that they might tell him truly the very facts of the case. . . . The diviner then asked the sticks, saying, 'Tell me, how old is the person who is ill?' And they said. But, as they have no mouths, they speak thus: If they say no, they fall suddenly; if they say yes, they arise and jump about very much, and leap on the person who has come to inquire. In this way they told John the character of his sister's illness, and traced out every little ramification of it which was known to John. So John assented, and left his shilling with the sticks, and said, 'This is what I want, that the diviner should tell me things which I know, without having asked me any question.' . . . Their mode of speaking is this: If it is asked where the disease has seized the patient, the sticks jump up at once and fix themselves on the place where the sick man is affected. If it has affected the abdomen, they fix themselves on the abdomen of the man who has come to inquire. If the head, they leap upon the head. They go over every joint of the body that is affected by the disease. Or if they are asked where the doctor is who can cure the disease, they leap up and lie down in the direction of the place where the doctor lives. If the owner of them knows for certain the name of a doctor who lives among the tribe to which the sticks point, he mentions the name to them; if it is he they mean, they jump up and down and fix themselves on their owner, and he knows thereby that they assent." It should be added that the sticks are usually about ten or twelve inches long.

It is hard to accept this statement, even though it satisfied the demands of the unbelieving John; but it is easy to see that if it be a piece of imposture it must be a very clever piece, for it is exactly the sort of thing that is calculated to impress a native.

Passing on, we now come to the mode of *divining by familiar spirits*. Our thoughts naturally turn to the Witch of Endor; but in South Africa no objective spirit is supposed to be raised from the tomb. The diviner seems to have the power of ventriloquism, and the effect of this on such simple people as the Kafirs is marvellous. Their excitement is so great when they fancy a voice comes from the roof of the hut that they are in a hopelessly uncritical frame of mind. And when the spirits make revelations to the diviners through dreams and trances there is an end of all argument: you cannot argue with a man who has a revelation, unless you have a more striking one to oppose to his. As the spirits of the departed can fight among themselves, get killed over again, or deceive one another, it is easy to see how a clever diviner can supply a thousand good excuses in case his words are proved to be

# The Witchdoctor

wrong; and human nature always remembers the few instances where the statement was correct rather than the many instances where the statement was found to be wrong.

Little need be said about *divining by means of the mantis*, or Hottentot god, as it is often called. The mantis is a small insect which looks exactly like a few pieces of green grass or yellow straw, the colour varying at times. The insect affords a very striking example of mimicry: frequently it is almost impossible to tell the difference between the insect and its environment, even when this is pointed out to an observer. South Africa is full of instances of this mimicry. I well remember having to spend a day at Maseru, near the edge of Basutoland. Strolling out into the veldt, I chose some rocks to lie down on in the warm sunshine. Suddenly a piece of the rock seemed to move. Rubbing my eyes to see if it were all illusion, I watched carefully, and again a part of the lichen-covered rock clearly moved. Turning over the little piece of moving rock, I found that it was a small insect, so perfectly marked with imitation lichen marks that even when the mimicry was discovered it was impossible to pick out the insect from the rock until the insect moved.

The insects called mantises have a habit of clinging to pieces of grass or dried straw, and they generally point in a certain direction with their head. It does not need a diviner to tell the Kafir how to use the mantis for divining purposes. Natives can frequently be seen by the road-side divining by means of the insect. A question is put to it, and the insect is disturbed from its position. It speedily settles itself to rest again, and if it points to the north this shows that the lost cattle have gone in that direction. It will also thus indicate the direction in which the needful doctor lives, if it be a doctor that is wanted. After all, this mode of divining is quite as good as " tossing up."

# The Essential Kafir

*Those who divine by subjective methods* need no outward helps : the patient sits before the diviner, who is supposed to tell the man what his trouble is, what the cause of the trouble, and what the remedy to be used. The natives naturally have great faith in such diviners, who carefully select cases where they can be successful. They can select their cases till they have suitable ones, because they can always say that the spirits either are, or are not, communicative. The natives will give marvellous instances where there could be no deception, and at first you are inclined to believe them; but a little more acquaintance with the natives makes you sceptical. The natives are so utterly uncritical in the weighing of evidence, and are so apt to believe what they have been led to expect, that their explanations of natural phenomena are grotesque.

We now come to the various forms of *ordeals which are used to detect the sorcerer*. In Chaka's days the diviner had a horn filled with oil, into the base of which a stick was inserted. The diviner took this to the people as they were sitting in a circle, and he tried to twist the stick round as each person touched the horn. The diviner declared that when the guilty person touched the horn the stick would not move at all, and thus the culprit was discovered.

Or sometimes a pot of water was taken, and medicine was placed in it, with two straws. Under certain conditions the water would bubble and froth up; but in other cases it would remain quiet: from this the supposed guilt of people was easily determined. Another plan was to make people lick a red-hot iron, and if the person was guilty the tongue was sure to get burned. The first person to be tested by this ordeal was always found to be guilty!

The ordeal by boiling water is much the same as that which was used in Europe not very long ago. A large beer-pot, made of native pottery, is filled with water, which is caused to

# The Witchdoctor

boil furiously, and some charms and herbs are placed in it. The suspected persons—the method is chiefly used for the detection of thieves—are arranged in a row as in the other cases, and they have to come up one by one and pick out a small pebble which the diviner throws into the boiling pot. It is needless to add that in this ordeal the first person to plunge in his hand is always scalded and so proved to be guilty. The people declare that sometimes it really does happen that the hand is not scalded; but I never came across an authentic case.

The poison ordeal which is so much used on the Zambesi was also in full swing in Chaka's days. The accused person on whom suspicion was fixed at the witchdoctor's dance the day before was made to take some poison. The moave bark was powdered up with medicines and made into balls about the size of lemons. The accused man had to eat these in the presence of the people of the kraal. He was first stripped entirely naked, lest he should conceal some antidote; and he had to eat the poison balls before sunrise, as he knelt with crossed hands in a circle of people. The people had sticks with which they used to beat the ground, saying, " If this man has practised magic, may the poison burst him!" Then his friends would say, " Yes: burst him!" Then some one would say, " If he has not used magic, then spare him!" and the people would all sing out, " Yes: spare him!" They kept up this chant until the man either vomited up the poison or died from it. If the man survived he would be declared guiltless, but would be expected to offer up a cock to the spirits; thus reminding us of Socrates, who before drinking his poison asked his friends to offer a cock as sacrifice to Æsculapius.

On the Zambesi the poison ordeal is a great institution. When a death has occurred in a village through an accident with a lion or a crocodile, the diviner is called in to smell out

# The Essential Kafir

the sorcerer. When suspicion is fixed on a person he has to undergo the poison ordeal, the theory of which is this: People use magic so as to eat human flesh without being detected. By magic they change themselves into crocodiles or lions, and lie in wait for the person they wish to eat; having eaten the person, they change themselves back into human beings again by magic. Now, it is supposed that if a person has human flesh in his stomach the poison will work inwardly and kill the person, for it combines with the human flesh he has eaten. If, however, he has eaten no human flesh the poison will be vomited up. Thus, a person who is accused of eating human flesh will say: "I am quite certain I have eaten no human flesh, and so the poison will be at once rejected by my stomach. Yes: give me the poison, that I may prove that I am innocent." People have been known to beg for this ordeal when they might have sought British protection. Their faith in the theory was so absolute that they preferred to demonstrate their innocence to all. There is a saving clause in the ordeal occasionally. A hen or a goat may be substituted for the man, and the poison is then given by proxy to the animal; if it dies under the test the man is declared guilty, but not otherwise.

This ordeal, of course, is strictly forbidden in British territory; but the policing of the country is so inadequate that it probably still goes on secretly, though not so frequently as of old. The people would never inform against their own kith and kin.

A strange kind of illness would seem, at this point, to call for some description. In Swazieland people are sometimes subjected to an epileptoid seizure which is attributed to ancestral spirits. This kind of sickness used to pass over the country in waves, and then for years it might be in abeyance, going completely out of fashion. When I first visited Swazie-

# The Witchdoctor

land, over a dozen years ago, it was very common; but during my recent visits to that country I noticed that it seemed to have quite died out. My introduction to this affair was somewhat thus:

We were taking advantage of a fine evening to push on with our ox-waggon journey, having rested, during the heat of the day, to spare the oxen. Soon after sunset we found ourselves skirting a crescent-shaped ridge of country which overlooked a vast plain, our view extending far away to the dark-grey hills on the horizon. Beneath us lay the sleepy country studded over with the beehive huts of the Swazies, from which lazy wreaths of smoke were curling in the air. "At one stride came the dark," which was punctuated, as it were, by scintillating spots of light, which showed that the women were cooking the evening meal inside the wind-screen enclosures of reed that surround their huts. Before long every sound had died away, and a thin mist filled the valley. The only noise that broke the stillness of the night was the cracking of the driver's whip and the creaking of the waggon as it lumbered on. The breathing of the oxen, straining and chafing against the awkward yokes, formed a monotonous background for the noise of the waggon.

Mile after mile we trudged along in silence, "our thoughts being our own playfellows," while away down in the dim sea of mist all was silent and asleep. Suddenly a murmur as of some angry ocean breaking on the shore was wafted to us from a hidden kraal. The noise became loud and discordant, and a spark seemed to glimmer from some hut; then the lurid glare of a torch was seen, and in a few moments some dozen other lights appeared. As we drew near we could see a crowd of half-naked savages dancing fiercely in a circle, while the excited shouts changed into a droning chant. It looked as if the dwellers from some lower world were celebrating a Corybantic

## The Essential Kafir

feast. In the middle of the ring could be seen a naked figure gesticulating furiously in the ruddy glare of smoking torches. The dancing became more and more excited and the singing more tempestuous, every one now singing the tune he knew best. We were by this time quite near the crowd; and the central figure suddenly stamped furiously and danced wildly in the circle, finally falling, foaming at the mouth. Within a few moments after the central figure fell, the bronze-looking people slunk off to their homes, while the patient was led off by a couple of friends to his hut. And in a few minutes the night was as quiet as before.

What had occurred was this. A man attacked by an epileptoid seizure had been immediately taken out into the open air. The natives who were living close by had caught up torches of grass smeared in fat, and had formed a circle round the person who was supposed to be possessed by spirits, which were stabbing him from inside with assegais. The people dance round the patient when he is attacked thus and make him furiously excited, and then ask him who the spirit is that is stabbing him from within, that they may pacify the spirit with the sacrifice of a goat or of a hen. Some people are specially liable to the seizure, and even children are known to suffer thus. Waves of this kind of illness seem to pass over the land " as if a spirit were travelling through the country and seizing people in its journey : " so a native told me. The natives say that it is not necessary to call in a diviner when people are attacked thus ; and indeed there is usually no time to call one, for the attack comes and passes quickly. If a doctor were present he would, of course, be the master of the ceremonies.

It must not be thought that all doctors are diviners or witchdoctors : some merely deal in medicines made from herbs, roots, and animal substances. These roots are often pointed out to the doctor in a vivid dream, and he gets up and takes

## The Witchdoctor

a long journey to get the coveted remedies. I remember meeting a doctor who was hurrying off at a great pace to hunt for some roots which (he declared) the spirits had shown him the previous night. He was in such a hurry that he would not wait to talk to me on the road. Other doctors see to the crops, kill the locusts, treat warriors, ensure successful hunts for game, and so forth.

The witchdoctor whose portrait is shown on plate 22 will be seen to have a cluster of buck-horns tied round his neck as an ornament. This necklace forms his medicine-chest. The horns are filled with various remedies for snake-bite. It would seem that the natives try to cure snake-bite by a homœopathic treatment. The doctor collects the heads of snakes of various kinds, and dries them in the sun, with the poison glands intact. When dry, the whole mass is powdered and mixed with herbs, roots, and pieces of fluff from the fur of various animals; possibly if he could procure a piece of crocodile or a lion's tooth, that would be powdered up and mixed in the medicine. The doctor thus collects the heads of a dozen different species of snake and keeps the powdered head and poison gland of each kind of snake in a different horn. If a person is bitten by a puff-adder the doctor takes the dried head of the puff-adder and rubs some of the powder into the snake-bite, also making the patient drink some of the same medicine. If the person had been bitten by a green mamba, then he would have to be treated with green mamba-head dried and powdered. Strange to say, the doctors seem to be fairly successful in their treatment: I have met white people who have been cured by them. The Bushmen were great at divining, of which wonderful stories are told. They frequently rendered people immune to snake-bites by injecting small and increasing doses of poison, until some antitoxin was formed or the people became accustomed to the poison.

# The Essential Kafir

The belief of the natives in their doctors is surprising. They will do the most silly things if a great doctor bids them. Thus, quite recently, some doctors told the people in Swazieland that they were on no account to have their cattle inoculated against rinderpest, or the oxen would be sure to die; if, however, they let their oxen die of the disease without inoculation, and would collect the bones of the dead animals, and pile them up in the cattle kraals, then after a certain time the spirits would raise up the cattle, and the people would wake up one fine morning and find their cattle grazing near the kraals. The silly people absolutely believed the diviners, and day by day waited till the dead cattle should rise up.

Not satisfied with this piece of imposture, the diviners again told the natives that the locust swarms could be completely cured for ever if only the people would dig great trenches and collect all the locusts they could find. When a large quantity was collected the doctors piled the locusts into the trenches and placed some medicine on them. The trenches were filled with earth and the diviners handsomely paid. The diviners assured the people that the locusts would never trouble them again. When the locusts swarmed on the mealie fields as much as ever, the diviners lost no prestige!

There is a classic illustration of the credulity of the people in the well-known case of a diviner named Umhlakaza. He used a girl, who stood in the water and pretended to receive messages from the spirits. The people from Delagoa Bay down to the borders of the Cape Colony seem to have been hypnotised, and believed implicitly in these messages. No doubt the whole thing was a plan of the chiefs to force the people, by means of starving, into a combined attack against the Europeans. It was in 1857 that this tragedy, which would seem without parallel in South Africa, occurred. The people were told that, if they would only destroy all their corn and cattle,

## The Witchdoctor

on a certain date these would rise again from the dead greatly increased, and that they would be able to destroy their enemies in vast numbers. The day when the cattle were to rise arrived; but there was no sign of the resurrection, and the wholesale starving which followed was very dreadful. It is said that over fifty thousand natives—according to some estimates, a hundred thousand—died of famine. It is difficult to induce the various native tribes to combine (a most fortunate thing for Europeans); but if some great diviner were to arise, and were to be used by a powerful chief to stir the people up, an ugly situation might result.

In Zululand an old man, who was a little unsound in his mind, recently assured the people that he had seen the Lord, who told him that people ought not to use red blankets, which were stained with the Lord's blood. The old man said that if they would burn all their red clothes the cattle which had died of rinderpest would rise from the dead. The people burnt enormous heaps of clothing to gain this end.

A Swazieland diviner, a few years ago, told the people that if they sold their hens at a small price to white men the native women would one day come back from the woods with enormous herds of milk-white cattle; and traders had a fine brisk time in their stores over this prophecy.

Not only do the people believe in the diviners: the diviners believe in themselves. They offer to do wonderful things. They will call spirits from the vasty deep. Turning lions and tigers out of the country is a trifle. They tell what is happening at a distance. No better case of this could be given than that recorded by Mr. David Leslie, hunter and trader, who travelled in South Africa for many years.

He had sent out his native elephant hunters with instructions to meet him on a certain date at a selected spot. He went at the appointed time; but none of his hunters arrived.

# The Essential Kafir

Having nothing much to do, he went to a native doctor or diviner who had a great reputation, just to amuse himself and see what the man would say. At first the doctor refused to tell anything, because, as he said, he had no knowledge of white men's affairs. At last he consented, and said he would "open the gate of distance, and would travel through it," even though it cost him his death. He then demanded the names and number of the hunters. Leslie demurred, but finally did as requested. The doctor then made eight fires, the number of the hunters being eight, and cast into them roots which burned with a sickly-smelling smoke. The man took some medicine and fell into a trance for about ten minutes, his limbs moving all the time. When he came round from his trance he raked out the ashes of the first fire, and described the appearance of the man represented by it, and said, "This man has died of fever, and his gun is lost." He then said the second hunter had killed four elephants, and described the shape and size of the tusks. He said the next had been killed by an elephant, but that the gun was coming home all right. Then he described the appearance and fortunes of the rest, and added that the survivors would not be home for three months, and would travel by a route different from that agreed upon. Leslie said that the affair turned out correct in every particular, and that, as the hunters were scattered over a country two hundred miles away, the man could hardly have obtained news of them from other natives. Nor did the diviner know that he was going to be consulted. Leslie was at a loss about how to explain the incident.

What shall we say to all these weird things? Shall we seek for some strange and unknown psychic influence to account for the statements made by the natives? Shall we deduce from these stories some nebulous theory of a sixth sense which Europeans have lost through civilisation? There are those

Plate 30.

SELF HELP.
1. Going.   2. Going.
(continued overleaf).

Plate 31.

SELF HELP (*continued*.)
3. Gone.      4. The Verdict, "Not Bad."

# The Witchdoctor

who, doing so, build on such asserted phenomena a belief in the spiritual nature of man; but surely we need not go so far afield for an origin of that conception. It is much easier to account for the facts by reference to natural causes which are known to us; and a little thought might have shown Leslie that his remarkable story was not inexplicable. He might have known the country and the people well enough to see that a diviner has sources of knowledge open to him over a far wider area than that mentioned. Such rare birds as elephant-hunters have their doings told far and wide, without their being aware of the fact, and no great doctor would fail to follow the fortunes of such marked men, and to hear the result of their shooting, or about their death. A little shrewd guessing was all that was needed to complete the clever séance. Deceit and fraud are the very breath of these diviners, the natives themselves being witnesses. It may be impossible to disprove psychic influences in such stories; but it is equally impossible to prove them. I started with the idea that there was some uncanny psychic secret known to these men; but maturer knowledge of the natives has led me to abandon my old theories. It seems to me that the witchdoctors, instead of knowing more than we do, know a good deal less.

CUSTOMS—BIRTH TO DEATH

Homo sum; humani nihil a me alienum puto

# CHAPTER V

### CUSTOMS—BIRTH TO DEATH

We off-saddled at a Kafir kraal at about three o'clock on a sultry summer afternoon. A dim blue haze veiled the sunlit landscape, and the faintest odour of burning grass pervaded the air. Knee-haltering our sturdy Basuto ponies, we left them to feed on the scanty and sunburnt grass, or roll at pleasure in the dust, while we joined a circle of drowsy men, who were doing their best to kill "the lazy leaden-stepping hours" by chatting in the shade of the cattle kraal.

Fine deep-chested fellows they were; their limbs supple and well-rounded; their physique shown to the best advantage by their lack of clothing, and by an unstudied grace or idleness, comfort rather than decorum determining their pose. One fine specimen of muscular humanity was extended at full length on his face, his head propped on one arm; he was chewing a piece of grass, and was quite unconscious of the fact that he was exposing to view a deep chocolate-coloured back, thick-padded with rich ripples of muscle. Another Kafir was lying on his back smoking, with one of his legs flexed, while his head rested on his crossed arms. A third man was sitting propped up against the cattle kraal; he was busily engaged in carving his knobkerrie, on which he had already expended a week's work. A delicious sense of drowsiness brooded over the whole scene. Even nature seemed tired. The very insects, whose noise and chatter is usually perpetual and insistent, were languorous.

# The Essential Kafir

In the distance, wending their way along the weary road, could be seen a Kafir and his wife. They were trudging through the dust in single file, the woman leading; on her head was a large bundle, for she was carrying the entire household furniture and stock-in-trade. The load contained a sleeping-mat, a blanket, a roll of tobacco, and a few trinkets; and perched on the top of the bundle was a three-legged pot—representing an entire kitchen and scullery—while a few awkwardly-shaped calabashes were tied to the bundle by home-made grass string. The lord and master walked behind his slave-wife in stately dignity, not encumbered by any impedimenta of travel, his very blanket being discarded in the heat. It would be thought as bad form in South Africa for a husband to carry the household goods as it would be for a man of fashion to carry his own baby in Hyde Park.

As this couple drew near to the kraal, they halted and held an indaba, the wife gesticulating and emphasising her meaning with natural and graceful action, the husband submitting with an ill spirit. The controversy having been settled, they walked up to the kraal, and the couple chatted with the women, after which the husband joined the circle of men who were near the cattle kraal, while the woman was carried off in triumph to the chief hut. The stranger explained to the men the cause which detained him on his journey, and received a few grunts in answer, while the women were all interest and excitement. When the first flutter had died down and the women were silent, the men resumed their endless talk about the cattle.

After a period of silence in the women's hut there arose a gust of excited talk, the dull mud walls filtering off most of the conversation, but allowing the clicks to pass as if they were X rays; no mud wall could stifle the clicks of an excited woman, who, when she is once under weigh, flings them

## Customs—Birth to Death

about the place much as rioters distribute bricks and stones. Fortunately, clicks break no bones.

There is much dispute as to the origin of these strange forms of speech, the most suggestive being that they have been imported into the Kafir language from the Bushmen and Hottentots. When the Kafirs made war on these primitive tribes they put all the men to death and kept the women as slave-wives; these women clung tenaciously to their own kitchen language. It is striking how many words connected with household affairs are full of clicks. As the clicks specially belong to the women, it is not to be wondered at that the men slur over them by instinct—and indeed it is sometimes difficult to detect clicks in some men's talk—while the women pronounce them with explosive force, in direct ratio with their excitement. It is the prettiest thing to hear the babies uttering these clicks. They do so with a softness and delicacy very bewitching; one sometimes asks them leading questions, so as to get them to answer with words in which the clicks occur.

Undoubtedly the women were excited. The clicks sounded like explosions from a motor-car, and the language was obscene. Suddenly a burst of satisfaction was heard, and half a dozen women came scampering out of the tiny hut door, all anxious to impress on the poor husband that his wife had presented him with a baby girl. The man received this intelligence with proper and decorous equanimity, merely making a grunt. He then turned to the men and told them that, unfortunately, this baby girl was mortgaged more than a year ago, for at his betrothal he had not sufficient cattle to pay for his wife; yet he added that he had been able to pay some four or five out of the dozen cattle, and so he would have a small balance over to his credit after selling the baby, who would be worth fully ten or twelve oxen by-and-by.

He then called out to the women to know how soon his

wife would be ready to continue her journey, because this delay was most awkward. In a surprisingly short time the good woman appeared with the baby strapped in her blanket, saying that she was ready to continue the journey. She was much flattered when the white men asked to see the baby, and with great pride showed a chubby little squalling creature of a colour strangely light, which had the dearest little pair of pink-white hands.

It is a common custom, the whole world over, to call babies after some event connected with their birth; among the Kafirs this is especially so. For example, if the wind is blowing strongly when the child is born it is frequently called " Wind." The late war has supplied many names for children: it is not only white men who call their children after heroes such as Gordon. Our Noels, Guys, and similar names have their counterparts among the Kafirs. So the woman declared she would call the baby after the white men who were present at the kraal when it was born.

The father then lifted the baby in the air above his head and kissed it on the thighs, calling out " My Cattle," for that was what it represented to his imagination. In olden days the father was not allowed to see the baby until some days after its birth; but this custom is rapidly dying out.

The wife expressed herself as being quite ready for the journey: so the three set out. The third member of the party was decidedly the noisiest, and consequently the man made his wife walk well in advance. By sunset the party reached home, and next morning, thanks to an open-air life and to healthy nerves, the woman was seen out at work in the fields, as if nothing had happened on the previous day. Such a thing seems incredible to those who have not actually witnessed it.

There are many customs to be observed at the birth of a baby, and to omit these would bring misfortune on the child

## Customs—Birth to Death

or on the family. When a Kafir wishes to marry he has to come to terms with the girl's father or guardian, for usually the girl is sold to the highest bidder. The number of cattle demanded for a girl depends upon the parents' position and upon the social status of the man. If the girl has a good physique, and is "fat and well-liking," the father may demand extra cattle before he consents to part with her. When she is married, the father gives the girl a special cow, which is said to belong to the ancestral spirits that preside over the fortunes of her house. In some tribes this cow is called "The Doer of Good." The animal is sacred, and its calves are neither killed nor sold so long as the cow is alive. In case of great family trouble, or when the woman is barren, the sacrifice of the cow is said to be specially acceptable to the ancestral spirits.

As soon as the child is born, a few hairs are pulled out of the tail of the cow and are made into a small necklace-charm, which has to be worn by the baby, to ensure good luck. The baby is then "washed" in cowdung, a practice supposed to be of great advantage to the child. Many willing hands volunteer to do this service of love. The ancient Zulu custom compelled the mother to be carefully secluded in her hut, while the people of the kraal were doctored by special medicines, lest they should be influenced for evil by the birth of the child. The seclusion of the mother lasted for a month, and it was called her "incubation" time; if she neglected it, she was considered to be certain to lose the power of child-bearing.

During the incubation time the women daily sprinkle the baby with decoctions of herbs, singing nonsensical chants as they do so. A fire of aromatic woods is prepared, and the baby is passed through the smoke in order that vigour and wisdom may be acquired. This rite is supposed to give the child valour and eloquence. Some old authors explained it as being a process whereby the spirit of the fire was enabled to enter into the child ; but there is no evidence that the natives have any conception of such a spirit.

The father was also bound to offer an ox as a sacrifice to the ancestral spirits, in order to induce them to take special charge of the new-born child throughout its life. A doctor was called in, and made an incision in the child's face, rubbing special medicines into the flesh, while he administered medicines to the mother. This course of treatment was continued for many days.

The baby is fed on sour milk during the two first days of its life, and after that it is allowed to take the breast. It is left to sleep on the floor, and is allowed to crawl about the hut and to take its chances of being killed in the struggle for existence. There is, therefore, a very drastic weeding out of the unfit.

The cruel mother-love performs all these disgusting rites for the baby: they are supposed to be good for the health of the child. The poor little creature will have to submit to many barbarous and degrading customs ere life's fitful fever is stilled and it is allowed to lie down in repose in the quiet grave. If the baby shows any signs of weakness or malformation it is exposed on the hills and allowed to die. Similarly, if a mother gives birth to twins, one is frequently killed by the father, for the natives think that unless the father places a lump of earth in the mouth of one of the babies he will lose his strength. The result of all this hardy and radical treatment is that a sickly or deformed person is but rarely met with among the Kafirs.

In olden days it was the custom to fix the name of the child long before birth, the ultimate form of the name being determined by the sex of the child. It was thought bad style to call a bride by her own name, and so people would call her " the Mother of So-and-So," even adopting this title when she was only betrothed.

## Customs—Birth to Death

Natives do not adopt children, though they frequently have foster-children who live in the kraal and drink the milk of the cows. In fact, if a rich man who had plenty of cows were to refuse to allow a child of a poor man to drink the milk of his many cows, he would run the risk of being punished for disgracing his tribe. There are countless small customs such as this which throw a great deal of interesting light on the character of the natives.

Many small customs are in force in different tribes. Thus, in some cases certain of the teeth are either extracted or chipped. The Damaras not only do this, but also cut off the last joint of the little finger, to give the child extra strength. Even in later life a Kafir will sometimes mutilate his little finger if he finds his hand growing weak: he thinks this adds to its strength. Mothers do the same thing to show sorrow for the loss of a child.

When the children are ten days old they have to undergo a peculiar ceremony. The mother selects a spot of ground on which there is a tree that has been struck by lightning; a hole is dug at the root of this tree, and the child is placed in the excavation. The mother chews medicines and spits them out on the child, after which she has to retire to a distance, never turning back to look at the child, no matter how much it may cry. To look back would bring endless trouble on the child. After a short time the mother returns, takes her baby out of the hole, and feels quite sure that she has thus instilled courage into its small heart.

A similar practice obtains when the children are about five years old, so that the ordinary fevers which afflict them may be averted. In this custom also it is said to be a very bad sign for the mothers to look back when they are walking away from their children, and when we come to discuss the practice of circumcision the same idea will be met with. The mind

# The Essential Kafir

naturally reverts to the story of Lot's wife, and, on examination, it is found that similar conceptions exist in nearly every savage tribe.

Turning now to the headman of the kraal, we ask him how many children he has. The old rogue bursts out laughing, or rather "chortles in his joy," for he tries to suppress his merriment at the question, and his inward convulsions reach the surface only in half-concealed chuckles. He calls a few small children to help him in his arithmetic, for the natives count by the aid of their fingers in the following fashion: Starting with the little finger of the left hand to represent one, they proceed to the thumb of that hand, and then pass on to the next, starting on that hand with the thumb. To hold out the thumb of the right hand signifies the number six. Ten is expressed by clapping the hands or by brushing them over one another. The headman, therefore, borrows the hands of one of his children, and, taking his wives in order, tries to enumerate all the various children. When he has exhausted the fingers of one child he calls in another, and when these ten fingers are exhausted he stops for a few moments to let off his merriment, for he considers the question extremely amusing. When he is refreshed he begins once more, and successively uses up the ten fingers of six children. He then says that he thinks he is near the end of the matter, and so uses his own hands. Finally there is a great addition of fingers, and the man tells you that he thinks he has sixty-seven children, more or less. His eldest wife is seventy and his youngest is seventeen.

It would never do to conclude from this isolated case that every man has sixty children. The great majority of men have but one wife and but three or four children. Yet in olden days large families were very common, and life must have been very complicated. It is hard to realise what it would be like to have sixty-six brothers and sisters and some twenty

## Customs—Birth to Death

mothers. Relationships would be very complicated in large families.

Such, then, is the introduction of the little Kafir into this strange world. How different from the entrance of a white child into its home of refinement! In England there are cradles, dresses, doctors, nurses, and all dainty soft delights; everything that luxury and forethought can do to welcome the little visitor is done with great pleasure. Love has been busily planning for a long time, and everything that could be wished for is lavishly supplied. But among the Kafirs the baby opens its eyes in a dark, smoke-begrimed hut; black faces surround it, and excited talk greets its ears; there is no cradle, no dress; there are no dainty fingers to tend it. Within an hour of its birth the baby may be strapped to its mother's naked back by a blanket, its nose being flattened in the process. Sour milk is administered, to its great disgust, and it may even start life mortgaged to some old ram of a polygamist who is now fifty years of age, and is already in possession of fifteen wives.

There can be no doubt but that the mothers love their children. To test this, I once proposed to a Kafir woman that she should sell me her baby for five pounds. The sum would have been a small fortune to the woman; yet, as she did not understand that I was but in play, she snatched up her baby with a scream, and hugged it to her bosom, and ran away to a safe distance, from which she assured me that the very thought was impossible. It was some time before she could be induced to laugh at the joke, and so long as I was at the kraal she kept eyeing me with jealous watchfulness, even though she eventually tried to laugh at the proposal.

Before long the small girl will have to nurse a baby not much smaller than herself, and will have to help the mother in her work. At a surprisingly early age she begins carrying weights on her head. She has to earn her salt by making

# The Essential Kafir

herself useful in the varied work of the kraal, helping her mother by carrying baskets of red clay, which acts as Pondo rouge, or bundles of wood.

### PUBERTY

The boys have a special department of work allotted to them. They have to herd the various animals possessed by their fathers. They have also to drive away the birds from the gardens, and in this duty, though not in the herding of the cattle, the small girls lend their help. The children are very precocious in hot climates, and they become men and women at a much earlier age than is customary in Europe. As the children grow up, they begin to be more careful about their dress, and become bashful in the presence of strangers.

Every year there is a time for circumcision—unless a young chief is growing up, in which case boys are kept waiting a year or two, to go through the ceremony with him. The ceremony is not religious; yet there is a sort of freemasonry between those who are circumcised the same year, and the young chief chooses his councillors—his "eyes" and "ears" they are sometimes called—from among their number. Boys circumcised in the same year form a kind of guild, and it is a great disgrace for them not to stand by one another throughout life. They are supposed never to give evidence against one another, and it is a great offence for any of them to eat food alone if their comrades are near. In fact, the friendship is greater than is that between men in England who go up to the University together.

The rite of circumcision is practised by most South African tribes, and in many cases the operation is performed on both sexes. Chaka abolished circumcision in Zululand; but the custom has survived in the great majority of tribes. The

## Customs—Birth to Death

season chosen for the rite is in the summer, when the crops show the first signs of ripening. The boys have to live in seclusion for a period of two or three months, and are not allowed to do any work in the fields during that time. But they may rob the gardens as much as they like; in some tribes they may even kill oxen with impunity. After the initial ceremony, in which the prospective prime minister is circumcised first, the chief second, and the man of next importance third, the boys are strictly isolated, and are allowed to eat only the entrails of animals. They receive many a good beating from older men, in order that they may learn to endure hardness bravely. When they show that they can bear pain well, they are allowed to eat other portions of meat, so that in after life a man will say that the right to eat such and such a part of the animal cost him a good beating. During the period of isolation the boys have to lie on the ground without mats, in order that they may be well hardened ; and so severe is the training that in olden days, when it was carried out with due rigour, many boys died under the discipline.

During the period of isolation the boys have to smear their faces with white clay, streaks of paint being rubbed over the eyebrows and other portions of the face, so that they present a very loathsome appearance, as will be seen from the picture on plate 32. Many of the customs connected with the rite are so hopelessly debased and demoralising that the Government has abolished them under heavy penalties, though what is still openly practised is so vile that a full description is quite impossible.

An old man is placed in charge of the boys, and when their period of isolation is nearly finished he makes them collect their blankets, into which white clay has been rubbed ; these blankets are then placed in a special hut, and the boys are dressed up in leaves taken from the date-palm. The whole group of boys then tours the country and visits every kraal represented by the boys, and the most obscene dances are held, in which the women stir up the passions of the lads. When the dancing is finished the man in charge gives them a long lecture on their duty to the chief and the tribe; he conjures them to keep all the customs of the tribe faithfully, and to stand by one another through life. After this he drives all the boys towards their hut, and makes them wash off their paint in a river. Then he takes them into the hut, where everything they possess is piled up in a heap, taking special care to include every shred of bandage or material used during the two or three months, and the whole is set on fire, lest some enemy should get possession of anything connected with the rite. If a magician can but get possession of any article used by the boys during their period of isolation, there is no limit to the evil he may work. The boys are given new blankets, and have to rush away from the burning huts without looking back, lest a fearful curse should cling to them. A great feast is made in the honour of these boys, who are sprinkled with special medicines. An ox is killed, and after the boys have eaten some of the liver of the animal to give them courage and intelligence, and a small portion of the skin of the forehead to give them perseverance, they are publicly declared men. They receive a number of presents from their friends, so that they may start in life; and never again need they herd the cattle, for this work is supposed to be beneath them, being the work of boys.

According to ancient native custom, a man cannot inherit any property unless he has been circumcised; nor would any one allow him to marry his daughter. He would be treated with universal scorn, especially by the women, who would regard him as a child. The whole period of circumcision is one of unmitigated licence; and any one who knows the natives will be able to guess how every restraint is removed when once

A TEMBU BOY.
He is painted with white paint for the circumcision rite.

Plate 33.

PONDO SWEETHEARTS.

## Customs—Birth to Death

the boys are allowed to steal and kill an ox. If that is allowed, then everything is permitted.

The customs observed when girls enter the period of womanhood vary very much in detail in different tribes; yet in practice the various tribes seem to vie with one another in the matter of obscenity. As Theal has pointed out, the very last traces of decency are stamped from a girl's mind by the customs she has to go through, and her womanhood is demoralised for ever. In Pondoland the natives seem to have sunk to the lowest possible depths of degradation in these matters, and I have heard Natal Kafirs, who were travelling through that country, express utter astonishment that such practices should be tolerated.

At the period referred to, a girl, if she happen to be in the fields, has to hide in the bush, avoiding all pathways with scrupulous care. She has to protect her face from sunshine, lest she shrivel up; and when she reaches her kraal the girls all rush into the cattle kraal and select the finest ox, which they promptly begin to prepare for slaughter. The men then run out and take the animal away, and, after a great deal of bargaining, substitute a less valuable one. This is killed, and a great feast is set going. The girl is kept shut up in her hut for about a fortnight. She is not allowed to drink any milk during that period; nor are her special maidens allowed to do so, lest the cattle should die. Notice is sent round to all the neighbouring kraals, and the people swarm up for the ceremonies. They can be seen coming from every quarter of the country, and tremendous dances are set going. Living in the country, one hears these dancing orgies night after night, and wonders how they can be kept going with such energy. At the dances the very minimum of dress is worn by the women, who are allowed on this occasion to carry assegais in their hands. Four girls advance into the circle of visitors and dance till they are tired, and then four men follow suit. This dancing is kept up till sunset, when most of the visitors retire for the night, though some women are allowed to choose sweethearts for the night, and dancing goes on till the small hours of the morning, accompanied by atrocious immorality. When any young woman refuses to join fully in every part of the ceremony the old hags choose a paramour for her and force her into the dances, which consist largely in lewd posturings of the body. Every lingering trace of virtue is thus effectively stamped out of the mind of the women. An old woman is sometimes set apart to train the secluded girl, who is made to carry heavy pots of water, that she may be strong to carry weights in her prospective husband's service. These old women also perform the minor operation which is thought necessary in some tribes. The treatment of the girl in whose honour these saturnalia are held varies very greatly; but, to put the matter in a nutshell, it may be safely said that nothing is left undone which could be expected to destroy any lingering remains of self-respect in the girl's mind. The last traces of chastity are consumed in the burning fire of unbridled lust. Henceforth the girl is but "a thing."

Europeans are frequently astonished at the rarity of illegitimate children among the Kafirs; but all authorities seem to agree that this is due to the fact that the native doctors know several very effective medicines which secure abortion safely, and to native customs which cannot be described in print. We must leave this subject with the remark that but a small part of the whole affair has been touched upon: a full description is quite impossible.

## MARRIAGE

Marriage among the natives is an event of the greatest importance, being the hub of life. It is the season of great

## Customs—Birth to Death

feasting and rejoicing to all the friends and relations, though sometimes it is anything but a time of joy to the girl who is concerned in the ceremony. However, to a good-natured girl it is a red-letter day. Her vanity is flattered by a sense of importance, for is she not the cause of all the commotion? Such a girl passes through life much more peacefully than one who is cross-grained and self-willed : no one will deny that in South Africa marriage is " the taming of the shrew."

Girls are married at what we would consider an early age, though this varies in the different tribes. In some tribes she is married as early as thirteen, and in others not until seventeen. If an average has to be struck it would be best to place sixteen as the average age for marriage. A girl may be engaged as early as four or five, or, indeed, may be mortgaged or " booked " before she is born.

The natives in some districts are very particular as to the marriage of relations. In most of the tribes near the coast a man may not marry a girl if even a distant relationship by blood can be traced. In fact, a man is not allowed to marry a woman who belongs to another tribe if she happens to have the same name as any blood relation of his. In other tribes this rule is absent, and a man may even marry the daughter of his father's brother. It is also a common custom not to allow any younger brother to marry until his elder brother has at least one wife. The reason of this is very simple. A father usually helps his sons to marry, giving them a number of cattle to pay as dowry. If a younger brother married first he might do an injustice to the elder brother, who might not be able to get help from his father. But once the elder brother has one wife the other brothers may marry as soon as they like, and may buy as many wives as they wish.

The proposal for marriage may come from the young man, his father, the girl, or her people. It was the custom for great

## The Essential Kafir

men to send, unasked, a daughter to a chief. To refuse to accept such a girl was taken as an insult to the great man making the offering; to send back too few cattle in return was also considered an affront. For example, when Rarebe sent his daughter to a Tembu chief and only received back a hundred cattle as dowry or payment, he declared war on the Tembu chief, to blot out the insult. A chief might be seventy years old, and he might have twenty or thirty wives; yet if some great man sent his young daughter of seventeen to this old chief, he would practically be bound to marry the girl, unless he preferred to meet the anger of the man offering her.

Among the common people it is usually the man or his father who takes the initiative in bargaining for matrimony. If the man's father is fairly rich he will send messengers to a girl whom he thinks suitable as a first wife for his son; these messengers take some cattle with them, and begin to treat and haggle over the price of the girl. If her people are satisfied with the bargain—the young man and woman are not usually consulted on the subject, and are forced by native opinion to fall in with their parents' wishes, though in the case of a man this only holds with regard to his first wife—they keep the cattle which have been brought to them, and send back an assegai as a token of agreement.

When the young man takes the initiative—and he does so now more frequently than in olden days—he sends the girl a snuff-box or some small present. If she accepts this present at the hands of the messenger, it is a token that she is willing to open negotiations; if she wishes to decline she returns the present to the man. The man, if provisionally accepted, may not drink milk at the girl's kraal, and has to attend to many small affairs of etiquette. If he intends to press matters to an issue he goes to her kraal with a party of his friends, and stands

## Customs—Birth to Death

at the gateway of the kraal. They wait there with their hands on their shoulders and their eyes cast down on the ground. By-and-by they salute the headman and ask if he will allow them to see the girl. She then receives these men in her hut, being escorted by a party of her maiden friends. They dance, and the young man does his best to show himself off to advantage. Sometimes the girl proves coy and hard to win, and in that case the man may go off to her father and calmly settle with him as to the number of cattle he will sell his daughter for. If the father is satisfied with the price, he may accept the offer, and the girl has to be married willy nilly. If there is a rival, the two men send up the cattle which they are willing to pay for the girl, and these cattle are reviewed by all the people of the kraal. The girl comes out of her hut dressed up in beadwork, and drives off the cattle of the man who made the smaller offer. This she does with a sense of importance, to show him how stingy he is, and how much greater her worth is than he fancied. Occasionally she persuades her people to accept the smaller offer, if she happens to love the sender; but it is easier for a girl in Vanity Fair to marry the poorer rival than for a girl in Kafirland to do so.

When the offer of marriage comes from the girl or from her people the customs are somewhat different. She first of all fixes her heart on some man, to whom she secretly sends a present of a few small ornaments. Next day some of her people go to the kraal of the young man, pretend to be passing by, and stop to talk about the news. During the conversation one of the girl's emissaries drops the remark that he has heard that a present from a girl was left at the hut on the previous day, and by the way the people answer the emissaries can tell whether the young man is prepared to enter into negotiations concerning marriage. The present is called " the mouth."

In the case of a girl sending a " mouth " to a chief, she

selects an athletic young man to take it; he has to present it to the chief as he is surrounded by a circle of his men. As soon as he has offered the "mouth" he must seek to escape, while all the chief's people try to catch him. If he manages to escape, the chief has to open negotiations about the girl; but if the man is caught the chief's people tie the present to his body, and he has to return to the kraal of the girl, to be heartily laughed at.

After this, a party of women (called "the spies") is sent to the kraal of the man who is willing to open negotiations concerning marriage. These "spies" come to the kraal and give a false account of themselves. They are asked to stay the night, and have a special hut set apart for them. They then begin to haggle over the price to be paid for the girl, and when matters are fairly well settled the girl herself has to come and be seen. She comes with a party of maidens and young men, who occupy the huts which had been previously set apart for the "spies." The girl has to appear in a circle of critical men; she kneels in the middle, having stripped off all clothing from the waist upwards, and she is then very freely criticised by the men. When they are satisfied, she has to go through the same ordeal in a circle of women, who are even more free in their comments than the men. As she retires from this ordeal she leaves behind a present for the men. The marriage ceremony is all that now remains to be performed. If everything is satisfactory, the people of the kraal kill an ox, and a feast is held; but if they are not satisfied with the bargain proposed they give the girl a burning brand, to show her, symbolically, that there is no fire at the kraal for her to warm herself at.

The dowry used to average ten or twelve cattle for ordinary people; but a chief would have to pay fifty or a hundred cattle—or more—according to his riches. A rich chief would often scorn to count the number, and would drive off a large herd of

## Customs—Birth to Death

cattle, which were taken to the girl's father. In many cases the full number of cattle to be paid by an ordinary man would not be demanded before marriage. He can let part of the payment of cattle stand over on giving an undertaking to mortgage his first baby girl. Until the full number of cattle are paid the girl's relations have the legal right of detaining her should they get possession of her without force. Warner long ago pointed out to the Government that this practice (called Ukuteleka) leads to a vast amount of domestic misery and wickedness. (It should be noted that this payment of cattle for a wife is quite a different thing from the payment of cattle for the temporary use of a concubine, and a different word is used for describing it.) Nor must it be supposed that once the cattle have been paid there is an end of all strife. On the birth of the first child the father of the young wife often demands extra cattle. If any of the cattle paid for the girl die before the end of the first year, fresh cattle are demanded from the husband. On the other hand, if the wife died before she gave birth to a girl, the husband could demand the cattle back, because the woman was evidently not worth buying: she has failed in her part of the contract and in the first duty of a wife. Sometimes the deceased wife's sister would be sent to the man and sold at a cheap rate, in recognition that the first girl was a poor bargain. If the wife should turn out to be barren, her husband can demand his cattle back, as the bargain was manifestly a bad one. Other instances in which the everlasting cattle appear will be given below.

### THE WEDDING

When all matters connected with the payment of cattle are settled, an ox is selected and killed, and some of the meat is sent to the men of the bride's party. This helps to ratify the

# The Essential Kafir

bargain and is sometimes said to be the thing which gives legal recognition of the engagement. Others maintain—and I think on the whole this is the commonest idea among the natives—that it is the transference of cattle which gives legal validity to the negotiations. The natives are never quite self-consistent in answering questions on such matters : the same man would give different answers on different days, according to what was uppermost in his mind at the time of speaking.

In the case of a chief, the wedding dance often immediately follows on the preliminary customs which have been described. These negotiations may take days or even weeks, and all the time the girl and her party would have been living in one of the huts assigned for their use. As soon as matters are settled, oxen are killed and the neighbours invited to feast for days or weeks. But in the case of men of medium importance, as soon as matters are arranged between the two families, the bride's party starts out from her kraal in full dress, in which beads play a prominent part ; this party tours the neighbouring country for several days, receiving hospitality everywhere. This preliminary tour is seldom held nowadays; but the bride's party sets out from her kraal at a fixed hour, so that the girl may reach the kraal of her betrothed after sunset,—a bride may not enter it by day. This party takes with it the semi-sacred cow which the father gives to his daughter at her marriage ; the cow belongs to the ancestral spirits, and it presides over the fortunes of the woman and her children. A hair from its tail has to be tied round the neck of her babies, to give them good luck, and the animal is generally considered sacred. If it dies, the event is taken as an omen that the ancestral spirits have deserted the woman's family; yet in times of great calamity the sacrifice of the cow is said to be the most acceptable offering to the ancestral spirits (see p. 201).

Arriving at the kraal of the bridegroom, the bridal party,

## Customs—Birth to Death

in olden days, would wait till every one pretended to be asleep. The bridal party would then enter the kraal singing, and find huts already prepared. Nowadays it is very common for the bridal party to camp out by the nearest river, where food is brought to them from the bridegroom's kraal. When the friends of the bride sleep at the bridegroom's kraal they have to go off early (long before dawn) to the river, where they have food sent to them.

When it is thought that the bridegroom's party is ready for the marriage ceremony some men from the bride's party go up to the kraal and pretend they are on a tour; but they stop to call the bridegroom good names, saying that he is a very handsome fellow. They then retire for a short time, only to come back with the headman who is giving the girl away; he says the previous talk of his friends was all nonsense; the bridegroom is quite an inferior sort of person, and should consider himself lucky to get such a good wife. He declares the bride to be the paragon of beauty and fatness. He extols her good qualities, and tells the people that they are getting her extremely cheap, that he never saw such a one-sided bargain before. The bridegroom sends down a petticoat which the bride has to wear during the ceremony; this is taken to her at the river bank. She dresses up with a marvellous array of beadwork, a veil of beads covering her eyes. A native bride is as hard to " bring up to the scratch " as any English lady, and she would be hopelessly late unless custom decided that the bridegroom should set apart a special man whose sole duty it is to hustle up the bride's party; this man is allowed to take all sorts of liberties which at other times would be deeply resented. He plays many pranks to make the people hurry up, and makes himself so thoroughly objectionable that the bride's party has to start off in self-defence.

The bride is hidden in the midst of her people, and as she

# The Essential Kafir

sings her people suddenly run away in all directions, leaving her exposed to view. The bride's party begins to dance, while all the others look on; and the bride takes this opportunity of going up to make her peace with her prospective husband's many wives, whom she begs to be kind to her. In true Kafir fashion, they answer that it all depends on how she behaves. She pretends to run away in horror and fear.

When the bride's party has finished dancing the bridegroom's party follows suit, and the men dance to their hearts' content. An interval may now be held for feasting. In the evening the bride skips round the kraal, having discarded her veil, pretending that she is trying to run away; her girl friends scamper after her, as if to rescue her from the bridegroom's party, who start in hot pursuit. Next day there is great feasting, and the bride comes out to dance. Ox races are held on this last day of the feast, and during the races the bride and two of her companions paint themselves with red ochre and strip almost naked, wearing only a small bundle of skins round the waist. The girl carries an assegai, and her companions hold a calabash which contains water and beads. The bride throws some of this mixture over the men after she has washed herself in it.

She is now allowed to let off all her spare steam, and she abuses the betrothed savage, calling him all the ugly names she can think of. A grim piece of humour this! She is allowed for the last time to enjoy the sweets of unmarried life, and so, if she is marrying a horrid old Mormon of a man, with two dozen wives, she abuses him for his hateful selfishness and bestiality. When she has to stop for lack of breath, she is supposed to have got rid of all the venom from her chest for life, and should she abuse him again she must take the consequences. She then tears a feather out of the headgear of the bridegroom, throws the assegai into the cattle kraal;

## Customs—Birth to Death

and as soon as the cattle are driven up the ceremony is over.

Then the bridegroom's party lecture her on her duties as a wife, and a mimic procession starts off to show her the way to her hut. One person carries a calabash, a second a heap of firewood, a third a bundle of thatching grass, while some carry cooking pots, brooms, and other articles of household use. They all mimic her new duties, and some young men go in front and take out all stones which may be in the path. Before she starts on this procession, and after she has thrown her assegai into the cattle kraal, she is allowed to make one last bid for freedom, and a certain young man is told off to catch her. Should he fail to do so, she is theoretically allowed to return to her father, and the whole performance has to be repeated; but the running away is usually a pretence.

Such are some of the customs connected with the marriage ceremony. The various events I have described may be spread over a fortnight, and may be modified in a hundred different directions, and contracted within the limits of a single day. Some parts may be left out and other ceremonies substituted, according to the tribe in which the ceremony is gone through. In the case of common people the whole affair may last only one day, and the feasting has all to be done on a single ox, which may be given by the bride's father. In the case of a chief the ceremonies may be lengthened for weeks, and hundreds of oxen may be killed for feasting the friends.

There is one variation which should be mentioned. When the bride is brought up in her beadwork dress to be finally established for life, she sometimes pretends that she cannot see her husband, on account of her beadwork veil. In that case she runs about chasing the young men: she is pretending that she cannot catch her husband. When she has caught him she carries him off in triumph to the headman, who is

## The Essential Kafir

stationed at the cattle kraal. Thus we find relics of two old usages. In the first place, we find distinct traces of the old custom of wife capture; and, secondly, we find traces of times when polyandry ruled the market, or at least when men were in great request. But before touching the question of wife capture, we must discuss a subject that has been kept in the background. It is this: Are the woman's wishes consulted, or has she to go invariably to the man who makes the highest bid for her?

It is very common to hear people talk of the hardship under which the woman labours—that she usually has to marry some horrid old man whom she loathes; that if she resists she is cruelly punished. This side of the story is specially emphasised by missionaries. No doubt there is much truth in the statement. Frequently a woman is forced to marry against her wish. But this is far from the whole truth. It would be as easy to find instances in which girls are forced to marry rich old men among the Kafirs as it would be to find similar instances in London, though one could find a good many more scandalous cases in South Africa than in London; yet it is undoubtedly true that most good-tempered Kafir girls can, as a rule, get out of a hateful marriage. A good many girls who are self-assertive and strong-willed may find difficulty, for men like to tame such characters and teach them lessons. If we expect to find among savage races the consideration we give to women in Europe, we shall be disappointed; but, remembering that these people are savages, one may safely say that the harm done is not nearly so great as we are often asked to believe. In the case of marriages with chiefs the girls are not consulted: things are arranged for them. And, strange to say, many Kafir women like this: it gives them a sense of their own importance. They like to feel that they are being sent to some great chief; they even like to feel that they are worth so many

## Customs—Birth to Death

head of cattle. But, on the other hand, it is also true that instances of the most brutal cruelty occur. The truth lies, as in so many cases, between the two extreme points of view. To say that women are never forced to marry against their will is as absurd as to say (with Lichtenstein) that there are no love marriages among the natives. It not infrequently happens that a girl is literally dragged off to be married to some man she hates—usually an old polygamist. There is no need to multiply instances: one will suffice to show that cruelty occurs, though I have no special desire to cross all the t's and dot all the i's in the matter.

A girl in Swazieland became a Christian, and engaged herself to a young man at the King's kraal. Her father was dead, and her brother received fifteen oxen and two horses for her from another man, who was a petty chief. The girl was sent up by her brother with a basket of mealies to the petty chief. As soon as she entered the kraal she saw that she was in a trap, for the men tried to catch her and marry her to the chief. But she escaped to a mission station belonging to a friend of mine. The brother came to the station and demanded the girl from the missionary. He, however, refused to give her up, but took her to the Native Commissioner, who in those days found himself between the fires of the Dutch and the English, and had, therefore, to be very guarded in what he did. He said that he had no power over the girl, for this was a matter of purely native concern. The Swazie Queen appointed a day to try the case, and the missionary went with the girl in order to see fair play. The case came off at the Zomboti kraal, and the Queen said straight off, with no preliminary inquiry: "So you ran away from your husband: did you? I will make you an example to wives to obey their husbands." She then ordered the young men to beat her; this they did till her features were quite unrecognisable. She finally gave in and consented to live with the man she hated. The Queen then said: "Let this be an example to all women who will not obey their husbands." No redress was to be obtained : an attempt to obtain redress would have been contrary to native law. It is well to remember that this cruelty was perpetrated by a Queen, not by a King.

I would contrast with this a case of another mission girl, whom her father tried to sell against her will. She bit her would-be husband so terribly that he thought it wise to lay aside all claims to such a vigorous Amazon. Instances could be given by the dozen which would tell on either side: all turns on the object one has in selecting cases. So we may safely say that each extreme side exaggerates the evil or the blessing of native marriages. The fact remains that on the whole the women are satisfied with their lot, and would give a solid vote for a continuance of the present custom, which may bring great hardness in isolated cases, but is a safeguard in favour of the women.

Coupled with this question is the subject of cattle marriages. Opinion on this point varies very much, and it is hopeless to try and convert strong adherents to either side. Such a mass of prejudice, and such clouds of words, thicken the air that a calm view of the matter is very difficult. It is no doubt degrading for a woman to be sold as so much property, with only the slightest, if any, reference to her wishes. But she gains certain things by this sacrifice of dignity. If her husband behaves badly to her, she can run home to her father's people, who will take her side. The husband will probably demand compensation for the cattle he paid for her. Her people will refuse, and if he has clearly ill-treated his wife the case will go against him. If the woman is manifestly in the wrong, and cannot persuade her own people to defend her, she will be driven back to her husband, lest he should demand repayment of cattle. But if he has ill-treated his wife, he will not be able to obtain a

## Customs—Birth to Death

refund of his cattle. The fear that if he ill-treat his wife she may run away, and that he may thus lose both wife and cattle, acts as a deterrent to a husband against ill-treatment of his wife. It is the heathen woman's one safeguard. Cattle have been paid for her, and possession is nine-tenths of the law. If she can make out a true case of ill-treatment, her husband will lose both his wife and the cattle he paid for her. The husband's power over his wife is almost unlimited ; but he has no right to take her life, and to do so would be to run the risk of a criminal action. Still, Kafirs sometimes kill their wives with impunity. If he beat her and thus maimed her, he might also be proceeded against criminally by the chief, for no one has a right to injure the chief's property ; and, of course, in ultimate analysis, a wife is the property of the chief, for she helps to keep the tribe alive. The chief would demand blood-money in that case, and the woman's relations might also demand extra cattle, and could keep her till these cattle were delivered.

If the woman refuses to live with a man because she hates him, the law cannot force her to do so, though the man may get his cattle back if she has borne him no children ; if she has borne him children the law will not award him any cattle even as a fine, for she has done her duty to the man. But if he has really ill-treated his wife, and she manages to get back to her father's kraal and can persuade her people to see things from her standpoint, then the husband will have a bad time if he tries to go and fetch her back. All the women of the kraal will scourge and whip him with their forceful tongues, and when they have exhausted their copious vocabulary will augment it with their teeth and nails. At best he will have a bad half-hour before he regains his wife, and will not rashly court a repetition of the scene.

It would seem, then, that the system of cattle marriages is

## The Essential Kafir

a very real safeguard to the women in a country where polygamy prevails, even though such a system seems to us to be degrading. The women would view with alarm any proposal to abolish the plan, and they pour scorn and contempt on a woman who has not been duly bought by cattle; they call such women old cats, for the cat is the only animal that natives consider unworthy of being sold.

On the other hand, it would seem that missionaries have a perfect right to abolish the custom among their converts. It is undoubtedly linked with the degradation of woman. Critics of mission work are always in the danger of assuming that missionaries are seeking to legislate for the nation. They are only legislating for their own church, entrance to which is quite voluntary. If they tried to abolish cattle marriages in the nation, while it was given up to polygamy, their action would be unwise. They are doing nothing of the sort. They have formed a small society of their own, and have a perfect right to legislate for entrance to that society, which no one is forced to enter against his will. In that society cattle marriages are useless and uncalled for, because woman takes a position there different from that which she has in heathen families. I admit that there are a few missionary cranks who are in favour of admitting polygamists into the Church, and to be consistent they should allow cattle marriages, and, indeed, should baptize heathenism wholesale. But I doubt whether one missionary in a hundred would advise the admission of polygamists into the Church. Of those who tentatively adopt the custom, nine out of ten change their minds after trying the method for four or five years.

If we must legislate for a polygamous *nation* we should allow cattle marriages as the woman's one safeguard; if we simply legislate for a *church*, into which polygamists have no entrance, then we should abolish cattle marriages, for in that society

Plate 34.

DRESSED FOR A WEDDING.
The shield is one that is used only for ornament and in dancing.

Plate 35.

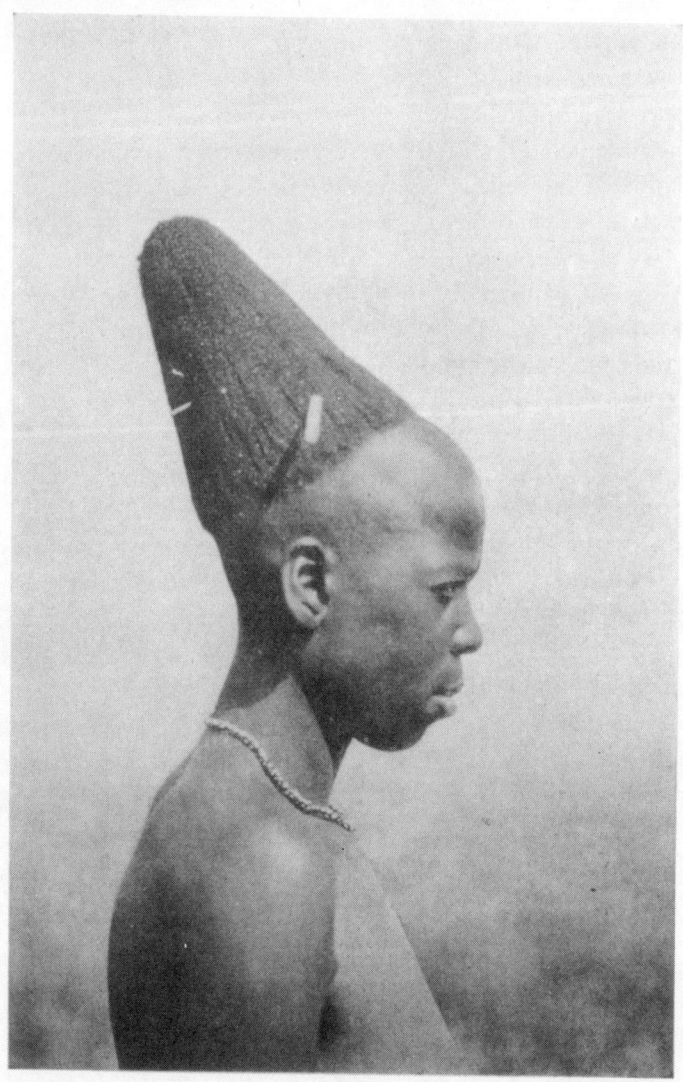

A MARRIED ZULU WOMAN.
The typical mode of dressing the hair after matrimony is here shown.

## Customs—Birth to Death

woman will be abundantly protected by more powerful and effective safeguards.

European influence is rapidly making itself felt in small colonies like Natal, and in such places the marriage ceremony is conducted in a very different way. The girl brings her prospective husband before the chief as he stands by the cattle kraal. The chief asks her, as a matter of form, whether she is marrying out of love or from compulsion, and, no matter what the truth may be, she has to say that it is from love. The chief then makes the couple join hands, and strikes the joined hands with a stick, saying "Let no man cut" (or divide). The girl gives presents to her husband and to his two male friends, to his other wives, and to his mother. She may also give some oxen to the chief if her father be rich. The presents are somewhat amusing, and indicate the dawn of civilisation. In one case they consisted of the following: a European shirt to the husband, soldiers' second-hand coats to the two men, paraffin lamps to the other wives, and handkerchiefs to the girls, besides sundry blankets and beadwork.

In very old times marriages were concluded by the mother of the kraal, who would place a cloth over the breasts of the girl to show that old follies were to be forgotten and covered up. Lichtenstein states that the marriage was ratified by the bride's drinking milk. As she drank it the people used to cry out, "She drinks the milk!" The woman was lectured and told to be silent under all misunderstandings, even when accused of witchcraft, which accusation was made by throwing ashes on the woman's head. The bride used to receive presents of a bowl, a broom, and a grinding-stone, while the man received assegais and an axe.

# The Essential Kafir

### DIVORCE

The least cause may lead to divorce. If the woman's friends think she is being ill-treated they may take her back and refuse to give up the cattle paid for her. If the husband dislikes her, or if she is barren, the husband may send her away, and even demand cattle back. Adultery is theoretically punishable by death; or else the husband may send the adulteress home and claim back the cattle which he paid for her. Or he may keep her and accept a fine. If she took milk out of the milk-sac he might consider it best to divorce her. If, however, she has borne him children he cannot claim the cattle back, for the children remain his property. There is but little difficulty in getting a divorce, provided one does not want the cattle back: that is the difficult point. And most Kafirs think far more of their cattle than of their wives.

### WIDOWS

In some tribes the brother of the deceased man takes his widow in order to raise up seed to his brother. This custom holds in Zululand, Swazieland, and Pondoland, but not among the Tembus and Gaikas. If the widow has children and wishes to return to her father, she has to leave the children with her husband's people ; and she rarely chooses to do this. If the brother of her husband does not wish to marry her, he may give her to a young man on the understanding that he does not own the children he may beget. If she returns to her father, and if she bore her husband no children, then the cattle paid for her have to be sent back to her husband's people, for she has failed in her duty as a wife. If, however, some one else marries her, the relations of her husband have to return the

## Customs—Birth to Death

cattle, for she is thus proved not to be a failure, and who, among the Kafirs, would marry a failure? A widow generally manages to bear children as if her husband were living, for frequently some man is told off to live with her; and she also has her recognised lover. But all children, no matter who the actual father may be, are supposed to belong to the dead husband. If the woman is married again she is generally sold at a reduced price. To exhaust the possible contingencies and arrangements concerning offspring and cattle would require an aged Kafir to write an encyclopædia.

### POLYGAMY

The women are, on the whole, in favour of polygamy. Sometimes a woman who has a dozen other "sisters," as they call fellow wives, will go to a woman who is the solitary wife of a man and ask her if she does not feel very lonely. No one can visit a large kraal, such, for example, as the king's kraal in Swazieland, where there are hundreds of huts, and not feel that there is a certain charm in the social life of the place. It is a sort of college life, and frequently my thoughts have reverted to my old 'Varsity days, and it has struck me that if one could imagine a set of men living in the Old Court at Trinity, surrounded by wives and children, with a social circle in which every one was related to every one else, one might get some idea of the sheer joy of life amidst a thousand relations. Fancy having thirty mothers, with over a hundred brothers, each of whom had a dozen wives! What an endless world of interest one would be in! But this state of things is becoming rare, even in South Africa, as sufficient men are not being killed off by war. So it is unusual to find men with more than one wife or two wives. The popular belief that every man has fifty wives is a mistake. The great majority of men can have only one wife, and it is mainly the chiefs and great men who have large households.

Naturally the natives have many proverbs on the subject of matrimony. Here are a few:

"*The prettiest girl often gets the ugliest man*"—a saying equivalent to our remark that "There's no accounting for tastes."

"*He was in such a rage that he married a toad.*" This is said of a man who does something silly in his anger. Many a husband marries a nasty woman when enraged with one of his wives. This he does that he may keep the unruly wife in order by means of a new and rival wife.

"*At length you have got married, bridegroom,*"—said of a person who has taken an inordinately long time to do a thing.

"*A stick has no kraal.*" In other words, a husband who ill-treats his wives will find it hard to gain others.

"*The knife and meat will never live together,*"—said as a warning against adultery.

## MARRIED LIFE

Until the birth of the first child the parents who received the cattle for the sale of their girl may not drink the milk of the cows. This practice is now well-nigh obsolete, I believe; but some connection is still kept up between the woman and her parents. If she is fined, for example, for using magical arts, it is not her husband's place to pay the fine. She must have inherited this evil propensity to use magic from her parents, and so they are responsible for the fine.

Kafir women usually have about three or four children. Dos Santos describes how in his days natives used to have very large families: it was a common thing, he says, for women

# Customs—Birth to Death

to have three children at a birth. He adds that he frequently saw men who were capable of suckling their babies. Lichtenstein talks of women having eight or ten children as an average; but we can believe as much or little of these tales as we choose. Lichtenstein seems to me a most untrustworthy writer on native matters; yet some modern scientific authors draw much of their information from his pages, and consequently come to marvellous conclusions.

If a woman fails to bear children her husband will sometimes exchange wives with another man for a certain period. This is said to be a very effective remedy for sterility. Violation of the marriage vow is a crime only with the wife: the husband may have as many concubines as he pleases without any sense of shame. He has to select these concubines from the ranks of unmarried girls or widows: to do otherwise would be to interfere in the cattle-purchased rights of some other man. It is not the women's rights that have to be respected: it is the rights of the man who has paid for the exclusive use of the women. These unmarried girls are quite as eligible for marriage as if they had never been concubines, and in the event of the girls having children—a very rare event, owing to the knowledge of drugs producing abortion—the man has only to pay a fine to the girl's father. Every married woman is allowed to have a lover, and no one thinks anything of this custom, which is hoary with the sanction of antiquity.

The question often arises as to whether the natives are moral or not. This all turns on what we mean by the word "moral." If we mean that word to connote the state of life allowed by the social opinion of the tribe, then, I suppose, every tribe under the sun is moral. In certain parts of the world marriage is a tribal concern. One tribe may be almost said to marry another. A tribe in Australia is reported to adopt this system. Intercourse between any members of the same tribe is regarded as immoral; any connection between people of the different tribes is legitimate and, from their point of view, moral. In Hawaii, sisters were the common wives of several husbands, or brothers the common husbands of several wives; that was what they considered fitting and moral. Any laxity beyond these bounds was called immorality. The great Chaka had five hundred girls whom he called sisters: they were his concubines. The people saw nothing immoral in this: it was fitting that a chief should possess these girls. If any one of the girls bore him a child, both mother and child had to be killed instantly. The people regarded this as quite right and moral : the chief ordered things thus, and the chief can do no wrong.

But if we mean by the word moral the relation of the sexes regarded as correct in England, then to call the natives moral is absurd. The man who poses as an authority on the Kafirs, and repeats the statement that the natives are moral and right enough if only missionaries would leave them alone, is either a knave or a fool. If he does not know the hundred disgusting and vile customs allowed to all, even down to the small boys and girls; if he does not know the filthy and putrid customs which boys and girls are subjected to at puberty, whereby the very roots of all decency are eradicated; if he does not know the erotic nature of the old men and the way they beg for aphrodisiacs; if he does not know the ghastly horrors and excesses which are perpetrated nightly in every kraal in the country under the protection of the word marriage—if he does not know these things, then he is a fool to pose as an authority. If he knows them, he is a knave to trade on the fact that such excesses are so utterly vile that they cannot be described in print, even in a self-respecting medical journal, or under the decent obscurity of a dead language.

When loud-talking white men pretend to defend Kafir

## Customs—Birth to Death

morality they have so little fact to draw on that they have to take refuge in the statement that adultery is punishable by death according to old Zulu custom. That this implies that the people are moral or pure-minded is a mistake. Adultery, as we conceive it, is committed every day among the Kafirs with impunity, and the ordinary punishment which follows is a small fine paid to the husband. Even this fine is not always demanded. In olden days the guilty persons were sometimes put to death, especially when the woman was a wife of a chief; and even in this case a fine would often put matters right, and the reputation of the guilty persons would be looked on as fully established. Let me quote a few passages from Theal, who is a cautious and cool-headed observer, and a man who knows the natives intimately. "Chastity," he says, "in married life can hardly be said to exist amongst the coast tribes. By custom every wife of a polygamist has a lover, and no woman sinks in the esteem of her companions on this becoming publicly known" (Theal's "History," vol. iii. p. 292). Again he says, in the fifth volume of the same work: "It is taken as a matter of course that a woman married to a polygamist, unless he be a chief of very high rank, will form a connection with some other man. She does not sink in the slightest degree in the estimation of the other women by so doing. The offence is punishable by native law, the lover being subject to a fine, and the woman to chastisement by her husband; but in most instances it passes unnoticed as an ancient custom of the people" (p. 413). So much for coast tribes. What of mountain tribes? In his third volume Theal says: "In the mountain tribes it is a common occurrence for a chief to secure the services and adherence of a young man by the loan of one of his inferior wives, either temporarily or permanently. In either case the children belong to the chief, who is regarded by law as their father. Another revolting custom of the

# The Essential Kafir

mountain tribes is that of polyandrous marriages. A man who has not the requisite number of cattle to procure a wife, and whose father is too poor to help him, goes to a wealthy chief and obtains assistance on condition of having joint marital rights" (p. 292). In olden days concubines were divided into two classes: those who were concubines by consent, for whom certain cattle were paid; and those who were so by order of the chief, who allotted them to his warriors. The offspring of concubines were not illegitimate, but of inferior rank; they could not inherit property except in case of the absence of male issue of the proper wives (Dugmore, in p. 45 Maclean's Compendium).

These extracts only touch the fringe of the matter. Medical missionaries could tell the most ghastly tales of native confessions which were made to them unblushingly, as if such excesses were perfectly normal to all people.

The accusation that missionaries encourage immorality among the natives is made so often in South Africa, and I have argued out its fallacies so many hundred times during the travels of the last dozen years, that I am heartily sick of the matter. Let me record a conversation which occurred in a certain district. A trader was using the stock arguments against mission work to a clergyman. He declared that mission stations were hotbeds of immorality. The missionary admitted that there was truth in the statement, though mixed with a great deal of untruth. It was true, he admitted, that under the old regimen, when magistrates were few and far between, and the chiefs used to kill off natives who showed interest in the new teaching, missionaries had in self-defence to buy large tracts of land, in order that they might have some area within which to protect their converts from the arbitrary cruelty of the chief. It was true that some of the worst Kafirs left the kraals and settled on these stations,

## Customs—Birth to Death

because they knew the missionary could not punish their adultery in a drastic fashion, and that it was very easy to hide their practices from white men. Hence it was only too true that the old system of mission stations led to very undesirable results. But on the more modern system the station was merely the home of the missionary, who, in the customary presence of white magistrates, no longer acted with authority. As he owned practically no land, natives could not take refuge with him. The trader began to object and to say that the natives were very moral till missionaries started work among them. The missionary turned round and said: "Look here: You have been a trader and I a missionary in this country for twenty years. Just tell me one thing: Do you believe that there is a single man or woman in the whole country whose talk from morning to night is not one mass of putrid obscenity? Do you believe there is one person in the whole nation who is pure-minded and chaste? You know that I know the natives as well as you. Bluff may help you in talking to others; but it is no use between us. Is there a chaste native in the country?" The trader saw that he had been talking rubbish, and admitted that the missionary was right.

One does not need to labour the fact that there is a sun in the sky: if a man is blind, our words are wasted on him: for such a man there is no sun. But it shines for the rest of the world for all that. If a man cannot see an obvious fact there is little use in trying to make him do so, especially when he does not want to see it. So one need say no more. Yet in case some one says that I have only mentioned the more southern tribes, and that the northern ones are different, let me state one fact. An intimate friend of mine was superintending some natives in Gazaland, who were building his hut. The women were treading the mud, and the men were doing the heavy work. These men came to my friend and said: "Cannot you give us some work to do away from the women? Their talk is so vile that we are ashamed to listen to it." Talk has to be very bad before a native thinks of feeling ashamed of it. And if women sink so low, we know what to expect from the men. I am fond of the natives, and want to say the best for them that I can; but it is impossible to say that they are moral in the sense in which we use the word in Europe. We may, of course, be very stupid in our conception of morality; objectors may even desire a very different state of society, in which free love is recognised. But, as things stand at present in Europe, the word morality has a certain meaning. In this sense Kafirs are not moral. In some tribes the people are scrupulously pedantic about marrying distant relations, and in this go far beyond us. But when that has been said we had better change the topic.

## MARRIAGE CUSTOMS IN OTHER LANDS

Before passing on to our next subject we must take a hurried glance at certain customs concerning marriage which obtain in other lands: they throw light on Kafir customs. Max Müller has well said: "Who has not wondered sometimes at the efforts of gentlemen in removing their gloves before shaking hands with a lady, the only object being, it would seem, to substitute a warm hand for a cool glove? Yet in the ages of chivalry there was a good reason for it. A knight's glove was a steel gauntlet, and a squeeze with that would have been painful." Thus is some ancient custom for ever throwing light on some modern one, and to understand our own customs we need to study the ancient history of our own race and that of others. Many seemingly capricious and senseless customs are thus justified. During the Kafir marriage ceremony the bride is apparently allowed to try and escape. This would seem to be

## Customs—Birth to Death

a relic of the custom of wife-capture which obtained in very ancient times and has in some races survived. It is represented in nearly all marriage ceremonies, right down to the occasion on which the family throws rice after the bridegroom as he drives off with his wife from her home.

There is no need to enlarge on the Rape of the Sabines, or of the daughters of Shiloah by the Benjamites, which were clear cases of wife-capture. Among the Arabs the woman makes a pretence of running away, or of unwillingness to go to the bridegroom. In East Melanesia, and among the Arabs, a sham fight is part of the marriage ceremony. In Khondistan, Campbell saw a lad carrying a girl in his arms; she was wrapped in red clothes, and the couple were being pelted with stones under the pretence that he was a wife-stealer. A similar custom was common in Java, New Guinea, Australia; among the Caribs, Tunguses, Kamchadales, Mongols, Esquimaux, Greenlanders; in Korea, on the Amazon, in Chile, Terra del Fuego, among the Fijians, New Zealanders, in the Philippine Islands, in West and North Africa. Wife-capture as a stern reality, or in pretence, survives in Hindustan, Central Asia, Siberia, Kamchatka, among the Northern Redskins, in Russia, and in Poland. A list of other tribes in which the custom prevails can be found in the writings of Lubbock and of Peschel, from whom I have derived this information. In one tribe the girl was mounted on a horse, and was given a certain start; then her lover had to try and overtake her on another horse; if the woman managed to escape the man lost his prize. Max Müller tells us that the old Norse word for "wife-catching" and the old German for "bride-racing" were used in the sense of marriage. This custom, then, is as widely scattered as the human race, and when the wife was sought by more gentle or persuasive means the old custom of capture would naturally be enshrined in the customs of the people.

# The Essential Kafir

It would seem that marriage was originally a communal concern, and that to take a special woman would have been an injury to society. But slowly capture of a wife from a rival tribe would be resorted to, and thus the interests of the clan would be respected. From this it was but a step to insist that marriage should be always sought outside the tribe; and in some races the man entered the woman's tribe, while in some cases she entered his. One reason why certain Kafir tribes do not allow their men to marry women of a different tribe when they have similar names may well be that in ancient days the people imagined this fact to be an indication that the women had once belonged to the same tribe as the men. Many habits have resulted from such ancient customs in connection with marriage, and one of these we must now discuss.

## HLONIPA

There is no fully-formed custom in Europe which is equivalent to the set of customs covered by the word Hlonipa. Therefore, we have to use that native word. It is true that we are familiar with certain emotions or feelings from which the custom gains strength; but for all that we must retain the native name. The word is derived from a root which means *shame*, and the custom enforces many restraints on men and women, especially women.

If a person rides up to a kraal and asks one of the wives to tell him the name of the headman whose kraal it is, she will not like to answer, but will call one of the children and tell it to explain the name of the owner of the kraal. She does not like to pronounce the name of her husband, and if she has to refer to him will mention him under the phrase of " the father of So-and-So." A daughter-in-law has to " hlonipa " her father-in-law and all her husband's relations in the ascending

## Customs—Birth to Death

line; she may not hold intercourse with them, or mention the emphatic syllable in their names. She may not even pronounce their names mentally to herself. If she refers to a word in which the emphatic syllable of their names occurs she must alter the word. Thus there arises a woman's language, which differs considerably from that used by the men.

Here is an example. An old woman was being taught the Lord's Prayer, and when she came to the phrase "Thy Kingdom come" she changed the word for "come." She used a word which made nonsense. The missionary—a lady who did not then understand the hlonipa custom—corrected the old woman, and asked her to repeat the sentence as revised. But every time the woman inserted the wrong word for "come." The missionary began to think that the woman was either silly or obstinate, and she noticed that all the other women were laughing. Soon one of them explained that the woman was not allowed to use the word for "come," as it contained the emphatic syllable of her husband's name. One day, soon after this, the missionary, whose name was Green, happened to say that the Cape gooseberries which the natives brought for sale were too green to use. Instantly the native women corrected her, declaring that she should express herself in a roundabout way and say the gooseberries were not ripe, for Green was her husband's name, and she should never mention it.

A hundred other petty little details are included in the custom of hlonipa. A woman may not sit in the same hut with the people whom she has to hlonipa, and she must be specially careful not to uncover in their presence any part of the body which is usually covered up. To uncover any part of her body in the presence of her mother-in-law would be considered very shameful, and she is not even supposed to look into the faces of the people she has to hlonipa. If she is walking along a

## The Essential Kafir

path and sees one of these people coming to meet her, she has to hide in the grass, or cover up herself as she best may. A woman who breaks this custom thereby loses caste, and when the witchdoctor is called in to "smell out" any one using magic this woman is sure to be the first person to be accused: why, it is argued, did she break the customs if not for evil purposes? In some tribes, such as the Basuto, this law only holds in its full severity until the birth of a woman's first child; after that she has a larger amount of liberty allowed to her. But women have to be careful not to mention the names of any of the male relations of their respective husbands. Natives have two names, as a rule: one is the birth name, which is given them before or after birth, and the second name is that which is given to them later, on account of some special characteristic which they show. The second name becomes their praise name after death. It is the birth name that has to be jealously avoided by the women.

There are also strict laws connected with the milk-sac, which all radiate from this central idea. Females who are not related by blood to the owner of a kraal dare not on any account touch the milk-sac. Nor are women, except under very special conditions and on specified occasions, allowed to enter the cattle kraal. Certain women are on no account allowed to cross those parts of the kraal over which the oxen walk. If but a drop of blood from a woman were to fall on the path, any oxen passing over it would run great risk of dying from disease. It thus happens that the women have special paths of their own, which run behind the huts.

On one occasion I wanted to induce a woman to stand in a certain part of the kraal, so as to get the light suitable for taking a photograph. She was quite alone in the kraal, and therefore not watched, but resolutely refused to go where I wished. She said she was not allowed by native custom to walk on that

## Customs—Birth to Death

spot. I threw down a box of matches on the spot, to see if that would induce her to break her custom; but she was proof against the temptation. I then threw down a sixpenny piece, and she refused to pick it up. So I dismounted from my horse and picked these things up and gave them to her, feeling that she well deserved the reward of her faithfulness.

A European lady friend was one day walking up to a kraal when she was attacked by several of the savage dogs which are to be found at all kraals. She called to a native woman to come and drive off the dogs. It was but a few paces to where she wished to go; but the native went a long détour round the back of the huts, and came up too late. When the English lady upbraided her for her slowness, she said, " I am a bride, having just married into this house, and so I was not allowed to cross that part of the kraal." If she had stepped on the forbidden ground she would have seemed to the natives to be far more mannish than a woman who deliberately goes into a smoking compartment of a railway train. Similarly, the women are not supposed to sit in certain parts of the huts, for these are the men's places. Certain women are allowed to walk over such places; but they are exceptions. Old women who are well past childbearing are allowed to please themselves, and indeed they are often called men. There is no longer any need to restrict them.

One day I was discussing this matter with some natives. I asked them whether a native woman on becoming a Christian was still bound by this piece of etiquette. They said that it turned a good deal on the character of the women. Native custom, of course, did not recognise Christianity; yet if a woman showed that she was in earnest, and if her husband was good-natured, no one would object. They would say to her, " You are now going along a new path, and you may go along it properly, and even break our customs." These women would be excused from taking part in sacrifices to the spirits; but then they would practically drop out of native life and be ignored. They would be regarded very much as strangers, for they would be cut off from all their heathen relations. Yet sometimes, if the woman was a hypocrite, the people would make her keep their customs; and so would some husbands enforce obedience to custom if they were bad-tempered, or if the wife was provokingly troublesome. In short, if the husband was a decent sort of man, and if the woman was good-tempered and sincere, but little difficulty would be placed in her way—a thing that speaks volumes as to the good sense of the natives.

Though women who are related only by affinity to the owner of the kraal have scrupulously to avoid touching the milk-sac, and may not walk on certain parts of the kraal, those related to him by blood may frequently pass over these parts, and touch the milk-sac, and even sometimes enter the cattle kraal.

The hlonipa custom also enjoins that the mother-in-law must avoid being seen by her son-in-law with her breasts exposed, for it is not seemly that the breasts that suckled his wife should be seen by him. She must not call him by his name, and he is expected to give warning, by clearing his throat, when he is coming into a hut where his mother-in-law is sitting. This gives her time to cover her breasts.

There are also restrictions placed on the son-in-law. He must not remain in the same hut with his mother-in-law, or mention her name; yet he is free to use the emphatic syllable of her name when it occurs in other words. He need not avoid any of her relations.

Again, people related to a man will not drink milk at the kraal belonging to any relation of his wife, and the same holds with regard to the wife's relations in respect to milk at kraals

Plate 36.

A SWAZIE HEADMAN AND HIS TWO WIVES.

BUSHMAN DRAWINGS.
On the walls of a cave in the Basuto Mountain.

## Customs—Birth to Death

of her husband's relations. I remember a good illustration of this custom in the case of a boy who was carrying a load for me. He became very thirsty and hot under the tropical sun. We stopped at a kraal, and the people gave me milk; but my boy refused to touch it, because the people of the kraal were connected in some such way with one of his relations.

But not only does the hlonipa custom apply to married life: there are also forms of national and tribal as well as family hlonipa. In Chaka's days the whole nation had to drop the usage of certain words, because the emphatic syllable in them was similar to that in his name. In other tribes the people at the king's kraal hlonipa the names of the chief and his father and grandfather (an exception to this rule is mentioned in the first chapter, where the Pondos freely mentioned the names of the old chiefs), and they alter all words in which the emphatic syllable is the same as in those names. Thus the language undergoes great alteration in the lapse of time.

Most writers on anthropology trace this custom to marriage by capture. A very real hatred would have existed in such times between the husband and the relations of his wife, and when the custom of wife-capture gave way to marriage out of the tribe the sense of strained relationship would still exist, for if the woman married into another tribe she was lost to her old tribe. Ratzel states that in nearly all cases where a man hlonipas his wife's people, and specially his mother-in-law, it indicates the fact that the man enters the wife's family—a statement that is hardly borne out in South Africa. I think it is undoubtedly the fact that the custom has deep connection with wife-capture; but this cannot account for all the facts. The theory is too small to cover such a large area of custom. There are elements in human nature which lie much deeper than such comparatively surface events as marriage into other tribes.

To start with, natives do not like to mention their own

## The Essential Kafir

name, and if you ask them what it is they will often call up a young brother to explain to you what the name is. A sense of shame is often experienced by a boy at school when he is asked his Christian name—or even his surname. This shrinking from mentioning one's name is almost universal. Coupled with it in native districts is the fear of being bewitched through one's name. A native will often try to put you off when you inquire about the meaning of a name by saying, "A name is a name and nothing more." Yet it frequently is a great deal more. If a man cannot get possession of some portion of a person's body wherewith to bewitch him, he can at least use the name to take hold of the person by. Bewitching through a name was in vogue in Europe till recent years. Yet this fear of being bewitched through one's name is also insufficient to explain all the facts of the hlonipa custom.

Speaking to Mr. Hogg, Mr. Wood, Mr. White, Mr. Hope, Mr. Faithfull, Mr. Waters, or other person with such a name, one naturally shrinks from using the word casually. Who would not try to press into service some synonym, rather than seem to play on the name of a friend? If your friend's name is Drinkwater, you will naturally avoid all allusions to drinking and water. From this deep-seated human feeling it is but a step to avoid certain sounds when speaking to people whose name reminds you of such sounds; and one would very naturally guard against using the sound of a person's name when not on the best possible terms with that person. No boy at school used to play upon my name unless he felt fairly sure that I could not thrash him. A consideration of that kind has probably helped to build up the hlonipa custom.

There is still another principle which is embedded deep in human nature. Men fear to mention the name of an animal or a thing which they dread, lest they should be punished for such levity. The Bushman is very much afraid of a lion,

## Customs—Birth to Death

and frequently calls him the boy with a beard. Something akin to praise or worship always follows in the wake of awe. The old Greeks dreaded certain seas, or places, and to prevent ill-luck gave them new names with a good meaning : witness the phrase Mare Euxinum. This innate feeling would tend to keep certain names—especially those of chiefs—sacred, and free from all approach of levity.

Another reason why women and men would respect relations would be to render the temptations to incest rare. In Zululand in olden days, to accuse a woman of lack of reverence for relations, and hint that she might possibly be tempted to commit incest, was such an insult that she was allowed to rush into the cattle kraal of the man falsely accusing her, and to kill the best ox she could find. To insist that a woman should keep out of the cattle kraal, where the men are frequently naked, and to make her keep to certain parts of the hut, and to oblige the mother-in-law to cover her breasts in the presence of her son-in-law—all tended to safeguard a man from temptation. It seems to me that these varied influences have been focused to a common point, and all are needed to account for the practice of hlonipa. No influence alone can be considered broad enough to act as a base for the varied customs of hlonipa.

With regard to this custom, it will help us to take a short glance at other nations, that we may see how universal the habit is in its main broad outlines. An Australian refuses to pronounce the name of his mother-in-law. In some North American Indian tribes father- and mother-in-law hide their faces when the son-in-law is present ; they will not even walk in the footprints he has left in the sand. Some American Indian tribes do not allow the mother-in-law to address her son-in-law, or even to look at him ; she has to address him through a third person. In some of the more southern tribes neither father-in-law nor mother-in-law may speak to the son-in-law, nor may he speak to them directly; they do not mention each other's names in company. In California the natives say that a man must not look in the face of his mother-in-law, or of his wife's relations; he has to step aside and hide if he sees them coming towards him. In Asia, among some tribes, the women must not speak to their fathers-in-law or sit in their presence. In some districts of Hindustan a woman may not speak to her mother-in-law; she has to make her meaning known by signs. In some parts of China the father-in-law never sees the face of his daughter-in-law after her wedding-day. If they meet by accident he has to hide himself. Similar customs obtain in Borneo and in Fiji. In some of these countries, as in some South African tribes, the custom is relaxed as soon as the young wife has borne her first child: she is then considered to have fully entered her husband's family, and all feuds are at an end.

### DEATH AND BURIAL

> Our vaunted life is one long funeral:
> Men dig their graves with bitter tears
> On their dead hopes; and all
> Mazed with doubt and sick with fears
> Count the hours.
> MATTHEW ARNOLD.

Death is indeed the King of Terrors in the natives' estimation. It is the one subject they dislike to talk about, and when a man starts upon it they say that he is not a good friend. Few men or women in Europe are able to meet the Man with the Scythe in equanimity, and very few in cheerfulness. To the natives death is the darkest of all gloomy subjects, and they try to forget it as much as possible. So much do they dread to have anything to do with death that they usually

## Customs—Birth to Death

desert a person whom they think *in articulo mortis*. In olden days they used to carry all dying people, except a few privileged persons such as chiefs or headmen, out of the kraal to the nearest bush ; there the person was allowed to die, and there he was left to be eaten by the hyenas, except in very ancient days, when the dead were burned.

The chief, however, always had a decent burial. Above the Zambesi he is still exposed on the top of the highest mountain. Farther south he used to be buried in a standing posture, with his head just above the ground. His grave was most carefully watched. The watchers had special cattle appointed for them, and neither the cattle nor the men were treated as common beings : they were specially privileged for life. The cattle were looked upon as the property of the dead chief, and the men were scarcely ever punished when they committed crimes.

When a great chief died many of his wives and cattle used to be killed off, to accompany him and administer to his pleasure in the lower world. When the chief is dying he is visited by all the celebrated doctors in the country, who sometimes wait ten deep outside his hut. As soon as one fellow has given the chief some medicine composed of powdered tiger's hair mixed with lion's blood, he makes way for the next doctor, who administers ground-up baboon's tooth mixed with roasted lizard- and snake-skin. He then gives way to another, who speedily gives the chief some very powerful medicine made out of porcupine quills, mixed with the claw of a leopard and the gall of a crocodile. Then another doctor is shown in, and he gives the dying chief some dried excreta of bats, mixed with powdered chameleon's eyes, while he applies a cowdung poultice to the patient's stomach. And so the game goes on till the poor chief must pray to be saved from his friends and to be allowed to die in peace. There are certainly drawbacks to greatness.

## The Essential Kafir

When a person is dead he is buried as quickly as possible, and in olden days some of his wives were killed to keep him company, and to make the people weep. When Chaka's mother died he wanted to kill off every mother in the country, to show his grief, and was with difficulty constrained to be satisfied when seven thousand had been killed. When the late Swazie Queen was about to order a wholesale slaughter in Swazieland on the death of her husband, she was told that the Great White Queen would not allow it: so she begged to be permitted to kill some hundreds of old women, for, as she said, they would not be missed badly, and would make the people cry a good deal; it was necessary that there should be a great deal of crying when a chief died.

This custom has recently become obsolete. The wives are simply considered unclean for a certain variable period; they have to flee to the bush or the mountains and burn all their old clothes, while fresh karosses are made for them. The women in this case may return to their kraals late at night when it is dark, so that no one may see them. They are not allowed to drink any milk till they have been duly doctored; and the huts the dead man lived in, as well as the huts of his wives, are deserted or burnt down. To use the wood of the deceased chief's hut for fuel would certainly lead to a charge of witchcraft. The wives are supposed to go clad in grass for a certain period. Soon after the death of the great Swazie King Umbandine I happened to pass near the queen's kraal, and saw a procession of about a dozen of his wives all clad in grass ornaments. The skirts were of grass; so were all the ornaments; and they each had a small skull-cap made of grass. The effect was weird.

In olden days the chief's entire kraal was burnt down at his death, and his wives and leading councillors were seized and thrown into the fire. Great were the excuses which men would

## Customs—Birth to Death

offer for absenting themselves when the king was thought to be dying. They would send messengers to express their intense sorrow at being unable to be present: inopportunely, some pressing business took them to the other end of the country, or some relation had died, or they were terribly ill themselves. The old chief would laugh and say that he thought these people were "weeping with one eye," which is their way of saying that sorrow is feigned.

But in the case of common people there is less fuss and commotion. If an old woman is thought to be dying she is carried out of the hut and left to die in the veldt: why should a good hut be defiled simply on account of the death of an old woman? A native does not care to go near people who are dying: he flees in terror. When a headman or man of importance dies he is allowed to do so in his hut, and all the people of the kraal have to shave their heads and be unclean till doctored. His dead body is never taken out through the door; a special hole is made in the wall, and his body is bundled out of it, and then the hut is burnt down. The only person whose deathbed is attended with real tenderness is that of a small child. In this case mother-love braves all the fears of death, and the child is treated with wonderful tenderness.

In some tribes when a man is seen to be *in extremis* his knees are bent up to his chin, and a net is thrown over his body. He is covered with skins, which practically smother him. His body is then hurriedly taken out of a hole in the side of his hut, and a shallow grave is dug in haste, and the man buried—sometimes before he is actually dead. So terrified are the people at the approach of death that undoubtedly they often bury people before they are dead. I know of an old man who was said to be dead. His anxious friends went to a mission station to borrow a spade and pick to bury him, and when they were putting him in the grave he sat up and objected

# The Essential Kafir

strongly. The people fled in terror. He lived after this for several months.

The grave is a shallow hole in which the body is placed in a sitting posture, with the knees bent up against the chin. The neighbourhood of the cattle kraal is the place chosen for burying the father of a family; other members of the family may be buried close by in the bush, or else just outside the kraal. The body is usually placed so as to look northward (whence the tribe came in olden days), though this is not invariably the case. All the personal possessions of the man are buried with him, his assegais being broken.

Natives dread to keep possession of a dead man's personal property, such as his snuff-box or his assegai. To keep such a thing would expose a man to the everlasting accusation of using magic, and of causing the death of the man in order to obtain possession of it. Even Christian natives feel a serious difficulty when they notice white men keeping souvenirs of the dead. They cannot conceive how our conscience should fail to condemn this practice—a fact worth the consideration of all religous cranks, for it shows how a matter of conscience may be mistaken.

A small calabash containing some grain is placed by the side of a dead man; and frequently his favourite dog or ox is killed, to give him pleasure in the new world to which he has gone. The earth is then filled in little by little, being well rammed down; and when the earth reaches the lips of the corpse a twig is placed in the soil, one end being allowed to stand up above the level of the ground. A little water is poured over the grave, and the people offer prayers, saying, "These are your things which we are placing in your grave; remember us from the place to which you are gone; send us prosperity and do not forget to take good care of us." The people hurry over the dark and gloomy funeral: they are terrified in

## Customs—Birth to Death

the presence of death, and remind one of sheep or oxen being driven into the shambles. They hasten to bury the dead out of their sight. A few hours ago they were talking to their friend, and as the sun is setting they feel that

> To-night he doth inherit
> The vasty Hall of death.

In Swazieland a small bush of thorns, and in other tribes a small mound of stones, is placed over the grave; doubtless to keep away the wild animals. If the dead man happened to be a petty chief, the son is lectured on his duty to the tribe or family, and is asked not to be unkind to the wives who are left behind.

The people in the kraal are all unclean. They may not drink milk, nor may they transact business with other kraals, until the doctor has cleansed them. Those who touched the dead body are specially unclean, and so is every implement which was used to make the grave with, or which the dead body touched. Those who touched the dead body, or the dead man's things, have to wash in running water.

A doctor is called in, and he offers a sacrifice to cleanse the cows, the milk, and the people; yet for several months the people are not allowed to sell any oxen. The doctor takes some medicine and mixes it with milk, making all the people drink the decoction; this is done at a spot far away from the kraal. If a white man has lent a shovel or a wheelbarrow, the natives will go and offer money so as to cleanse it. On one occasion they went to a friend of mine and borrowed a wheelbarrow. Later they came up with two shillings, "to cleanse away death," they explained. When my friend said he was glad to lend it to them without payment they begged to be excused, and pointed out that they were not ungrateful, but that it was their custom to pay, and if they did not some calamity would happen

# The Essential Kafir

to the kraal. On a second occasion another friend lent them a sledge and four oxen to take the dead body away on, and the people came back with a cow, which they paid to cleanse away death. Natives are very slow to part with money or cows, and their fear must be very great before it overcomes their disinclination to part with these things.

The women are not supposed to wash themselves after a death. On one occasion an American lady I know met a horribly dirty old hag in Swazieland, and expostulated with her for not washing; the dirt was hanging from her in great scales. The dame cried out in horror, "What! Wash myself? Would you have me wash away my sorrow for my husband?" The American lady asked how long it was since her husband had died. " Only three years," the native answered. She had not washed since her bereavement.

A husband is supposed to be unclean for about a week after the death of his wife, though the wife is unclean for twice that period after her husband's death. If there is a death in the kraal, no member of it may go to the chief's kraal on any account, though he may go to the kraals of ordinary people.

A great feature of funerals is to be found in the wailing of the women. It is performed with truly Eastern vigour and insincerity. The men sit by in stolid, dull, leaden silence; the women start their threnody, and wail for hours at a time. Every now and then they have a pause for refreshments, or at least for laughing and for gaining breath. They crack jokes and have a good laugh before they set out again on their lamentation. This they do as if their very hearts would break. Not to wail is taken as a sign that the woman is not sorry; not to be sorry is an indication that she is glad; to be glad is a sign that she has helped to cause the death of the person through magic; to be guilty of magic is to be worthy of death.

If a man is at a distance from the kraal when his father dies,

## Customs—Birth to Death

every time he returns to the kraal during the next six months he has to start wailing as he enters the kraal. He may even keep up this practice for years. The Damaras have a strange custom, which consists in dancing backward and forward over the grave in order to ward off any evil influence which may come from it; and every tribe has its peculiar practices in this connection.

A friend of mine saw a strange ceremony at a funeral in Natal. When the man was just on the point of death the people of the kraal drove up the oxen and made them smell him, and then they drove the cattle away. It frequently happens that the oxen are driven up to the grave of the dead man; but in this case they seem to have been driven up to the dying man. On being asked what the custom meant, the people said that it made it easy for the spirit of the dying man to enter into the cattle; the spirit would then soon find an occasion of entering into the snake in which the Amadhlozi, or ancestral spirit, is supposed to live.

Another strange case was told me. At the funeral of a small child the people buried the blankets and ornaments used by the child, and then went and fetched the door of the hut in which the baby had lived. This also they buried, substituting a new door for the old one; they said they did so to bamboozle the spirit of the baby. When it came wandering round at night it would find a new door on the hut, and would think it had made a mistake; whereupon it would wander about until it found the old familiar door in the earth, and would then settle down contentedly, and not trouble the people in the kraal. This reminds one of the Angoni custom on Lake Nyassa, where people make an image of the dead man, and bury it with great noise and weeping, while some one, at the same time, buries the corpse in secret. The spirits are thus baffled, and cannot injure the dead man. Natives frequently

# The Essential Kafir

try to bluff the ancestral spirits. They offer some worthless ox, and will cry out to the spirits to notice what a splendid ox they are offering up, what splendid proportions it has, and what a fine colour.

A very ancient custom of the Kafirs, living in what is now Cape Colony, was as follows. As soon as any one was ill, people would blow into the ears of the sick man, hoping to drive out the disease. If this failed, the invalid was taken out to the bush, and watched day and night by his wife (or the wife by her husband). She made a fire in the bush, and threw cold water over the sick man, to try and revive him. The fire was not allowed to go out on any consideration, and when the man was dead the woman would go at night and burn her old hut down, returning to her solitary fire in the bush. At the end of a month she would discard her clothes, and, having scratched her body, would rub in medicine, and then gird herself with clothing made out of rushes. She then went to the kraal and asked for fire. The people first made her drink milk, mixed with medicine, with which she had also to wash her mouth out. The cow that supplied the milk was considered sacred. In the case of a husband losing his wife he had to do much the same, though he only had to mourn for a fortnight, after which he took some hair from the tail of an ox and twined it round his neck.

The Bechuana used to make the women stay outside the town on the death of the husband, and they had to drink a little milk which was taken from every cow; the various samples were mixed up, and the woman had to boil some of it with her food, and smear her body with cowdung and medicines. If she failed to do these things the cattle were sure to die.

As long ago as 1684 the wives of chiefs were killed at the death of their husbands, and Dos Santos describes how all the women kept a private supply of poison for the occasion. No

## Customs—Birth to Death

one was allowed to work in the fields the day after a death. In Chaka's time when a man was sick a reed would be placed outside the hut as a sign that no one was allowed to enter unless invited. The chief used to be buried in great state. The people would gather up and greet the dead body as it was pushed through the hole in the hut, and they would say, "Fare thee well, chief." Gardiner mentions that people were usually buried after sunset—a practice, I believe, long ago obsolete.

There was also a custom in virtue of which all the people of the kraal had to assemble nine days after the death of any person. A spade or hoe would be made red-hot and plunged into a pot of beer, and every one had to drink a little of this, to become immune from infection. The doctors frequently cleansed people after a death by scarifying the flesh and rubbing medicines into the wound.

With regard to the wearing of mourning, the natives on the Zambesi place a small circle of white cloth round the head. This custom was common in Zululand in olden days. In southern tribes the people allow their hair to go untended, and the men do not polish their head-ring. Grass ornaments take the place of metal ones.

# GENERAL CUSTOMS

Plate 38.

A SWAZIE BEAUTY.
She was very fat, and the natives considered her one of the most beautiful girls in Swazieland.

Plate 39.

EXTRACTING A THORN.

# CHAPTER VI

### GENERAL CUSTOMS

### CLEANSINGS

THE universal way in which people of all nations feel the need of cleansing after wrong-doing or pollution unites men into a common brotherhood. They may differ in their conceptions of right and wrong; but within their respective areas they all feel the need of some readjustment after wrong-doing, if not to One outside them, at least to something within the sphere of their own consciences. Even Socrates, who loved to rout out fallacies and shams from the dark corners of the mind, while he ruthlessly exposed slipshod modes of thought, felt the need of squaring matters with Æsculapius as he was about to drink the poison, though he could not reduce his feeling within the boundaries of a syllogism. He must, to say the least, have doubted the efficacy of the ceremony; yet he felt some impulse from his human nature urging him to fall in with human custom. Instead of lowering himself in our eyes by this rather trivial performance, he seems never so much bone of our bone and flesh of our flesh as when he accepts his kinship with world-wide human nature. He felt dimly some need of readjustment to those whom Dolly in "Silas Marner" called "them as are above."

A Kafir seems to gain in self-confidence as he conforms to the customs of cleansing which his fellows adopt. The act enables him to face the world once more. His self-respect is

# The Essential Kafir

restored, and he feels clean, even though there be but little readjustment of his moral nature.

When a Kafir has injured a man, he feels ill at ease until the chief makes him pay a fine. Thereupon he feels relieved in mind. Before he paid the fine he would not care to look his fellows in the face; having paid it, he is as good as any man he may meet in a day's march. Or he may have committed adultery with another man's wife. He feels guilty until he has made restitution by paying an ox. After that he feels quite comfortable. After killing a man in war the fellow recognises the fact that he is polluted, and he would feel unable to take his place in society without some cleansing process. This may vary very much as to detail. One tribe considers it sufficient for the warrior to wash in running water ; another orders him to roast some flesh of an ox, mixed with bitter herbs or bark. He has to eat this and then rub his face with the ashes. After washing in water and rinsing his mouth with milk he may rejoin his fellows in the kraal.

On the death of a wife the husband is unclean for a short time; the wife is unclean for a longer period when her husband dies. These people may not rejoin society until they have cleansed themselves. On other occasions a man will shave his head, lest the pollution should cling to him through his hair. A Bechuana will often cleanse himself with the gall of an ox; he will also purify himself after a journey, lest by chance some pollution may have clung to him unobservedly. The Basutos even fumigate the oxen taken in war by lighting branches of leaves and passing the cattle through the smoke. This cleanses the captured animals, and makes it safe for them to mix with other cattle.

These customs may seem to us very silly and ineffective; but are they much worse than the common European idea that a man who has failed and ruined others may clear himself

## General Customs

and again become a respectable person by simply passing through the bankruptcy court? Does that process change his moral nature? The respect paid to constituted order may be a trifle; but it is better than nothing. To ignore responsibility would be more degrading.

The Jews seem to have had the loftiest conceptions concerning cleansings; yet how very gross these ideas were for ever becoming! Because the Kafirs practise some customs which the Jews adopted, many writers, chiefly missionaries, maintain that they received these customs from the Jews. In fact, some of the early Dutch settlers naïvely suggest that the Children of Israel must have passed through South Africa on their way from Egypt to Palestine. It is, of course, well known that the Dutch regard themselves in some measure as the Chosen People. As examples of so-called Jewish customs I here present a few, given by various writers. Campbell cites seven points about the Kafirs which indicate a Jewish origin. They are as follow: (1) The rite of circumcision; (2) the custom of espousing long before marriage; (3) the custom of purification by water and by shaving the head; (4) the supposed transference of impurity to animals which are afterwards slain; (5) the custom in which a brother raises up seed to his deceased brother; (6) the habit of the chief to try cases at the gate of the kraal; (7) the custom of women going out to greet the returning warriors.

In addition to these, other writers have mentioned the custom of raising heaps of stones to mark a grave, or to commemorate a victory; the custom of worshipping the Queen of Heaven, which is thus supposed to be a relic of the story of Jephthah's daughter; the worship of snakes; the custom of the Feast of First Fruits; wailing for the dead; patriarchal rule in the kraal; and a dozen minor rites, such as sprinkling the huts to ward off evil.

# The Essential Kafir

It needs but a moment's consideration to show the absurdity of the claim. Take circumcision, for example. It is natural that South African missionaries should imagine that the only other race under heaven which has adopted this custom is the Jewish one. Missionaries in South Africa know more about the Jews than, for example, about the Chinese or Australians. But the custom of circumcision is found in Egypt, Syria, Central America, on the Amazon, in Australia, among Papuans and Phœnicians, in New Caledonia, the New Hebrides, Friendly Islands, Fiji, &c. Did all these varied nations get the custom from the Jews? Raising seed to the deceased brother is practised only by a few South African tribes—not by all. The custom, however, is found among the Mongols, in Brazil, North West of America, Northern Russia, among the Papuans, &c. Did all these get the custom from the Jews? As an example of the fantastic ideas which religious writers put forward, here is what Backhouse, quite a sober man in all other things, says. Speaking of the Kafirs, he writes: "Their practising circumcision at about fourteen years of age seems to point strongly to a descent from Ishmael; and they have much of the character of having their hand turned against every man, and every man's hand against them." Forsooth, because the Kafirs circumcise at the age of fourteen and the Jews at eight days, there is a strong probability that the Kafirs obtained the custom through the Jews! This is strange logic. Again, every savage nation shows the Ishmaelitish practice of turning their hands against all others: therefore, the Kafir nation, which also shows it, is descended from Ishmael! The proposition does but need to be clarified to become manifestly absurd.

In other chapters we have pointed out how custom after custom is simply world-wide in its application. All the supposed Jewish argument amounts to is that the Jews were very human—a statement which no one doubts. In what

A NATIVE EVANGELIST.
This is *not* the evangelist referred to in the text.

Plate 41.

A ZULU WARRIOR.

## General Customs

country in the world may not a man espouse a woman at an early age? In what country do not people cleanse themselves ceremonially in water? In what primitive nation do they not transfer evil to animals or other things? In what savage country do not people try cases at the gate of the village? Where do not women occasionally go out to greet returning warriors? What land is without its stone memorials to the dead, or its pillars marking victories in war? Where is the nation that does not wail for its dead? One might as well argue that the Kafirs are undoubtedly descendants of the Jews because both nations eat food, sleep at night, practise polygamy, and till the ground.

### THE SCAPEGOAT

When men are ill among the Kafirs, and the witchdoctors can do them no good, natives sometimes adopt the custom of taking a goat into the presence of a sick man, and confess the sins of the kraal over the animal. Sometimes a few drops of blood from the sick man are allowed to fall on the head of the goat, which is turned out into an uninhabited part of the veldt. The sickness is supposed to be transferred to the animal, and to become lost in the desert.

### HUT SPRINKLING

When it is thought that a witch has been at work to injure a kraal, a doctor is called in, and he sacrifices an ox. According to strict Zulu custom, Captain Gardiner tells us, an ox is not allowed to be killed in the cattle kraal except when it is to be offered to the ancestral spirits; but this custom is frequently departed from nowadays. The people hold a feast until the evening, when one or two men help in preparing a decoction made out of the contents of the stomach of the ox. This stuff is mixed with medicines, and the priest dips the tail of a cow into the mixture and sprinkles all the huts, the people having previously been carefully shut up inside them. Woe to the person who is not inside the hut! He will probably absorb the full force of the evil exercised by magic on the kraal by the unseen enemy.

Many are the means used to ward off epidemics. Sometimes the doctor makes the people swallow small portions of the powdered bone of an ox; this is administered to the healthy as well as to the sick. On other occasions the doctor will walk through the kraal with a bowl of water in which special medicines are mixed, and will sprinkle all the people in the place. The Bechuanas prevent a disease from entering a town by placing pointed stones outside the town; a cross-bar is then placed at the entrance of the kraal, and smeared with medicines. It is thought that the sickness cannot pass this barrier. The natives sometimes inoculate for small-pox. They choose a person who has had the disease slightly, from whom to inoculate the people. This practice may be derived from Europeans. When the natives offer a hen in sacrifice they may not, as a rule, take one of their own for the purpose, but have to go and buy one from a neighbouring kraal; and diviners say that they are not allowed to treat their own children, but have to call in some outside doctor.

### MUTILATING A FINGER

It is a common custom in some tribes to cut off a joint of a finger, generally the little finger; the blood is caught on a cake of cowdung, and the amputated joint is then hidden in the cowdung and plastered up in the roof of the hut for luck. This ceremony counteracts the evil magic of enemies. A joint of the

## General Customs

finger may be cut off for many other reasons, one being to show sorrow on the death of a child, and another to add strength to the remaining fingers.

The belief in magic is said to be a remnant of the stone age, and consequently a small piece of metal, such as a horseshoe, is very efficacious in warding off magical influences. Strange to say, I have been unable to trace any similar idea as to the virtue of metal among the Kafirs.

### BINDING GRASS

In Swazieland I frequently noticed at the side of the footpath portions of grass which had been tied in wisps. The natives said that they tied grass thus when they were pursuing a runaway wife. The moment a man finds that his wife has disappeared, he calls his friends; and they run out all over the country, "binding up the paths" by this innocent method, fondly imagining that the wife cannot double or turn back over paths which are thus protected. The belief in this custom must be absolute: otherwise a man would not waste his time in the chase. In other parts of the country the grass is tied into knots, to give good luck on a journey, and to ensure food at the kraal ahead. It is supposed to delay the cooking, which cannot be concluded till the traveller arrives. This brings us to a curious custom.

### IZIVIVANE

This untranslatable custom is of great interest, and forms the subject of endless speculation. In every part of the country the traveller comes across small heaps of stones which are placed by the side of the road. As natives pass these unpretentious heaps they pick up a stone, sometimes spit on it and offer a short prayer, and then throw it on to the heap. Sometimes they omit the spitting and the prayer. The natives vary immensely in their account of this custom. Some say they do it simply because it is a custom, and know not what the object is. In Basutoland the natives tell you that it ensures good luck on your journey. Sometimes they say that it ensures your getting food at the kraal to which you are going; or it prevents the food being cooked and eaten before you arrive. On the Zambesi I saw no heaps of stones, but found small piles of sticks, and noticed that our native carriers always stopped, picked up a small stick, and threw it on the heap. Occasionally they rubbed their legs with the stick before throwing it on to the heap. Sometimes they would stop at a large tree, place a small twig or stone in the fork of a branch, and pass on. They said it was a very ancient custom, and brought good luck. Sometimes the natives will rub their leg with a stick, and throw the stick on the heap, "to get rid of fatigue," they avow. Others say that throwing a stone on the heap gives one fresh vigour for the journey. They sometimes stop at the heap and pray for plenty of cattle. In Bechuanaland the traveller sometimes places a stone in the branch of a tree, or puts some grass in the road and places a stone on the grass to prevent its being blown away. They say it ensures their obtaining food at the next kraal. If going a journey on some difficult business, they will tie the grass in knots by the roadside, to ensure good luck.

So much for the group of customs which cluster round the one idea. It is supposed to be of Bushman or Hottentot origin, as far as South Africa is concerned. The Hottentots used to declare that a semi-mythical hero called Heitsi-Eibib (*see* Appendix) died and rose again from the dead many times; that he has consequently many graves in the country, and over each of these has been placed a heap of stones. They say that the act of throwing a stone on to his grave is their way of worshipping him. It would seem that the custom of raising

## General Customs

these cairns was imported into the Kafir tribes through the Hottentot women taken in war. In passing a certain tree which looks very old and large, the Ovaherero bow down to it, and either place green twigs in the branches, or cast them at the trunk of the tree. They talk to the tree, and declare that it answers them; they hold the tree sacred, believing that from it mankind sprang forth. They never sit under its shade, fearing to do so. The Ovambo throw grass and twigs on a similar tree, because they believe that a hero was buried beneath it.

A very old Zulu told a friend of mine that invading armies always raised heaps of stones to mark the extent of their invasion, and my missionary friend, of course, came to the conclusion that the custom was Jewish in origin—did not the Jews adopt a similar practice? But similar practices are observed in all parts of the world. Thus, in the Island of Timor, people who are on long journeys fan themselves with leaves or stones, and then throw them on certain spots, in order to get rid of fatigue. In the Babar Archipelago tired people stroke their legs with stones, which they throw on certain heaps of stones, to transfer their weariness. In the Solomon Islands the natives throw sticks on certain heaps, saying, "There goes my fatigue." In Nicaragua the Indians throw grass on heaps of stones, to get rid of weariness and hunger. In Guatemala people gather a bundle of grass, rub their legs with it, and place it on a heap of stones, adding a stone to keep the grass from being blown away. This restores vigour to their limbs. In Nyassaland the natives rub their legs with a stone and place it on a pile, to make their legs "light." Cowper Rose stated that the Xosa Kafirs told him they threw stones on these heaps to regain vigour. In Norway cairns (Telemarken) are raised where anything terrible has happened, and passers-by are expected to throw stones on the heap. In

# The Essential Kafir

Sweden such cairns are raised at places where people indulged in illicit love. In Central Asia similar heaps are raised at spots where people were murdered, and passers-by add stones to the piles. In Borneo spots at which people told egregious lies, or scandalously failed to keep engagements, are marked by similar cairns, and passers-by throw stones on the heaps. Similar customs obtain in Ireland, France, Spain, Germany, Bohemia, Lesbos, Morocco, Armenia, Arabia, India, North America, Venezuela, Bolivia, Celebes, and New Zealand. (*See* Frazer's "Golden Bough," vol. iii. pp. 2–14, from which these details are taken.)

Other writers describe similar customs in Peru, Bolivia, Burmah, Thibet, Mongolia, &c. It is thus clear that the human mind has travelled along somewhat parallel lines in vastly different regions, the Jews being no exception, but taking their place with the rest of humanity.

It is by no means easy to give a full and lucid explanation of the group of customs described above. Probably many influences went to form the habit of casting sticks or stones on cairns. To start with, the practice is very frequently performed to delay the cooking at the next kraal, and stones placed in trees may be thought to retard the course of the sun by sympathetic magic, for natives in many lands indicate the time by placing stones in the branches of trees to mark the altitude of the sun. Misconceptions as to the nature of cause and effect are so great that savage races would not regard the fallacy in our scientific light. Some tribes seek to delay the sun by knotting bundles of grass, and this may partly account for the Kafir custom of knotting the grass when going on a difficult journey.

Then, evil spirits, or angry ancestral spirits, are supposed to haunt such spots, as we see in the case of Heitsi-Eibib of the Hottentots. Stones may be placed on his many graves to act

## General Customs

as a sort of offering. The fact that Kafirs pray at such heaps of stones would suggest some appeasing of ancestral spirits. Or the natives may seek to drive away evil spirits by the throwing of a stone. Or, yet again, they may feel that the action helps them to collect into a concrete focus all their fatigue, their pollution, their fears, or other ills, which they symbolically, or more than symbolically, throw away on the heap of stones. Thus it would be merely one of the many ways in which savages transfer evil from themselves to other things. But a full discussion of this matter would land us far from our theme.

It is difficult to exhibit any argument on such a subject to Europeans, who do not find it easy to enter into the conceptions of savages concerning the subject of magical practices and the all-pervading presence of spirits. To us, the world is an orderly sequence of cause and effect; to the native it is but the crazy result of a thousand conflicting and capricious spirits. It is rare to find any European who is able to detach himself quickly from the system of Western scientific thought. And unless he can do this and become, for a time, a Kafir in thought, he is but a poor judge as to the value of an explanation of a Kafir custom or belief; nor is it possible to explain the subject if there be not abundance of space and time at one's disposal.

### THROWING THE SPEAR

In Swazieland—I have not heard of it in any other tribe—a custom is observed when the young chief comes into his place of authority. The custom is called "Throwing the Spear." The ceremony, the details of which were told me by a white man who witnessed it when Bunu became king, is as follows:

# The Essential Kafir

All the soldiers of the nation are called to the king's kraal, and are formed into three sides of a square, the fourth side being left open. At a sign from the young chief a fine black bull is chased by unarmed men, who have to catch the infuriated animal, and drag him into the hollow square formed by the soldiers. If the bull escapes from its pursuers it is thought a very bad sign. In the case recorded the bull escaped thrice. The ceremony was, therefore, postponed till the tide of luck should turn. On the next occasion the bull was caught and dragged, panting and snorting, into the square. A hundred naked warriors, jumping, gesticulating, and shrieking, threw the bull to the ground, and cut off one of its shoulders while it was yet alive. The animal was then forced to get up on its three legs, and the naked warriors chased it round the hollow square, beating it to death with rods. As soon as the ox was dead the chief or king advanced into the hollow square, and threw an assegai in the direction of the foe he meant to attack first. The people in Swazieland were afraid lest the young king Bunu should thus declare war on the whites by throwing the spear in the direction of the little European town of Bremmersdorp. However, he threw the spear in another direction. The night that Bunu held this ceremony, the old queen died. She had previously told people that she would die that night, for there could not be two queen-mothers in a nation, and she had hitherto been queen while the king was a minor. Now that Bunu was king, his own mother was to be queen. Whether she poisoned herself or was killed no one knows. But she died that night. Jewish influence is proposed as the root of this custom, and the fact that Asa put away the queen-mother is quoted. It is all a question as to whether one puts the horse before the cart or the cart before the horse. A custom like this is world-wide for very obvious reasons, and the Jews, being gifted with a

Plate 42.

A SWAZIE WARRIOR.

Plate 43.

ZULU CHILDREN SETTING BIRD-TRAPS

# General Customs

very strong human nature, naturally adopted a world-wide custom.

## FEAST OF FIRST-FRUITS

The ingathering of the crops is a most important event in all countries, and specially so among the Kafirs. Consequently, in some tribes no one is allowed to eat the new crops until the chief has celebrated certain ceremonies which mark the event. The Tembus, the Geikas, and the Gcalekas, however, do not observe the custom. In olden days, people were placed by the chief as spies to see whether any one broke the custom: to do so was to be accused of witchcraft, and, of course, was punishable by death or expulsion from the tribe.

The feast is divided into two portions, the Little and the Great Festivals. Sometimes only one of the customs is observed; whence arise the confused statements of writers who seem to contradict one another.

## THE LITTLE FESTIVAL

This is held when the mealies are soft, which is generally about the time of the New Year. If the moon be full the king sends certain men down to the sea, in order that they may bring back some sea-water. As soon as the messengers return the king calls together many of his warriors—not all at this season—who assemble at the Great Place. The national priest, or doctor, takes a bulb, somewhat like an onion, and squeezes the juice into the sea-water. He washes the body of the king with this " Intelezi," or medicine, that he may be strong to overcome other kings.

It is but the great men of the nation who are called to this festival, which may be the only ceremony held; or else the little festival may be omitted and the great festival alone may be observed. Custom varies much in different tribes and in different years.

### THE GREAT FESTIVAL

When the great festival is to be held the king calls up his warriors to the Great Place, and any soldier staying at home would be put to death. All go up armed as if for war, and at the conclusion of the festival many old regiments of warriors are allowed to marry, and new recruits are enrolled. This was the case in Chaka's days.

As soon as the people have all gathered at the chosen place they go down to the river and wash, calling to the king to come; and then they return to the kraal and sing and strike shields with assegais to salute the king, who sits and looks on at the performance.

The next day the people rest, and on the fourth day the great dance is held. The king is clad in grass, leaves, corn-sheaths, and herbs, and stands at the head of the kraal, dancing backwards and forwards thrice; he is accompanied by a band of boys who whistle as loudly as they can, the tune, apparently, being optional. When this part of the ceremony is over, the men fetch two bulls, which are made to fight. Sometimes they kill a single animal, which, however, has to be killed without weapons and cooked over a fire made by friction. The two sticks which are used for this purpose are considered sacred. They are jealously guarded by the national witchdoctor or by the chief, and are kept for a future occasion. During the feast the chief places his power and majesty on one side, and people are allowed to insult him with impunity. The men may not eat the meat of the ox, lest the king should be injured by his enemies; but the boys are allowed to eat it. During the dances which are held, men posture as animals, and pretend to stab one another, making gurgling sounds in imitation of those

## General Customs

of the dying animals. The doctor gives the king the gall of the ox to drink, that he may be strengthened to meet his enemies. After this other cattle are killed and there is a general feast. Sometimes the first bull that is slain is burnt entire with its skin on ; but sometimes it is eaten by the boys.

At a certain sign the chief declares the feast over, resumes his kingly place, and advances to the cattle kraal, dancing and praising himself. This is the true native form of poetry. If a Kafir does not sing his own praises and blow his own trumpet, who will do so for him ? The doctor gives him a calabash which is filled with boiled specimens of the new crops, and the king breaks the calabash—sometimes he breaks three calabashes in succession—by throwing it on the ground at the feet of one of his warriors. He then sprinkles the people with the cooked food, frequently spitting it out on them. The man at whose feet the calabash falls considers himself very lucky. The king "gives out the notices," telling one regiment to wear the head-ring, and allowing another veteran regiment to marry. The people rest at the Great Place all the next day, after which they are allowed to return to their kraals and eat the new crops. The special dress worn by the chief during the ceremony is burnt at the close of the festival. Arbousset describes how the chief would come out on the occasion of this feast and spit at the sun in contempt and scorn; but the custom seems to have lapsed. The whole ceremony is rarely celebrated now in anything like its ancient completeness. Variations of the true old Zulu custom are found among the Matabele, the Bechuana, the Basuto, and other tribes. But there is no need to enter into the *minutiæ* of these different ceremonies. Sometimes the king takes great mouthfuls of the cooked food and spits it out over the people. Then, again, in other tribes a special song, called "the chief's song," is sung. It may not be used on any other occasion except when rain

# The Essential Kafir

hinders an army in its manœuvres. This song is supposed to bring down the rain only where it is needed, and if rain does not immediately follow the people say that it will not rain for many days—very much like our myth of St. Swithin's Day. It is a striking thing that the chief's songs as sung in Swazieland are all chanted in the old Zulu tongue, and not in the Swazie dialect ; and, indeed, all songs at the king's kraal are said to be sung in pure Zulu.

The ways in which different nations practise customs at times of harvesting are very interesting. Frazer has made a special study of these customs, and any one wishing to gain a bird's-eye view of this so-called " Jewish " ceremony should read the second volume of " The Golden Bough," where over a hundred pages are devoted to the subject, so world-wide is the group of customs which are practised in many European countries as well as in all other parts of the globe. To give the briefest outline of the customs as observed in other lands would require more space than I can afford.

### OMENS

It is quite impossible to give a full list of the various things which are taken as omens of good or evil, because their number is inexhaustible. Whenever any domestic animal happens to do something a little unusual, the natives suppose that there is some deep and hidden import in the omen. Assume their conception of nature to be correct, and grant that the very trees and stones are radiating occult influences every moment, and it becomes impossible not to assume that every unusual accident has some important significance. If a cock should crow at an unusual hour it is certain that the cattle or the people of the kraal are about to fall ill. If a cow should enter, or try to enter, a hut, it is a bad sign: not so if a calf

## General Customs

should make the attempt, for calves are frequently kept inside Pondo huts when they are young. When a sheep bleats as it is being killed, the people fear some evil to be impending, and not infrequently the meat is thrown away. If a bird or other animal should happen to cross the path, especially when a hunter is pursuing game, the omen is considered to be very bad. A dream is a most powerful omen, and should never be disregarded. If the people find but little gall in the gall-bladder of an animal they think that the ancestral spirits must have previously sucked it out.

Lichtenstein states that the natives draw omens from the lines of a person's hand, and in this seem to resemble the gipsies. When a native treads on a thorn he will sometimes eat it, in order that he may be the better enabled to avoid other thorns. If a frog enters a hut a death is expected to happen shortly. It is a very bad sign when a goat is seen to jump to the roof of a hut. If the first animal a hunter kills happens to be a female his luck is thought to be very bad; if the first one killed is a male the hunter is sure to be successful for the rest of the day. If a man misses his aim twice running, he considers that the ancestral spirits are opposing him, and will abandon his hunting for the day.

A man can tell what luck he may expect by using dice to see whether the omens are favourable or not. Should an army on the war-path notice any action of an animal which they consider unusual they will refuse to fight, for the war in the unseen world which is carried on between the ancestral spirits is frequently regarded as more real than that which is carried on in the flesh. The ancestral spirits are supposed to be fighting in the air just above the heads of the warriors, and the victory depends more on them than on the actual soldiers.

It is possible to bind evil influences so that they may be unable to affect certain people. Thus, a mother, on leaving her

## The Essential Kafir

baby for a short time, will frequently place a few drops of milk on its head, to keep it "sleeping" and free from harm. To eat milk (the sour milk of the natives is *eaten*, for the liquid portion is strained off) during a thunderstorm attracts the lightning to the kraal. The greatest discrimination is necessary to know what to eat. To eat the whiskers of a leopard with ordinary food leads to certain death; to eat it with leopard's flesh will ensure the absorption of the good qualities of the leopard. Lobengula made it a capital crime to kill crocodiles, for small portions of the animal were supposed to cause the death of people, if mixed with their food.

A witchdoctor has only to advance some fantastic explanation of an omen, and the people are completely satisfied for the time. The belief in omens is but a corollary of the belief in magic. If the doctor can prove himself a master in the one art he must also be a master in the other. And so the entire life of a native is filled with uncanny feelings and fears concerning witchcraft; and the whole world is filled with omens of deep import for those who have eyes to see. No Jacob Behmen ever saw such conflicts in the heart of things. The whole world is filled to overflowing with meaning of the most fantastic kind.

# MENTAL CHARACTERISTICS

# CHAPTER VII

## MENTAL CHARACTERISTICS

THE whole mental furniture of a Kafir's mind differs from that of a European. His outlook upon life is different; his conception of nature is cast in another mould. It is quite common for Europeans to think that they can soon sound the depths of a Kafir's mind; but maturer experience always reveals the shallowness, not of the Kafir's thoughts, but of our first and hasty impressions. There are depths beneath the shallows of a native's thought. The most incompatible things seem to be able to dwell together in harmony and peace in the muddy and turbid stream of his thoughts. He is a complete stranger to Western conceptions of clear thinking, and is as ignorant of logic as he is of the moons of Jupiter. His conceptions of cause and effect are hopelessly at sea, and, as all primitive religions are based on such conceptions, his religion is a confused mass of ancestor-worship coupled with dread of magic. He cannot distinguish between coincidence and causation; he will argue that because he had a headache yesterday and a cow did something unusual, therefore the headache was caused by the weird action of the cow.

One of the commonest generalisations made by hasty observers is that the natives are but overgrown children. There is, of course, some truth in the statement—just sufficient to make it very untrue. It is easy to bring forth a dozen traits in which the native is like an overgrown child; yet the statement is not very brilliant. A little more experience convinces most people that he is not so much an overgrown as a misgrown child, and misgrown with a vengeance. There is nothing at all childish in the strength of his vices, in the cleverness of his cunning, in the sententiousness of his wisdom, in the geniality of his humour, in the cleverness and fairness of his legislation on such matters as property, in the keenness of his capacity for bluffing.

The next phrase under which he is dismissed is that of non-moral. It takes a very little experience to convince one that, though he may be immoral, he is by no means non-moral. Very ignorant he is, doubtless, and very mistaken. But he is usually fully aware that he is doing wrong, until his conscience becomes hardened.

Lastly, we are for ever being told by people who do not know the native in his own home that he is an utterly lazy creature. This point must be left undiscussed for the present. There is truth in all these three statements; but there is more error than truth.

## THE SEAT OF VARIOUS QUALITIES

It may be well to collect systematically details given throughout these pages which show what the natives regard to be the seat of the various qualities and emotions. Bravery or courage is the most royal of all qualities in the estimation of the natives. It is co-equal with the virtue of obedience to the chief. These two qualities are of a high order, especially in savage life. The liver—sometimes the heart—is said to be the seat of courage, and the gall is a fluid which contains its very essence. Arbousset declares that the Basuto consider the gall to represent the anguish of death; but it seems problematical whether the natives have any conception of such an abstract thing as the anguish of death. The gall is regarded in most

## Mental Characteristics

tribes as the seat of courage and boldness. When the natives wish to describe the bravery of a great man they say that he has a large liver. Perseverance, that elemental faculty in human nature, is coupled in the native mind with perspiration; and, as the first place this is seen is on the skin of the forehead, they frequently consider that its seat or "centre" (as physiologists would say) is there.

Intelligence or enlightenment is also sometimes considered to reside in the liver; but I fancy the sort of intelligence that is referred to is that which is displayed in battle. Strength is often considered to reside in the heart, as well as in other organs peculiar to men. Vigour is sometimes thought to reside in the marrow of the bones; but this is not often referred to. Life is sometimes thought to reside in the blood; the idea is probably not a purely native conception, but a notion imported by white men. The brain may be the seat of some quality; but I have not heard any function applied to it. The natives are not overburdened with brains. Nor do I ever remember natives talking about the seat of affection, though a mother would probably place it in her breasts. For much the same sort of reason, a little European girl, on being asked where she loved her aunt, rubbed that portion of her small person which is generally supposed to be connected with digestion—and cake—and answered, "Down here." Arbousset declares that the natives place the conscience in the pleuræ; but it is quite common to hear them speak of it as residing in the heart, which, by the way, they consider to be placed in the throat. The reason is very simple. When a person is overcome by sudden emotion he is apt to feel the tumultuous pulsations of the carotid arteries in the throat.

Cassalis states that the Basuto place feeling and will in the heart. A large heart implies an intelligent man; a long heart a patient man; a short heart an irritable man; a strong heart a brave man; a white heart a happy man; a black heart an unhappy man. These last two expressions are very common among other tribes: often a man looks as sour as vinegar and as black as thunder: he will tell you that his heart is sore and black within him.

The Basuto are said to place emotion in the lungs. A man who feels elated will say that his lungs are uplifted; a man who is overcome by feeling will say that his lungs prevent him from speaking. The spleen "bites" or "accuses" people, and much sickness is traced to that organ. The man who is capable of enduring hardness is said to have a hard liver; those about to die are said to be losing their heart, while on recovery the people say that the man's heart is coming back again.

We now come to a consideration of some mental characteristics *seriatim*, and we had better start with

### MEMORY

Natives have the most marvellous memories for facts that interest them. Having no written language, they have to rely on a memory which is not burdened in childhood by the discipline of board schools. The function of memory is strengthened by use, and the natives carry out Lord Beaconsfield's receipt for a good memory—namely, Never make a note—a rule, I fancy, he did not keep himself. I have seen a council of chiefs and great men discussing a legal case. Some controversy arose over an ancient precedent. Immediately the old men recited the minutest details of the case, which happened sixty or seventy years before. They knew the exact colour of the various cattle which had been the subject of dispute. One could see them mentally travelling back over the landscape of the past, and after ten minutes' talk the old case was made to live again, so that all who heard the discussion would remember

## Mental Characteristics

the various points for another sixty years. The old men, who were children at the time, were unanimous as to the judgment given and all the various technicalities of the case: there was not a dissentient voice in the gathering.

### MENTAL POWERS

Kafir boys are very quick in absorbing new ideas, and not infrequently make more rapid progress for a time than European boys. It is a strange (and I must say unwelcome) sight to visit Lovedale and see white and black children doing lessons together. Sometimes the native children are very precocious in the rapidity with which they absorb knowledge; but at puberty there generally comes a gradual falling off in capacity, and the white boys then easily outdistance the black. The energy of the native seems to be absorbed in merely bodily functions—nutritive and sensual—as soon as he reaches the age of puberty, when the development of his brain, as a rule, comes to a standstill. Whether this is caused by purely mechanical means, owing to the formation of the bones of the skull, or not, must be left to men of science to settle; yet the fact of stunted mental development remains. Not that it is universal or invariable. One occasionally meets a native who could read, say, the *Nineteenth Century* or the *Fortnightly*. Yes: read, and quite appreciate the articles. Yet this is very rare. Such men are usually trained from early age in some European atmosphere.

Once a native has grown up in ignorance, it is very hard to knock any knowledge into his thick skull. The natives vary in this respect; but as a rule it is a very slow and tedious matter to teach a grown-up man to read or write, especially an oldish man. The old men will sometimes start learning to read, thinking it will take only an hour or so. A lady on a

# The Essential Kafir

mission station was trying to teach an old man the elements of the New Testament, and came to the subject of angels. She spent a good half-hour trying to knock into the head of the old fellow, who was, however, very dull, some idea as to the nature of angels. The work was probably one of supererogation. At length, after endlessly dinning the same facts into his head, she said, " And what are angels ? " The old man looked very serious, and said very slowly, with a pause between his words, " Angels—are—birds." And on another occasion, after listening to a long dissertation on sin, which was likened to the weeds in the garden, he was asked what sins were, and he said in the same deliberate way, "Sins—are—weeds—in—the—garden." After all, Dante spoke of the angels as the birds of God.

With regard to such qualities as the critical or logical faculty, the natives seem hopelessly deficient. They have very little mental stability, though they are very shrewd. Nor have they much power of imagination or invention; yet they can copy well. Natives on the Zambesi will make a coat, or a pair of boots, if they are given the material and the thing to copy from, and they will faithfully reproduce every detail. When a native was given a pair of store-bought boots to imitate, he made them perfectly, even down to the two little holes at the heel, which had been caused by the thread used for hanging them up in the shop. Natives do not stop to think : they imitate slavishly.

The natives are frequently quite incapable of seeing pictures at first, and wonder what the smudge on the paper is there for. When they see that it represents something they are very excited. Some see a picture instantly, while old men frequently fail to see anything at all, no matter how long and patiently one tries to explain the matter to them; occasionally they become quite irritable because others say they can see the

## Mental Characteristics

picture. They feel as much injured as a person who cannot see a joke that others are laughing at. They have almost no sense of the beautiful, and are devoid of all art, the Bushmen far surpassing them in this. Their poetry and chants are of a low order as a rule, with a few striking exceptions. Their songs are much like the following specimen, which a missionary heard some women chanting as they walked off to hunt for a lost cow:

> Our cow let her come, we are calling her:
> We say, let her come, let her come, we are calling her:
> Let her come to me, then let her come:
> Our cow, let her come, we are calling her.

They have a strange lack of any sense of proportion or of values. When Queen Victoria was to send a present to the old Swazie Queen, her Majesty's advisers presumably gave her a hint as to what would be suitable. So a priceless cashmere shawl was chosen. When the Swazie Queen received it she cut it into four and gave it to her daughters, having first soaked it in fat and red ochre.

### CONSCIENCE

It would be safe to say that the natives generally have very real and very troublesome consciences. They are quite familiar with the whole gamut of emotions which gather round the conscience, such as inward misgiving, searching of heart, scruple, inward warning of approaching evil, struggle with temptation, fear of the consequences of wrong-doing, repentance, penitence, self-reproach, remorse, callousness, hardening of the heart, searing of the conscience, and drowning of conviction—with all these they are familiar, and so cannot be considered to be non-moral. Of course, the vast majority of grown-up people have virtually smothered the voice of conscience; yet it haunts some of them even to old age.

# The Essential Kafir

The texture of a Kafir's conscience is very hard to describe. His thoughts are but rarely tinged with philosophic or reflective doubt, for he rides roughshod along the pathway of life. When he feels qualms of conscience, they usually seem to him to come as unreasoned checks, almost *ab extra*. It is as if he suffered from some alternation of personality, or as if some faculties of his soul had suddenly arisen out of the strange hidden depths of his own personality, and made themselves felt in his consciousness. Frequently it seems to him as if a voice were arresting him, somewhat in the style of the Demon of Socrates, and, as in his case, it warns him what *not* to do, and does not urge him to positive duty. Or it may be that a dream is the cause of a man's misgiving, and this wretched dream haunts him day after day, giving him no peace. That is a very common cause which determines a native to go and listen to a missionary, though many missionaries seem strangely ignorant of the fact. I have often asked missionaries if any of their converts began attendance at the mission on account of dreams, and they have usually said that they thought not; yet on my calling up the different members of the church and cross-questioning them, it became clear that a great many began to go to the mission from this cause. The conscience of a Kafir slumbers for the greater part of his life ; but when it awakes it does so energetically.

Still, as the natives' ideas are confused, their uninformed conscience is not much guide to them. A Bushman was asked what he considered to be a bad action, and he promptly answered that it was a bad action for another man to steal his wife. And a good action ? Why, that he should steal another man's wife ! But I regard this answer as an illustration of Bushman humour rather than of his conscience.

The natives generally describe conscience by saying that they have two hearts: one of these speaks in a gentle voice,

## Mental Characteristics

and restrains them from doing certain things; the other is a hard heart which speaks in a rough, imperious voice. Here is a picture of a Swazie girl (Plate 38). Every one will admit that the human and kindly juices are well developed in her case: she should not be specially neurotic. The natives consider her to be a beauty, chiefly because she is so fat. Yet she used to say that she would frequently hear her soft heart—she called it her "little heart"—speaking in a gentle voice, telling her not to do certain things. But then her other heart would speak out in a very loud and boisterous fashion and quite drown the voice of this little heart, so that she did not know what to do. Natives will sometimes say that when they do wrong they feel that they are not responsible for it, for the matter is not theirs, but His who put that hard heart in them: they say that one day they find a gentle heart within them, and another day an evil, hard heart: it is, therefore, not their business, but is wholly the look-out of the One who put that heart in them. These hyper-Calvinists will tell you that once they heard the gentle voice restraining them, but that it is long since they heard it, and that the responsibility cannot rest upon their shoulders. The strange thing is that a native will steal your necktie with cunning, and feel uncomfortable while he is doing so, yet later will come into your presence with your necktie round his own neck, and without a blush or trace of embarrassment: truly a case of a misgrown and anomalous conscience.

### SENSE OF TRUTH

Deceit is the air in which a Kafir lives. It is a smart thing to deceive so long as a person is not found out; if he is detected in his deceit he is shown to be very silly. A native father will enjoy seeing his children deceive people cleverly. It reminds one of a saying common among the Dutch: when the parents

# The Essential Kafir

hear a child tell a splendid lie, they will sometimes say, "See how prettily he lies!" But natives do not tell lies to a chief, and there are many natives who would never deceive a white man whom they are fond of or respect. There are natives, though not many, whom I should absolutely trust to tell me what they thought to be the truth. Even when they tell what they consider to be the truth, they are very apt to mislead, for imagination enables a Kafir to see what he is looking for. Because he tells you that a dozen cockroaches came out of his brain half an hour ago you must not jump to the conclusion that he is purposely trying to tell a lie. He may believe it fully; but, being absolutely uncritical, his word is worth little, and it is easy to account in this way for some of the marvellous tales recorded by travellers. As observers of fact the Kafirs are hopelessly incompetent, and their evidence in such matters is as light as the wind.

### SENSE OF JUSTICE

This sense is very strong among Kafirs; it is as marked as their strong memory. If a white man thrashes a Kafir when he has not done wrong the native will never forgive him for the injustice; if the native was in the wrong and knows it, he will like the man the more for having given him the thrashing. In this respect he resembles a dog, which rarely hates a person who punishes it when in the wrong. It is here that the Dutch get such power over the natives. They rarely beat a native who is not in the wrong, but beat him well when he is. It consequently happens that among the Dutch one finds natives who have spent their lives with their master and would not think of leaving him, even though they are often severely handled. The Dutchman is always even in his treatment of the native, and, unlike the Englishman, does not spoil him to-day to thrash him the harder to-morrow.

# Mental Characteristics

It may seem to Europeans that the natives are very unjust in torturing people found guilty of witchcraft. But take their point of view, and recognise the enormity and reality of the crime: then the affair takes on a different complexion.

### SENSITIVENESS TO RIDICULE

Natives are very susceptible to ridicule, which is to them as gall and wormwood. They are, consequently, very much pleased with a little praise. It is much more easy to wean a native from a habit by laughing, than by preaching, at it. Ridicule was a more effective weapon against the early Christians than persecution and martyrdom. A Bushman will get terribly angry when laughed at, for his sense of vanity is egregious.

### EYESIGHT AND HEARING

It was always supposed that these functions were very much keener in natives than in Europeans; but experiment has proved that this is a mistake. It is true that a native can see game much more quickly than Europeans; because he knows what to look for. An English sailor can detect land on the horizon when a landsman can only see clouds; because the one is accustomed to look for it and knows by experience what it is like, while the other does not. When natives are tested by rigid experiment in matters with which they are not familiar they show slightly less acuteness than Europeans. When out hunting, a native detected a crocodile on the river bank, while I only saw what I thought to be greyish rocks; and when I shot at the seeming mass of rock, and saw it rise and plunge into the water, the native told me where my bullet hit the crocodile. As soon as I became accustomed to the appearance of a crocodile, the native was no longer superior

# The Essential Kafir

in this direction. A Bushman is so used to follow a spoor through the bush that he will tell that an animal has passed by that way recently, his judgment being based on the slightest bending of twigs or displacement of stones. He can do this in a most marvellous way as he runs along, simply because he has been trained at this special work all his life. The European is not trained to observe the slight indications that guide the native.

### CRUELTY AND SENSE OF PAIN

It is a trite saying that all savages are cruel; yet it is well-nigh impossible for highly civilised nations to judge the matter fairly. It is necessary that we should form some conception of the dull condition of their leathern nerves before we can estimate their sensation of pain, and so judge fairly concerning their cruelty. Natives vary greatly as to their sensitiveness to pain; yet on the whole they feel it far less acutely than we do. The strange thing is the way they seem sensitive to certain modes of pain and not to others. It reminds one of a photographic plate, which is far more sensitive to blue rays of light than to yellow, green, or red. Here is a native who had a corn on his toe. The pain irritated him so much that he went to borrow a chisel from a white man. Bringing this home in triumph, he called one of his wives and told her to give the chisel a good thump with a stone while he held it over the toe-joint. She objected to do so, and he calmly took up the stone and cut off the joint of the toe, and then looked quite satisfied with his work. That corn would never trouble him again! This case, which happened in Swazieland, presents a strange problem. Why should the pain of the corn seem so acute that the man preferred to suffer the pain of amputation rather than put up with the corn? The native will wince when he gets a friend to pull out a thorn from the thick pad

## Mental Characteristics

of skin which covers his hoof-like foot (see photograph on plate 39); yet he might bear a more gruesome operation with fortitude. In some such way, the elephant will pull up a tree by the roots to brush off a fly that settles on its thick hide, which a Martini-Henry bullet will not pierce. Manifestly it will not do to judge of native cruelty from the point of view of some sentimental girl who weeps over drowning flies. When we have made every allowance we can make, the fact remains that the native is callous to pain in others.

The man who can enjoy to the full his love of inflicting pain is the chief, for no one would dare to interfere with his pleasure. Chaka, that Napoleon of South Africa, is the centre of a thousand ghastly tales. He would kill people for the slightest offence. If a man sneezed in his presence he would instantly order the offender to be killed; if the relations showed any signs of sorrow they were killed also, for what right had they to show to the chief " a will most incorrect ? " People used to go to the doctors for bitter roots, which, they thought, drove sorrow away, lest they should mourn over the loss of friends. Chaka would without any compunction make men kill their own wives or brothers, or make women kill their babies. On one occasion he killed off all the old men of a kraal, saying that they were no use and only consumed food which might otherwise be eaten by his soldiers. He would even argue that this was a charitable thing to do, as the old men were no good for fighting. He was an apostle of evolutionary ethics. He told the relations of the people he was killing that he would now see whether they loved their kinsmen or their chief the better. We have already mentioned how at the death of his mother he wanted to kill every mother in Zululand, but was appeased when some seven thousand were slaughtered. His love for his mother was the one redeeming trait in this monster, though it led to such slaughter. If a man happened

## The Essential Kafir

to get his limb dislocated in a hunt, Chaka would merely grunt out that it showed what a useless fellow he was, and what poor limbs he had. He would then add, " I suppose that now you are an old woman I shall have to find a wife for you," the young active warriors not being allowed to marry. Chaka himself never married, though he had hundreds of girls whom he called "sisters." On one occasion somebody pointed out a child who was a son of Chaka's. He was furious at this true statement, and took the child up by its heels and dashed its brains out on a stone, and ordered the mother to be killed on the spot. When, in a buffalo hunt, men got trampled on and killed in the king's service, he would merely say that it was the best way to get rid of cowards. Yet this man raised up one of the most efficient armies the world has seen. If a regiment was beaten it was slaughtered on its return to the king's place. If any man lost his weapon in war, he was killed for cowardice. If the chief wanted to see what kind of weapons were most successful he would order a sham fight, in which real lives would be lost.

His brother and successor, Dingan, was a worthy follower in all cruelty practised by Chaka. He used to keep a magnifying glass, and for sheer fun would burn holes in the arms or flesh of his warriors. Cetewayo reduced many old punishments, and enacted that people should be killed for witchcraft only; other offences were to be punished by cutting out the eyes of the guilty persons, and a special knife and fork were kept for the purpose. Another chief, Panda, saw a man in a regiment with his hair a little too long, and ordered him to be slaughtered on the spot for that offence. In olden days a man would kill his own wife for no greater crime than cutting a small piece out of his blanket.

Lobengula, the late Matabele chief, whose power was broken by the Chartered Company, probably ran Chaka close

## Mental Characteristics

in the record for cruelty. Out of a thousand instances of his conduct let one suffice. A man drank of the king's beer. The chief called the man up and said, " Did those lips dare to touch the king's beer ? Then cut those lips off." The executioner speedily did so. Lobengula then said, " Did those ears not hear the king's order ? Then off with those ears." After this he repeated the same barbarity with the nose that dared to smell the king's beer, the eyes that dared to look on it, and the tongue that dared to touch it. Then the poor sightless wretch was turned out into the veldt and left to die.

The late Swazie king, Bunu, also was a fiend incarnate. He would say to a man, " Would you like to die ? " And the fellow would answer, " Yes, chief, if it be by your hands, or for your pleasure." Bunu would then have the fellow bound, and would give a packet of needles to one man and tell him to plunge them into the tenderest parts of the body ; he would give another man a packet of pins and get him to continue the process, all the time laughing at the poor wretch's torture. One packet of needles would be put into a man's legs, another into his arms, a third into his chest, and so on, till the man was riddled with needles ; and then, when the victim implored to be relieved of his misery, the king would get some one to dash his brains out with a knobkerrie. When he was tired of this sort of thing, he would take another man down to the water—well do I know the spot—and he would get his warriors to hold the man under the water till nearly dead. The man would then be taken out and allowed to revive, only to be again held under the water, while Bunu laughed at the bubbles of breath floating up through the water. He would even torture cattle in the most abominable ways, and impale men on thick sticks ; he would cut some men's throats and hang them up to the trees ; others he would have beaten to death with sticks, and even rip up women in sheer fiendishness.

# The Essential Kafir

Nevertheless, traders have turned to me and said that the natives are quite happy and well enough off without the interference of missionaries or Government!

This strain of cruelty comes out even in native evangelists, who grasp the aggressiveness of religion better than its lofty ideals. Even anthropoid apes could develop aggressiveness. In Swazieland an evangelist was preaching on the words "root and branch," and was describing in the most vivid colours how people would suffer if they did not "believe." "What does this verse mean?" he asked. "It means that God will take up you mothers and will burn you with fire for ever and ever; He will take up you old men, who are the roots, and He will burn you with fire for ever and ever; He will take your children, even the babes at the breasts, for they are the branches, and He will burn them with brimstone and fire for ever and ever; He will take up the babes which are only as old as my little baby, and He will cast them into the lake of fire. This is what He will do, if you women do not believe. How would you like this, you mothers?" &c. &c.

The missionary in charge heard of this affair, and, sending for the evangelist, asked him to account for his terrible sermon, saying that he did not find any such horrible doctrine in the Bible. "But I do," said the man with a cruelty like that of an aggressive anthropoid ape. "Where do you find it?" inquired the missionary. The excited native said, "Korah, Dathan, and Abiram." "But you cannot argue from that case in such a way," expostulated the missionary. "Yes: I can," said the native; "and my interpretation is as good as yours."

On another occasion a native convert, who had lost a leg in earlier days in a fight, asked his missionary if he would have two legs in the resurrection. The unsuspecting missionary said he supposed he would. "Then, that's all right," said the

Plate 44.

A GAZALAND GAME-TRAP.

Plate 45.

STRIPPING THE MEALIE FIELD.

## Mental Characteristics

fellow : "I shall be able to punch the head of the man who broke this leg of mine years ago."

After all, these latter instances are no worse than scenes which still are witnessed in Italy. As I was drafting this chapter I happened to read in a magazine the report of a Roman Catholic priest in Naples who wished to make his preaching about hell forcible, and so arranged stage lightning, and got people to clank chains, and groan and shriek, during his sermon. It is only fair to say that when this caused a panic the priest was rebuked by the authorities.

The natives have no shadow of idea that animals should be treated with kindness. They hardly seem to recognise the fact that they feel at all, far less that their feeling is any concern of ours. So they are often brutally cruel to animals.

### EMOTIONAL NATURE

The natives are very emotional under certain conditions : once the barriers have been removed a whole flood of excitement rushes forth. To see natives in the midst of an old-fashioned Wesleyan revival is a thing that can never be forgotten. It would rejoice the heart of a Cornish Wesleyan. The natives lie about the floor in heaps, crying, shouting, laughing, gesticulating, struggling, praying. All order is blown to the winds, and emotion runs riot. There is no holding the people in once they are in full gallop : they have to be left until the storm wears itself out. Eschatology is the one thing which appeals to their imagination, especially when the references to fire are vivid. They would rejoice in a Salvation Army after-meeting, provided the noise were plentiful. The result of this emotional tornado is frequently bad for the character of the people.

# The Essential Kafir

## SENTENTIOUS WISDOM

To understand the wisdom of a people, it is necessary to glance at their proverbs. Let me, therefore, give some native sayings which will illustrate this aspect of Kafir character. The proverbs are collected from many sources, the most valuable being taken from the pamphlet referred to in the Bibliography and from Casalis' *Les Bassoutos*. Some of the proverbs sprinkled through the pages of this book are gathered here so as to show their cumulative force.

" The last partridge to rise gets the most sticks thrown at it ": that it is to say, the last man to run in war is most likely to be killed.

" A stick has no kraal ": said of an irritable man who cannot obtain wives.

" The weasel has pride, the snake having gone out of its hole " : When the cat's away the mice will play.

" The buck has got out of the pot " : There's many a slip 'twixt the cup and the lip.

" He milks the cow in calf ": He tells a lie.

" You are big in the mouth ": You boast.

" Pots are made while the clay is in good condition ": Make hay while the sun shines.

" The cow licks the one that licks her ": Kindness brings its own reward.

" A chip killed an elephant ": Get out of harm's way.

" The potter eats out of a broken dish ": The shoemaker's children go worst shod.

" You have held a buffalo by the horn for me ": You have rendered great help.

" You begin with the meal before the water is boiled ": Do not count your chickens before they are hatched.

## Mental Characteristics

"I am a lopped tree": said in times of great disaster.

"The old corn is sprouting again": said when a ruined man gets a fresh start.

"Let the bottle of the ear be filled": Tell all; make full confession.

"Old mills are thrown away for new ones" (at the death of a chief the people destroy old grinding-stones): A new broom sweeps clean.

"He gathers firewood with centipedes in it": a threat to a meddlesome man.

"The cow eats its milker": Be sure your sin will find you out.

"A repetition will be by accident": Once bitten twice shy.

"I returned with only a feather": There's many a slip 'twixt the cup and the lip.

"It is better to turn the enemy back on the hill than to drive it out of the village": Prevention is better than cure.

"We are wandering in the belly of a bullock": Groping in the dark.

"A dog of the wind": a person with no settled home.

"It is the foot of a baboon": the sign of a treacherous person.

"You are creeping on your knees to the fireplace": said of a dangerous course of action.

"He weeps with one eye": He is insincere.

"I am with a head": I have a headache.

"You kindle a fire and leave it": You are a tale-bearer.

"The walls have come into collision": There is a dispute between great people.

"The heads being cut off, let us leave the rest": The main points being settled, let us proceed.

"One does not become great by claiming greatness."

# The Essential Kafir

" You are lighting a fire in the wind ": said of a person who favours strangers rather than his own people.

" The obstinate man will see by the bloodstain."

" No clever man ever licked his own back ": Do not try impossibilities.

" Clever men do not bargain with one another."

" The hut of a man who professes, but does not perform, leaks."

" He has a cockroach in his ear ": He is always in trouble.

" The eye crosses a full river ": Desire goes beyond the possible.

" We shall ask for it when it is cooked ": Events will prove.

" Height is not reached in a hurry."

" There is no beast that does not roar in its own den."

" The adhesive grass will cling to you ": said of bad habits.

" The well ahead is not to be depended on."

" The lion which kills is not the one that roars."

" He is a calf of the old cow ": A chip of the old block.

" There is blood in the dregs of the cup ": Too much beer drinking leads to quarrels.

" The point of the needle goes through first ": Attend to accuracy in small details, and do not try to evade the point by evasive words.

" All countries are frontiers ": Wherever you are you are exposed to danger ; said to grumblers.

" Water is never tired of running ": said to a person who talks too much.

" To-morrow will become the day after to-morrow ": said to procrastinators.

" The knife and the meat will never be friends ": a warning against adultery.

# Mental Characteristics

"Hunger is hidden under the sacks of corn": said to people who are vain about their wealth.

"Lions scold in eating": Grumblers are never happy.

"Harness is never tired": Travel has no ending.

"A thief catches himself": Murder will out.

"Stolen goods do not increase."

"Human blood is weighty."

"If a man has been killed secretly the grass of the field will say so."

"Anger is a warmth which lights itself."

"Right has no age."

"Quails nest in the garden of the lazy one."

"The lent knife never returns alone": One kind deed brings another.

"Death does not know kings."

"The most abundant sources can be slow in coming."

"Scarcity lives in the house of the quarreller."

"Two dogs will not let a fox escape": Unity is strength.

"Two mouths correct each other."

"The thief eats thunder"—attracts the lightning.

"The miser is a thief."

"A good name makes a person sleep well."

"The road is king": Do not hinder a traveller.

These proverbs show how sententious is the wisdom of the natives, and how very shrewd their thoughts are. The very maxims which are current in Europe are to be found among the Kafirs, though dressed up in different clothing. The Kafirs naturally express their thought in terms which are familiar to them; yet they do this with admirable brevity and force.

# WAR AND THE CHASE

Plate 46.

IN THE HARVEST FIELD.
Some Pondos are seen stripping the outer husk off the mealie cob.

A PONDO WOMAN WITH A BASKETFUL OF GRAIN.

# CHAPTER VIII

### WAR AND THE CHASE

## WAR

In all savage tribes war is the great occupation. On it the very existence of the tribe depends. Every able-bodied man has to take his place in the defence of the tribe, and this compulsory training is undoubtedly one of the causes of the fine physique of the native tribes. The weak must go to the wall, the "wall," of course, being their grave. If a large percentage of men fall in battle, there is all the more food for those who are left, and, what is as important in their eyes, the more wives. The influences which go to the development of the physique of the men tend to the destruction of the altruistic sentiment, and consequently the nation makes no progress through the centuries. Muscular energy rules the market, and intellectual and emotional qualities have no chance in the struggle.

No account of South African warriors would be complete without a rapid survey of the military system of Chaka, who was devastating South Africa at about the period in which Napoleon was filling Europe with bloodshed. It is calculated that he must have killed fully a million people in his wars, and there are still districts where the effect of wholesale slaughter is manifest.

Chaka, who is supposed by Grout to have been born about 1787, kept a force of about a hundred thousand men, half of

# The Essential Kafir

whom were always ready for an immediate call; he was troubled with no tardy War Office, with its red tape. There were no telegraphs, or war correspondents, or newspapers to become hysterical over his doings: so his iron, cruel, ruthless will was omnipotent all along the line. If a regiment disgraced itself he ordered no inquiry, but sent a veteran regiment to wipe it out, and he put all defeated soldiers and all cowards to death. To make the men come to close quarters, he abolished the long-throwing assegai, and substituted for it a short stabbing weapon; and if a man had the ill-luck to lose this in the fight he was promptly put to death. Chaka kept spies all over the whole country, and knew exactly how to attack every kraal of importance. Nothing was left to luck at the last moment. He divided his warriors into regiments, whereas before his time they fought in masses with little discipline or order. He kept the soldiers in special military towns which contained about a thousand huts, and some five thousand men were thus kept living together; they were fed on beer in the morning and on beef at night, all supplied by Chaka himself. No children were allowed in these towns, lest the men should grow soft-hearted. Warriors were forbidden to marry, for the same reason; but when they had served him for a long time, and had distinguished themselves, Chaka would give orders for a whole regiment to get married. However, his warriors were allowed concubines to any number, though these were placed under certain rigid restrictions when war was imminent.

The different regiments were dressed in varying styles. One would have a head-dress made of straw, somewhat in the shape of the hats worn by the Malays in Cape Town, and in the hats were placed some feathers. Another regiment would wear a cap made of otter-skin adorned with blue crane feathers. A third would have white shields; a fourth would have black shields; and a fifth would be called the Bees, and as they

## War and the Chase

went along the warpath the men forming it would make a noise like the buzzing of insects. The white regiment was formed of veterans, and these were allowed to have wives in times of peace. When the men went to war the wives would fasten up the mats and pillows of their husbands in the sunshine, and would tell by the length of the shadow whether their husbands were killed or not.

While the spies reported full information to a council of warriors, Chaka kept his plans to himself, and only informed the general selected for a special piece of service what the plan was, just as he was going off to the fight.

Many of these customs are still preserved in Swazieland, and close to the king's kraal there are huge stacks of grain for feeding the army.

I have seen the Swazie impi, or army, on parade, and met them when holding a sham fight. The sight was too impressive ever to be forgotten. The men were dressed in special colours, the shields of one regiment being made from the hide of brown cattle, another from black, a third from black and white. The warriors wore long rings of hide of the same colour over their shoulders. These masses of men raced over the ground with earthshaking tread, chanting a war-song as they ran. They came along like a whirlwind, dancing up in the air at certain parts of the chant, and then stopping to spear, in imagination, some down-trodden foe, every man plunging his assegai at the ground with a great whir; they would restab the imaginary foe again and again. It was not a case of "thrice he slew the slain"; they did it a dozen times, bragging loudly of their prowess and bravery. Whir, Whir, went the assegais, accompanied by a similar sound from a thousand deep-throated voices; then all would jump in the air and yell, and stab at the fallen foe again. Having finished this histrionic performance, they continued their journey, and the noise of

## The Essential Kafir

their tramping ranks sounded like some "deep multitudinous murmur that swells from the soul of the seas." The impression left on one's mind was that of overwhelming, irresistible force sweeping over the veldt, and tramping out every living thing on its surface. It seemed as if nothing could withstand that whirlwind of fury. Yet if a rabbit ran out in front of this huge force, or if a calf did something unusual, the whole army would be filled with fear at the bad omen, and refuse to fight that day. After all, mind is ten times more powerful than muscle.

Every kind of deceit and treachery was practised by Chaka, whose all-devouring ambition and cruelty knew no bounds. He would promise quarter to besieged men and ruthlessly slay them all in cold blood when they surrendered. Lichtenstein describes how that in ancient days it was considered degrading to take a mean advantage over an enemy. He says that if one army was not quite ready for the fight the other would chivalrously wait till it suited their convenience to receive the attack; that it was thought mean to capture all the cattle of a defeated foe, for they would starve under these conditions. He says that women and children were never killed. Where he got these ideas from it is hard to tell: if these customs ever existed it must have been very long ago, for natives consider anything fair in war. Chaka would wait until his foe could be taken at a disadvantage, and would slaughter every man, woman, and child if he wished; he would stoop to any depth of treachery, and generosity never seemed to loom above the horizon of his mind.

Some tribes used to accustom themselves to live on raw meat. They would creep up to a kraal and hide in the long grass, eating uncooked meat, so as not to betray their presence by the smoke of fires; and at night they would creep into the kraals as soon as they thought the inmates were asleep, and a few men would stand at the door of each hut, while others went behind and set fire to the huts. The frightened people had to

Plate 48.

A ZULU WOMAN THRESHING KAFIR CORN.
The baby on her back enjoying the motion.

Plate 49.

A PONDO WOMAN WINNOWING THE CORN.

## War and the Chase

creep out through the low doors of their huts on their hands and knees, and in this defenceless position the warriors would kill each person as he came out of the burning hut—not a very generous mode of attack!

But no impi could fight unless it had been properly doctored previously. This operation raised the boldness of the natives to a high temperature.

The war doctor was the national priest, and to disobey his orders was to declare oneself a wizard; the punishment came hot upon the heels of such a crime, and the man's whole kraal would be "smelt out" and burnt for the offence. All his relations also would be put to death. So many are the various modes of doctoring the army that one despairs of reducing them to anything like order. To start with, the warriors would be put on a general course of purgatives and emetics, to expel from their systems anything injurious to the future operations of the doctor. Then, if any things belonging to the enemy could be obtained by stealth, these articles would be doctored so as to injure the enemy. Great delight would be felt if some of the blanket of the opposing chief, or some paring of his nails, or some article which had been in contact with his body, could be stolen. It is possible to "work" on such things and deprive the man of intelligence and power.

The doctor concocts ointments which render the body invulnerable or invisible. He makes a small fire, and throws roots and medicines into it, and the warriors have to step through the smoke, in order that they may render themselves invisible to the enemy. The assegais also have to be held in this smoke, that they may be invisible to the enemy, and so prevent his dodging them.

When war is imminent this general doctoring gives way to very special ceremonies. The warriors are summoned by the chief, and stand round him in a large circle. The doctor then takes a huge calabash and places medicines in it ; with the tail of a gnu, or ox, the doctor sprinkles the people with the decoction, and after this ceremony warriors may not on any account live with their wives till after the fight. If they did their eyes would "become dark," and they would be surely slain in battle. The warriors have to eat portions of wild animals, so as to assimilate their qualities: lion's heart, tiger's blood, and other things are taken to give the warriors sagacity, swiftness, boldness, agility, and so forth. The chief then harangues the people, telling them to be brave and face the enemy, and adds that if any of them return with wounds in their backs they will find their own chief become their enemy.

But before the army can start out the doctor "trains the mind." He chooses a black ox, which the warriors have to throw down by sheer force. One of its shoulders is then cut off while the animal is alive, and long strips of this are roasted over a fire, and mixed with bitter roots. Every man has to eat a portion of this sickening mess, and if he spits it out he is instantly killed, as he gives power to the enemy by so doing. The doctor then makes incisions in the flesh of the men and rubs the medicated meat into the wounds. The ox is chased about until it is dead, and the longer it takes to die the better for the luck of the army. When it is dead it is cut up and roasted. The doctor blows the sparks of the fire at the warriors, to "doctor" them. The bones are burnt, and no woman is allowed on any account to touch the meat of the ox ; in fact, the women have to keep at a long distance, except a few old ones who have long passed the age of childbearing; they are allowed to go where they like. Men who have recently been married are often sent back to their homes, and are told not to fight until after the birth of their first child. This is partly to keep the family alive, and partly because men who are just

# War and the Chase

married are supposed to be tender-hearted, and therefore a hindrance to the army.

The ancestral spirits are interceded with, and begged to help in the war; indeed, many natives seem to think that there is far more real warfare among the ancestral spirits of the rival armies than among the actual warriors. It has been pointed out previously that these ancestral spirits are sometimes supposed to be fighting in the air just above the heads of the people, and if only the warriors can be persuaded that their ancestral spirits are with them they will fight with immense bravery and confidence. At the end of the ceremony of doctoring the army, the men all dance up into the air with yells, brandishing their weapons, declaring how well they will fight. They rush up to the chief, whom they are allowed on this occasion to jeer at, and they flauntingly boast that he will soon hear of the marvellous prodigies they are about to perform, and if not—if they are defeated—then they devote their heads, their possessions, their kraal, to the chief, who may do as he pleases with them. Thus men devote whole villages to the chief on such occasions. They will break rods in the face of the chief, which action is a form of oath; if they are defeated after this, the chief may treat them as he wishes. During the various parts of these ceremonies, which may be spread over many days, the men have to fast in the bush, so as to get into fighting trim; and one of the last ceremonies is performed by the chief when the whole impi, or army, is ready to start.

The doctor brings out the chief's calabash, which contains special medicines. These are then churned up. If the mixture froths over it is a sign that one side will be victorious; if it does not froth over it shows that the other side will be victorious. Or else there may be two calabashes selected, which represent the two sides. Whichever calabash froths over first decides which army will be victorious. If the vessel which represents

# The Essential Kafir

the chief froths over first, then the omen is good. If the omen is bad the army is kept waiting, and all the ceremonies may have to be repeated. They would not dream of going to war if the omens were unfavourable. Sometimes the diviner places two sticks in the ground, and these are made to represent the contending sides. If the wind blows over the stick which represents the enemy, then the omen is excellent. Practices such as these are performed by many tribes in different parts of the world. Thus, the Maoris are said to adopt the very same method of divining the success of a projected war.

But it is not only the soldier who has to be doctored. The chief has to undergo a long course of doctoring to enable him to overcome the enemy. He selects medicines, called Intelezi, made from different plants which are supposed to have magical properties; he takes these to a river and pounds them up with a small stone till he expresses some of the juices. He holds the medicines above his head, and allows the juices to trickle down his arms and over his body. He takes some of the juices in his mouth, and spits them in the direction of his enemy. The chief thus wards off the evil magic, and turns the scales on his enemy. When he has washed himself thus, he takes a vessel and churns medicines in it, saying to himself all the time, " Now I am overcoming my enemy ; I have overcome him, in fact ; he is here in my vessel ; he is vanquished ; I am treading on him ; I am conquering him just now ; in fact, he is killed already by my magic ; I can see this by the churning of my vessel." If the chief can manage to get possession of anything belonging to the enemy, he places this substance in his vessel, believing that thus he controls his enemy most forcibly. (For other details, the reader should consult Callaway's " Religious System of the Amazulu.")

When all is ready, and the omens are good, the warriors are painted with a little red ochre over their eyebrows, and

## War and the Chase

the advance is ordered. But should any unlucky omen be observed by the priests or doctors who accompany the army, the expedition is deferred. The natives fight with the most marvellous bravery when they are assured by their doctors that success is certain; in fact, everything turns on the sense of impending victory, for the natives lose heart quickly in a forlorn hope. They are either stupidly and magnificently brave or ridiculously timid and fearful. They do everything in superlatives.

When the war is over the defeated chief is brought home in triumph by the soldiers. The victorious chief calls in a doctor, that he may strengthen himself to meet the conquered chief, who is, however, being brought home bound. Yet, though he is bound, his medicines and magic may overcome the victorious chief and make it impossible for him to face his defeated foe. Nothing can be done without doctoring. When the defeated chief is within striking distance the victorious chief leaps in the air and stabs and restabs the poor wretched man, thus showing his prowess. If the defeated chief was conspicuous for bravery certain portions of his body are cut out and made into medicine, and these are said to give the chief kingly qualities. The chief chars certain portions of the dead man's body and eats them out of his fingers. As he is eating the human flesh he stops now and then to spit out portions of the flesh in the direction of his enemies. The head of the slain chief is kept and made into a vessel to hold the medicines of the victorious chief, for to keep medicines in a skull increases their effectiveness.

Warriors who are wounded have, in certain tribes, to undergo a course of cleansing, and so do those who have killed men during the fight. They may not see the king or drink any milk until they are doctored. An ox is taken, and the intestines, gall, and other portions, are boiled with roots. The

## The Essential Kafir

wounded men have to take three gulps of this nauseous decoction, and are told with unconscious humour not to take too much. The rest of the medicine is sprinkled on their bodies. The wounded man has then to take a stick, spit on it three times, and point it at the enemy, saying "Eczie" three times; he then throws it in the direction of the enemy. After this he takes an emetic and is declared clean.

In Bechuanaland, after a fight, the men who have killed people during the war have to go to the chief's village, each bringing with him a portion of the skin of the man he has killed. The part selected is the navel, with some skin adjoining it; these portions of skin act as a passport, without which no warrior is allowed into the cattle kraal. The doctor takes an assegai and makes a gash in every man's thigh, one gash being made for every man he has killed. This mark is coveted as much as the Victoria Cross. After this performance the men have to eat the portions of skin they have taken from their enemy.

There are a thousand and one other ceremonies connected with war, every tribe having its special customs in this connection; but the above account will suffice to show the spirit of the thing.

Many other ceremonies are used to prognosticate success or failure. For example, two sheep are skinned alive, and they are made to represent the contending armies; the sheep which lives the longer indicates the side on which victory is about to rest.

Hostile armies are also kept at a distance by magic, which, however, only acts on the defensive. Thus, the Bechuana tribes take a black bull once a year, sew up its eyelids, and let it wander about for three days; then they kill it and eat the flesh. The gall is made into medicine with some roots and herbs—the bodies of twins being specially useful in this direc-

## War and the Chase

tion—and the mixture is smeared on poles which are planted in the ground. A bladder and a horn are filled with the mixture, and suspended from poles likewise. No enemy is supposed to be able to come near the poles, and all magic of evil-wishers is counteracted and turned back on the heads of those using the black arts.

### THE CHASE

The sporting instinct is well developed among the Kafirs. One of the very first things the small boys learn to do is to set bird-traps. Here is a photograph of some small Zulu boys near Lake St. Lucia (plate 43). Look at these boys : are they not perfect little animals rejoicing in the lust of killing ? The traps are made with great simplicity and efficiency. A dozen small pieces of reed are stuck in the ground in a circle, and their ends are all collected at the top, so as to make a small cage of the shape of a bell-tent. Some grain is placed on the ground in the midst of these pieces of reed, and at one side a small opening is made, so that the bird cannot get the grain without putting its head through a noose, made from a hair of a cow's tail. The noose is so lax that the bird can easily push its head through ; but the moment it withdraws its head the slip-knot tightens, and the bird is securely caught. These boys hide at a distance, having thrown down some grain as bait to allure the birds to the traps; and as soon as a bird is caught they run up and kill it and eat it, either raw or slightly cooked over the fire. Of course, they eat feathers, entrails, and all : these things are too good to be wasted, and improve the flavour.

When the boys grow up a little they are taught to use the knobkerrie (or bow and arrow, if that weapon is used by their tribe). The Bushmen poison the tips of their arrows, using various substances, such as snake poison, caterpillar juice, and

## The Essential Kafir

poisonous roots. The puny arrows made from reeds are thus converted into deadly weapons. Some tribes kill animals by placing poison in the pools at which the animals drink. The Euphorbia plant supplies a juice which will kill zebra but not other animals. In the mountains of Basutoland the natives put certain roots into the pools, and the effect is to make the fish silly, when they can easily be caught ; but most native tribes refuse to eat fish, the Tongas being a noted exception. The children are taught how to make game-pits, which are made of a conical shape in order that the animal which falls into the pit may get its legs so caught that it will be unable to get out again. A stake, or pile, is placed in the middle of the pit if the elephant or rhinoceros is to be caught. The natives surround the captured animals and seek to kill them with assegais, sometimes as many as a thousand being used to kill an elephant. Old travellers declare that lions have been seen to come to the rescue of some luckless member of their species which has fallen into the pit, dragging it out by the mane, the theory being that they learned this plan by stealing buck out of the pits in a similar fashion.

In travelling through the country north of Delagoa Bay one frequently comes across an artificial hedge made of thornbush, which runs for many miles over the country. Every here and there an opening is made, and a heavy branch of a tree is placed so that it must fall down and crush the animal that touches a small lever. Here is a photograph of one of the game-traps : this type of trap is common above the Zambesi. (See plate 44.) Sometimes the game are driven up against this artificial hedge, and naturally run along until they find an opening. Large holes are often made in the ground at such points, and covered over with twigs and leaves. In this way hundreds of buck fall into the snare, and the natives have an enormous feast for days.

## War and the Chase

The Bushmen are, however, the kings of hunting; they make their home where the game has been killed, and the mothers run along after the hunters, following their spoor, and bringing up the babies and the movable furniture. The Bushmen will run for days after game, covering incredible distances, and then, when they kill the quarry, they feed till all the meat has gone, after which they sleep till the pangs of hunger force them to get up and hunt once more. The Bushmen dress themselves up in the skins of ostriches, and, thus concealed, walk up to a group of these birds and suddenly throw off their disguise and shoot the ostriches with their poisoned arrows. The skill which Bushmen show in stalking game and in imitating animals is marvellous: they can mimic every animal they know, and will spend a whole day in stalking a large buck. The Bushman is most particular not to allow his shadow to fall on the dead game, as he thinks this would bring bad luck; and he discards an arrow that has missed the mark, while he almost venerates one that has been successful. The arrows are small flimsy things, and the shooting is not at all accurate: but Bushmen stalk the game so well that they rarely miss, for they come to very close quarters. They will often offer up a little meat as an offering to the spirits before they eat, and can manage to swallow and digest meat that is utterly putrid: it has no ill effect on them, for they have become immune to ptomaines.

As soon as the small boys show efficiency in throwing the kerrie—which is a heavy stick with a huge knob of wood at one end—they are allowed to help in the outskirts of a proper hunt. The way these small boys throw the kerrie is marvellous. I have seen them knock flying birds over at forty or fifty yards; and, in fact, they can do far more damage with their kerrie than an average English schoolboy can with a catapult. That amateur weapon was, in my schooldays,

## The Essential Kafir

very good for breaking windows and for missing birds. But a Kafir boy becomes very expert at hitting birds even when on the wing. Natives often break the leg of a buck with one of the kerries, and after that it is easy work to catch the wounded game. When boys wish to shoot small birds with arrows, they put a wooden knob on the point of their arrow, and so the bird is not broken to pieces, but simply stunned.

Any kind of wild animal awakens the sporting instinct of a Kafir, and it is very amusing to see how cannily natives set to work to catch a crocodile. Here is a quaint account of the process given in " Pinkerton's Voyages," a book long out of print.

When the natives want to catch crocodiles " they prepare a piece of wood two feet in length, and of tolerable breadth; lengthwise, through this, a hole is bored for a cord to pass, at the extremity of which is a large hook baited with fresh meat; this they cast into the river. Soon as the crocodile perceives the meat, it immediately swallows it, and, fancying that all it sees is of the same nature, endeavours to seize on the wood also; but this, sticking in its maw, prevents the jaws closing, when the water, rushing without impediment down its throat, drowns the animal. The fishermen, when they perceive it at the last extremity, draw it on shore and despatch it with clubs. The Caffres notice when the animal is being killed that it groans and cries like a reasoning being, whence doubtless the proverb of 'crocodile tears' to express a forced lamentation." The writer continues, and gives a delightful account of a mermaid, thus :

" At a distance of fifteen leagues from Sofala, among the islands Boccias, a fish is found, denominated by the islanders the *mermaid*, or *woman fish*, the flesh of which is of excellent flavour when eaten boiled like other meat, and which also serves to make highly savoury sausages. From the waist to the neck this fish much resembles the human species; the

## War and the Chase

females suckle their young in the same manner as women, but the fish has neither arms nor hands, and as to its features, they bear not the slightest resemblance to those of the human countenance; but its head is rather like that of a maid or thornback, and its mouth full of teeth like that of a dog, but with four of them projecting the length of a foot in the same manner as the tusks of a boar. These teeth have the property of staying a flux of blood, and softening the painful sensations which attend the piles. The proof of it is easy, and the remedy common : all that is requisite is to wear them near that part of the body where the pain is felt. This fish originated the fable of the Syrens in the works of the poets ; but they gave by far too great loose to their imagination when they attributed to it a long head of hair, a hairy body, a human face, and a voice so musical as to enchant mariners ; for this sea monster has neither hair on the body nor the head; its head is monstrous, and nothing resembles the human countenance : and as to singing, it neither sings nor speaks, being, like every other fish, condemned to eternal silence." (See " Pinkerton's Voyages," vol. xvi. p. 700.)

But the great event is a true tribal hunt, in which the chief decides to surround a large area of country and drive the game found therein to a common centre. The descriptions given by Dos Santos in the seventeenth century are exactly equivalent to the customs still in force in Zululand.

Standing near a kraal in the St. Lucia district, I noticed two boys who were about sixteen years old. They had certain red circular patches on their arms, and on being asked what that signified the natives said that the boys were sent by the chief to give notice of a great hunt to be held two days later. The marks were official badges to show that the boys had been sent by the chief. Every able-bodied man had to come to the hunt when called thus.

# The Essential Kafir

On the day of the hunt some natives dressed up as animals and crawled about before the chief in imitation of the animals to be hunted.

At the first blush of dawn there was an ominous sound of natives assembling in the neighbourhood, and very many dogs were to be seen lurking about. They knew what was coming, being kept half-starved so as to ensure their keenness in hunting.

Crowds of natives could be seen wending their way, single file, along the Kafir footpaths, all tending in the direction of the chief's kraal. Every one was well smeared with fat, to make his body lissome and active, and the odour did not improve matters. Surrounded by his chief indunas, the chief was sitting in his hut, waiting to receive the hunters, who came up in families to the different gates of the kraal. All were yelling and dancing in great excitement. The doctor was present, looking very important: on him more than on any one depended the fortunes of the day—at least, so the natives thought. There was furious barking and counter-barking of dogs as family after family came up, and a plentiful supply of oaths and shouts followed, with not a few blows to silence the dogs.

The chief then walked out into the centre of the kraal, and one batch of natives received the word to pass in. They burst into the cattle kraal like a tidal wave, and tore round it howling and yelling, and gesticulating with intense energy. They carried on these grotesque antics, every man boasting of his own wonderful prowess and swiftness in running, until the chief asked, in pretended ignorance, who those fine fellows might be. He affected to be quite delighted when he heard their names, and praised them up as the finest specimens of humanity he had ever seen. He flattered the people inordinately, and then the huntsmen all greeted the chief and brandished their assegais, stabbing scores of imaginary buck, and boasting of the marvellous

## War and the Chase

feats they were about to perform during the hunt. When they had let off all their superfluous steam they sat down in a crescent near the chief, while the next batch of men was admitted. These men tried to outdo the performances and boasting of the predecessors, and were in turn complimented by the chief, who pretended at first not to know who such extremely swift, agile, manly fellows could be.

When all the various parties had been introduced to the chief, he retired with his headmen and decided what part of the country should be surrounded. These men know every shrub in the district, and map out, with words, the area to be surrounded, and apportion every man to his exact spot behind this or that shrub. Sometimes an enormous area is surrounded, and all the game are driven to the middle.

As soon as the chief had settled the details, a sign was given, and the whole crowd of huntsmen—perhaps five hundred or more—tore as fast as they could to the gates of the kraal shouting, "Bo, Bo, Bo, Bo, Bo, Bo!" This was done so suddenly that it almost resembled an explosion. The whole crowd tore off at a furious rate to a tree about half a mile away. Then they began to strip off its bark, which is very bitter, and to chew portions, spitting out the substance in all directions with explosive sounds. This bark is supposed to strengthen the wind of the runners, and to ward off evil practices enemies may be using to bewitch them. When they were quite satisfied that the spitting out of the bark had been thoroughly done, they formed into a large circle. The doctor knelt on the ground, and mumbled out a prayer to the ancestral spirits, especially to those who were renowned for hunting when on earth. The people all grunted assent to the sentiment of the prayer. The chief then walked out before the people, and pointed his assegai (he uses a gun if he happens to have one) down to the ground; and simultaneously the whole

# The Essential Kafir

five hundred men stabbed the ground in front of them with their assegais, making a very loud hurricane of noise and fury, for they added to the sound of the quivering assegais a tremendous shouting of "Whir-r-r-r-r-r-h, whir-r-r-r-r-h!" After this the chief explained the portion of country to be surrounded, and entered into the most minute particulars and details, telling each man what he had to do. The crowd dispersed at a hundred tangents, shouting, screaming, gesticulating.

Mile upon mile of country was surrounded, and every bush was searched, and the buck * were driven out. Slowly, amid much shouting, the circle grew smaller, and the buck took refuge in fresh clumps of thorn-bush. But the hunters rushed about as if they were mad, and the dogs shared in the excitement.

I have seen two men give chase to a buck in mountainous country in Swazieland, and without any dog they chased the animal, and, after the most marvellous exhibition of running I have witnessed, they actually caught the buck alive. It is quite impossible to describe the activity of a native when his whole heart is in his business. Yet some anthropologists say that Kafirs cannot run, and then invent a reason. These men simply flew like the wind up steep mountains, and down over broken rocks, as if they had been gazelles.

As the circle of the hunters slowly narrowed, the buck ran about in terror, and when the circle was very small they rushed right on to the assegais, or even up to the muzzles of the guns, with their tongues hanging out of their mouths. One could see terror and desperation in the faces of the poor creatures, which had no chance of escape. In a silly, dazed way, they ran from side to side of the small circle, or right past the chief, who was placed in the centre, and shot with his gun at the

* The word, thus used, will sound absurd to British sportsmen. In South Africa wild animals of certain species are classed as "buck," without regard to sex.

## War and the Chase

animals when they were only a few yards off. He took no trouble to aim, but fired away into a mass composed of fifty buck, which were mixed up with struggling, shouting, sweating men, who might get shot for all they or the chief cared, so excited were they. The graceful buck impaled themselves on assegais, and fell dead or dying. I never saw such an utterly disgusting sight in all my life, and had to turn away with a sense of nausea. I had been trained years before to stand any sight the hospitals can afford, and thought I should never feel sick again at the sight of pain; but to see these graceful buck running, dazed, stupefied, and dead-beat, right up to the muzzles of the guns, or impaling themselves on assegais, was too much for me.

As soon as any man wounded a buck, he carried it up to the chief, threw it down before his feet, and claimed it as his. Any one wishing to dispute the matter had to come and state his case, and the chief's word was final.

The theory is that the man who inflicts the first wound has the right to the animal; but if some one comes to his help, or lends his dog to help, he may claim a leg of the animal. It frequently happens that a poor fellow half kills a buck, and as it is dying a dozen men stab it with their assegais, or set their dogs on it, and each of the twelve claims a leg! If a man kills a buck outright, he places it on his head and rushes up to the chief regardless of any guns which may be pointing in his direction, and claims it as his. Some rascals wait till every one is occupied, and then steal wounded buck, and hide them in the bush, going afterwards to carry them home as trophies of their skill and prowess.

If the first hunt proves a failure, and only a few beasts are caught, the doctor again prays for good luck, and the whole operation is repeated. At the close of the day's hunting the natives gather round the chief, carrying the buck they have killed, and each section dances once more, even after running, possibly, some forty miles since dawn. They surround the chief with terrible enthusiasm, shouting, sweating, and gesticulating ; many of them are stark naked, for every rag has been torn to shreds in the bush. They tell the chief how many head they have killed, and return home chanting a song, which is all about meat from beginning to end. As they come to the kraal they begin to blow their own trumpet with egregious brazenfacedness. The women have large fires ready for their returning husbands, and far into the night there is a royal feast, the men gorging till they can eat no more. There is no end to the talk about the hunt ; and the chief, for days to come, is flattered in the most fulsome way as to his wonderful shooting. But what can a chief do that is not worthy of endless praise ?

And these perspiring, shouting, dancing natives, who run their forty miles, are said by white men to be lazy !

Plate 50.

A PONDO WOMAN GRINDING MEALIES.

Plate 51.

A NATIVE BLACKSMITH ON THE ZAMBESI.

# ARTS OF PEACE AND DOMESTIC MATTERS

# CHAPTER IX

### ARTS OF PEACE AND DOMESTIC MATTERS

AGRICULTURE is mainly the work of the women, for in olden days the men were occupied in hunting and fighting. The women do but scratch the land with hoes, sometimes using long-handled instruments, as in Zululand, and sometimes short-handled ones, as above the Zambesi. When the ground is thus prepared, the women scatter the seed, throwing it over the soil quite at random. They know the time to sow by the position of the constellations, chiefly by that of the Pleiades. (They date their new year from the time they can see this constellation just before sunrise.) The staple foods grown consist of mealies (Indian corn) and Kafir corn, which is a small round russet-coloured grain about the size of hempseed. Kafir corn is the special grain used in making beer, though other grains are used when that is unobtainable.

A good many other vegetables are grown. In nearly every mealie field the natives rear pumpkins, which reach an enormous size, as well as sweet potatoes, of which there are at least four varieties, red, white, pink, and brown. Gourds, beans, yams, sugar-cane, sweet reed, and poco are grown, and in Zulu kraals pineapples are frequently to be seen near Lake St. Lucia. There is also a waxy sort of potato called amadumbe, which seems to be made of a specially tough kind of guttapercha, so fearfully solid and indigestible is it; yet a native thinks it digestible. Occasionally the natives grow lemons, limes, bananas, and melons, as well as tomatoes, though

## The Essential Kafir

they pay no attention to these things, but accept them when they grow at their doors. Rice is cultivated on the Zambesi, and tobacco in nearly every kraal in South Africa. The old men cure the tobacco in a rough and ready way, and often grind it up, with the ash of the aloe, to make snuff. Dacca, (Indian hemp) grows wild, and is smoked.

Gardens were not allowed near a great chief's kraal in olden days: it was supposed to be beneath the dignity of his oxen to be herded and kept out of gardens.

The weeding is done by the women; but birds are driven away from the crops by the girls and small boys. For this purpose, a booth (pempe) is erected in the fields or on some elevated ground, and the children spend the day in it, shouting at the birds, or throwing stones at them. Sometimes the pempes are two-storied, and the children have grand times as they are watching the birds. If the boys can manage to get some matches it is a good thing for them, but a bad thing for the grass. It is amusing to notice how grass fires abound when a white man travels through a country purchasing eggs from the boys with matches.

The fields are frequently doctored in order to make them fertile. In Bechuanaland it used to be the custom to select a man, who was promptly made drunk. He was then killed and his blood burnt with his body, the ashes being sprinkled on the fields to make them fertile. In the Basuto mountains I once saw the natives pour beer into the edge of the field to propitiate the ancestral spirits, and to put them in a good humour. In other tribes the doctors light fires at the edges of the fields, and place charms in them, believing that the smoke will ward off blight. Some of these customs are said to be relics of ancient sun-charms; but the natives have lost all such definite ideas.

The gathering-in of the harvest is a great event, and all

## Arts of Peace and Domestic Matters

hands are "in-spanned" for it. The mealie cobs are piled on the ground, and the natives sit down in the sunshine and strip off the white outer sheath. The effect in the sunshine is very dazzling, for the sheaths are snow-white; and the contrast with the dark chocolate colour of the natives is shown up to great advantage. In the photographs all the charm of colour is, of course, lost (see plate 46). The mealies are stripped from the cob and placed in the mealie pits, which are excavations in the ground of the cattle kraal. The fluids from the cattle kraal percolate into the ground and turn the grain sour, which prevents the weevil from attacking it. The flavour of mealies taken from one of the pits is too disgusting for words; yet the natives like it. Sometimes the grain is stored in large huts either inside or just outside the kraal.

When the Kafir corn is to be threshed, the women place it while still on the stalk on a portion of ground which has been well smeared with cowdung to make the surface hard and clean. They then bruise it with sticks, an operation in which the men sometimes help. When the crop is very large the Kafir corn is placed, while still on the stalks, on a large piece of ground which has been specially cleared, and oxen are turned on to the mass, and hunted round till all the corn is threshed. Then the grain is collected and winnowed by the women, who pour it from one basket to another, the wind blowing away the lighter chaff and dirt. A good deal of grit and dirt still remains mixed up with the grain; but so much the better—it swells the quantity and adds to the flavour. The women often beat out the grain with a baby strapped on their backs. Indeed, a baby will be noticed in nearly all the photographs connected with the work of women. In no case have the natives been "made up" for the photographs.

When the women wish to grind corn for beer or for mealie porridge, they take a large stone which has been scooped out

# The Essential Kafir

into a hollow shape by ages of use; the grain is placed in this hollow, and a little water is sprinkled on it by flicking the damp fingers; then a small round stone is held in the hands, and used in very much the same way that a European cook manipulates a rolling-pin; the grain is thus ground, and when it is considered fine enough it is pushed out in front on to a dirty grass mat, and then collected. There is so much small stone grit in the grain that it frequently makes Europeans dangerously ill; but the cast-iron insides of the natives do not object to it at all. (See plates 45-50).

The natives are not very particular about cooking their food. If we may judge by the folklore of the people in prehistoric ages, they used to cook by means of hot stones. This plan is not now practised. Meat is often roughly roasted over the ashes, or else boiled in a pot. "Mealie pap" is made by stirring the meal into a large pot of boiling water, any dirty old piece of stick that is at hand being used as a spoon. As soon as the meal is well mixed with the water, the lid is placed on the pot, a small space being left to allow the steam to escape, and the whole pot is left severely alone. The result is that a thick crust of porridge burns at the bottom of the pot, and suffuses a faint flavour of burning through the mass. The porridge is not stirred again, or the flavour would be too strong. When the food is cooked it is turned out on a wooden dish and eaten from the fingers. The burnt crust at the bottom of the pot is a great delicacy. It serves as dessert, liqueur, and coffee all combined.

Sometimes the natives roast the mealies on the cob, especially when they are young and tender. This is a favourite dish of many Europeans, who, however, usually boil the mealies. It forms the famous dish known as "green mealies."

When beer is to be made the women place some Kafir corn in water till it sprouts; they then dry and grind it up, mixing

## Arts of Peace and Domestic Matters

it in huge calabashes with water. In some districts the natives add ferments extracted from the roots of certain plants, to help the brewing. The result of the operation is a thin, dirty, nauseous, watery gruel which serves for both food and drink. The natives can absorb the most prodigious quantities of this stuff; but, after drinking for a day and a half without any needless intervals, they are apt to become very quarrelsome. They sometimes drink till they can hold no more, and then lie out in the sun to get rid of the liquid by perspiration, when they set to work once more. This process may be kept up for days together. Beer drinks are equivalent to our garden-parties and other social ceremonies all rolled into one.

No one need wait to be invited to a beer drink unless he happens to be some great personage. In that case he would expect a special invitation to be sent to him. People passing through the country all gravitate to these great drinks. The women bring out huge pots holding immense quantities of beer. A small calabash and a skimmer is supplied, and one man blows or skims off the scum and takes out a small dishful of beer, and after drinking his fill passes the pot on to the next man. In olden days it was customary for the host to drink some beer first, to show that it was not poisoned. If the pot is not too large to drink from directly, the natives take long draughts out of it, and this plan has the manifest advantage that no one knows quite how much is taken at a time.

When the men get quarrelsome tribal fights begin, and broken heads are sure to be the result. It is surprisingly difficult to break a Kafir's skull. I have seen natives fight with heavy knobkerries, and hit one another as hard as they could on the skull; but they did not seem to feel it much. It is a sort of scratching of the head which is not unpleasant, apparently, though the blood flows freely.

The result of a beer drink is that the people have a famous

appetite for beef, which they will consume in large quantities when the beer is finished.

Next to beer the favourite beverage is sour milk, which is wholesome, though the natives can drink it in a state of sourness that would make a white man wince were he to taste it.

## MANUFACTURES

The natives used to be able to work in iron in a very creditable fashion; but since traders have opened stores they do very little of this work. Above the Zambesi a great many smiths are still to be met with, and their work is very good. The apparatus used is of the simplest nature, the bellows consisting of the skin of a goat, while the stone-tipped horn of an ox serves as the blast, which feeds a charcoal fire placed in a hollow stone. The anvil consists of a hard stone, and the hammer is frequently made of iron. The natives on the Zambesi turn out very fair silver and gold work, which trades they learned from Jesuit missionaries in past centuries. They make good leather articles.

Pillows are made in all parts of South Africa by cutting blocks of wood with knives bought from traders, these pillows being carved in fantastic shapes. Mats for sleeping on are made from grass or thin reeds. The women make a rude kind of pottery which stands the heat of the fire very well. The pots are made in immense sizes, and then baked in hot earth. The natives derive several proverbs from this art, saying, " The potter eats out of a broken dish," a proverb equivalent to our own which declares that a shoemaker's children go worst shod. They also say, " Pots are made when the clay is in good condition," which is equivalent to our proverb about making hay while the sun shines. A Kafir would never express such proverbs in our way; for in that

# Arts of Peace and Domestic Matters

sunny country when does the sun not shine, and who needs to wear boots? The men frequently carve milk-pails out of solid blocks of wood, and make dishes in the same way. Some of the articles are very well carved, and, as specimens can be seen in nearly every museum, photographs are not needed to show what they are like. String is made from grass, and also from bark of a certain tree, which the natives cut into strips and chew; after doing this, they twist the strands by rubbing them along the outside of the thigh with the edge of their hand. This string or rope is extremely strong. Above the Zambesi the natives spin a little of the cotton which grows wild.

### DOMESTIC MATTERS

Poultry are to be found in every kraal. I know not when they were imported: Vasco da Gama found them in Natal when he landed. They are of a poor breed, and the natives generally sell a bird for sixpence. The bird is not worth more. The women and children have annexed the hens as their special care. When some superannuated hen is condemned to be sold to the white man there is tremendous excitement among the boys of the kraal, who run among the hens and chase the poor devoted old lady with tremendous clatter and noise

The bigger boys take care of the goats and cattle. Of old the natives used to teach the cattle to dance, run in circles, lie down at word of command, and run races with no one on their backs. But they rarely do these things now. They used even to decorate the cattle by cutting their skin in fanciful designs, bending the horns into fantastic shapes. They knew the voice of every ox in a huge herd, and frequently bought one for no other reason than its beautiful voice. The Hottentots are said to have no fewer than thirty-two words to describe the colour of the oxen; yet they would call the sky and the veldt

# The Essential Kafir

the same colour. It is risky to deduce too much from this fact. Unwarrantable conclusions were drawn from the fact that the Bushmen had words to count up to three only. It was supposed they could count no higher—a deduction not quite so mistaken as the supposition that because the French count on the decimal system they cannot count above ten.

The hour of milking cattle is referred to elsewhere, and we need only add that it used to be the custom to milk into baskets which were watertight, so well woven were they. When a cow is difficult to milk the calves are driven up and allowed to drink a little, so as to start the process.

The cooking falls to the women, and if a man felt that his wife did not keep him well he would stand at the door of his hut and proclaim aloud to all listeners that she was a very shabby woman and did not give him enough to eat. This was a sure remedy for the evil. Likewise, when a man ill-treated his wife, she would stand at the door of her hut and proclaim his cruelty.

An old custom used to consist in sending the breast of every ox to the chief. The men were forbidden to eat swine, hares, fish, hens, ducks, geese, turkeys, which were thought unclean. The women might eat all of these except fish. The men eat their food first. Then the women are allowed to finish what is left, though they are not allowed to eat the breast, heart, head, or feet of oxen. A visitor always eats out of the common pot. To offer him food in a separate one is regarded as an insult: it looks suspiciously like foul play. The head of the kraal is responsible for providing strangers with food.

Sometimes the people make small huts for the hens, and these are generally plastered with cowdung; the habit still survives in Pondoland, while above the Zambesi pigeon huts are found in nearly every village.

# Arts of Peace and Domestic Matters

### ARTISTIC POWERS

It is surprising how little artistic talent the Kafirs show. The only tribe in South Africa that makes any serious attempt at drawing is the Bushmen, and these people have left records on the walls of caves in many parts of the country. The drawings are crude, yet wonderfully suggestive in outline, a small amount of shading being added. Still, the majority of drawings are but outlines filled in with a little reddish-brown paint. The photograph given on Plate 37 was taken in a small cave in the Basuto mountains. Very few white men have seen this cave, and when the natives heard that I had photographed it they went to destroy the paintings, lest they should attract Europeans up into the forbidden fastnesses of the mountains. The paintings are of a dull yellowish red or brown, and might easily be passed without being noticed, as they are so faint, and so little relieved in colour from the rocks. They must have been done ages ago: it is a long time since the Bushmen were turned out of the mountains by the Basuto.

Occasionally one sees an attempt at drawing on the walls of the hut of some progressive Kafir; but the attempt is very rude when compared with the drawings of the Bushman. Why this race of pigmies should be the only tribe to draw is unexplained.

Yet most of the native tribes contain men who can carve fairly well, and I have frequently seen the Pondo children making small clay oxen to play with. Sometimes they bake the clay images of oxen and stretch a piece of the intestine of an animal over them, allowing the membrane to dry; then, the clay casts broken, the oxen stand forth in a semi-transparent gelatinous form, having been previously teased into little dots and ridges by a sharp piece of bone. Some natives

# The Essential Kafir

carve respectable heads of men or of animals on the hard wood which they use for walking-sticks.

As the natives have no writing, they are sometimes slow in grasping the idea that signs can convey meaning. When the early settlers sent messages to one another by writing, the chiefs considered it the most marvellous witchcraft they had ever heard of. It happened, on one occasion, that a white man sent five loaves of bread to another white man by a native boy, who took a note stating the number of loaves he was sent with. On the way, the boy ate two of the loaves, and was astonished when the white man accused him of eating two loaves. When the boy was sent, on another similar occasion, he sat on the note, so that it might not see him eating the loaves. The white man again detected the theft. The boy was surprised, and said that he sat on the note, so that it could not possibly have seen him eating the bread : he was sure the white man must have bewitched the piece of paper.

MUSIC

The natives have several rude musical instruments. The Damaras tie a piece of twine round a bow till it is very tight, and then strike the bow with a small stick; they thus admirably imitate animals, walking, trotting, cantering, and galloping. They delight more in rhythm than in melody. At Inhambane, in Gazaland, the natives have two forms of " piano." One of these is made by supporting different lengths of a special wood over two strings ; when the pieces of wood are struck with a hammer they emit musical notes which vary with the length of the piece of wood. The other form of " piano " is made by fastening a good many pieces of iron of different lengths into a hollow calabash ; this is decorated with many pieces of shell which jingle when the apparatus vibrates. By twanging the

## Arts of Peace and Domestic Matters

pieces of iron various notes are produced. These pianos are to be found in many parts of South Africa, chiefly above Zululand.

There are many kinds of reed instruments which are used, some in the shape of a rough flute, and others resembling the reed instruments of the "Punch and Judy" men. For hour after hour they will "grate on their scrannel pipes of wretched straw." Another instrument is made by taking a piece of wood six inches long and an inch thick. The edges are bevelled, and a thong is fixed to one end; when this is whirled in the air it makes a weird noise. The big boys love to frighten babies thus, declaring that wild animals are approaching; and the mothers make them cease, for they say that the noise will attract a gale of wind. The Bushmen use bones of sheep as flutes. They take a stick for another instrument. A long string is tied tightly down the whole length of the stick, and at one end of the string a piece of quill is fixed: the player has to suck in the air over this piece of quill, thus causing it to vibrate and emit a sound. I have seen the instrument used in Pondoland; but the music was very rude, and it required an immense amount of energy to bring it forth at all. The Bushmen called it a Gorah, but the Pondos an Ugwali.

The chief instrument in general use (called an Igubu) is made from a long stick which is bent like a bow by a string; the stick is fastened to a round gourd; the gourd is placed on the breast, and acts as a sounding-board. When the string is struck with a piece of reed the instrument gives out a sort of "ting, ting, ting" sound which is most monotonous. The natives will play it for hours, as they walk over the country. Occasionally one finds natives making use of hollow bones as musical instruments.

The natives have endless chants. As the Machilla boys carry a traveller they keep up a sing-song chant all day.

# The Essential Kafir

Natives sing as they row their canoes, and chant as they run with a load; yet all the time their words are practically devoid of meaning. The natives laugh at our singing, and say that it is very strange; yet they pick up our tunes very quickly, the men falling into the bass parts without any effort or training. When they hear white men sing for the first time they often burst out laughing: they think our performance very comical. Some specimens of their songs and odes have already been given on pp. 93, 94, and 283; but the most impressive of all their songs is the "Hymn of the Afflicted," which is here taken from Arbousset.

The women cry:

> We are left outside,
> We are left for sorrow,
> We are left to despair,
> Which increases our misery.
> Oh, that there were a refuge in heaven!
> That there were a pot there and a fire!
> That there were found a place for me!
> Oh, that I had wings to fly thither!

The widow adds:

> O foolish woman that I am,
> When evening comes I open my window: (a hole above the door)
> I listen in silence, I watch,
> I fancy that my husband returns!

Then all the women chant:

> Alas! are they really gone?
> Have they left us here?
> But where are they gone,
> That they can return no more
> To see us again?
> Are they really gone?
> Is hell insatiable? (Hell is the cavern in the earth where the dead go.
> Will it never be full?

# Arts of Peace and Domestic Matters

This song, I fancy, gains much in the graceful translation ; yet it will show what the Kafir imagination is at its very best.

### GAMES

A race of people without games would be inadequately human. It is true that cricket and football are unknown to the Kafirs, except in the neighbourhood of towns, and even then it is only the small boys who play the game ; but in kraals the natives have their own games, which differ a good deal from our sports.

The girls, of course, play with dolls, which are the most ridiculous-looking creatures. A mealie cob is taken and covered with a small portion of the mother's blanket, surreptitiously stolen from her. Some pieces of thread are teased out of the edge of the blanket, rubbed well with oil and red clay, and made into hair. Two beads are placed in the head to represent eyes, and the thing becomes quite human.

The small boys play at making huts inside the cattle kraal. Some old pieces of wattle and a few wisps of grass are roughly put together, and form an endless source of amusement. Then, they have a game something like hopscotch. Sometimes they play at soldiers, and once in Swazieland I saw a splendid " awkward squad " being drilled by a small urchin in true chiefly dignity and importance.

As the boys grow a little older they play a game of spitting, which takes us down to the bed-rock of human nature. Two or three boys sit on the ground, and one quickly passes his hand before his mouth, spitting on the palm as it passes. The other boys have to guess where the spittle hit the hand. They play this game for long periods with great merriment. Who could help being delighted with the disingenuousness of the game, and with its utter naked simplicity, in spite of the

## The Essential Kafir

dirty habits it revealed? In the picture on Plate 54 the central boy has just been spitting on to his hand. He holds it up so as to hide the palm from the boy on his right-hand side. He is saying, "Where did it go?" The boy on his right (the observer's left) is pointing to that part of his hand which indicates the part on which the spittle fell on the central boy's hand. He is saying, "It fell here." The other boy is looking on, laughing at the fun; and great ringworm patches can be seen on his head. The geological record of human nature is revealed in this game. It is just what European boys at a certain age would like to do, if they felt sure that no one would see them. The boys have great fencing matches with sticks, every boy using two sticks, one to parry with and one for thrusting. They manage the sticks with wonderful agility, and it is a practice which is useful to them through life. The boys play at animals; some represent lions and tigers, and others represent dogs. A certain area is marked off as "home," and then the fun begins. Sometimes the boys run races on calves, and if they are sent on an irksome errand they will draw lots with pieces of grass, and thus decide who must go on the errand.

I shall never forget my first Sunday spent in the Port Herald district above the Zambesi. We arrived late on a Saturday night at our destination, and in an hour or two the news spread around all the villages that some white men had arrived. Next morning we were awakened at dawn by a group of small boys all anxious to see the white men. There must have been some thirty or forty boys outside the house. They began to play at leapfrog, and when they were tired of that they played at horses, in a novel fashion. As the game is well worth importing into England, I will describe it. A boy stands straight up, and another comes behind him, placing his hands on the shoulders of the boy in front. Then

Plate 52.

A PONDO PLAYING AN UGWALI OR GORAH.

This instrument is made by stretching a piece of string of grass along a stick. A small piece of quill is fastened to the string at one end, and the breath is drawn in over the quill, causing it to vibrate and emit a weird sound.

Plate 53.

A ZULU WOMAN PLAYING THE IGUBU.

This instrument is made by stretching a string across the chord of a bent stick, which is fixed to a gourd. The player strikes the tense string with a piece of reed, and the sound is increased in volume by the gourd acting as a sounding board.

## Arts of Peace and Domestic Matters

a third boy jumps up on to the arms of this second boy, and away the fellows run. They are specially fond of playing at "chiefs," who shake hands as they pass one another on horseback (Plate 55). When tired of this game the boys began to play at frogs in a most delightful and comical way; then they all began to stand on their heads (Plate 55), and when the blood got too much into their thick little skulls they played at catching an india-rubber ball made from a rubber-vine which grows in the country. These balls are lively things, and will bound to an immense height. The boys scorned to use both hands, and showed the most marvellous dexterity in catching—any boy who missed his catch being chaffed immoderately. If they were to perform at Lord's or at the Oval they would be well cheered for their performance. They made surprisingly clever catches.

When they were tired of catching balls they started to play "touch," or a game of a similar kind. In other parts of the district the boys played at King of the Castle, using ant-heaps some ten feet high for the "castles."

When boys grow a little older they play other games. A favourite one used to be for a company of boys to go into one of the huts belonging to the girls; they stripped half-naked, or rather ninety-nine per cent. naked, and squatted down on their haunches; they would then move about the upper parts of their bodies with violent jerkings and contortions, until the perspiration ran off from them to the ground; the boy who managed to make his stream of perspiration go farthest was praised by the girls, and was a hero for the rest of the day. They play a sort of "Follow-my-Leader"; but instead of running about they kneel down and bend over from side to side, and the boy who bends over the farthest is the winner.

Another game consists in holding a stone in one hand

behind the back; after a good deal of shuffling both hands are quickly thrown out, and the other person has to guess which hand contains the stone. They do this with surprising rapidity, and keep up the game half the night with tremendous excitement. Then, there are wrestling matches, in which the boys sit on the floor cross-legged, much as is the method used in "cock-fighting" on board an ocean steamer. Sleight-of-hand tricks cause great interest.

There is a "round" game played by a number of people. All sit in a large circle, and a boy in the middle has to guess in whose hand a grain of Indian corn is, as it is shuffled by the players. Hide-and-seek is, of course, played; it is universal. The boys sometimes sit down and throw stones into the air, catching them as they fall and throwing them up again quickly, so as to see who can keep the greatest number of stones in the air at one time; sometimes five stones are kept going in this fashion.

The most popular game for the grown-up natives is played with a large flat stone, in which holes are scooped out in rows. They sometimes use holes in the earth, or pieces of wood with holes in them instead. The players have to move about a certain stone, and the game proves very exciting, being somewhat like our game of draughts. An American missionary was so struck with the game that, I believe, he patented it in America, where it had a certain vogue. This game is played all over South Central Africa, and I have heard that it is common even up as far as Egypt. The game is said to be of Hottentot origin; but the exact nature of the rules I could never grasp, the natives always laughing when asked to explain them. They say that they cannot describe the rules; but this excuse is false.

Over and above these games, the natives are fond of making labyrinths or mazes in the dust, and one is reproduced from an

# Arts of Peace and Domestic Matters

ZULU LABYRINTH
From native drawing which appeared in *The Natal Colonist*

# The Essential Kafir

old Natal paper, to show how ingenious the natives are at this game.

### NATIVE TELEGRAPHY

It is well known that the natives occasionally—but not often—learn news with amazing rapidity, sending information concerning the main outline of certain events over large tracts of country even faster than it is conveyed by telegraph. There has been endless dispute as to the mode in which this is done.

I was told of one of these instances by a magistrate who had been at King Williamstown during the great border wars. He told me that one day the son of the chief we were fighting against came into court with his head shaved. (This native was a clerk in the office.) The magistrate quickly recognised the sign of mourning, and asked what relation was dead. The youth stated that his father had at last been killed in the war, and even mentioned the spot where the body was lying. The magistrate thought the whole thing strange, for he had heard nothing by telegraph. However, soon after a telegram came giving details of the news, which fitted in with the description given by the native.

Mr. Blackburn investigated some cases of this nature, and wrote an interesting letter to the *Spectator*. Here are two cases which he records:

CASE 1.—At 9 A.M. on a Monday, a Kaffir herd-boy was attacked by a bull. He defended himself with a' crowbar. Kaffir and bull were dead by 10 A.M. At 12 the same day B, a farmer residing forty-two miles from the scene of the tragedy, wrote to A a business letter, appending this postcript: " My Kaffirs are saying your herd-boy stabbed your red Devon bull with a long knife and that both are dead. Hope it is only a Kaffir yarn." That letter was despatched by mounted messenger before half-past 12 the same day.

CASE 2.—A Kaffir was being tried for manslaughter at Johannesburg. At 5 in the afternoon an old Kaffir woman on a Boer's farm thirty-eight miles

## Arts of Peace and Domestic Matters

from Johannesburg told me and others that the boy had been acquitted, and that the principal witness against him had been taken to prison. As the Kaffir had pleaded guilty at the preliminary hearing and was to be undefended, this result seemed extremely improbable. Later we learned that the Kaffir was given counsel at the last moment, the plea of guilty withdrawn, and he was acquitted at 3.15 p.m. At 4 o'clock that afternoon the principal witness was knocked down by a cab in the street and taken to the jail hospital, where he died.

In each of these cases the accurate news travelled in less than half the time that would have been required by the fastest horse, bearing in mind the broken, almost virgin, and roadless country that would have to be traversed.

Various explanations have been given. Some mystics think that the natives have a weird telepathy. This word is one of those with which " we decorate our ignorance ": we think that if we give a phenomenon a name and put it in some pigeon-hole in the brain we are explaining it. Though Mr. Blackburn does not exactly say that the natives convey news by mystical methods, he seems to hint in this direction, for he ends his letter by saying, " That news is sometimes transmitted under conditions unknown to Europeans is, I am satisfied, a fact; but the explanation lies neither in the legs of a horse nor the lungs of a Kafir."

The common theory is that the natives shout the news from hill-top to hill-top. And undoubtedly very much can be done in this way. The Bushmen used to admit openly that they transmitted news by lighting fires on certain hill-tops, thus signalling to their friends, and I have often heard natives shouting information across immense distances; they carried on quite a full conversation when I could not hear the slightest suspicion of an answer, although I imagine that I have normal powers of hearing. Mr. Blackburn says, scornfully, that this explanation is offered always by Europeans, and never by colonials or those who know the country. I can only say I have heard scores of true colonials, and people who have

## The Essential Kafir

lived for twenty years or longer among the natives, give this explanation.

Yet it is not certain that this is the true explanation of all cases, though it may well be the means adopted where news is expected concerning an important event. To be quite fair to Mr. Blackburn, it should be noted that he rules out many cases which might be accounted for in this way. The news of General Buller's defeat at Colenso was told by natives sixty miles away within two hours, and Mr. Blackburn writes such a case of, as it might only be a shrewd forecast—or surely a case specially arranged for. Mr. Rider Haggard has recorded a case which occurred during the Zulu War. In this case, Mr. Haggard says, "the theory that intelligence is conveyed with extraordinary rapidity among the Bantu peoples by men calling from height to height would, however, appear to be falsified by the fact that in this instance it must have come across the great plain of the high veldt."

Following on these explanations comes one advanced by Mr. Hugh Clifford. He would boldly postulate a sixth sense which has been lost to Europeans through civilisation.

In an extremely interesting letter to the *Spectator* he couples the well-known phenomenon of "going Fantee" with this mode of sending news by telepathy. I take him to mean that in races of low civilisation there is an extraordinary power possessed by certain people of "feeling" things at a distance, and of impressing their thoughts on others. This mental characteristic would enable people to impress others at a distance with their thoughts by "telepathy," and would also over-ride the bulwarks of the personality of a European, under certain conditions, forcibly drawing out latent streaks of heredity which had long lain dormant. These streaks of heredity suddenly awake with terrible force under the influence of some strong psychic-tide exerted by the uncivilised native

## Arts of Peace and Domestic Matters

society in which the European finds himself isolated and surrounded and mentally overpowered. In a moment the white man finds the barriers against animalism, which civilisation had erected, demolished, and he is carried off his legs, as it were, by some strong psychic-tide. The idea is very interesting; but it is surely no more than the most tentative suggestion, with scarcely a shred of scientific evidence in its favour, as yet. One shred—though Mr. Clifford does not refer to it—might consist in the fact that Bushmen are said to possess the sense of locality in a way quite unknown to most Europeans. If they are blindfolded and taken to a great distance, they take a bee-line to their home when the bandages are removed from their eyes; in this respect being much like carrier pigeons. Civilisation has robbed most of us of this sense, which is no longer needed in the struggle for existence; and if one sense is lost why should another not have been similarly eliminated? What I should like to lay stress on is that, while Mr. Blackburn and others may be proved ultimately to be quite correct in their ideas, it seems by no means proved that any of the cases brought forward is impossible on the simpler theory of native messages conveyed by the human voice or by arranged signs or signals. And by the law of parsimony we are forced to accept, provisionally, the simplest notion that will cover theoretically the phenomena brought forward. There can be no doubt as to which is the simpler notion. Legs of horses and lungs of Kafirs are much better known things, to say the least, than sixth or seventh senses. Let us not adopt mystic causes till we have quite exhausted natural ones.

And in favour of the natural system of sounds or signals I can bring forward the very well-known fact that even to-day the natives in some parts of the country convey intelligence by means of drums. These drums were common in Zululand till com-

## The Essential Kafir

paratively recent times, and travellers have stated that in olden days the Zulus conveyed certain items of information by means of the drums. Be that as it may, *I know the natives on the Zambesi do so still.* They have a regular code of signals which they can beat out on drums, using instruments of different sizes and various modes of beating the instruments. I think, though it is four years since I heard it, that I could tell with certainty when natives were having their midday meal at a distant kraal, by the " rumble of a distant drum," for the notes and rhythm are very significant, and quite as distinctive as the bugle-call to dinner used by military men. They have also a certain style of drumming which warns people at a distance that a white man is approaching.

I know a man who wished to make a surprise visit to his wood-cutting station on the banks of the Shire River, and he kept his purpose quite secret till late at night. Then he awoke his machilla crew, and made them start off in silence through the bush. But he noticed that as he left every native village the drums were set working in a very peculiar fashion, and their rhythm was repeated without any exception right through the whole journey, village after village turning out in the dark to see him pass. When he reached his destination and made his "surprise" visit to his native wood-cutters in the dawn, he found them strangely busy and hard at work, and soon found out that they knew of his approach hours in advance, and so were not to be caught napping.

I think there can be no doubt but that the natives have a system and code of signalling by drums ; that this code is developed to a very surprising extent ; that it is very efficient ; that it was in use in Zululand years ago. If so, it would be but a short step to signalling by means of voice or gesture, or beating pieces of wood, or lighting fires, whose smoke could be seen sixty miles away, or by a dozen simple methods that the

## Arts of Peace and Domestic Matters

unsuspicious European would never think of coupling with a signal code. And the law of parsimony would compel us, if we wish to have even a show of being scientific, to exhaust this possible mode of communication before we make such *ex cathedrâ* statements that colonials or those who know the country never adopt this explanation. The fact remains that in many cases they *do* adopt it, even though they may ultimately be proved to be mistaken in their ideas.

In conclusion, we need to remember how frequently the news is untrue, half true, or sadly deficient in detail; how much of it is expected, and how slowly it travels compared with the rapidity which might be expected by mystic modes of communication. And no one seems to record instances in which news unexpected by the Kafirs, which therefore cannot well be conveyed by signals, is thus transmitted. For example, the natives were astonished to hear of the Queen's death, though it might easily have been communicated by telepathy to the place I was staying at in Tembuland at the time: the news arrived by *post* before the natives knew of the event. The Queen's death appealed most strongly to the natives' imagination, more strongly if possible than the death of one of their own chiefs; yet I know of no cases on record in which it was conveyed by other means than horses' legs, Kafir lungs, or telegraphs. The subject has not been sufficiently examined in a strictly scientific manner, and consequently no dogmatic statements are yet justified—except through faith in future evidence.

### SMOKING

The natives are very fond of smoking tobacco and Indian hemp, which is usually called dacca (or dacha) in South Africa. On the Zambesi the natives make small cigars from tobacco which is wrapped up in banana leaves. The Portuguese call these "carrotes," I believe, and the word is to be found in some old books. I have never seen carrotes south of the Zambesi. The natives wear them behind their ears, just as a clerk holds his pen. When natives meet, one of the carrotes is produced, and each native takes a few whiffs, and passes it on to his neighbour. They never seem to smoke to excess.

Farther south the natives are very fond of tobacco, which they smoke in pipes. They usually buy these from traders, but in olden days used bones of animals, or else made elaborate pipes from wood, decorating them with rough carvings. The women, as well as the men, smoke.

The favourite material to smoke is Indian hemp. The men make rough tchibouqes and draw the smoke through the water to cool it. They show great ingenuity in the way they make these smoking-horns. When they are travelling they use bamboos, which they bend into bow-shape with a string, placing some water in the tube; they then fix on a small stone pipe at one end and draw the smoke through the water to cool it. Sometimes they draw the smoke through the damp earth. When living at home they usually make their pipes out of horns of oxen, a hole being made near the apex of the horn, which is held downwards. A stone pipe is fixed on to a piece of bamboo, which is inserted into the hole in the horn. Water is then poured into the horn, and men draw the smoke down through the water to cool it. They are very fond of inhaling the smoke into their lungs, and frequently smoke in couples. One man fills his lungs with smoke first, and hands the pipe to his friend, who fills his lungs. Then they take small hollow reeds and exhale the smoke through these reeds, making bubbles with their saliva. One man blows the smoke out and forms a row of bubbles on the ground, and his friend tries to outflank him by making his row of bubbles encircle the first line. So they go on, each trying to win. The

## Arts of Peace and Domestic Matters

game is something like a form of chess played in a dirty fashion.

The effect of the Indian hemp is to make them cough very violently and become excited. It induces a mode of intoxication, and is very injurious to the health. From the photographs it will be seen at a glance how the game is played. (See plate 56.) It is said that the natives thus play at labyrinths.

# LEGAL MATTERS

# CHAPTER X

### LEGAL MATTERS

### GENERAL REMARKS

In this chapter it is intended to give a condensed account of the native legal code, trifling details being omitted that the leading conceptions may stand in the clear relief.

The natives are very respectful to constituted authority: whatever is, is right. As there is no written language, special men sometimes make it their business to remember past precedents; but there are no true lawyers, for every man has to defend himself and his friends. Some conception as to the strong sense of justice among the natives may be formed by noticing the fact that several Bechuana tribes were in the habit of paying tribute to the pigmy Bushmen when they killed game: they recognised that the Bushmen, by their priority in occupation of the country, had acquired rights over the game. It need hardly be said that Europeans have not sought to strengthen this view of the matter.

There are various kinds of courts of justice. The people are divided up into clans, tribes, sub-tribes, and families; and there are, consequently, several courts, which answer to these divisions. The chief's decision is final in all cases; and if a case happens to be given against a man in a lower court and he thinks it well to appeal to the chief, he will have his fine increased if he loses his case a second time.

In theory, the mother is responsible for her small children,

## The Essential Kafir

and she has to give account to the father; he, again, is accountable to the headman of the village or kraal; and this man is responsible to the councillors of the chief. Every native is supposed to be acquainted with the affairs of every one else, and thus to be virtually a policeman; but the supposition is somewhat exaggerated. It holds in theory; but it is not always true in practice, especially in case of people who were circumcised at the same season.

Cases are tried in the open air just outside the cattle kraal, or close to the gate of the village, and the accused is considered guilty until he can prove his innocence. The Kafirs cannot grumble at the "law's delays." Justice is meted out in a rough and ready fashion while the subject is still warm. A man used to be allowed, under certain circumstances, to administer justice on the spot, especially if he detected a man committing adultery with his wife, or stealing his cattle. The chief Gaika stopped these practices in his tribe at the beginning of the nineteenth century, and declared that to kill a man who was caught in the act of committing adultery was to commit the crime of murder. Retaliation was declared to be illegal. In olden times the hut of the chief councillor was a harbour of refuge, and any one fleeing to it was safe as far as his' life was concerned: he could be fined, but not put to death, once he reached that haven. This custom, I believe, was confined to a few tribes.

### CLASSIFICATION OF CASES

Offences are roughly divided into two classes, criminal and civil. All offences committed on the person of any subject of the chief are considered to be criminal, and have to be tried by the chief himself; no one is allowed to accept payment privately to settle such a case. The people are the property of

Plate 54.

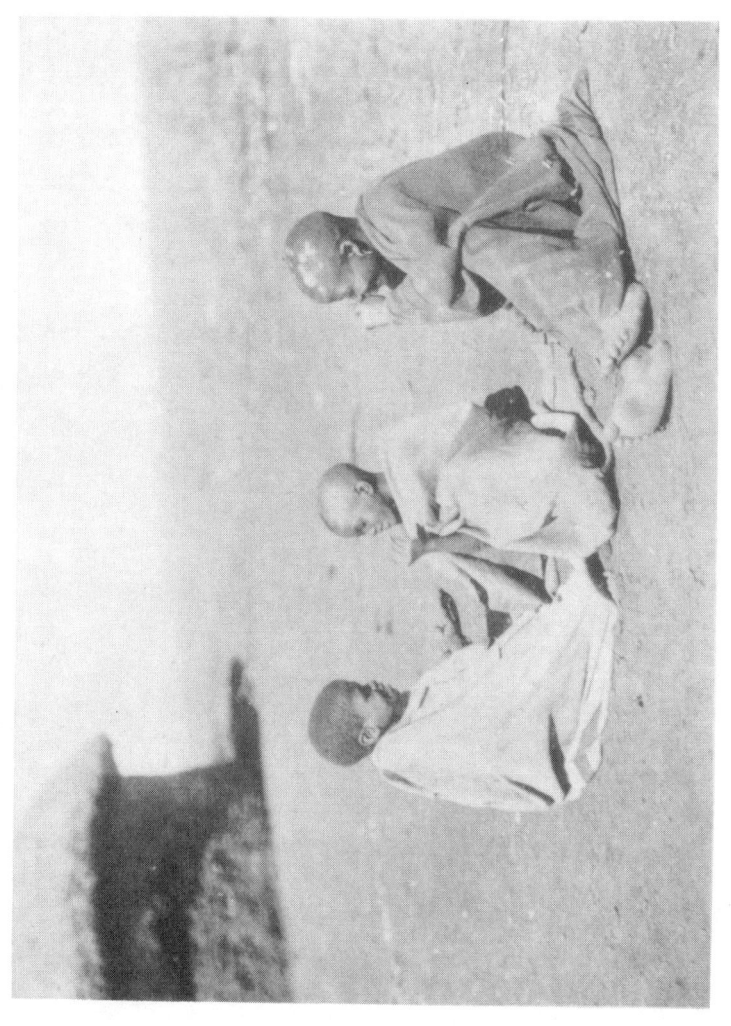

THE SPITTING GAME.

Plate 55.

*Upper.*—ZAMBESI BOYS PLAYING AT HORSES.
*Lower.*—ZAMBESI BOYS STANDING ON THEIR HEADS FOR FUN.

## Legal Matters

the chief, and anyone damaging the person of a subject injures the chief's property, and is, consequently, accountable to the chief. The following offences are, therefore, considered criminal: homicide, assault, rape, procuring abortion, incest, treason, witchcraft, speaking against the chief, cowardice in war, and acting as a spy to the enemy. Many of these offences in olden days were punished with death. To speak against the chief, or in very tyrannical times to cough, sneeze, blow the nose, or even to stand, in his presence, was punishable with death; and Chaka frequently put people to death for smaller offences. All criminal cases are prosecuted by the chief.

Civil cases are prosecuted by the plaintiff, and comprise such things as the following: adultery, theft, injury to property, debt, and minor offences. But all "blood belongs to the chief," and if a man cuts a person's arm off the chief receives the fine, and not the wounded man, or his family; they say, "We cannot eat our own blood."

In theory all the land, cattle, and people belong to, or are vested in the name of, the chief, and when a man does not wish to sell some article, he will say that he cannot do so because it does not belong to him. If asked to whom it belongs, he will say, "To the chief." Yet for all that, if he is offered something that catches his fancy, he will freely sell the thing that he has just declared cannot be sold because it belongs to the chief. The natives are delightfully illogical in such matters.

This respect for the chief is their fundamental conception of virtue. It is a serious offence to lie to him; yet they may lie to any one else to their hearts' content. When a man is carrying on a civil case before a petty court he may lie as much as he likes, and make the worse case appear the better. But when he is answering the chief he has to tell the truth—at least theoretically!

# The Essential Kafir

A missionary asked a young warrior in Swaziland when he would become a Christian, and the fellow answered gaily, "When my chief sets the example." The missionary unwisely said, "But suppose your chief goes to hell?" "Then I will go there with my chief," was the spontaneous answer. Any one who knows the natives will admit, I think, that this showed true native virtue, and not lack of moral tone. Something can be done with the man who talks like this. The *man* is not dead in him, and the missionary who reproves him for such a remark undoes in one moment the plodding work of years. It is their lying, thieving, cruelty, conceit, and lust, and not their loyalty to the chief, that make one wish the natives to say,

> Oh, that a man would arise in me,
> That the man that I am might cease to be.

But to return to the law. There sits the old chief at the gate of the kraal, looking like some patriarch of old. A case is being tried, and the natives are all in a state of interest and excitement. The accused man has to conduct his own case, though his friends will supply any detail he may forget on the spur of the moment. The natives speak with extraordinary eloquence, suiting the action to the word in a way that would rejoice the heart of a Hamlet. Gifted with a marvellous memory, the native pours forth a torrent of fact, argument, and mere words, adding to the dramatic effect by perfectly natural and unstudied gesture. Gesture is a thing he never thinks about, and consequently, being lost in his subject, he uses it in consummate perfection. He strikes a full chord extending over the entire gamut of the emotions; every possible argument is exhausted, for his life depends upon his skill in presenting his own case. The chief sits surrounded by his councillors, looking provokingly cool and calm. Witnesses are

# Legal Matters

called on each side, and the whole case is thoroughly sifted; the chief's verdict is final, and satisfies every one, even the accused if he is found guilty; for a chief can do no wrong.

The following brief extract is taken from Maclean's "Compendium of Kafir Laws," which gives the opinions of such well-known men as Dugmore, Warren, and Brownlee (published in 1858). Some details are inserted from old writers, such as those who knew Chaka personally, or who are specialists with regard to certain tribes, such as Macdonald, Grout, Theal, Thomson, and Leslie.

### CRIMINAL CASES

*Homicide.*—Murder and accidental death are not clearly distinguished (even if the law separated these crimes, the chief might not). The punishment usually was seven cattle for killing a man, or ten cattle for killing a woman, whose value to the tribe is great. Sometimes the culprit's whole property was confiscated for murder. The fines in all criminal cases go to the chief.

*Assault.*—Both parties are fined, unless one did not resist; the fine is about five or six head of cattle.

*Rape.*—The fine is one to four head of cattle.

*Procuring abortion.*—This is very common, yet rarely found out by the chief. The fine is variable. Thomson says there was no fine for this offence. The doctor as well as the father was fined. Putting a child to death soon after birth was recognised as murder.

*Treason or witchcraft.*—This is punishable by death; especially was it so in olden days; in fact, the natives do not seem to have noticed that it was better to kill a man outright than run the risk of being accused of doing so by witchcraft. But who would expect to be accused of this crime?

# The Essential Kafir

Gardiner says that in Chaka's days the three crimes punishable by death were adultery, witchcraft, and speaking evil of the chief. Thomson says that the custom of putting men to death for adultery lapsed about a century ago.

Added to these criminal cases were many offences, such as stealing, disrespect, errors of judgment, mistakes in carrying messages, violating native customs, want of attention during dances, &c., which, Isaacs says, were punished according to the passing whim of the chief, sometimes with death and sometimes with very severe beatings. To overshadow the king by standing in his presence was an offence worthy of instant death. The chief would be at the mercy of assassins unless this law were rigidly carried out. If a chief made himself very unpopular he would find his subjects deserting to rival chiefs, who would gladly welcome such refugees. The fear of this acted as a wholesome restraint on many tyrannical chiefs. Even Gaika had to repeal some of his own laws because public opinion was strongly opposed to them.

## CIVIL CASES

With regard to civil cases, the plaintiff has to go with a party of his friends to the kraal of the defendant, and lodge his accusation in the presence of all the people. The whole day might be spent in preliminary skirmishing, neither side giving itself away by producing too much information. The process is repeated day after day. Finally the case is tried before some suitable court; if that court felt unable to decide, or if the person who lost wished to appeal to the chief, the case would be sent up to him. There would be endless torrents of words used before any conclusion would be reached. The chief has no legal claim to any share of the fines in civil cases; yet he generally manages to get a good slice of

## Legal Matters

them. Here are some of the more common fines for civil cases :

*Adultery*.—The fine is three or four head of cattle (Brownlee says one to ten head of cattle and more in case of the wife of a chief). If pregnancy follows the child belongs to the husband. Sexual abuse is only a crime as committed with a married woman. Seduction of virgins is not punishable, nor disgraceful. If pregnancy follows, the father or guardian of the girl demands an ox. The child then belongs to its father, who has to leave it at the girl's kraal and pay for its keep, redeeming it when grown up by a few head of cattle. If the offender is uncircumcised the fine is heavier, and still heavier if the man was undergoing the rite of circumcision.

*Theft*.—Stealing forcibly in retaliation is not theft ; but property so taken must be restored or compensation given. The fine for cattle-stealing used to be ten cattle, even if only one animal were stolen. The fine of ten cattle when paid would often consist of half a dozen oxen and some calabashes, assegais, axes, &c., which were called "cattle" for the occasion. A man staying at a kraal as a guest holds the owner of the kraal responsible for all theft of his possessions while under his roof. Long credit is given for payment of debt, and when a man cannot pay, his relations have to help him ; his debt descends to his son after death.

This conception of responsibility for all that is done in the kraal is sometimes exaggerated in recent books. It is true that a man is responsible for what his son does, and that sometimes he would have a finger cut off when his son was found guilty of stealing : the headman is also, theoretically, responsible for all that happens in his kraals. But the practice of holding the people responsible for stolen cattle whose spoor can be traced to their kraal is quite a recent importation, and is European in origin. It is hardly a native characteristic. The custom was introduced by Gaika on the representation of the European authorities, who complained that the natives were stealing their oxen. This law came into force in 1817. The plan instituted then was this: If people were following up the spoor of stolen cattle, and could trace the marks to within about six hundred yards of a kraal, they would give over the pursuit, and call on the people of that kraal to carry it on, or else point out the spoor for a similar distance from their kraal. If they refused to do this they came under suspicion, though the chief would by no means invariably fine them for refusing to take the matter up.

To receive stolen goods is punishable; but it is allowable to eat the meat of stolen oxen unless this is done to hide the thieves.

*Injury to Property.*—Compensation has to be made to the full. In olden days it was said that a person had to give an eye for an eye, and a tooth for a tooth. But it is hard to see why this should have been the custom, for such injury is criminal and is an offence against the chief, who would hardly injure his own property—and the guilty man was, after all, but the property of the chief. This may be but one of the illogical things the Kafirs do. Injury to property which is purely accidental and inevitable is not punishable; this does not allude to bites by dogs, grass fires, or damage done by cattle to the gardens. Retaliation was allowed in the case of cattle straying into the gardens of others; the women used to be allowed to drive the oxen back into the gardens of their owners.

To make a false accusation is actionable.

*Divorce.*—A man may divorce his wife at pleasure without stating his reason. But he would run the risk of not getting back the cattle which he paid for her. If she has borne him children he cannot demand cattle back; yet the children are

## Legal Matters

his property. As a rule a man would prefer to keep the troublesome wife, and make her work hard, humbling her by taking an extra-masterful wife, who would side with the husband and oppress the troublesome woman. The natives rarely divorce a wife for adultery, as it is a much better bargain to get some extra cattle through the fine. If a woman leaves her husband for ill-treatment he cannot get the dowry back unless she marries again.

The chief's final way of keeping order when all other means fail is "eating up" the troublesome people. They may escape to a rival chief if they can; but even he will make them pay him a preliminary fine. When a chief wants to eat people up he sends for some men who live for a time at the chief's Great Place; they leave their wives behind, and the chief sends out to have some girls collected, who have to act as concubines as long as the men are busy on the chief's errands. This custom is called *Upundhlu,* and is another instance of Kafir "morality."

If a son behaves in a disgraceful way the father may disown him publicly, and after that he cannot inherit property.

*Land Tenure.*—The natives have very sensible laws on this subject. No man can sell or pawn land; yet the chief allows to every man as much as he needs for his kraal and for his garden. All other land is free for public grazing. If a man does not keep his land in cultivation it can be taken from him; but as long as he takes care of it, it is virtually his, though he has no power to sell it or negotiate with it in any way. The owners of cattle are responsible for all damage caused by them, and have to provide herds to watch and keep them from the gardens. One result of this land law is that there is hardly any poverty of a distressing character, though there may be great inequality as to wealth. A man or his wife can always grow enough food to support life. The people have to provide for their chief, who may even order his subjects to go and work for others, pocketing nearly the whole wages; or he may give the people who have earned the money a portion of it. While this system of land tenure prevents distressing poverty, it hinders the natives from progressing. They are shielded from the economic pinch of European life which does so much to spur men to activity and work.

*Inheritance and Family Matters.*—The merest fringe of this subject can be examined. The eldest brother is supposed to help his younger brothers to buy their first wives; the younger brothers are servants of the elder even when married, and they, theoretically, give even their earnings to him. This custom is rare now. With regard to wives, if a man has not paid up all the cattle to his wife's father, his first daughter is claimed as part payment. A woman cannot inherit property, for she is but "property" herself, and property cannot inherit property. In case of divorce, as pointed out before, the demand of the husband for a repayment of cattle all turns on his treatment of his wife—whether she have borne him children, and whether she get married again or not.

The eldest son of the great wife (who, it will be remembered, is often taken late in life, after the man has several other wives) is the heir presumptive. The eldest son of the right-hand wife lays the foundation of a new house, and a certain part of the tribe is allotted to him, and on his father's death he has jurisdiction over that portion. Yet he admits the superiority of the eldest son of the great wife. This twofold division of the tribe is of great antiquity; but Gaika introduced a third wife of importance. The son of this third or left-hand wife was called the representative of the ancestors, and the councillors of his deceased father clung to him as the representative of the man they had served, and so greatly helped to consolidate his power. Thus now it is common to

## Legal Matters

find three main houses, and if there are fifty wives there are but the three houses, the lesser wives being added as "Rafters" to one of these three main "houses." One house may "wither" and so cause endless disputes with regard to property. The Kafirs have a Salic law; yet, strangely, they allow a woman to rule while the king is a minor.

Property descends in much the same way as heirship to the chieftainship; but when a man has only one wife the eldest son is the heir. When a man dies without an heir his next brother succeeds him. So keen is the trouble in regard to property that when a man buys a new ox he states before all the people to which son it shall go after his death. The eldest son of a house inherits all the property left to that house, and hence comes great inequality in wealth. If a man dies without making a will, the eldest son of his great wife takes all the property, but has to provide for all the various children. He virtually becomes the father. On a man's death all his wives become the property of the heirs, and cannot marry again without their consent. Children belong entirely to the father. The dowry paid for a girl whose father is dead goes to the dead man's heir, and in Basutoland the maternal uncle gets a share of all cattle paid for girls. If a man die without children his father succeeds to his property; if the father be dead the eldest brother of his house succeeds to it. If he has no brother by the same mother the eldest son of his father's great wife takes the property; failing all relations, the chief takes the property.

While the coast tribes usually make their chief an absolute despot, who rules by means of councillors, the mountain and inland tribes frequently exert great power over their chief by pitsoes, or public debates. When a chief is a despot the people still have a hold on him: if he is cruel or tyrannical they threaten to desert him and so strengthen a rival chief.

FOLKLORE

The World is too much with us ; late and soon,
Getting and spending, we lay waste our powers :
Little we see in Nature that is ours ;
We have given our hearts away, a sordid boon !
This sea that bares her bosom to the moon ;
The winds that will be howling at all hours,
And are up-gathered now like sleeping flowers ;
For this, for everything, we are out of tune ;
It moves us not.—Great God ! I'd rather be
A Pagan suckled in a creed outworn ;
So might I, standing on this pleasant lea,
Have glimpses that would make me less forlorn ;
Have sight of Proteus rising from the sea ;
Or hear Old Triton blow his wreathèd horn.
WORDSWORTH.

Tis fable, therefore truth.
ROBERT BROWNING<br>(Fifine at the Fair).

## CHAPTER XI

#### FOLKLORE

MAX MÜLLER has said that, "in order to know what man is, we ought to know what man has been." And the folklore of a country preserves, as in some series of geological strata, evidences of the past national life. Many of the customs mentioned in old Zulu folklore stories have vanished, and are never practised now in the country; but among the Polynesians many of the customs described in Zulu legends are still being practised. This strange fact points to a time, very remote, when these two stocks had not completely separated, a period far outdistancing all historic records.

The Hottentots and Bushmen are the great people in South Africa for nursery tales and folklore. Any one wishing to study the subject should seek to get a second-hand copy of Bleek's " Hottentot Fables "; the book has long been out of print. A few of the stories it contains concerning Reynard the Fox, which are very much akin to the well-known stories of " Uncle Remus "—indeed, they may have been the result of some European importation of ideas—will be found in this chapter. The Zulus have borrowed not a little from these people with regard to stories and customs.

As the aim of the present book is but to catch the spirit of a Kafir's mind, only a few stories taken from an endless fund are given; but these are characteristic, and are given mainly in the words of previous writers, who took them from native sources. The natives, unfortunately, are rapidly forgetting their own stories, and it is only some old woman here and there who can now tell them at all perfectly. The influence of European civilisation has been to destroy all such memory-records. Even these old women confuse the stories, and that is why I prefer to borrow from others, instead of supplying my own accounts. The people are ashamed of telling the stories in the presence of the white man. Many of the tales I quote I have also heard in garbled form, one portion of a story being incompatibly tacked on to another, with endless variations interpolated.

Here is a well-known story told by Edwards in the old "South African Folklore Journal":

### MASILO AND MASILONYANE

It is said that once upon a time Masilo and Masilonyane went to hunt. They arrived at a place where two roads parted. Masilo said to his younger brother, "Take that road: I shall take this one: and this evening we shall meet here again."

Masilonyane then walked, and walked, until he was tired, when he saw a village, into which he entered. He went into the first hut, and found it deserted; he entered the second, with the same result. When he was about to despair, he found a number of pots reversed. He went to this one and turned it over, he went to the next and turned it over; then he went to the largest of the number, and tried in vain to turn it over. His girdle parted. He sat down and mended it. Again he tried; again his girdle parted. He sat down and mended it. Then he tried once more with all his might, and turned it over, and found a small old woman underneath, grinding snuff.

The old woman spoke, and said to him, "Put me on your back, child of my child." He put her on his back, and walked until he arrived at a pool of water. There were springbucks there.

# Folklore

Masilonyane said, "Grandmother, let me put you down, that I may go and kill a springbuck from among these, to procure a skin in which I can carry you on my back." The old woman agreed. He put her down on the ground; after which he called to his dogs, and set them on to the springbucks, and followed them. No sooner was he behind the rise than he recalled his dogs. Seeing an ant-bear's hole, he crept into it, and hid himself from the old woman.

While in hiding, he suddenly saw the old woman appear, saying, "Here is the footmark of the child of my child, and here is the other!" Then she said to him, "Put me on your back," and he put her on his back. He walked, and walked. They saw hartebeests. "Grandmother, here are hartebeests! Let me kill one, and obtain a skin to carry you in." He put the old woman down, set his dogs on, and followed them. No sooner was he out of sight than he hid himself. Again he saw the old woman suddenly appear, who ordered him to put her on his back, which he did.

Masilonyane was now out of patience and tired. At that moment he saw a leopard.

"Grandmother, let me kill this leopard, that I may prepare a pretty skin to carry you in!" He left her and gave chase to the leopard. He ran a long distance, and then hid himself. While he was hiding again, as before, the old woman came, saying, "Here is the footprint of the child of my child, and here is the other!" Masilonyane said, "What? I shall see a good many things! My dogs, seize her and kill her!" The dogs then seized her and killed her. He ran towards her with his battle axe; and, her big toe being very large, he chopped at it. Cattle came out. He chopped again. Cattle came out. The third time he chopped, there came out a beautiful beast of many colours.

He then drove the herd of cattle to the meeting-place

agreed upon with Masilo; when he found him, Masilo said, "Where did you get all these cattle? I have been all over the country, but have seen nothing. O, give me, please, that many-coloured beast, my younger brother!" Masilonyane said, "No, my elder brother: take all the rest; but this one is my fate. I will not give it to you." Notwithstanding all Masilo's entreaties, he remained obdurate. There being a pit close at hand, a thought came to him. "Here, Masilonyane! Hold me by my legs, while I drink, and I will do the same for you." After he had drunk, he held his younger brother by the legs, until he had reached the water, when he let him loose, and he was drowned in the pit.

Masilo then drove the cattle homewards; while driving them, he was startled by a bird settling on the horn of the many-coloured beast, whistling and saying, "Masilo has killed Masilonyane for the sake of the many-coloured beast of his herd!" He took a stone and killed it, and went a little way. It came to life again, and did as before. Again he killed it and ground it to dust, drove on his cattle, and reached home.

The people all crowded round him saying, "Hail, son of a chief! Where is Masilonyane?" "Nay: Masilonyane, since he and I parted at the pit, I have not seen. I thought he was already at home." They went to the cattle. "O, look! What a beautiful beast that is! Look at its colours!" said the people.

When they were still standing and admiring, the same bird came fluttering, and settled on the horn of the many-coloured beast, whistling, "Masilo has killed Masilonyane for the sake of the many-coloured beast of his herd!" Masilo took a stone and attempted to knock it over. It avoided the stone and slipped aside. The people said, "Leave the bird and let us hear!" It again said, "Masilo has killed Masilonyane for the

# Folklore

sake of the many-coloured beast of his herd!" The people said, "So you have killed your younger brother!" Masilo only hung his head. The people dragged him out of the village and killed him.

### THE CLEVER TORTOISE

As an example of a fable with a strong Hottentot flavour the following abstract of a long story told by Mr. Bain, also in the "South African Folklore Journal," will be found interesting.

Once upon a time there was a drought, and the lion told all the animals to scratch a large hole, in order to catch the first rain. Next day the leopards, hyenas, baboons, hares, and tortoises began to work; but the jackal refused to help, saying it did not mean to dirty its nails by grubbing in the earth. Still, when the rain came it went to drink from the hole, and even purposely muddied the water, and bathed in it. The lion then told the baboon to watch the water and to beat the jackal with a kerrie if it dared to come to the water. The baboon hid itself near the water and watched for the jackal. When the offending jackal came it saw through the stratagem and devised a plan of hoaxing the baboon. It knew that baboons are very fond of honey: so it walked up and down near the pool, and put its fingers into a pot, saying that, as it had such nice honey, it did not need any dirty water. The baboon heard this and grew covetous of the honey. The jackal then said that it would only give the baboon the honey on condition that it was willing to give up its kerrie and be bound. To this the baboon foolishly agreed, when the jackal began to beat the baboon and steal the water, telling the baboon that it was a great fool to be so simple and so easily taken in. When the animals appeared they were angry with the foolish baboon and gave it more beatings. . . . (Many other animals tried to catch the jackal, and all similarly failed.)

When a new plan had to be devised of catching the jackal, the tortoise offered to help. The animals thought it too silly until it explained its plan. It said it would cover its back with a sticky matter found on beehives, and hide near the pool. The plan was decided on, and the tortoise hid itself in the mud, looking just like a stone. When the jackal came down he thought it very kind of the animals to place a stone for it to stand on, and promptly walked on the back of the tortoise. His feet stuck fast, and the tortoise put out his head and began to move away. Only the front legs of the jackal had stuck to the tortoise's back, and so the jackal threatened to stamp on the tortoise with its hind legs, and hurt it. The tortoise told it to do so by all means if it wished. So the jackal began to stamp on the tortoise, and only entangled its back legs for its trouble. In anger it told the tortoise that it still had its mouth and teeth to fight with, and threatened to eat the tortoise, who simply told him to do so, then. The enraged jackal bit the back of the tortoise, and found its mouth and nose glued together with its feet. The tortoise then walked to the top of the bank, that all the animals might see how successfully it had done its work. The lion ordered the hyena to put the jackal to death; but the jackal begged one last favour, namely, to have his tail shaved and greased, after which the hyena should swing him round his head and dash his brains out against a stone. The lion consented, and the jackal's tail was shaved and greased. The hyena then took hold of the slippery tail, and the jackal escaped with the greatest ease. All the animals gave chase, and the lion outran them and caught up the jackal, who devised a further mode of escape. The jackal ran to an overhanging precipice, and stood on its hind legs and pretended to be propping up the jutting rock, calling to the lion to help him,

# Folklore

as the rock would otherwise fall and kill both of them. The lion put his back to the rock and exerted himself to the utmost. Then the jackal waited a little, and proposed that he should go and get a stick to prop up the rock with, so that the lion might be relieved from the strain. The jackal crept out and vanished, leaving the lion holding up the rock in fear, until he was starved to death.

### THE WOMAN WHO BECAME A LION

As a specimen of a Namaqua story the following is quoted from Anderson, who in turn takes it from Alexander. It is one of the most characteristic stories that could be selected.

Once upon a time, a certain Namaqua was travelling in company with a Bushwoman carrying a child on her back. They had proceeded some distance on their journey, when a troop of zebras appeared, and the man said to the woman, " I am hungry, and as I know you can turn yourself into a lion, do so now, and catch us a wild horse, that we may eat."

The woman answered, " You'll be afraid."

" No, no," said the man: " I am afraid of dying of hunger, but not of you." While he was speaking, hair began to appear at the back of the woman's neck, her nails assumed the appearance of claws, and her features altered. She set down the child.

The man, alarmed at the change, climbed a tree close by, while the woman glared at him fearfully; and, going to one side, she threw off her skin petticoat, when a perfect lion rushed out into the plain. It bounded and crept among the bushes towards the wild horses; and, springing on one of them, it fell, and the lion lapped its blood. The lion then came back to where the child was crying, and the man called from the tree, " Enough! Enough! Do not hurt me. Put off your lion shape. I'll never ask to see this again."

# The Essential Kafir

The lion looked at him and growled. "I'll remain here till I die," exclaimed the man, "if you don't become a woman again." The mane and tail began to disappear; the lion went towards the bush where the skin petticoat lay; it was slipped on, and the woman in her proper shape took up the child. The man descended, partook of the zebra's flesh, but never again asked the woman to catch game for him.

There is, however, no one to whom we owe so much in the direction of folklore tales as to the late Bishop Callaway, whose works on the "Religious System of the Amazulu" and "Nursery Tales of the Zulus" are now extremely rare, several guineas being asked for second-hand copies of the former. It is sad to think how much more he could have given us if only the money for printing and publishing had been forthcoming. It is now too late to collect stories on a large scale—so many have been forgotten by the natives. Here is one of his stories, taken from the "Folklore Journal."

### THE ROMANCE OF UNYENGEBULE

Unyengebule had two wives. They went to fetch firewood. When they reached the forest they collected firewood. The younger discovered some honey. They took it out of the hole; when they had finished, both sat down and ate it. The older one went on eating, and at the same time set some aside. When they had done eating, they went to their firewood. When they rose up, the younger wife saw the elder one had some honey in her hand; she said, "Why did you not ask my permission to eat and set aside?" The elder said, "You? As you have only a husband for a child" (As you have given birth to no children, and have only a husband to take care of), "do you ask why I did not seek your permission? It was you who should have remembered your husband. As for me, I am

Plate 56.

PONDO MEN SMOKING INDIAN HEMP.

A ZULU WOMAN CARRYING WATER.

conveying honey for my children." So they tied up their firewood. The elder one tied up the honey in small branches with her firewood; they put it on their heads and went home.

On reaching home, the elder went to her house and the younger to hers; they threw down their burdens. The elder went indoors, and found the husband there; she gave him the honey. He ate and said, "Thanks, thanks! My own wife." He said this though he was thinking of his beloved Inquandamate. (This name means, She who prevents the flow of saliva: that is, She who suppresses desire by gratifying it.) He went on eating till he had finished the whole.

He immediately went out and ran quickly to the house of the younger wife. He was full of hope, saying in his heart, "Since this woman brought me honey, she will have brought much more; for she knows I live in her house" (that is, I live in her hut).

He went in and sat down. He remained sitting a long time; but Inquandamate did not bring forth any honey. At length he asked, "Where is the honey?" She answered, "I have not brought any." He started up with a stick and beat her; the blows resounded. It happened, as she was preparing to be a diviner, that she had an Isala on her head. (An Isala is an ornament made of a bunch of feathers.) The Isala fell. He beat her and so killed her. He buried her.

Whenever he had buried her, he went for his sticks, thinking to go to the friends of the wife he had murdered, hastening to recover his cattle. The Isala, which fell from her head when he was killing her, turned into a bird, and, as he was on his way, came and said:

> I am the little Isala of the diligent wood-bearer,
> The wife of Unyengebule;
> It is I who was wilfully killed by the head of the house
> When he was asking me about the honeycomb.

# The Essential Kafir

The bird continually came to the path; sometimes he threw sticks at it. It constantly did so, until at length he hit it with a stick and killed it; he threw it down and went on his way.

After a time it came back again, and sang the same song. He was mad with passion; he threw at it and killed it; he buried it, and went on his way. As he was travelling, it came again to the place where he was, and said:

> I am the little Isala of the diligent wood-bearer,
> The wife of Unyengebule;
> It is I who was wilfully killed by the head of the house
> When he was asking me about the honeycomb.

He was perplexed now, and asked, "What can I do to the bird? It constantly annoys me by this thing which I do not like." He thought in his heart, and said, "I will kill it now and put it in my bag." He threw at it and killed it, and put it in his bag, and fastened it firmly with the string, and went on his way.

At length he reached his wife's village. When he arrived, they were dancing. Ah! he forgot that about which he was in such a hurry. He went up to his wife's female relations, and was in a hurry now to join in the dance. His wife's relations asked him for tobacco. He said instantly, "Untie my bag yonder." He had forgotten the bird, which he had placed in it. As soon as they untied it, the bird came out; for his part, he was engaged in dancing. It made a whir and pitched on the poles of the entrance to the cattle kraal; where it sang the same song, saying:

> I am the little Isala of the diligent wood-bearer,
> The wife of Unyengebule;
> It is I who was wilfully killed by the head of the house
> When he was asking me about the honeycomb.

# Folklore

He heard it, and many heard it. He hastened to run away. The people rushed on him and seized him, and asked him what he was running from. He answered, "For my part, I was coming to the dance. I do not understand what is said by the bird."

The bird again sang the song, hovering over the people who had caught him; it said:

<blockquote>I am the little Isala—&c.</blockquote>

They said to him, "What does the bird say?" He replied, "I do not know." They killed him.

Cannibalism has left its trace in a marked way in the stories of the natives, and our stories of "Fee, Fie, Fo, Fum" can be easily matched by the Zulus. Here is one, also taken from the "South African Folklore Journal":

### KGOLODIKANE

It is said that maidens, having gone to the river to fetch water, hid their beads in the sand. To one of their companions, who had delayed coming up, they said, "We have thrown our beads into the river; do you the same." She took them off and threw them into the river. As soon as she had done so they unearthed theirs, and laughed at her, saying, "She has thrown her beads into the water; where will she find them again?" They took their pitchers on their heads, and went home, laughing at her.

She went down the river, saying, "Pool! pool! Show me my beads that have passed this way." The pool said, "Pass on!" She went along until she became tired, and then came to a large, deep pool. She said again, "Pool! pool! Show me my beads passing this way." The pool was silent. She spoke the second time, and the water was disturbed. She spoke the third time, and the pool opened and said, " Enter ; your beads are here ! "

She entered and found an old woman, covered with wounds, who was half eaten up by Dimo (a kind of supernatural being). She had only one arm and one leg. As soon as the girl appeared, the old woman hopped in front of her and said, " Laugh at me, laugh at me, my little sister." The girl had compassion on her and would not laugh. Then the old woman said to her, " Come here and lick my sores." She went up to her and licked them. The old woman said, " You young maid, that are so beautiful, have also a compassionate heart ; you have pity on a thing like me ; I shall preserve you. I am living with Dimo ; he has gone to hunt for human beings, that he may eat them. You will know when he is coming by a light wind that will blow, and a few drops of rain that will fall. Take and eat, and when you have finished, hide yourself behind this wall."

When she had hidden herself, in very truth a light wind did blow, and a few drops of rain fell. Dimo appeared and looked awful. He had long hair ; his mouth was red ; his teeth looked like the tusks of a wild pig. He ran round the house saying, " I smell a human being ; I smell a human being ! " He took fire and burnt the sores of the old woman, saying, " I smell a human being ! " The old woman replied, " There is no human being here. You may kill me as you have always killed me." Dimo wished to devour her, as he was hungry, not having been successful in hunting that day. But he was loth to do it, for he would have no one to cook for him. He then went to sleep. The next morning he arose early, and went to hunt for human beings.

The old woman then took the young maiden and decorated her with beads, and anointed her head with grease, put brass rings on her legs and rings on her arms, and adorned her with

# Folklore

elbow bracelets and anklets of beads. She dressed her in a new kirtle, a pretty one, and an apron of kid-skin, also a copper fringe. She gave her a robe of jackal skins, and a mantle of the silver jackal skins. She then gave her a small round stone, and said, " This round stone, as soon as you have emerged, take and rub your armpits with. You must not look back. As soon as you have rubbed your armpits, throw it back over your shoulder into the pool. It will return to me. Before you may look back, one will give you water to drink. If you do as I instruct you, Dimo will not catch you. Go in peace, my friend, and may rain fall upon you ! "

Verily, this child did as she was instructed, and arrived at the place where she had thrown her beads into the river. Her younger sister found her there. " Are you my elder sister ? Where do you come from ? Where did you get all your pretty things ? Believe me, you have been sought for again and again." The elder sister replied, " Give me some water to drink." Her sister gave it. They then went home.

Her parents and people of the village crowded round her, inquiring where she had been, and where she had obtained all the beautiful things she had on her person. She told them all. Some were pleased ; others were jealous and said, " It is like her fortune. If it had been any of us it would not have happened."

Her uncle's children went to the place where she had been, but did not follow her instructions. They laughed at the old woman when she said, " Come and lick my sores." They replied, " What ! Are you mad ? Shall we lick such a thing as you ? What has become of us ? Give us beads. We are going: we have not time to delay. We came for beads." The gain for which they had travelled they did not obtain. The old woman, being angered, gave them over to Dimo, who devoured them.

# The Essential Kafir

In another story of a similar nature a young man went to court the two daughters of a cannibal woman who had devoured all the people of the country. The two girls dug a hole in the house and hid their sweetheart, after telling him not to be afraid of their mother, who had a large toe which would come in front of her. The lover had no sooner been safely covered up when, sure enough, there was a great noise, and a huge toe came into the hut; the woman came in after it and rolled on the ground and began to smell the earth, saying, "Eh, eh, but I smell the delicious odour of a man; my children, whom have you got in the hut to-day?" The girls pretended to be very angry, and said, "Don't bother us, as if it were our business; we have had no one here to-day; you are quite mistaken." The cannibal woman hunted round the hut, but could find no human flesh, and during the night the young man crept out of the hole, killed the cannibal, and carried off the two girls, whom he made his wives.

No naughty boys should read the next tale.

It is a story of which the natives are particularly fond, and it is called

## LITTLE RED STOMACH

Long, long ago, there was a little boy who was very clever and precocious, whose name was Red Stomach. His mother told him never to drink out of a certain pool, for it belonged to a terrible monster who loved to swallow little boys who were naughty and disobedient. However, Red Stomach laughed at his mother, and told her that he was not afraid of any monster, for he could take care of himself quite well. His mother, of course, said the usual things that all mothers do say to such bad boys. The boy felt very thirsty one day, and said to his mother that he intended to go and drink from the forbidden pool. His mother warned

# Folklore

him of his danger; but he said he did not care at all for all the monsters in the world. No sooner had he swallowed the water than a great monster of fearful proportions and of hideous face came running up to the pool and grew furiously angry with Red Stomach. Opening its huge mouth, it swallowed Red Stomach at a gulp. This most edifying and moral tale should end here ; but, unfortunately, it has only begun. Little Red Stomach proved himself a very obstinate morsel to digest, and so the huge monster began to feel great pains in its stomach, and at last grew so bad that it decided to summon all the animals which lived in the pool and to address them. They all came, bedecked up for the occasion; and the monster made a speech to them explaining how it had such a bad stomach-ache that it was sure to die, and then no one would protect them. The frog began to cry and ask who would protect them after his death, and the monster could not say. After a great deal of pain the monster died, and Little Red Stomach pulled out his knife, which he had secreted in his dress, and cut open the monster. Coming out into the light of day, he went home and found his mother, who was explaining how disobedience is punished, enforcing her lecture by pointing out the sad death of Red Stomach. He, however, came in and astonished every one by explaining how he had escaped. All his mother could do was to say, weakly, that she never knew he had any plan formed for escape.

## A CANNIBAL STORY

Arbousset tells a Bechuana tale which I have heard in Tembuland, and indeed some of its features are universal throughout South Africa, though tacked on to other legends. It is somewhat like this. A man had a daughter whom he loved, and he said to her that he was about to start off to build

# The Essential Kafir

a hut in a different part of the country, and added, " My child, you will go with us." He started off with his wife ; but his wilful daughter refused to budge. She said that the house was so prettily ornamented with nice things that she could not think of leaving it. Besides, it was very cold sleeping in the open air at night, and she feared the hyenas. Anyhow, she did not mean to follow her father : was she not well able to take care of herself? The mother gave her a truly motherly lecture on disobedience ; and added a warning to keep her hut closed if she permanently refused to come, for there were cannibals in the country.

Day after day the self-sacrificing mother came with bread, and told the girl to open the hut and receive it, which the ill-tempered lass did. This happened many days, until at last a cannibal came and said in a coarse, rough, husky voice, " My daughter, open the door and take this bread." Instantly the girl called out that she knew the voice to be that of a cannibal : it was not at all like that of her mother. The cannibal left disconcerted, for the girl pointed out to him that the door of her hut opened on a precipice, and thus could not be forced. So the cannibal went away and swallowed a red-hot assegai-point to clear his throat. (This is a very favourite method in many cannibal stories, and it is said to make the voice very gentle and soft.) After this operation he came back and repeated the same command to take the bread. The girl said that his voice was much softer, but that it was not her mother's voice, and so she would not open the door. The cannibal then went away and swallowed a red-hot hoe, and this time his voice was so soft that the disobedient girl thought it was her mother. She opened the door, and the cannibal quickly jumped in and caught her. He put her into the large bag which all well-regulated cannibals carry. He went away home with the girl in his bag, promising himself a good feast. But as he passed

Plate 58.

PONDO WOMEN THATCHING A HUT.

A woman is standing inside the hut pulling through the wooden needle which the woman on the roof pushes from above.

Plate 59.

A GAZALAND CARRIER.

# Folklore

by the hut of the aunt of the captured girl—he did not know that it was the aunt—he went in, as they offered him some beer. He drank too much and got quite drunk, and while in this state the aunt looked into the bag out of pure womanly curiosity; to her astonishment, she saw her own niece. There and then they rescued the girl, and filled the bag with vipers, dogs, poisonous insects, snakes, and other delightful animals, which every one keeps ready against such emergencies. Closing the bag, they hid the girl until the cannibal should awaken from his drunken sleep. When he awoke he was so drowsy and silly that he shouldered his bag and went home. Calling his wife, he made her fill a large pot with water in which to boil his prey. He then told the woman to shut the door tightly and securely, so that no one could come in. When this was done he opened the bag, and all the creatures jumped forth and stung, bit, tore, and wounded him. He cried out, "Uch! Uch! King! King! Och! Och!" and shouted to his wife to open the door. But it was so securely fixed that this could not be done: so, seeing a hole in the roof, he jumped out, and ran through the village to a mud-heap, on which he threw himself. He was instantly changed into a tree. The wild bees now live in the bark of that tree.

The modifications are endless; but this story is to be found everywhere among the native tribes.

Instead of detailing a hundred stories, let me give a short extract of the different limbs, organs, or parts of such stories. Out of these thousands of permutations and combinations can be made. The details help to indicate the bent of the Kafir mind. They form the seed-plot in which fresh stories germinate.

(1) A company of boys are killed and become changed into birds, buck, crocodiles, &c., and so escape from cannibals.

# The Essential Kafir

(2) Whenever a person goes into a hut which he finds empty, he gets into trouble with cannibals.

(3) An assegai stuck in the ground stands upright if all is well; it vibrates if there is a little trouble, and falls down when any one dies.

(4) People can say, "Hut, grow up," and instantly a hut appears fully formed.

(5) When pursued by cannibals, throw an egg on the ground; it will become a mist.

(6) If chased by cannibals throw off your cloak; it will run one way while you run another, and the cannibal will always follow the cloak: or else, throw a dozen articles down, and they will all run in different directions and puzzle the cannibal.

(7) A person pursued by cannibals changes himself into a stone: the cannibals always break their teeth over such a stone, and then in anger throw the supposed stone over the river, when it becomes a man again.

(8) In times of trouble always ask an old woman, a bird, or a mouse, and you shall have the information needed.

(9) Mice are most self-sacrificing creatures: whenever they see a person in trouble they say, "Kill me, and throw my skin into the air"; this always opens up a way of escape.

(10) To make a flood of water behind you when fleeing from pursuers, throw down a milk-sac: it instantly becomes a flood of water to hinder the pursuers.

(11) If you are chased and come to a river, all you have to do is either to step over it in one stride or to turn yourself into a stone; in the latter case your pursuer will throw you across the river.

(12) Rocks open and close when you speak the right word to them.

(13) Birds can make milk by pailfuls when you need it; they can undo the whole of a day's work done in the garden.

# Folklore

They say "Ground, be mixed," and all the day's ploughing is undone.

(14) Crocodiles always keep houses under the water for people who are in trouble: they always welcome visitors!

(15) Impudent bold-faced *girls* always get the worst of it: not so the *boys*.

(16) Girls who break native customs always come to grief in fairy tales.

(17) Women can give birth to crows, snakes, or other animals. Boys can be born with no arms or legs. The arms and legs always grow, later, in a moment.

(18) If an old woman proposes to boil you, always suggest playing at the game. They will want to pretend to boil you first: let them start: then, when you are getting uncomfortable, say that it is time to change places: the women always consent, and you naturally refuse to let them out when they begin to scream. This ruse recurs again and again in the native stories, and greatly amuses the people.

(19) Children who are precocious monsters always manage to smear some guiltless person with blood and thus escape punishment.

(20) There are endless stories of the usual European pattern which run as follows: "Stick beat dog: dog eat cow: cow kill rat," &c. Or, again, a poor boy lends a stick to another; it is his only stock-in-trade. The borrower breaks the stick: a blanket is demanded in exchange: the blanket is lent to a man who tears it and has to make restitution with an ox: the ox is killed by somebody, and a whole kraalful of oxen is demanded: and so forth. The poor boy is soon a prince at this rate.

I have some thirty or forty more points of this nature noted down; but these will abundantly show the type of story which delights a native's mind.

# The Essential Kafir

We may close the chapter with a few tales concerning Reynard the fox, of Hottentot origin, taken from Bleek and others.

### THE LION'S ILLNESS

The lion, it is said, was ill, and they all went to see him in his suffering. But the jackal did not go, because the traces of the people who went to see him did not turn back. Thereupon he was accused by the hyena, who said, "Though I go to look, the jackal does not want to come and look at the man's sufferings." (Animals frequently call a lion a *man* in Kafir folklore. The jackal always calls the lion his uncle.)

Then the lion let the hyena go, in order that she might catch the jackal; and she did so, and brought him.

The lion asked the jackal, "Why did you not come here to see me?" The jackal said, "O no! When I heard that my uncle was so very ill, I went to the witchdoctor to consult him, whether and what medicine would be good for my uncle against the pain. The doctor said to me, 'Go and tell your uncle to take hold of the hyena and draw off her skin, and put it on while it is warm. Then he will recover.' The hyena is one who does not care for my uncle's sufferings."

The lion followed his advice, got hold of the hyena, and drew the skin over her ears, while she howled with all her might, and put it on.

### WHICH WAS THE THIEF?

A jackal and a hyena went and hired themselves to a man to be his servants. In the middle of the night the jackal arose and smeared the hyena's tail with fat, and then ate all the

BLANTYRE CHURCH.
The building shows what natives can do when trained.

SAWING MAHOGANY NEAR PORT HERALD.

Plate 61.

# Folklore

rest of it which was in the house. In the morning the man missed the fat, and he immediately accused the jackal of having eaten it.

"Look at the hyena's tail," said the rogue, "and you will see who is the thief." The man did so, and then thrashed the hyena till she was nearly dead.

### FISH-STEALING

Once upon a time a jackal, who lived on the borders of the colony, saw a waggon returning from the sea-side laden with fish. He tried to get into the waggon from behind; but he could not. He then ran on before, and lay in the road as if dead. The waggon came up to him, and the leader cried to the driver, " Here is a fine kaross for your wife."

"Throw it into the waggon," said the driver; and the jackal was thrown in.

The waggon travelled on through a moonlit night, and all the while the jackal was throwing the fish out into the road. He then jumped out himself, and secured a great prize. But a stupid hyena, coming by, ate more than her share, for which the jackal owed her a grudge: so he said to her, " You can get plenty of fish, too, if you lie in the way of a waggon as I did, and keep quite still whatever happens." "So!" mumbled the hyena.

Accordingly, when the next waggon came along from the sea, the hyena stretched herself out in the road.

"What ugly thing is this?" cried the leader, and kicked the hyena. He then took a stick and thrashed her within an inch of her life. The hyena, according to the directions of the jackal, lay quiet as long as she could; she then got up, and hobbled off to tell her misfortune to the jackal, who pretended to comfort her.

# The Essential Kafir

"What a pity," said the hyena, "that I have not such a handsome skin as you!"

### CLOUD-EATING

The jackal and the hyena were together, it is said, when a white cloud arose. The jackal ascended upon it, and ate the cloud as if it were fat.

When he wanted to come down, he said to the hyena, "My sister, as I am going to divide with thee, catch me well." So she caught him, and broke his fall. Then she went up and ate there, high on the top of the cloud.

When she was satisfied, she said, "My greyish brother, now catch me well." The greyish rogue said to his friend, "My sister, I shall catch thee well. Come down."

He held up his hands, and she came down from the cloud, and when she was near the jackal cried out (painfully jumping on one side), "My sister, do not take it ill. O me! O me! A thorn has pricked me, and sticks in me." Thus she fell down from above, and was sadly hurt.

Since that day it has been said that the hyena's left hind foot is shorter and smaller than the right one.

### THE LION'S SHARE

The lion and the jackal went together, hunting. They shot with arrows. The lion shot first, and his arrow fell short in its aim; but the jackal hit the game, and joyfully cried out, "It is hit." The lion looked at him with his two large eyes; the jackal, however, did not lose his countenance, and said, "No, uncle: I mean to say that you have hit." Then they followed the game, and the jackal passed the arrow of the lion without drawing the latter's attention to it. When

# Folklore

they arrived at a crossway, the jackal said, "Dear uncle, you are old and tired : stay here." The jackal then went on a wrong tack, beat his nose, and, in returning, let the blood drop from it like traces of game. "I could not find anything," he said; "but I met traces of blood. You had better go yourself to look for it. In the meantime I shall go this way." The jackal soon found the killed animal, crept inside it, and devoured the best portions; but his tail remained outside, and when the lion arrived he got hold of it, pulled the jackal out, and threw him on the ground with the words, "You rascal!" The jackal rose quickly again, complained of the rough handling, and asked, "What have I now done, dear uncle? I was busy cutting out the best part."

"Now let us go and fetch our wives," said the lion; but the jackal entreated his dear uncle to remain at the place, because he was old. The jackal then went away, taking with him two portions of the flesh, one for his own wife, but the best part for the wife of the lion. When the jackal arrived with portions of the flesh, the children of the lion saw him, began to jump, and, clapping their hands, cried, "There comes uncle with flesh!" The jackal threw, grumbling, the worst portion to them, and said, "There, you brood of the big-eyed one!" Then he went to his own house and told his wife immediately to break up house, and to go where the killed game was. The lioness wished to do the same; but he forbade her, and said that the lion would himself come and fetch her.

When the jackal, with his wife and children, had arrived in the neighbourhood of the killed animal, he ran into a thorn bush, scratched his face so that it bled, and thus made his appearance before the lion, to whom he said, "Ah! what a wife you have got! Look here: how she scratched my face

# The Essential Kafir

when I told her that she should come with us! You must fetch her yourself. I cannot bring her." The lion went home very angry. Then the jackal said, "Quick! let us build a tower." They heaped stone upon stone; when it was high enough, everything was carried to the top of it. When the jackal saw the lion approaching with his wife and children, he cried out to him, "Uncle, while you were away we have built a tower, in order to be better able to see game." "All right," said the lion; "but let me come up to you." "Certainly, dear uncle; but how will you manage to come up? We must let down a thong for you." The lion tied himself to the thong, and was drawn up; but when he was nearly at the top the thong was cut by the jackal, who exclaimed, as if frightened, "O, how heavy you are, uncle! Wife, go and fetch a new thong." ("An old one," he said aside to her.)

The lion was drawn up again, but again came down in the same manner. "No," said the jackal: "that will never do: you must, however, manage to come up high enough, so that you may get a mouthful at least." Then he ordered his wife to prepare a good piece, but aside told her to make a stone hot, and to cover it with fat. Then he drew up the lion once more, and, complaining that he was very heavy to hold, told him to open his mouth, whereupon he threw the hot stone down his throat. When the lion had devoured it, he entreated him to run as quickly as possible to the water.

### A FABLE SHOWING EUROPEAN INFLUENCE

The Basutos have a legend which runs as follows: Once upon a time there was a monster called Kammapa, which set to work devouring people. It was so big that its whole body could not be seen at one gaze. It devoured so many people that at length there was but one woman left on the earth. She

# Folklore

went into a stable and gave birth to a child, who instantly sprang up to the full stature of manhood. His name was Litaolane, or the Diviner.

When the monster saw this child he swallowed it at one gulp. But Litaolane cut the entrails of the monster from within, and so killed it. When he began to cut his way out of the body of Kammapa a strange thing happened. Every time he cut the body of the beast there was a cry heard, which emanated from the people previously devoured by the monster. Voices kept calling out to Litaolane that he was killing them. Finally he disregarded the voices and cut his way out to the open air. Then all the people who had been previously devoured came to life and followed him.

Instead of the people showing gratitude to their deliverer, they began to oppress him, because, forsooth, he had never been an ordinary child. They laid traps for him, and tried to catch him, that they might put him to death. So he hid in a bed of reeds. The people saw him one day in the open country, and chased him. He ran to a river, and when he saw the people he turned himself into a stone. The people imagined that he had crossed the river, and so took up the stone and threw it across the river, intending to kill him. And by this means he escaped out of their hands.

In this story it is easy to trace a resemblance to the Christian conception of the Virgin Birth of the Deliverer, who was rejected by the people whom He came to set free. In a similar way, many Zulu tales contain clear traces of such stories as Pharaoh's attempting to cross the Red Sea.

These stories lose a great deal when they are met with in print. It is very interesting to hear the people tell them, and to watch the signs of intense curiosity in the faces of the listeners.

# THE KAFIR—WHAT IS TO BECOME OF HIM?

## CHAPTER XII

### THE KAFIR—WHAT IS TO BECOME OF HIM?

THIS question becomes of increased importance every year. At present the natives outnumber the Europeans in South Africa four or five times over. They are multiplying at a very rapid rate; the land on native territories is slowly becoming filled up; and, though it would carry a vastly greater population if the agricultural interests were more scientifically developed, the natives are so slow to adopt new ideas that the time is not far distant when the shoe will begin to pinch. The natives are wonderfully submissive to constituted authority; but no one can say what they would do if threatened with a famine of great proportions.

There is as yet no sign that the native is likely to diminish in his rate of increase. Every tribe is extremely prolific. It may be that the Kafirs' physique will suffer in consequence of the way they are now shielded from the stern struggle for existence. When native wars reduced the population, the physique was splendidly developed: the fittest alone survived.

European clothing will undoubtedly have a great effect on the health of the people. Pneumonia and other diseases are on the increase among the dressed natives. Cotton shirts and pneumonia go together in the mines. Any one who has visited the Kimberley or Johannesburg mines and has seen the natives emerge from the bowels of the earth, covered with profuse perspiration and damp cotton shirts or blankets, will understand that when these natives sit about in order to cool down, chills are sure to supervene. And the sick Kafir, depressed and gloomy, is a pitiable sight.

The natives are distinctly flabby, though they look so muscular, and they are strangely unable to stand extremes of heat or cold. They have not the reserve forces which most Europeans possess : nor can they carry out sustained work of a heavy nature. If there should ever be a struggle between the natives and Europeans, the natives will be sure to go to the wall.

We have already seen that the Kafir is as a rule incapable of developing mentally beyond a certain stage, and consequently it is very difficult to say what the future of the native races of South Africa will be. If Weismann is correct in maintaining that acquired habits are not capable of being preserved by heredity, we can form no theory of value as to Kafir possibilities until we know what latent capacity for " variation " they possess. On this point we have scarcely any light at present. The Kafir is in that respect an unknown quantity.

The first question to be examined before we can form any judgment as to the future of the Kafir Races is :

ARE THE KAFIRS LAZY?

The modern Kafir tells us no straightforward story, no manifestly simple tale : he is no clear and unmistakable printed page that he who runs may read. He is some obscure palimpsest, the original writing of his nature being partly effaced and rendered illegible by recent European influence and unnatural development. From this disfigured page it is not easy to discover his true nature.

All admit that he is incapable, at present, of sustained and heavy work, though he can perform the most extraordinary feats in a spasmodic way. When this has been said for the

## The Kafir—What is to become of him?

Kafir, most people in South Africa add that he is a hopelessly lazy creature. But I quite agree with Sir Harry Johnston in his statement that the Kafir is not really lazy.

And now for first impressions. It is very difficult to take the Kafir seriously, for he is a most provoking fellow. First appearances are all against him.

On landing at Cape Town the traveller is amazed at the seeming laziness of the Kafirs. While he is waiting in the docks to get his luggage passed through the customs, the visitor sees a gang of Kafirs at work. It may be that some twenty of them are busily engaged in moving rails from one heap to another. Instead of finding a few white men working with a will, he sees some twenty natives, all dressed in old sacks, standing in a group, chatting and laughing over a heap of rails. The white overseer says, "Now, boys, hurry up," and the natives all advance in a well-dressed line to the first rail, and then begin to chant a droning tune. At a certain note in the song all twenty natives stoop down and take hold of the rail, chanting as they stoop. When this is done they continue the chant, and, at another note, all raise the rail with great merriment and fun. They then continue the chant and at another note all raise their right feet, and when the chant comes to the next period they advance one step, and laugh again. Continuing the chant, they lift the left leg this time, raise it high in the air, laugh, chant, and take a step forward. When they have moved the rail to the new position they chant till they come to a certain phrase or "motif" in their Wagnerian song, and, with a yell and volley of sound, drop the iron rail into its place, and then look at one another and laugh. They slowly return to the heap of rails, hold a short indaba, and proceed to take up the next rail, which is treated in exactly the same fashion as the last. The newcomer looks on spell-bound at the weird sight, and then

## The Essential Kafir

suddenly bursts into a laugh and walks off, inwardly chuckling to himself. The first impression is all against the Kaffirs. A new-comer cannot take these men seriously, but looks upon them as only big babies, grinning and grunting at one another over their work. Their ways, like those of Bret Harte's Heathen Chinee, "are peculiar."

The next time the visitor comes into contact with the natives is, perhaps, after he has settled into expensive lodgings in Johannesburg. His only servants are two or three native boys. One is cook, one is houseboy, and the other is nothing in particular; he seems to help the others in doing nothing. English servants are soon surrounded by a halo of glory in the observer's mind, and he forgets all the worries he had with them before he left the old country. He gives a note to one of his boys to take to a friend a few streets off. The native looks at him, and then looks at the letter as if he thought it might sting him. At last he takes it up and stands still, not quite knowing what to do. The master repeats his instructions, using abominable kitchen-Kafir, which even makes a native grin. The boy starts off with the note, and the master waits half an hour—an hour—an hour and a half;—but there is no sign of the boy. He wonders whether his boy is climbing the lamp-posts or playing marbles like a decent English boy-messenger. All this long time the Kafir is chatting to the native cook at the house to which he has been sent. He had first gone round to see a few friends, and to have a good look at the shop windows. Having lost his way, he went up to a white man in the street and offered him the letter with a grunt. The white man read the address and shook his head, saying, "Not for me," as he passed on. After showing the address to a dozen white men, at last he was put on the track of the right street, and finally arrived at the right house. Here the European heard that a boy had come with a note,

## The Kafir—What is to become of him?

and said, "Then let him wait." A Kafir's time is worth nothing. I have seen a trader keep a messenger for hours outside his shop for no earthly reason whatever, except that the messenger was a Kafir.

The boy smelt a pleasant odour in the kitchen, and his friend the cook allowed him to sample the various pots on the stove. The white man eventually read the letter, and sent a note to the boy, telling him to take it off to his master. But the boy sat chatting with the cook; and finally returned home, having left the note in the kitchen of the house he was sent to. Again appearances are all against the Kafir: no one can take him as seriously as he takes himself.

The next stage is to see the native in his own kraal. Here first impressions are just as bad. We shall suppose that the observer visits native kraals. He finds the men all lying about in the shade, smoking, snuffing, and chatting, while their wives are tilling the ground. The Kafir kills time with a consummate grace. Walking off to the nearest trader's store, the visitor sees twenty lazy men sitting about, chatting over the news concerning some calf that was born last week. Perhaps a Kafir is seen walking about the place with an umbrella, taking care of his complexion; or two or three Kafirs are engaged in gossip, wasting the hours, which seem to pass without *ennui*. Their wives are all at work in the fields.

### SECOND IMPRESSIONS

A little reflection, however, will show the new-comer that most of the hard work of the docks where he landed is performed by Kafirs. If he doubts this, let him stand by the dock-gates at sunrise, and see them streaming in to work. The railway he travelled over, on which he thought of the lazy Kafirs, whom from the train windows he could see

# The Essential Kafir

lolling about in their kraals, was built by native sweat. The present position of Johannesburg would have been impossible without their labour. Who is it that does the hard work on the farms while the Dutchman is drinking his coffee on the stoep? It is the native again. These "lazy" creatures have done an amazing amount of work.

In olden days even the Zulus did a good deal of the hard work in the gardens, until Chaka stopped them and made them adopt the profession of arms as their main work in life. Thus it came about that when England stopped all tribal wars the women kept the men. In many districts one can still find the men working in the fields, and the number of men who are working thus is increasing rapidly. Only a small proportion of men have more than one wife—they say 3 per cent. in the Transkei and 11 per cent. in other districts. So men cannot wholly depend on the slave labour of their wives.

To judge the question fairly, we need to consider what work the women do, what work the men undertake; what they used to do in olden days, and why they do less now than formerly. We need to compare these matters with the position of affairs in European countries.

### THE WORK OF WOMEN

Women are responsible for the house work; the cooking falls to their lot, and nowadays most of the work in the fields. They have to grow and cook the food. As there are no coal-merchants or waterworks in the country, the women naturally fetch the firewood and water which are needed in their special work. In short, everything in connection with household affairs falls to the lot of women. But then they have no houses to dust and clean, no silver to polish, no plates to wash up, and practically no needlework to do.

# The Kafir—What is to become of him?

The women plaster the huts with mud, though they do not cut the wattles or build the framework of the huts. In fact, the men give them all the work which they consider undignified, and even the women would resent any alteration in the division of labour. The women do the thatching of the huts.

If we compare this work with what European women do, we shall not find very much difference, except with regard to the tilling of the soil and the thatching of the huts and mudding of the walls. Even tilling the soil is done largely by women in many European countries.

The women in England do all the household work, and would laugh at the proposal that the men should henceforth manage that department of labour. The average colonial wife has to work quite as hard as the average native woman, who has plenty of time to sit about smoking and chatting.

## THE WORK OF THE MEN

In olden days the men shared all the work with the women, until military necessities compelled them to attend to the duties connected with fighting. In this way war became the main work of the men; and in adopting that department of work they were, in their estimation, doing the hardest work, while they thus provided the women with all they needed, even, in war time, capturing women who might slave for them and save their own wives from excessive toil.

In those days a man could call his wives, cattle, and grain his own only so long as he could defend them and protect them from rival tribes. Consequently, the men felt they were doing the hardest and most dangerous work in attending to the profession of arms while the women applied themselves to the agriculture. It is computed that Chaka killed over a million people in his wars, and the killing of such an

## The Essential Kafir

enormous number of people, who were most unwilling to be killed, took a good deal of elbow-grease out of the nation. Men do not tamely submit to be slaughtered without resistance, and the endurance and toil of these old warriors was simply homeric in its magnitude. The rivers ran, not in school-book parlance, but in terrible reality, with blood. No one who has happened to get in the way of a Swazie or Zulu impi, when it was on the warpath, will be inclined to call the natives lazy. Nor will any one do so who has seen these people at one of their amazing tribal hunts for game. The amount of perspiration and muscle used up in war and the chase is incredible.

But the work of the man does not stop here. He does more than merely fight and hunt. He cuts the wattles for the huts, fixes up the framework of the building, and gives what he considers the light work to the women only when the heavy work is done. As the natives have not even the faintest conception of sanitation, they have to move their kraals very frequently, and leave the old place exposed for a few years to the sun and rain. Hence building takes up a great deal of time.

The men look after the cattle, and when the natives had thousands of head of cattle this took up an immense amount of time. Rinderpest has robbed them of cattle, and so another portion of their work is taken from them. Yet they make the fences; and when their chief wants his extensive fields weeded or hoed up he sends for his warriors, who turn out in hundreds, glad to work for their king, considering that the finicking work of women is elevated by the fact that the work is being done for their chief. To use an Americanism, they "enthuse" over the work in the gardens on such occasions, as though they loved the work above all things on earth.

Plate 62.

GOING TO SCHOOL IN TEMBULAND.

**THE LESSON.**
This is the same Tembu boy who appears on plate 10. He is doing "home-work."

## The Kafir—What is to become of him?

When the natives go to towns like Durban to pull "Lickshaws" (as the natives call the Japanese articles), they run up the hills so fast that they very soon injure their hearts; they used to die off rapidly from this cause. Not even Durban men accuse *these* boys of being lazy.

It is true that the men might do the mudding of the walls and the thatching of the huts; but it will take time to educate them up to this. We all know the story of the small boy who asked his mother whether God made the elephants. On being told that He did, he asked, "And did He make the flies?" When he was told that He did this also, he was silent for a few moments, musing; then he said, "Mighty fiddling work making flies after making elephants!" That is what the Kafir thinks about mudding the house after he has built it. I am not wishing to make people believe that the Kafir is a paragon of virtue and activity. No one who has read these pages could fairly make this assertion. The fact that he is lazy and indolent *in certain directions* has been emphasised.

The men also do most of the heavy carrying work for Europeans, though women do it for their own husbands. A man looks utterly lazy as he stalks behind his wife who has a heavy bundle on her head. But do not call him lazy till you have walked hundreds of miles with boys who carry your load of seventy pounds on their heads for thirty miles a day. At the end of the day's march these boys come into camp full of good spirits and climb the first tree they see, and cut off the top branches, just to show you that they are in fine fettle and not tired out: after this exhibition of superfluous energy they run back over the road to take the load from any young boy who is not as accustomed to his work. I have seen this so often that I hesitate to call them lazy.

When we reflect on the work men do in Europe we find very little difference between them and the Kafirs. European men do the building, the hunting, the fighting, and take care of the animals, and earn money. These things fall to the lot of men among the Kafirs also.

We may conclude, then, that while the Kafir differs from Europeans in his ideas as to what constitutes profitable labour, and is much better off in relative riches compared with Europeans who cannot rest content with what the Kafir considers ample comfort, he is not utterly lazy. The moment there is what *he* considers an adequate inducement to work he rouses himself and begins.

If, then, the Kafir is not hopelessly lazy, it should be possible to give him new ambitions and new occupations. Much of his old occupation has gone from him, and at present he is seen at one of the awkward "joins" in history. He stands midway between the shattered ideal of the past and the unformed ideal of the future. We must not look at him solely in the light of the labour problem : this (to quote a Zulu proverb) "dies like the moon and rises again." But it takes a different shape at every resurrection. At one time the great problem was how to get sufficient labour into Natal to supply the needs of Durban. The burning question was whether this supply of native labour would come from the Transvaal or not. Mr. David Leslie suggested that the Natal Government should buy large farms in the Transvaal, on which natives might stay as they were flocking into Natal. He pointed out that they could thus be lodged and shielded from the rapacity of the Transvaal Boers. In those days labour could be secured in Durban at the rate of five or ten shillings a month. An ox could be bought for an axe, and a native would carry a load of 100 lbs. for three days for a copper bangle. But, though the labour problem is constantly changing and presenting new aspects and protean forms, the great *native* problem still looms up ominously in the background. What

## The Kafir—What is to become of him?

place is the native to take in the fabric of a United South Africa? Is he to be a hewer of wood and a drawer of water, or is he to take his place as a full-grown citizen of the country? Is he to compete with carpenters, masons, and other tradesmen of the country? The Johannesburg difficulty is but passing, while every year the great native problem grows more insistent and important.

At present some few Kafirs have the benefits of the franchise; for example, those who live in Cape Colony, and own property which is valued at £75 or earn a fixed salary of £50 a year, are allowed to vote. But the great bulk of the people are quite unfit for this privilege. They are also unfit to sit on sanitary boards, for they are living a good many centuries behind the times, and develop but slowly. They have no grit or balance; nor have they any ambitions worth naming. It is our work to create these ambitions and needs, and to lead the natives into new occupations. Already ploughs are making their way into some districts, and, though the natives are slow to change, they cannot but see the advantage of such labour-saving implements.

The Glen Grey Act is an experiment full of hopefulness. By that Act natives in a certain district can own land under certain restrictions. When land-tenure is a tribal concern the natives have no inclination to cultivate specially well. When they have a personal stake in the country they show more keenness in their cultivation of the soil. Tribal tenure, also, naturally tends to strengthen and consolidate the power of the chiefs, for on this system they allot the land to the people. Much might be done in the direction of the cultivation of tobacco, rubber, coffee, tea, sugar, cotton; and the natives should do admirably on cattle ranches and in purely agricultural pursuits.

To show what natives can do, a photograph of the interior

# The Essential Kafir

of Blantyre Church is given (see plate 60). This was built by native labour under white supervision. Another photograph shows natives sawing timber (see plate 61): strange to say, they frequently object to work in a saw-pit, and so the timber (a log of native mahogany in this case) has to be propped up on a special staging.

But before the Kafir can make any substantial progress there are two things which must be eliminated from his life: the first is the eternal fear of magic and witchcraft, and the second is the practice of polygamy.

To get rid of his fear of and belief in magic, education is necessary. There are some great drawbacks in education, for the school-Kafir is frequently a very objectionable person. He is apt to suffer from self-conceit, and is therefore cordially hated by most white men.

It is comparatively pleasant to see the small Kafir boys going to school in their blankets, with slates slung over their shoulders (see plate 62). The thing has a picturesque aspect. It is also interesting to see a boy doing his lessons when he is clad in a white night-shirt (see plate 63). But when he leaves the school and comes into contact with Europeans the effect is unpleasant. Here are two letters written to a friend who wanted a school-teacher.

The first is from a fond parent asking for a rise of salary for her daughter:

DEAR SIR,—I want to say to you to raise the girl's money I am not enough for the money of the girl if you do not raise the money of the girl I will refuse the girl I may stop there with great salutations—I am

Yours truely.

The second is from a woman applying for the post of teacher, which she did *not* get:

DEAR SIR,—You are most humbly implored and pleaded to receive my application tenderly imploring you to consider and approve the same. I

# The Kafir—What is to become of him?

possible employ me as an Interpreter and school mistress under your mangement. I would be glad to succeed Miss . . . and can assure you am competent re what am applying for,

Yours.

The effect of such letters is to make Europeans regard education as anything but a blessing.

But we cannot keep the natives from learning something, and the question is, What shall they learn? Advanced technical knowledge is unnecessary. All that is needed is the very elements of learning, with a small amount of instruction which may help to dispel the ideas entertained concerning magic. At present a native fears to grow too rich, lest he be accused of doing so by magical practices: thus all initiative and ambition is crushed in the bud.

Polygamy is slowly vanishing, because but few men are now being killed in tribal fights. But so long as the animal and sexual nature of the natives absorbs all their thought, and fills all their conversation, progress is impossible. Limitation is an essential factor in life, and the man whose mind for ever broods on such matters finds that all his thought becomes occupied with them, as Cicero long ago pointed out. The natives must be taught the lesson of restraint; and, of course, this work is the special care of missionaries.

It would be an excellent thing if the natives could be left alone to some original and natural mode of civilisation suited to their natures; but the presence of Europeans in the country makes this difficult or impossible. They are forced to adopt some elements of our Western civilisation. The natives must be more or less the drudges of the white men, owing to their inherent inferiority and incapacity. It is impossible to expect the Ethiopian to change his skin or the leopard his spots.

I know that an educated Kafir will occasionally come up and say, " I have been watching my face in the looking-glass,

# The Essential Kafir

and I really think I am becoming a little whiter." I know one man who said this with great gravity. I have also seen a native looking at a picture in which a small boy was depicted in a bath, scrubbing himself with a wonderful soap: wherever he had washed himself the black skin had become white. The native looked at this picture with great hungry eyes. An educated native will try to make himself white; but we should be able to prevent that calamity.

After all, the feat is impossible. No man in his senses would suggest that we should give our daughters to black men; no one would wish to have them sitting at our tables as a regular thing; no one would care to take a native into partnership. It is a thousand pities that we cannot banish all European clothing from native territories, and allow the Kafirs to evolve naturally, and form a society of their own, just as the Malays have been doing in Cape Town. Such a plan would be better for both black and white. Native manufactures would then develop naturally.

I know one missionary—needless to say he is American—who wished to keep his Kafirs away from beer-drinks, and thought the most practical method to adopt was to keep them busily employed. So he asked one man what work he could do. He said he could only make baskets. The American missionary instantly said he would undertake to buy every basket he made. The next native could only make mats: the missionary undertook to take all he could make. And so on. He then gave them seed of new vegetables, which would need attending to just when the beer-drinks were most frequent, and thus began to raise his natives. Could not this be done on a large scale? It would be easy to teach the natives how to make their baskets and mats a little better. They would soon pick up new ideas, and thus natural industries might be fostered, and a normal growth of personality be obtained.

# The Kafir—What is to become of him?

This would solve the problem of the native vote. At present one would no more think of giving the native a vote on European matters than one would think of giving fourth-form boys at school a vote in the management of lessons.

The Kafir is a thriftless person, "a buck of an endless forest," as he vividly describes a man who is improvident and careless about the future. He will use up all his grain for beer, wasting it in the process; and then, when a time of drought comes, he has to starve. He is most wasteful and prodigal, and in his own light-hearted way squanders his grain while it lasts and never thinks of laying up provision for a rainy day—or a rainless day, as we ought to say in true South African style. At the mines, as in his kraal, he freely gambles away his possessions, and when he is "like a lopped tree" he will trust that his tide of luck may change and lead him on to fortune.

It may be possible to give him some degree of self-management in his own internal matters by-and-by. At present it seems to me to be out of the question to think of suggesting that he should take his place in the political life of the country. There are so many contending and conflicting interests that if the Kafir were to be allowed to complicate matters he might upset the vessel of State in a short time. No one who has watched the erratic development of the Ethiopian Church movement could take these people seriously. This strange sect started out from Churches with but little in common with the Church of South Africa, and after a short and flickering life has come to rest in the bosom of that Church. A ship will run into any port in a storm, and it is probably a good thing that these unstable people are now under the strong control of rigid ecclesiastical authorities.

The Kafir has made but little progress during the last few centuries. As we look into the " dark backward and abysm of time" we find that the descriptions of the Kafirs given by ancient writers would apply wonderfully to the tribes as we find them to-day. As we look into the future we see many dangers ahead, and find it hard to prophesy as to the fortunes of these strange people. The present is all that we can see quite clearly, and there can be but little question that our duty has been pointed out by Carlyle. "Of this thing be certain," he says: "wouldst thou plant for eternity, then plant into the deep infinite faculties of man, his fantasy and heart; wouldst thou plant for year and day, then plant into his superficial faculties, his self-love, and arithmetical understanding, what will grow there." And, yet again, "that there should one man die ignorant who had capacity for knowledge, this I call a tragedy, were it to happen more than twenty times in the minute, as by some computations it does."

We must now part from our light-hearted companion. We have traced his life and customs, and have seen that he is drifting along the surface of time in a rudderless bark, which is frail indeed. He is in the presence of mighty and restless forces which the economic development of the country has liberated; he is a misgrown child in the presence of races superior to him in all respects; and it is our task to help him to unlearn what he has wrongly learned, and to teach him how to use his limited powers to the best advantage. His good-natured indolence and his helplessness call to us to help him in his ascent, and we shall surely find that in helping him we are advancing the interests of the country which has passed through so much trouble, and has seen such lavish expenditure of life and treasure. When the gold mines have been worked out at Johannesburg, it may be found that our chief asset in South Africa consists in the native population.

# APPENDIX

Click signs used in this chapter: ‖ the Lateral, ! the Cerebral, ‡ the Palatal, ǀ the Dental.

## HEITSI-EIBIB, A HERO OF THE HOTTENTOTS

A SHORT account of Heitsi-Eibib and the Hottentots may prove interesting, and a note is therefore given in which some of the chief names of the Supreme Being occur. Many of the names are purposely left out, in order to simplify the account. Much of the information is derived from Hahn.

The word Hottentot is of doubtful origin. Frequently it is said to have been coined by the early Dutch settlers, who could make nothing out of the strange "clicking" language of the natives: they thought the talk was all made up of words like Hot and Tot. Hahn derives the word from the Frisian or Low German word *Hütten-tüt*, to quack. He says the Dutch used this word because they thought the language of the people sounded like the talk and jabber of parrots, and so they called it gibberish. Other Dutch settlers described the talk of the Hottentots as much akin to the cackling of geese.

According to Hahn the Hottentots are divided into two tribes, one the Koi-koi, whom he calls the true Hottentots, while strongly objecting to the term; and the Bushmen, or Sān. The Koi-koi are pastoral and nomadic, while the Sān are hunters. The word Koi-koi means Men of Men, or Men *par excellence*, the Bantu or Kafirs being in their estimation creatures of a very low order, whom they call *things* or *dogs*. The Kafirs call them monkeys in return. The word Hottentot includes the Griquas, the Namaquas, and the Koranas, these being Hottentots as much as the Koi-koi. It is said that some Bushmen can only count up to two, and, though they were said to be able to count to three, this word really only means *those*, being a derivative from a Koi-koi word. When they learn to count up to twenty, as they sometimes do, they use the decimal system, which is probably due to

# The Essential Kafir

Mashona influence, though, as they use the fingers for counting it would be an obvious system to adopt. It would seem as if they never felt the need of counting while they were merely hunters; but the moment they kept stock they felt the need of numbering their possessions. The words " to count " naturally took on the meaning of *to respect*, for the man who had most possessions was considered the greatest. Similarly, a fat man was a rich or important one, because only a person who was comparatively rich could have sufficient food to grow fat and to smear himself with grease. Consequently, fatness became an essential in the conception of beauty.

Though the Hottentots are much inferior to the Kafirs in physique and worldly possessions, they are immeasurably superior in the gift of imagination. Their ideas concerning the Supreme Being are very interesting, though somewhat obscure to us, as so few of those who knew the language made any serious attempt to discover what the Hottentots thought. Heitsi-Eibib is a great hero; but he is frequently confused in Hottentot thought with other beings, and specially with Tsuni-||Goam.

Thus, for the Good Being we find the following names: Tsuni-||Goam, Tsūi-||Goab, Tsui||kuap, Uti'kuap, Tsoei'kuap, Tshu'koab, Tsoeikwap, Tsū-||Goab, Tsui-||Khoab, Tsu-||Goa, Tsūi-||Goam, and a dozen similar forms, all of which were supposed to mean " Wounded Knee," " Sore Knee," or " The One who inflicts Pain." This will be seen to be a mistaken idea.

Continuing the list of names, we find the following, all of which apply to the Good Being: ǃKhūb, the Rich One, the Chief, the Ruler; |Nanub, the Thunder Cloud, or the Pourer; ǃGurub, the Thunder Cloud, or the Coverer of the Sky; ||Khāb, the Returner, or the Moon, which was worshipped as a visible god; |Gur|khoisib, the Only One, the primitive man (thus fusing the conception of ancestors with gods); ‡Eixa|kha||nabiseb, the Man with a Brass-coloured Spine, the Lightning; Suquap, the One with a Sore Knee; Thikqua, Thukwa, Thiko-Theuke, Tiqua, Thuickwe, Tuiqua, Tigoa, Tanquoa, all of which have reference to " Wounded Knee," or " The One who inflicts Pain "; this word gave rise to the Kafir Utixo.

We find many other names for the Good Being, such as Khourra, Chuyn; and compound words like Gaunia-Tiqua. Heitsi-

# Appendix

Eibib is also known by the word Kabib, while ‡Eixa|kha‖nabiseb is the same as Gurikhoisib.

With regard to the names of the Bad Being, we find the following: ‖Gaunab, ‖Gaũab, Kaunaam, Damoh, Dangoh, ‡Gama-‡Gorib. These names represent wickedness, oppression, mischief or ruinous lightning which kills people and destroys crops. ‖Gaunab is a ghost who troubles people, and he seems to have been worshipped long before the Good Being; his name is found with but little alteration in all branches of the original stock, while that of the Good Being varies greatly, and can be traced to the best-known ancestor of the various divisions of the tribe. Again, Damoh was a cruel black chief who used to oppress the people.

‡Gama-‡Gorib was a chief who oppressed the Hottentots, and he fought with Tsuni-‖Goam, who was defeated several times (though he finally overcame the cruel chief). These wicked black chiefs were naturally confused with the darkness and death (which the Hottentots declare to be only a sleep). This Evil Being lives in the dark heaven, or black sky, and seems sometimes to be confused with the thunder clouds, or the lightning which kills people. In nearly all the oldest legends the Good Being was killed several times, but came to life again, being able to change his form at will. He has endless names and appears under many varied personalities.

It was thought that the true meaning of most of the names for the Good Being was "The One with a Wounded Knee." Hahn, however, thinks that it is derived from two words which mean "The Red Dawn." Heitsi-Eibib was thought to mean "The One who Foretells, the Prophet"; others suggested that it meant "The Messenger"; but it would seem to mean "The Dawn Tree," and so refers to the rays of light which stream up into the sky at sunrise. This explanation readily fits in with Hahn's idea that the word Tsuni-‖Goam and its many derivatives mean "The Red Dawn," and not primarily the "Wounded Knee."

The Evil Being is the darkness, or the night, and the Hottentots always said that he lived in the dark heavens, whereas the Good Being lived in the beautiful or Red Heaven, referring, of course, to the Dawn. In olden days the Hottentots rose at the first streak of dawn and worshipped the Good Being from the cover of the nearest bush, the women

# The Essential Kafir

daubing themselves with red paint in honour of the Red Dawn. I have never seen it suggested, but this custom may well have been passed on to the Kafirs, and may be the ultimate cause of their painting themselves habitually with red ochre. The Hottentot women daubed themselves with red paint when they worshipped at the grave of their ancestor, and even painted the stones of his grave red.

Since Heitsi-Eibib is the Dawn Tree and Tsuni-‖Goam is the Red Dawn, we see how natural it is that these two personalities should become confused in the minds of the people, and hence Heitsi-Eibib, who was but a great chief at one period, became a divine hero, and people considered it to be a religious duty to throw stones and to place twigs of trees on his graves.

In all the myths of these most interesting people, who are—sad to tell—rapidly dying out, the Good Being held many a fight with the Evil Being, and but slowly overcame him. And as the Red Dawn slowly overcame the Dark Night the sky became suffused with red light, which was taken to represent the blood shed in a real conflict. And since the Hottentots, owing to the immense fat-reserves on their buttocks, walk with the knee well in advance of the rest of their body, they considered that the Night wounded the Dawn in the knee, or advancing part of the body. The Hottentots declare that the Red Dawn was not the original name of the Good Being, which has been forgotten. The Good Being was a chief who delivered them from an oppressor who was naturally fused with the darkness, or night (‖Gaunab). Thus, as they forgot the name of their ancestor, they confused him with the Infinite, and all unconsciously raised him to the rank of a god.

The Kafir name for this ancestor is Utixo (the word is the Kafir form of Tiqua, the x being a click which is not sounded as in European languages); yet they did not understand the conception of the Day overcoming the Night, but caught at the surface idea of the " Wounded Knee," and consequently supposed this to be a complete account of the matter, and constructed their idea of the Supreme Being on the mistake.

The Hottentots worshipped this Tiqua as their invisible god; yet they considered the moon to be a visible god, and danced in its honour. It has been recorded that they would sing as they danced, " Be

# Appendix

welcome, give us plenty of honey, give us grass for our cattle, that we may have plenty of milk."

Not only did the Hottentots throw stones on the graves of their old hero Heitsi-Eibib: they also did the same at certain spots where their ancestors had great luck in hunting. Thus these Izivivane, or piles of stones, which the Dutch thought to be heaps of stones raised by the Israelites as they passed from Egypt into Palestine, turn out to be the most interesting relic of a bygone age.

Heitsi-Eibib is the great mythical hero of the Hottentots. His birth came about thus: One day a cow (some legends say a maiden) was eating sweet grass, and suddenly became pregnant and brought forth a bull. The people ran after it to kill it; but the bull ran down hill and vanished at a spot where an old man was found. He was carving a milk-pail, and was no other than the bull, which had thus transformed itself into human shape. The pursuers asked him where the bull had gone to, and he said that he did not know. All the time the man knew that he was no other than Heitsi-Eibib, who had changed himself into a bull and then into an old man. Later he changed himself into a pot, and when the people cooked meat in it the vessel absorbed all the fat. Thus Heitsi-Eibib became fat and rich.

According to one story Heitsi-Eibib was a small baby: his mother was carrying him on her back, when suddenly he grew large and overpowered his mother, committing incest with her, and then grew small again. This story is a rendering of the obvious fact of the New Moon riding on the back of the Sun. The moon slowly grows larger and becomes greater than the sun in size. After this it begins to dwindle again. The idea is met with in the folklore of many countries.

One day Heitsi-Eibib was travelling with his family, and they all came to a certain valley where raisins grew. Heitsi-Eibib died from eating these raisins, which proved to be poisonous. As he was dying he told his son, "The Whitish One," to cover his grave with soft, smooth stones, and never to touch the fruit of the raisin-tree again. The son did as commanded and covered the grave with stones.

The family then moved on to another place, and as they were unpacking their household things they heard a voice singing thus:

> I, the father of Vrisib,
> Father of this unclean one,

# The Essential Kafir

I, who had to eat these raisins and died,
And dying, live.

The young wife noticed that the voice came from the direction of the grave of Heitsi-Eibib, and sent her son to look. He saw traces of his father's footsteps and returned home. The young wife then told the son to creep round to leeward and intercept the old man on his attempt to get into his grave once more. When he did this, Heitsi-Eibib, who was all the time up in the raisin-tree, jumped down and tried to get into his grave. But the son caught him. The father cried out, " Let me go—for I am a man that was dead—lest I infect you." But the wife said, " Hold the rogue." They brought him home, and he became quite well.

There are endless tales of this Heitsi-Eibib. He was once looking for his people near the place of ‡Gama-‡Gorib, who sent a hare to him to ask him to join in a certain game which is played thus: If one man quarrels with another he fills his hand with dust, and offers both hands to his opponent. If the adversary is bold he dashes the dust to the ground, and then the two men fight. This is what happened with ‡Gama-‡Gorib. At first Heitsi-Eibib was thrown into a hole ; but he said, " Hole of my ancestors, heave up your bottom a little, and give me a lift, that I may jump out." It did so, and Heitsi-Eibib jumped out. This happened twice, after which Heitsi-Eibib threw his adversary into the hole, after hitting him first behind the ear. Then Heitsi-Eibib said, " Hole of my ancestors, heave up your bottom a little, that my children may come out," and it did so, and all his children who had been previously destroyed came out. After this Heitsi-Eibib cursed the hare and told it that henceforth it should eat only by night.

Heitsi-Eibib then went on to the kraal of ǀHauǁGai‡Gaib, and, when asked what he was doing, said that he was looking for his people. Here also there was a hole, and it was the custom of ǀHauǁGai‡Gaib to place a stone on his own forehead, and ask people who were passing by to take the stone and throw it at his forehead. When they did so the stone bounded back and killed the thrower. Heitsi-Eibib was invited to throw the stone. He promised to do so if ǀHauǁGai‡Gaib would shut his eyes. Then Heitsi-Eibib hit him behind the ear and killed this evil person on the spot, who fell into his own hole. Passing on, he came to a lion. In those days lions used to fly, and Heitsi-Eibib saw one of the

# Appendix

flying lions in a tree : thereupon he burnt the tree down, and caused the lion ever after to walk on the earth. Another version of the way in which lions lost their power of flight is as follows :

Heitsi-Eibib noticed a lion which had been flying in the sky : it pounced down on an ox and devoured it. This made the lion so heavy that when Heitsi-Eibib chased it the lion could not fly, and so Heitsi-Eibib cut off its wings.

According to another variation, Heitsi-Eibib was angry with ǂGama-ǂGorib because he worked so much evil on earth. Heitsi-Eibib managed to distract his attention, and when his rival was not looking Heitsi-Eibib hit his enemy behind the ear. After that the people lived happily. But Heitsi-Eibib was wounded in the knee during the fight, and ever after limped.

As people pass his grave they throw on it some pieces of their clothing, or dung from a zebra, or flowers, or branches of a tree, or stones, and if they are hunting they pray thus :

> O, Heitsi-Eibib,
> Thou our grandfather,
> Let me be lucky,
> Give me game,
> Let me find honey and roots,
> That I may bless thee again.
> Art thou not our great-grandfather,
> Thou, Heitsi-Eibib?

Sometimes they leave small offerings of honey or game at his graves, and think that, as Heitsi-Eibib's spirit walks on the earth, he is pleased to hear people praising him.

# BIBLIOGRAPHY

*A list of books consulted, with short notes which only indicate the value of the books from the point of view of the study of native character*

## BOOKS WRITTEN BEFORE 1850

1. ARBOUSSET, Rev. T., with Rev. F. DUMAS.
    *Narrative of an Exploratory Tour to the North-east of the Colony of the Cape of Good Hope.* (Cape Town. 1846.)

    This book gives a delightful description of Basutoland and the adjoining parts of Natal, together with some account of Basuto and Bechuana customs. A chapter is devoted to the Bushmen. The object of the journey was missionary work.

2. BACKHOUSE, JAMES.
    *A Narrative of a Visit to the Mauritius and South Africa.* (London. 1844.)

    The aim of this writer was religious; yet there are some interesting references to native customs scattered through the book. The man was a shrewd observer with no tendency to exaggerate. The book contains a most extraordinary jumble of subjects—Korrana Villages, Uses of Cowdung, Missionary Wives, Queen of the Mantatees, Conviction of Sin, Measles, the Weather, Kafir Tortures, &c.

3. BARROW, Sir JOHN.
    *An Autobiographical Memoir.* (London. 1847.)

    This book is not very useful for our purpose, nor is it very trustworthy.

# The Essential Kafir

4. BURCHELL, WILLIAM.
    *Travels in the Interior of Southern Africa.* (2 vols. London. 1822.)

    These two large volumes are very quaint. There is a naïve sense of self-satisfaction and humour running through the book. The first interest of the writer was outward nature, and the reader has to wade through many pages to glean much information concerning native character. Theal describes it as one of our most trustworthy books. It was published at Nine Guineas, and is hard to obtain. The writer, after telling us in his preface that his language might have been arranged "in smoother periods and expressed with more fashionable elegance," starts off thus : " Our sails, filled with the gentle gale, bore the gliding vessel over the blue waters of the deep, and forced its foamy prow through the yielding waves." Still, read the book by all means.

5. GARDINER, Capt. ALLEN F.
    *Narrative of a Journey to the Zoolu Country, Undertaken in* 1835. (London. 1836.)

    A most interesting and trustworthy book, showing what Zululand was like in the days of Dingan. There is much information concerning customs at the King's kraal. Capt. Gardiner's first love was missionary work, though he held a civil appointment.

6. ISAACS, NATHANIEL.
    *Travels and Adventures in Eastern Africa, Descriptive of the Zoolus, their Manners, Customs, &c., with a Sketch of Natal.* (2 vols. London. 1836.)

    These volumes are most valuable, for they give us first-hand descriptions of Chaka and Dingan. Isaacs was trading in Zululand and had much intercourse with Chaka.

7. LICHTENSTEIN, HENRY.
    *Travels in Southern Africa in the Years* 1803, 4, 5, *and* 6. Translated by Anne Plumptree. (2 vols. London. 1812.)

    This author is often quoted as one of prime authority by anthropologists. He is condemned by others, and I think justly. The book must be read ; but great caution is needed in accepting his statements, which seem to be frequently mistaken.

# Bibliography

8. MOFFAT, ROBERT.
    *Missionary Labours and Scenes in Southern Africa.* (London. 1842.)
    This book is too well known to need any description. It must be read, for it deals with life among the Hottentots, Bechuana, and Matabele, and is valuable in many directions.

9. OWEN, Captain.
    *Narrative of a Voyage to Explore the Shores of Africa, Arabia, and Madagascar.* (2 vols. London. 1833.)
    Parts of these volumes are well worth reading, especially the chapters dealing with Portuguese East Africa. But native character is quite a side issue with this writer.

10. *Pinkerton's Voyages and Travels.* (1814.)
    The 16th volume contains reprints and translations of other works, notably an account of the Hottentots by Thunberg, written in 1795, and above all a history of Eastern Ethiopia, originally written in Portuguese by the famous Rev. Father Joano dos Santos, which was published in 1684. It deals with events as early as 1506, and describes visits to Sofala, Sena, and Tete, with details about the gold-mines of those days. A most useful book.

11. SPARRMAN, ANDREW, M.D.
    *A Voyage to the Cape of Good Hope towards the Antarctic Polar Circle, and round the World, but chiefly into the Country of the Hottentots and Caffers, from the year 1772 to 1776.* (2 vols. London. 1784.)
    These delightful volumes are full of dry humour and shrewd observation of men and things. Yet much of the information about the natives is from hearsay, and therefore not of high value.

12. SUTHERLAND, Lieut.-Colonel.
    *Original Matter contained in Lieut.-Colonel Sutherland's Memoir on the Kaffirs, Hottentots, and Bosjemans of South Africa.* (Cape Town. 1847.)
    The "original matter" proves to be mainly large extracts from dos Santos, which occur in full in Pinkerton. The misdoing of the Dutch settlers is the main concern. The book is tedious and the writer full of fads, so that Theal rather savagely describes the original matter as a curiosity of literature.

# The Essential Kafir

13. THOMPSON, GEORGE.
    *Travels and Adventure in Southern Africa.* (2 vols. London. 1827.)

    A very suggestive book. It is not very useful from the point of view of native customs; yet Theal describes it as one of the best books ever written on South Africa. Much of the light thrown on natives is second-hand.

## ANTHROPOLOGY, &c.

14. FRAZER, J. D.
    *The Golden Bough.* (2nd edition. 3 vols. London. 1900.)

    These three volumes are invaluable, and full of suggestion. One cannot afford to leave these volumes unread. Be sure to get the latest edition.

15. LANG, ANDREW.
    *The Making of Religion.* (London. 1898.)

    With all respect to so great a writer, I feel bound to say that he frequently misunderstands the Kafirs, and gives their ideas a wrong flavour. But the volumes are suggestive, and have a charm of their own.

16. LUBBOCK, Sir JOHN (Lord Avebury).
    *The Origin of Civilisation and the Primitive Condition of Man.* (2nd edition. London. 1870.)

    An intensely suggestive book; yet the evidence frequently *seems* to be selected in order to fit the theories advanced. The book should certainly be read, for everything this author writes is valuable.

17. MAX MÜLLER.
    *Chips from a German Workshop.* (4 vols. London. 1867.)

    The second volume contains excellent papers on Comparative Mythology and Folklore, Zulu tales, as well as manners and customs of Zulus—all deeply interesting.

# Bibliography

18. PESCHEL, OSCAR.
    *The Races of Man and their Geographical Distribution.* From the German. (London. 1876.)

    A most useful book, though rather out of date.

19. PRICHARD, J.
    *The Natural History of Man.* (London. 1848.)

    This book is interesting as showing the views held on ethnological problems before the introduction of Darwin's theories. Otherwise this voluminous book of 600 pages is not worth reading, for it throws but little light on South African tribes.

20. RATZEL, Prof.
    *The History of Mankind.* (3 vols. London. 1896.)

    This laborious compilation is probably unique. It is very ponderous, and is written in true German style. The description of the races I know is as grotesque as the illustrations are. The rest may be better. Not worth the toil of reading.

21. VOGT, CARL.
    *Lectures on Man: His Place in Creation and in the History of the Earth.* (London. 1864.)

    The book is out of date, yet may be consulted by those who wish to know how people measured human skulls before the days of Huxley.

22. TYLOR, E. B.
    *Primitive Culture.* Researches into the Development of Mythology, Philosophy, Religion, Language, Art, and Custom. (3rd edition. London. 1891.)

    This work is too well known to need any advice as to its value. A new edition is advertised as I am writing. All must read it, and also the two following works by the same author. They are all very valuable.

23. TYLOR, E. B.
    *Researches into the Early History of Mankind, and the Development of Civilisation.* (London. 1865.)

24. TYLOR, E. B.
   *Anthropology: An Introduction to the Study of Man and Civilisation.* (London. 1892.)

## BOOKS ON SOUTH AFRICAN TRIBES WRITTEN LATER THAN 1850

25. ANDERSON, C. J.
   *Lake Ngami.* (London. 1856.)

   An account of travels and hunting expeditions in South Africa. The author's first love was hunting. Yet there is useful information concerning the Damaras and Namaquas scattered through the pages.

26. *Anthropological Institute, Journal of.* Vol. XIX.

   This contains a valuable article on methods of salutation and other South African customs.

27. *Anthropological Society, Journal of.* Vols. VII. and VIII.

   An article by Hamilton and Price in vol. viii. is frequently quoted from; but it is inaccurate. The volumes are not worth consulting for information concerning the Kafirs.

28. BLEEK, W. H. I.
   *Hottentot Fables and Tales.* (London. 1864.)

   This delightful book of Hottentot tales concerning the Fox was also published, by some mistake, under the title of "Reynard the Fox in South Africa." Having obtained a copy of the book under the former title for some twelve or fifteen shillings, I discovered that a number of copies had been bound up under the second title and were to be obtained for two shillings at a second-hand shop in St. Martin's-le-Grand.

   These stories will delight all who take the trouble to obtain a copy of this out-of-print book. It is very much in the style of the well-known book, "Uncle Remus," though the stories are told from a South African standpoint.

# Bibliography

29. CALLAWAY, The Rev. Canon.
    *The Religious System of the Amazulu.* (London. 1868.)

    This book is of the greatest value. It was published in four parts, the fourth never being completed. The first volume contains information about Unkulunkulu and the tradition of Creation; the second volume is on Amatongo, or Ancestor Worship; the third volume is on Izinyanga Zokubula, or Divination; and the fourth and incomplete volume is on Medical Magic.

    It is customary for people in South Africa to laugh at the book; but, for all that, it is the highest authority on matters within its province. It has perfectly caught the native spirit, and the flavour is excellent. "Zulu Cologne" and "Eau de Pondo" are the two phrases which occur to one on reading the book. It smells of the natives. Unfortunately, the book is long since out of print and extremely hard to obtain; *but it must be consulted if possible, even if no other book is read.*

30. CALLAWAY, The Rev. Canon.
    *Nursery Tales of the Zulus.*

    This book is quite inimitable, but, unfortunately, out of print and very rare. My copy is not complete, and so the title given may not be correct, as it is missing. It was advertised as above. Every one should read this book if possible.

31. CAMPBELL.
    *Travels in South Africa.* (2 vols.)

    These volumes describe missionary journeys undertaken early in the nineteenth century. The missionary element is predominant.

32. CASALIS, E.
    *Les Bassoutos.* (Paris. 1859.)

    A well-known work in French by a pioneer missionary. Must be read. There is a translation, I believe, though I have been unable to find a copy.

# The Essential Kafir

33. CHAPMAN, JAMES.
    *Travels in the Interior of South Africa.* (2 vols. London. 1868.)

    The author's main interests were centred in hunting and travel; yet there are some interesting facts recorded in these pages, though in a slipshod way. Detailed information is absent. The book is worth reading only by those who wish to know all that can be found out concerning the Bushmen, the Hottentots, the Damaras, and the Bechuanas.

34. DECKLE, LIONEL.
    *Three Years in Savage Africa.* (London. 1898.)

    The best part of this work is the title. Many of the conclusions arrived at are very immature. It is the hasty journal of a hurried traveller, and reports are apparently accepted for facts without due examination. The accounts of travel are interesting.

35. EVANS, MRS. FRANK.
    *Some Legendary Landmarks of Africa.* (London. 1893.)

    This is a thin book of some hundred pages which will appeal to folklore specialists only.

36. *Folklore Journal, The.* (Cape Town. 1879–1880.) Vols. I. and II.

    These pages, long out of print, are very interesting and of great value. They should be consulted if possible.

37. GALTON, FRANCIS.
    *The Narrative of an Explorer in Tropical South Africa.* (London. 1853.)

    Some valuable references to the Damaras are scattered throughout the three hundred pages, which mainly describe shooting and travel. Valuable for those studying the special tribe referred to.

38. GROUT, REV. LEWIS.
    *Zululand, or Life among the Zulu Kafirs of Natal and Zululand.* (London. 1861 [?].)

    This work contains a good deal of information concerning the Kafirs, though it is not at all exhaustive in its treatment of the subject.

# Bibliography

39. HAHN, T.
    *Tsuni‖Goam, the Supreme Being of the Khoi-Khoi.* (London. 1881.)

    This volume is of the greatest possible value to all who wish to study the Hottentots and the Bushmen.

40. HOLDEN, Rev. WILLIAM C.
    *The Past and Future of the Kaffir Races.* (London. 1866.)

    A very useful book, though not brilliant. It is written by a well-known Wesleyan missionary, and is in the main trustworthy.

41. HOLUB, Dr. EMIL.
    *Seven Years in South Africa.* (2 vols. London. 1881.)

    This is a translation by Ellen E. Frewer. The book is frequently quoted from, but is mainly occupied with hunting and travelling experiences. It need not be read.

42. LESLIE, DAVID.
    *Among the Zulus and Amatongo.* (2nd edition. London. 1875.)

    A valuable book written by a shrewd observer. His chapter on the Hlonipa custom is generally considered to be one of the best to be found.

43. LIVINGSTONE, DAVID.
    *Missionary Travels and Researches in South Africa.* (London. 1857.)

    This book is too well known to need a description. All Livingstone's books are worth reading.

44. MACLEAN, Colonel.
    *A Compendium of Kafir Laws and Customs.* (Compiled by Maclean.)

    This is a most valuable compilation relating to the laws and customs of Kafirs, information being supplied by such eminent authorities as Dugmore, Warner, and Brownlee. This small book is packed full of information, and must on no account be skipped. Every missionary should read it.

# The Essential Kafir

45. MARTIN, MINNIE.
    *Basutoland, its Legends and Customs.* (London. 1903.)

    A chatty little book, written with the strangest disregard of King's English. Much of the information tastes as if it had been gleaned through Europeanised natives, and is of but little value. The unwary reader will frequently be misled, especially if he has not read extensively on the subject.

46. MASON, G. H.
    *Life with the Zulus of Natal.* (London. 1855.)

    A book of but little value, though the author states that Colenso borrowed from him and praised his work highly.

47. SHOOTER, REV. JOSEPH.
    *The Kafirs of Natal and the Zulu Country.* (London. 1857.)

    This work contains a good history of Chaka, and has a valuable, though very dry, account of native customs.

48. *Stanford's Compendium of Geography and Travel: Africa.* By A. H. KEANE. (2 vols. London.)

    Contains a superficial account of the various tribes of South Africa.

49. THEAL, GEORGE McCALL.
    *Kaffir Folk Lore.* (London. 1882.)

    A series of Kafir stories as told by natives. They are of great interest, though not so charmingly put together as Callaway's tales, which are far richer. The tales in this book are modifications, in the main, of stories to be found in Callaway. The book should be studied, if possible.

50. THEAL, GEORGE McCALL.
    *The Beginning of South African History.* (London. 1902.)

    This is the latest of Theal's works. It contains a very valuable description of the Bushmen, Hottentots, and Kafirs, though the account is somewhat cold and formal. It is very valuable for all who wish to examine the skeleton of Kafir character. The main portion of the book is concerned with the Portuguese in South-East Africa.

# Bibliography

51. THEAL, GEORGE MCCALL.

   *The History of South Africa.* (5 vols. London.)

   This is one of the standard histories of South Africa, and contains much information concerning the natives and their past. The contents are roughly as follows: Vol. I., 1486–1691; Vol. II., 1691–1795; Vol. III., 1795–1834; Vol. IV., 1834–1854; Vol. V., 1854–1872.

   The method of this writer is coldly historical, and native affairs are treated from the outward aspect. The inwardness of the whole thing might be non-existent as far as the writer is concerned. But the volumes are excellent. It may be well to add that the first volume contains, among other things, an account of wrecks along the coast; Vol. II. contains a *description* of native races; Vol. III. contains a *history* of native races down to the early years of the nineteenth century. The fourth volume treats of Kafir wars. There is no need to advise students to read these volumes: they will do so as a matter of course.

52. *The Natives of South Africa: Their Economic and Social Condition.* Edited by the South African Native Races Committee. (London. 1901.)

   This volume is of great interest to those who wish to study native economics. It is edited by a committee, and consists of papers from different pens. Consequently, the contents of the book are unequal in interest and in value. The student must remember that the description of native customs holds only for a few isolated tribes, and by no means represents all the races of South Africa.

53. TYLER, JOSIAH.

   *Forty Years among the Zulus.* (Boston and Chicago.)

   An American missionary's views of the Zulus. The book is not of high value, being somewhat superficial; yet it is worth reading for the descriptions of Zulu customs.

# The Essential Kafir

54. *Zulu Izaga, and Zulu Customs.* Three pamphlets reprinted from the *Natal Colonist.* One is dated July 1879, and another is dated 1880 ; the third is undated.

    These proverbs are invaluable, and I have borrowed largely from the list given, leaving scores to those who care to take the trouble to read the pamphlet. The pamphlet on Customs is not so good as that on the Proverbs, which is superb.

*In addition to the above-named books, I have consulted many articles in magazines and South African and other daily papers, together with Blue Books and masses of manuscript, &c.*

# INDEX

Abortion, 355
Absorbing qualities by eating, 140, 309
Abusing ancestral spirits, 91
Abusive talk of women, 24
Accusation of incest, 243 ; magic, 148 ; witchcraft, 238
Action at a distance, 10, 311
Adultery, punishment of, 357
After death, 68
Age, gauging the, 29
Agriculture, 323
Almanac, Pleiades as an, 323
Amadhlozi, 99,
Amatongo, 92,
Amputation of finger joint, 203
Ancestor worship, 79 ; mode of origin of, 79
Ancestors, cow of the, 201, 216 ; house of, 13 ; spirit of, in snakes, 85
Ancestral spirits, 82, 91, 133 ; sacrifice to, 42 ; sickness due to, 137
Angels, one-legged (Swazieland), 108
Animals in hut, 48, 49
Anthropomorphism, 88
Apologising to elephant, 84
Appearance and dress, 18
Are the Kafirs lazy ?, 394
Armchair critics, 73
Army, doctoring the, 305
Arrows, poisoned, 311
Artistic powers, 331
Arts of peace, 323

Assault, 355
Assegais, women allowed to carry, 209, 218

Baby, doctoring the, 201 ; instilling courage into, 203 ; mortgaged, 199 ; washing a, 52
Babies killed for medicine, 151
Baboons used for magical practices, 146
Backbone of man becomes snake, 87
Backward-looking disastrous, 203, 208
Bamboozling the spirits, 251

Bantu huts, shape of, 14
Basuto ideas of creation, 108
Beating the idol, 74
Beauty in nature, sense of, absent, 53
Bechuana, customs at burial, 252 ; ideas of creation, 107
Beer, 57, 326
Beer drink, 327
Best man, the, 217
Bewitching a person, through his photograph or possessions, 144 ; through a name, 242
Bewitching, food as a means of, 143
Bewitching medicines, 174
Binding grass to influence travellers, 263
Binding up the skies, 115
Birds shot with bow and arrow, 313
Bird traps, 311
Birth customs, 201
Blackbeetles and sickness, 139
Black men, inferiority of, 105
Blacksmiths, 328
Bluff, 65
Boasting, 307
Boots, use of, 20
Bow and arrows, shooting birds with, 313
Boys, 25 : awkward stage of, 26
Bunu, 291 ; as rainmaker, 116
Burial customs, 248, 251, 252
Burial, Kafir, 79 ; of chief, 245
Burying dead man's possessions, 248
Burying oxen by eating, 44
Burying people alive, 247
Bushman legend of death, 78
Bushman's idea of nature, 108
Bushmen and ox waggon, 4
Bushmen's poisoned arrows, 311

Calamity through diviners, 190
Cannibalism, 143 ; practising by magic, 149
Catching crocodiles, 314
Cattle, 329 ; hours of letting out of kraal, 59

# The Essential Kafir

Cattle marriages, 211, 222; needless among Christian natives, 224
Causation, mistaken theory of, 5
Cause or coincidence, 5
Chaka, and medicine, 137; as General, 301; kills 7000 women, 246; song in honour of, 94
Chaka's cruelty, 289
Chameleon, legend of, 76
Champion eater, 44
Changes of fashion, 19
Chase, the, 301, 311
Cheering little wheel, 4
Chief, burial of, 245; death of, 253; defeated, facing the, 309; greeting a, 36; illness of, 245; visit to a, 37; working for, 400
Chief's attendant, 39; cruelty, excuse for, 143, 289; dinner, 39; dish of medicine, 307; "eyes" and "ears," 206; modesty, 40; oxen not herded, 324; song, 271; soul, 83; wives killed at his death, 245, 252
Chiefs, list of, 41
Chiefs favour killing witches, 150
Child, father not allowed to see, 200; naming a, 200, 202
Childbirth, 199
Children, 15, 17; counting his, 204; foster, 203; illegitimate, rare, 210; number of, per wife, 19, 228; sceptical, 90; temporary burial of, to obtain rain, 117
Circles, 11
Circumcision, 206
Civil offences, 353
Clay modelling, 331
Cleansing, after lightning, 125; Swazie mode, 125
Cleansing away death, 249; victorious soldiers, 310; wounded warriors, 309
Cleansings, 255
Clicks, origin of, 199
Clothing, effect of European, upon natives, 393
Colour of skin, 31
Colour sense excellent, 14
Colours of oxen, Hottentot words for, 329
Concealing emotions, 28
Concubines, 215, 229, 230, 232
Connection of body and soul, 84
Consulting a diviner, 160
Contradictory ideas not incompatible, 74
Cooking food, 326, 330
Copying, power of, 282
Corn, grinding, 325; threshing, 325; winnowing, 325
Councillor, a begging, 42

Counting, mode of using fingers in, 204; his children, 204
Courage, 28; instilling into baby, 203
Courts of justice, 351
Cow of the ancestors, 201, 216
Cowdung, smearing floor with, 42
Creation and Umkulunkulu, 76, 96
Creation, Basuto legend of, 108; Bechuana's ideas of, 107; Damara ideas of, 107; myth of, 104
Credulity of natives, 190
Criminal offences, 355
Critical faculties, 70, 282
Crocodiles, 149; catching, 314; as medicine, 150
Cruelty, 288-292; of Chaka, 289; of chief, excuse for, 143
Crystal-gazing, divining by, 179
Custom, breach of, leads to accusation of witchcraft, 59; power of, 66
Customs, Jewish origin of, examined, 259

DAMARA customs at burial, 251; ideas of creation, 107
Dance, a witchdoctor's, 170, 173
Dandy, hair of Pondo, 34
Dead, mode of life of, 87; praise of, 89; wailing for, 250
Dead man's possessions, 82, 248
Death, Bushman legend of, 78; cleansing away, 249; dread of, 76, 244; Hottentot legend of, 77; origin of, 76; uncleanness at, 249
Death of chief, day of rest after, 253
Deceiving the spirits, 252
Delicacy, sense of, 21
Demons, 126
Developing native trades, 406
Dingan, ode to, 93, 290
Disaster through looking backward, 203, 208
Discussing the news, 57
Disease, extracting cause of, 166
Dislocated joint, reducing, 136
Disobedience to war doctor, 305
Dispelling false notions, 5
Display, love of, 28
Distance, opening the gates of, 192
Diviner, consulting a, 160
Diviner, extracting cause of disease, 166; finds lost cattle, 178; "smelling out" a witch or wizard, 169
Diviner's failure, 166; methods, exposure of, 163, 168
Diviners, calamity through, 190; die violent deaths, 117; dress, 160; faith in, 190

430

# Index

Divining, by asking questions, 159; by bones, 178; by crystal-gazing, 179; by familiar spirits, 182; by lifting basket, 180; by ordeals, 184; by sticks, 181; by subjective methods, 184; by the mantis, 183; instance of, 192
Divorce, 225, 358
Docks at Cape Town, work in, 395
Doctoring the army, 304; the baby, 201; the chief, 308; the fields, 324
Doctors and wizards, power of, 147
Doctors, hail, 121; storm, 122
Dogs, 40; as napkins, 45
Dolls, 335
Domestic matters, 329
Dowry, the, 212
Dreams, 83, 89
Dress and appearance, 18
Dress, bizarre, 27; European, inartistic, 25; of diviners, 160; used in mourning, 246
Drought caused by neglect of ancestors, 89
Drowning, mode of rescue from, 111
Dying, treatment of, 245, 247, 252

EARRINGS, 16
Eater, a champion, 44
Eating, absorbing qualities by, 140; as a form of prayer, 90; hours of, 58; putrid meat, 44
"Eating up," 173
Education, 404
Emotional nature, 293
Emotions, concealing, 28
Epidemics, warding off, 262
Epileptoid seizure, 186
Esedowan, 126
Esemkofu, 128
Eternal duration not a native idea, 88
Ethiopian Church, the, 407
Etiquette, native, 34
European clothing, effect on natives, 393
European dress inartistic, 25
European influences, 80, 225
Every man a policeman, 352
Evil, transference of, 145
Existence, struggle for, 201
Extracting teeth, 135
Eyesight, 287

FACING the fire, 46
Faith in diviners, 190
Fashion, changes of, 19
Feast, a Kafir, 43; of first-fruits, 269
Feet, thick soles of, 21
Fencing, 336

Festivals, 269, 270
Finger joint, amputation of, 203, 262
Fingers, sucking, 47; used in counting, 204
Fire-making by friction, 51
Folklore, 365–389
    Cannibal story, 379
    Clever tortoise, 369
    Cloud-eating, 386
    Fable showing European influence, 388
    Fish-stealing, 385
    Lion's illness, 384
    Lion's share, 386
    Little Red Stomach, 378
    Masilo and Masilonyane, 366
    Romance of Unyengebule, 372
    Which was the thief, 384
    Woman who became a lion, 371
Folklore plots, plan of, 381
Food, cooking, 326, 330; forbidden articles of, 330; sharing of, 31; staple, 323; as a means of bewitching, 143; for visitors, 330; placed in grave, 248
Forbidden articles of food, 330
Foster children, 203
Franchise, Kafirs and the, 403
Fruits, 323
Future life, 84; of the Kafir, 393

GAME, pits, 312; right to wounded, 319; traps, 312
Games, 335
Gauging the age of a Kafir, 29
Gazaland huts, 14
German induction, 60
Girls, 15, 18; age of, at marriage, 211; lenience to, 19; sold in marriage, 212
Goats, 329
Golden Age, a, 78
Gorah, or Ugwali, 333
Grain, 323; stores, 325
Grave, a native, 248; food placed in, 248
Great festival, 270
Great Place, the, 36
Great wife, 13
Greediness, 43
Green mealies, 326
Greeting a chief, 36
Grey hair, extracting, to ward off old age, 29
Grinding corn, 325
Grunting, possibilities of, 38

HAIL, 119; doctors, 121
Hair-dressing, 31; mode of men, 33; mode when married, 33

# The Essential Kafir

Hair, extracting grey, 29; mica schist for, 32; of a Pondo dandy, 34
Harvest, the, 324
Haunted wood, 128
Haunting spirits, 126
Headaches, how to cure, 137, 156
Head ring, 33
Hearing, 287
Heaven above the tree tops, 81
Heaven herds, 121; queen of, 112
Heitsi-Eibib, 264, 266, 409
Hens, 329
Hili, 127
Hlonipa, 236; breaking custom of, 238; customs in other lands, 243; tribal, 241
Homicide, 355
Horses, playing at, 336
Hottentot god, 183
Hottentot legend of death, 77; words for colours of oxen, 329
Hottentot's dance to the new moon, 110
House of ancestors, 13
Houses, "withering" of, 361
Hunt, a tribal, 316
Hut-making, playing at, 335
Hut sprinkling, 261
Hut tax a wife tax, 14

IDEAS, contradictory, not incompatible, 74; on religion, 41; topsy-turvy, 3; vagueness of, 74
Identifying ancestor from appearance of snake, 87
Idleness of Kafirs, 57
Idol beating, 74
Idols, Kafirs have none, 91
Igubu, 332
Illegitimate children rare, 210
Illness of chief, 245
Ill-treatment of women, 221
Immorality of natives, 230; on mission stations, 232
Incapacity to see pictures, 282
Incense, 90
Incest, accusation of, 143
Incubation time, 201
Indian hemp, 324
Inferiority of black men, 104
Influence through spitting, 11
Inheriting property, 208, 360
Injury to property, 358
Insult to manhood, 33
Intelezi, 269, 308
Intellect, dulness of, 281
Isitshakanamana, 127
Isolation of wives at death of husband, 246

Izivivane, 263

JEPHTHAH'S daughter, 112
Jewish influences, supposed, 112
Jewish origin of customs examined, 259
Johannesburg, effect of upon natives, 27; native servants at, 396
Justice, courts of, 351; sense of, 286, 351

KAFIR, beer, 57, 326; boys, 25; children, 15, 17; consciousness, 71; dogs, 40; feast, 43; the future of, 393; girls, 15, 18; idleness, 57; letters, 404; logic, 88; nakedness exaggerated, 14; odour, 34; pianos, 332; problem, the, 393; servants, mistakes of, 6; spirituality, 30; trinity of delight, 41; women, 18
Kafir, the, a valuable asset, 408; an unknown quantity, 394; in his kraal, 397
Kafir's skin turning white, 406; thoughts, difficulty of understanding, 62
Kafirs, and the franchise, 403; are they lazy, 394; are without idols, 91; have no writing, 332; how they die, 245; red, 31; thriftless, 407; work done by, 397
Killing the time, 60
Kissing, 37
Knobkerries, 316
Kock, 53
Koolukoolwani, 103
Kraal, derivation of word, 12; shape of, 11, 12, 13; structure of, 12; visit to, 15, 46
Kraals deserted when struck by lightning, 125
Kreli, 35

LABOUR problem, the, 402
Labyrinths, or mazes, 338
Lack of mercy, 9; truthfulness, 8
Land tenure, 359
Language, no written, 70
Law-abiding people, 351
Left-hand wife, 13
Legal matters, 351
Legislation for polygamist nation, 224
Lenience to girls, 19
Letters of Kafirs, 404
Lightning and thunder, 119; cause of, 120, 121
Lightning, cleansing after, 125; kraals deserted when struck by 125; warding off, 121
List of chiefs, 41

# Index

Little festival, 269
Lobengula, 34, 290
Logic of natives, 88
Logical faculty, 282
Love philtres, 155

MACHILA, A, 170
Magical practices, baboons and tiger cats used for, 146
Magic, 133; accusation of, 148; differentiated from witchcraft, 148; elimination of belief in, 404; mimetic, 140; practising cannibalism by, 149; sickness caused by, 139; sympathetic, 140; working on a symbol or representative, 145
Magondi, 102
Manhood, greatest insult to, 33
Mantis, divining by, 183
Manufactures, 328
Marriage, 210; age of girls at, 211; custom, ancient, 245; daughters sold in, 212; originally communal, 236; proposals for, 211; restrictions as to, 211
Marriages, cattle, 211, 222; cattle, needless among Christian natives, 224; forced, 220; in Natal, 225
Married life, 228
Married woman, mode of dressing hair, 33
Matoome, 107
Matoomyan, 107
Mbona, 102
Mbona's prophetess as rainmaker, 118
Mealie pap, 326
Mealie pits, 325
Mealies, green, 326
Meat, eating putrid, 44
Medicine, bewitching, 174; Chaka and, 137; crocodiles as, 150; killing babies for, 151; the chief's dish of, 307
Medicine by proxy, 136
Medicines kept in skull of enemy, 309
Medicines, native, 135, 140; serpents sit upon, 116
Memory of natives, 41, 280
Mental characteristics, 277
Mental fog, 73, 96
Mental powers, 281
Men, mode of dressing hair, 33; newly married not allowed to fight, 306; old, 29; work of, 399
Mercy, lack of, 9
Metal, influence of, 263
Mica schist for hair, 32
Military matters, 301

Milk sac, restrictions, 238
Milk, sweet and clotted, 59; tabooed, 209, 228, 240, 246, 249
Milking, hours of, 58, 330
Mimicry, 183
Mistakes of Kafir servants, 6
Mission stations, immorality on, 232
Modelling in clay, 331
Molungu, 102
Monkeys once human, 108
Monsters, fabulous, 126
Moon, eclipse of, 109; new, Hottentots dance to, 110
Morality of natives, 229, 354
Moremo Morimo, 102, 107
Mother love, 205
Mourning customs, 250, 252
Mourning, dress used in, 246
"Mouth," the, 213
Music, 332

NAKEDNESS of Kafirs exaggerated, 14
Name decided before birth, 202
Name, dislike to mention, 242
Names, 242
Naming a child, 200, 202
Natal, marriages in, 225
Native bluff, 65; carriers, 401; conception of virtue, 147; labyrinths, or mazes, 338; medicines, 135; problem, the, 403; servants at Johannesburg, 396; string, 329; telegraphy, 340; trades, developing, 406
Native doctor's mode of curing sickness, 138
Natives, credulity of, 190; prolific, 393
Nature alive, 112
Nature, native explanation of, 108
News, 57
Ngwali, 102
Night in a Kafir hut, a, 47

ODOUR of Kafirs, 34
Offences, civil, 353; criminal, 355
Old age, respect to, 22, 29; warding off, 29
Old men, 29
Old Moliwash, 30
Old women, 22; called men, 239
Omens, 272, 307
Ongeluck's Neck, 53
Opening the eyes, 38
Ordeal, poison, on Zambesi, 185
Ordeals, divining by, 184
Ornaments, 19
Ovaherero, 265
Ovembo, 265

433        2 E

# The Essential Kafir

Oxen of chief not herded, 324
Ox waggon and Bushmen, 4

PAIN, sense of, 288
Peace, arts of, 323
Pempes, 324
Photography, dislike of, 111
Physique, 28
Pianos, Kafir, 332
Pictures, incapacity to see, 282
Piercing ear to improve hearing, 20
Pigeon huts, 14
Pillows, 32, 328
Playing at horses, 336; at hut making, 335
Pleaides, 110; as an almanac, 323
Poison ordeal on Zambesi, 185
Poisoned arrows, 311
Poisoning game, 312
Policeman, every man a, 352
Politeness, sense of, 8
Political instability, 407
Polyandry, 220, 232
Polygamist nation, legislation for, 224
Polygamy, 227; a hindrance, 405
Polynesians and Zulus, 365
Pondo, dandy, hair of, 34; kraal, shape of, 13; rouge, 206
Possessions of a deceased man, 82, 248
Power of copying, 282
Praise, examples of, 93; love of, 92; of dead, 89; to ancestors, 89
Prayer by eating, 90
Praying, native mode of, 90
Presents, 38
Prime Minister begging matches, 43
Property, inheriting, 208, 360; injury to, 358
Proposals for marriage, 211
Proverbs, 7, 31, 32, 57, 122, 177, 228; selection of, 294
Puberty, 206
Punishments for witchcraft, 175, 355; of theft, 357

QAMATA, 101
Qualities, absorbing, 140, 309; seat of, 141, 142, 278
Queen of Heaven, 112
Questions, divining by asking, 159
Quotations
  Callaway, 163, 308
  Carlyle, 408
  Frazer, 139
  Gardiner, Allen, 103
  Kinglake's "Eothen," 50
  Leslie, David, 191
  Lubbock, 91

Quotations—*continued*
  Max Müller, 365
  Old writer, an, 34
  Owen, 84
  Pinkerton's Voyages, 314, 315
  Santos, dos, 81
  Shakespeare's "Macbeth," 150
  Theal, 99, 100, 177, 231

"RAFTERS," 14, 360
Rain, stopping, 118; temporary burial of children to obtain, 117
Rainbow, explanation of, 112
Rainmaker's excuses, 116
Rainmaking, 113
Rape, 355
Rarebe, 212
Red clay, 31
Red Kafirs, 31
Reed fence, 14
Religion, native ideas on, 41
Repartee, 39
Responsibility, 352
Riddle, a South African, 50
Riddles, 60
Ridicule, sensitiveness to, 287
Riding, mode of, 9
Right-hand wife, 13
Rival armies, sticks representing, 308
River spirit, 10
Rouge, Pondo, 206
Runaway wives, 221

SACRIFICES, 80
Sacrifice, for sickness, 169; to ancestral spirits, 42
Salic law, 361
Salutations, 37
Scapegoat, the, 261
Sceptical children, 90
Seat of qualities, 141, 142, 278
Sense, of beauty absent, 53; of colour excellent, 20; of delicacy, 21; of justice, 286, 351; of pain, 288; of politeness, 8; of relative values deficient, 5; of truth, 285
Sensitiveness to ridicule, 287
Sententious wisdom, 294
Serpent worship, 85
Serpents sit on medicines, 116
Shadow mistaken for soul, 83
Shadow of mat representing a man, 83
Sharing of food, 31
Shaving with broken glass, 18, 33
Sickness and blackbeetles, 139
Sickness, caused by magic, 139; due to ancestral spirits, 137, 138; explanation

434

# Index

of, 133; extracting cause of, 166; sacrifice for, 169; transference of, 146; without causation, 134
Skies, binding up the, 115
Skin, colour of, 31
Sky, the, nature of, 108
"Smelling out," 169, 173
Smoking, 345; indian hemp, 346
Snake bites, treatment for, 189
Snake, identifying ancestor from appearance of, 87
Snakes as the abode of ancestors, 85
Snuff, 55
Soldiers, training the mind of, 306
Soles of feet thick, 21
Song of the afflicted, 334; of the chief, 271
Songs, 283, 332
Soul, the, 83; leaves body in sleep, 83; of chief lives in horns, 83
Spear, throwing the, 267
"Spies," the, 214
Spirit, conception of, 84
Spirit voices, 156
Spirits, bamboozling the, 251; deceiving the, 252; divining by familiar, 182; haunting, 126; of ancestors, 82
Spitting at enemy, 10; game, 335; in river, 10
Sprites, 126
Stars, shooting, 109
Sticks representing rival armies, 308
Stone-throwing in river, 10
Stories, &c.
    Baboon as sorcerer's agent, 175
    Body and spirit, 84
    Bunu's eating competition, 44
    Bushman and wind, 110
    Bushman smashing wife's head, 84
    Bushmen and waggons, 4
    Captain Cook at Tahiti, 5
    Cases of witchcraft punished, 175
    Chaka's medicines, 44, 137
    Cheering little wheel, 4
    Dark suit causing rain, 5
    Deaf woman, 67
    Diviner baffled, 166
    Diviner deserts dying patient, 158
    Emetics dispel ideas, 5
    Esemkofu. David Leslie, 128
    Extracting lizard from abdomen, 166
Forced marriages, 220
Gates of distance, 192
German induction, 60
Hlonipa story, 237, 239
Kafir filling kettle through spout, 6

Stories, &c.—*continued*
    Kafir lighting fire in oven, 6
    Kreli, 35
    Lunatic, 84
    Matabele and engine, 4
    Medicines act at distance, 136
    Medicines by proxy, 137
    Origin of death, 76
    Safety-pins bearing children, 5
    Soapsuds mistaken for boiling water, 5
    Torture for witchcraft, 176
    Unicorn, 8
    Witchdoctor outwitted, 174
Storm doctor at work, 122
Storm, fighting a, 122
String, native, 329
Struggle for existence, 45, 202
Sucking fingers, 47
Sun and stars, 108
Sunrise, a, 53
Swazie huts, shape of, 14
Swazie, impi, 303; mode of cleansing after lightning, 125
Swazie queen, 35; killing old women, 246

TEETH extracting, 135
Telegraphy, native, 340
Texo, 104
Theft, punishment of, 357
Threshing corn, 325
Throwing the spear, 267
Thunder and lightning, 119; cause of, 120, 121
Tickoloshe, 127
Tico, 104
Tiger cats used for magical practices, 146
Tobacco, 324
Totem, modified, 84
Training the mind of soldiers, 306
Transference, of evil, 145, 259; of sickness, 146
Treachery in war, 304
Treason, 355
Tribal hlonipa, 241; hunt, a, 316
Truthfulness, lack of, 8
Truth, sense of, 285
Twins, 202
Two hearts, 284
Tyelinzima, 36

UGWALI, or Gorah, 333
Ukuteleka, 215
Umbandine, 115
Umkulumcande, 101
Umkulunkulu and creation, 76, 96

# The Essential Kafir

Umkulunkulu, meaning of word, 96; used as an excuse for vice, 98
Umkulunkulus, various, 97
Unvelinqangi, 100
Upundhlu, 359
Urezhwa, 78
Usondo rains, 118
Uthlanga, 100
Utixo, 100

VAGINO, 138
Valuable asset, a, 408
Vegetables, 323
*Vestige, a*, 9
Vice, Umkulunkulu as an excuse for, 98
Victorious warriors, cleansing the, 310
Villenangi, 103
Virtue, native conception of, 147
Visit to a chief, 37; to a kraal, 15, 46
Visitors, food for, 330

WAILING for the dead, 250
Waistcoat, the use of, 27
War, 301; doctor, disobedience to, 305; paint, 308; prognostications for, 310; treachery in, 304
Washing a baby, 52; method of, 52
Wedding, the, 215
Weeding done by women, 324
Wesleyan native revival, 293
Whirlpool, 111
White men, origin of, 105
Widows, 226
Wife, the "great," 13; the left-hand, 13; the right-hand, 13; capture, relics of, 219, 235
Wind, 110
Wisdom, sententious, 294
Witch, " smelling out " a, 169

Witchcraft, accusation of, 59, 90, 238; belief in, 67; differentiated from magic, 148; punishments for, 175, 355
Witchdoctor, 155; functions of, 155; initiation of, 156; not a wizard, 155
Witchdoctor's dance, 170, 173; roguery, 158
Witches, chiefs favour killing, 150
" Withering " of houses, 361
Wives, isolation of, at death of husband, 246; runaway, 221; various, 360
Wives, killed at death of chief, 245, 252; killed at death of husband, 82; not washing after death of husband, 250
Wizards and doctors, power of, 147
Woman, married, mode of dressing hair, 33
Woman's father responsible for her crimes, 176
Womanhood, entrance to, 209
Women, 18; abusive talk of, 24; allowed to carry assagais, 209, 218; curse of 22; ill-treatment of, 221; lifting weights, 56; rights of, 22
Women, old, 22; called men, 239; sad lot of, 22
Women's paths, 238; work, 56, 324, 398
Wood-carving, 328, 331
Work, done by Kafirs, 397; in the docks, Cape Town, 395
Working for the chief, 400
Wounded game, right to, 319; warriors, cleansing the, 309
Wrecks on coast, effect of, 75
Writing, Kafirs have no, 332

YOUNG men, 26

ZAMBESI huts, 14
Zulu kraal, shape of, 12
Zulus and Polynesians, 365